Brigadier General
John D. Imboden

Brigadier General John D. Imboden

Confederate Commander in the Shenandoah

Spencer C. Tucker

THE UNIVERSITY PRESS OF KENTUCKY

Publication of this volume was made possible in part
by a grant from the National Endowment for the Humanities.

Copyright © 2003 by The University Press of Kentucky

Scholarly publisher for the Commonwealth,
serving Bellarmine University, Berea College, Centre
College of Kentucky, Eastern Kentucky University,
The Filson Historical Society, Georgetown College,
Kentucky Historical Society, Kentucky State University,
Morehead State University, Murray State University,
Northern Kentucky University, Transylvania University,
University of Kentucky, University of Louisville,
and Western Kentucky University.
All rights reserved.

Editorial and Sales Offices: The University Press of Kentucky
663 South Limestone Street, Lexington, Kentucky 40508-4008

07 06 05 04 03   5 4 3 2 1

Frontispiece: Brigadier General John D. Imboden. (Courtesy of the U.S. Army)

Library of Congress Cataloging-in-Publication Data
available from the Publisher or The Library of Congress

ISBN 0-8131-2266-X

This book is printed on acid-free recycled paper meeting
the requirements of the American National Standard
for Permanence in Paper for Printed Library Materials.

Manufactured in the United States of America.

Dedicated to Dr. Beverly B. Tucker

Contents

List of Maps   viii
Introduction   ix
1. Early Life to the Civil War   1
2. Initial Military Service   23
3. First Battle of Manassas   44
4. Forming a Partisan Command   69
5. The 1st Virginia Partisan Rangers (1862–1863)   94
6. The Spring 1863 Jones-Imboden Raid into West Virginia   111
7. The Gettysburg Campaign   139
8. Imboden's Second West Virginia Raid   173
9. The 1864 Shenandoah Valley Campaign   193
10. Destruction of the Valley   222
11. Final Confederate Service   262
12. Post–Civil War Career   289
Conclusion   312
Notes   315
Bibliography   351
Index   363

Maps

The Virginia Theater   27
The Shenandoah Valley   32
The First Battle of Manassas, July 21, 1861   47
Jones–Imboden Raid, April 20–May 27, 1863   118
The Gettysburg Campaign, June–July 1863   142
New Market, May 15, 1864   211
Piedmont, June 5, 1864   238
Lynchburg, June 17–18, 1864   255

Introduction

John Daniel Imboden figured prominently in the Civil War in Virginia. In a letter of 1884, Imboden claimed to have been a participant in a total of "67 encounters with the enemy, battles, affairs, etc., in which the fighting was hard." He was slightly wounded twice.[1] The major battles included First Bull Run (Manassas), Gettysburg, New Market, and Piedmont. Although he had no prior military experience other than limited militia training, Imboden rose to the rank of brigadier general in the Confederate Army. He proved a capable and aggressive cavalry commander, especially in advance guard and independent commands. Imboden, his four brothers, and their brother-in-law all served in the Confederate Army and have sometimes been referred to as "Six Brothers in Gray."

Imboden initially distinguished himself at the July 21, 1861, First Battle of Bull Run (Manassas). The next year he organized a cavalry unit, the 1st Partisan Rangers, which fought under Maj. Gen. Thomas J. "Stonewall" Jackson in the 1862 Shenandoah Valley Campaign, one of the major feats in the history of American arms. Imboden participated in the Battles of Cross Keys on June 8, 1862, and at Port Republic on June 9. During Lee's invasion of the North that summer, Imboden assisted in the capture of Harpers Ferry (September 15, 1862).

Promoted to brigadier general on January 28, 1863, Imboden showed considerable enterprise and ability in semi-independent command. On April 20 of that year Imboden led a 3,300-man force into western Virginia,[2] in conjunction with another force of 2,200 cavalry under Brig. Gen. William E. Jones. Their joint raid cut Baltimore & Ohio Railroad lines, captured large amounts of livestock, and ravaged the Kanawha Valley petroleum fields.

Imboden then took part in Gen. Robert E. Lee's 1863 invasion of Pennsylvania. His forces helped screen the Army of Northern Virginia's left flank during the advance but arrived in the vicinity of the battlefield of Gettysburg only on July 3. When Lee was forced to depart Gettysburg, he assigned Imboden the vital duty of covering the Confederate withdrawal. Imboden's men performed this task well, engaging in a fight at Williamsport that helped prevent Union forces from capturing the Confederate baggage trains and wounded.

In October 1863 Imboden raided into West Virginia for a second time and captured the Union garrison at Charles Town. This action won him a written commendation from Lee. In May 1864 Imboden's cavalry played a key role against Union Maj. Gen. Franz Sigel's thrust up (that is, southward) the Shenandoah Valley. On May 11 his force surprised and captured nearly five hundred Union troops in a cavalry regiment on outpost duty near Port Royal. Operating with Confederate Gen. John C. Breckinridge, Imboden helped defeat Sigel in the May 15 Battle of New Market. He fought in the June battles of Piedmont and Lynchburg and then participated in Confederate Lt. Gen. Jubal A. Early's June–July Valley Campaign, in which Rebel forces threatened Washington. Imboden also fought unsuccessfully to stem the subsequent advance of Union forces under Maj. Gen. Philip A. Sheridan up the Shenandoah Valley. In late 1864 Imboden contracted typhoid fever. On his return to duty, he closed out his war service in command of Confederate prisons in Georgia, Alabama, and Mississippi.

After the war Imboden entered business. He also wrote a number of articles for *Battles and Leaders of the Civil War* (4 volumes; 1887–1888). But he spent most of his post–Civil War life trying to restore the economic well-being of his native state through the development of its natural resources. In 1872 he published *The Coal and Iron Resources of Virginia*. Imboden realized that new rail lines would be crucial in the development of these natural resources. He worked tirelessly to promote the extension of rail lines, and he sought to overcome the proliferation of different gauges by inventing a car lifter that was adopted by a number of lines. He traveled extensively to secure investment for the development of the state's natural resources. Imboden founded the city of Damascus in southwestern Virginia, which he hoped to make into a new iron and steel center. Married five times in the course of his life, he died at Damascus on August 15, 1895.

Imboden has both his defenders and detractors. Some have praised him as a daring and resourceful leader; others have found much to criticize. Harold R. Woodward Jr.'s *Defender of the Valley: Brigadier General John Daniel Imboden, C.S.A.* (Berryville, Virginia, 1996) is a comprehensive and well-researched study, but Woodward finds no fault in his subject. Prolific Civil War author William C. Davis, while incorrectly bestowing on Imboden the rank of major general, says he was a "rare man" who, though not blessed with extraordinary talents, did realize his own limitations.[3]

Others have not been nearly as kind and have called into question Imboden's postwar recollections, citing what they consider to be fabrications or at least attempts to stretch the truth. Imboden's own views of the campaigns in which he participated found extensive distribution and were much cited in secondary accounts, thanks to the wide circulation of *Battles and Leaders of the Civil War.* Two eminent biographers of Confederate Lt. Gen. Thomas J. "Stonewall" Jackson, Robert K. Krick and James I. Robertson, have been scathing in their assessments of the worth of Imboden's postwar writing, especially in the instance of Jackson's purported dismantlement of the Baltimore & Ohio Railroad and a meeting Imboden claims he had with Jackson before the Battle of Port Republic. Krick writes, "Imboden's postwar declarations are almost completely worthless for historical purposes."[4] Robertson has observed that Imboden's postwar writings "must be ignored in most instances or handled with extreme caution in the other cases." Robertson noted, "The impeccable Jed Hotchkiss in later years wrote of Imboden (whom he had known in postwar Staunton): 'I do not like to say that my friend is unreliable; and yet the truth of the matter is that his statements will not bear the tests of criticism. . . . He writes from a confused memory and never takes the trouble of verifying his statements by a reference to documents.'"[5]

Such a conclusion is troubling for the biographer. Certainly Imboden was writing well after the fact and much of it from memory. As he noted in 1894, "All my military papers were lost or burnt after the surrender of Gen. Lee's army in 1865." Apparently these papers were with his brigade, which was scattered from Harrisonburg to Fincastle in Botetourt County when the war ended. Imboden assumed they were secreted or burned. In any case, all efforts to recover them had been unsuccessful.[6]

I have tried in my own account of Imboden to note such discrepancies. Certainly, three salient characteristics marked Imboden's life: his great ambition to succeed (which may have helped prompt his later embellishment of his own role in events), his determination to follow through on projects, and his concern for others, especially those in his charge. This latter trait is perhaps best shown in his efforts at the end of the war to alleviate the suffering of Union prisoners at Andersonville, even to the point of releasing some of the men. It is also revealed in his efforts to promote industrialization in Virginia after the war.

Imboden's men appear to have been intensely loyal to him. His chief leadership traits were his strong sense of duty, his concern for his men and desire not to risk their lives unduly, his awareness of the strengths and limitations of his subordinates, and his willingness to share the hardships of his troops.

There are two excellent master's theses on Imboden, both helpful to me in writing this book. Each covers a different aspect of Imboden's life. The first, by William D. Hager, "The Civilian Life and Accomplishments of John Daniel Imboden" (James Madison University, 1988), treats the pre–Civil War and antebellum years; the second, Clayton Malcolm Thomas III's "The Military Career of John D. Imboden" (University of Virginia, 1965), examines Imboden's Civil War service. Also quite useful is Robert J. Driver Jr.'s *The Staunton Artillery—McClanahan's Battery*, especially for Imboden's early service. There is only one biography of Imboden, Harold Woodward's aforementioned *Defender of the Valley*.

Archival records of Imboden papers are found at the National Archives, the Library of Congress, the Virginia Historical Society, the libraries of Washington and Lee University, the Virginia Military Institute, Case Western Reserve, and the Universities of Kentucky, North Carolina, Tennessee, and Virginia. Particularly valuable to this book have been the extensive holdings of family papers gathered by Imboden descendant T. Gibson Hobbs Jr. of Lynchburg, Virginia. In addition, there are Imboden's own writings on the war (with the caveat noted above), diaries, and numerous secondary books, articles, dispatches, and reports in the *Official Records of the War of the Rebellion*. These latter are particularly helpful to the researcher for they often reveal glaring discrepancies in the situation as reported at the time and as recalled years after the fact.

I am grateful to the Virginia Military Institute for its support of my work and to the following individuals for reading the manuscript and making helpful suggestions and corrections: William Hager, Gibson Hobbs, Richard Halseth, Keith Gibson, Dr. Steven Woodworth, and my wife, Beverly. I take full responsibility, however, for any errors or omissions.

Chapter 1

Early Life to the Civil War

John Daniel Imboden was born on February 16, 1823, at Christian's Creek near Fishersville, Virginia, a small community not far from the Augusta County seat of Staunton. Augusta County is situated on the westward slopes of the Blue Ridge Mountains in the central Shenandoah Valley, which takes its name from the Shenandoah River. Named for an Indian word meaning "Daughter of the Stars," the river is unusual in that it flows north rather than south.[1]

The first white settlers, predominantly of English stock, crossed the Blue Ridge from the Piedmont area of eastern Virginia and arrived in the Shenandoah Valley in 1716. Early in the nineteenth century another wave of immigrants arrived, largely Scotch-Irish and German in origin and predominantly from the northeastern United States. They established small ethnic farming communities in the Valley. The Germans quickly learned English and assimilated into the mainstream British culture.[2]

The name Imboden is Germanic in origin and means "of the valley." John Daniel Imboden's great grandfather, Johannes Imboden (1733–1819), was born in Henau, Switzerland, and arrived in Philadelphia from Rotterdam aboard the ship *Two Brothers* in 1752. The ship's captain apprenticed him to a rich farmer in Lebanon, Pennsylvania, as payment for the voyage. Johannes Imboden later married Eleanor Diller, his employer's daughter. He fought as a private in the Pennsylvania Militia during the Revolutionary War, and he and Eleanor had eleven children: seven sons and four daughters.

One of these sons, John Henry Imboden (1765–1838), and his wife, Catherine Williams Fernsler, moved to Augusta County, Virginia, in 1795. In May 1796 they bought from Gilbert and Lucy Christian a 195-acre farm on Christian's Creek, some five miles east of Staunton. The creek was named after the earliest white settlers there, and reportedly the farm was close to the site of the area's oldest fort erected for settlers' protection against Indian attack. The farm was also situated near the town of Fishersville and the Old Tinkling Spring Presbyterian Church.[3]

John Henry and Catherine Imboden had eleven children, seven of them sons. Their fifth son was George William Imboden (1793–1875). Although his other brothers moved west, George chose to remain in Augusta County, and in May 1822 he married Isabella Wunderlich, the daughter of close neighbors, whose forefathers had also come to America on the *Two Brothers,* although on a different voyage.[4]

On February 16, 1823, Isabella Imboden gave birth to their first child, John Daniel Imboden (1823–1895). George and Isabella Imboden would have eleven children. John Daniel's siblings were Susan B. (1824–1832); Polly Jane (1826–1832); Benjamin (1828–1847); Henry (1831–1832); Eliza Catherine, known as "Kate" (1833–1892); George William (1836–1922); David (1838–1851); Francis Marion, "Frank" (1841–1922); James Adam, "Jim" (1843–1928); and Jacob Peck, "Jake" (1846–1899). Benjamin probably died of typhoid fever at Buena Vista during the 1846–1848 Mexican War; Susan B., Polly Jane, and Henry all succumbed to scarlet fever in 1832.

In 1827, George Imboden purchased the three hundred–acre farm belonging to his father-in-law, also located on Christian's Creek some five miles east of Staunton. It remained in the family until 1852, when they sold it to William M. Simms and moved to Lewis County in western Virginia, with three of their younger children: Frank, Jim, and Jake. John, Kate, and George William remained in Augusta County. In 1855 George and Isabella Imboden sold an additional six hundred acres that they had acquired in Augusta Springs. Shortly thereafter, they moved again, this time to Braxton County, which adjoins Lewis County to the southwest. They were brought back to Virginia by their sons during the Civil War.[5]

The population of Augusta County was overwhelmingly rural. In 1820 the one thousand–square-mile county had a population of only 16,742, less than a tenth of whom lived in Staunton. Life on the farm was financially difficult at times, but the Imboden children seem to have been relatively well off. By all indications the family was close-knit and happy. Money was probably in short supply—much of the trade was by barter and there was no bank in the county until one was established in Staunton in 1847—but the children were never without food or clothing.[6]

John Daniel grew into a handsome, strong, well-built, tall (standing well over six feet), and intelligent young man. Children on the farm were expected to work from an early age and, as the firstborn son, John Daniel assumed an increasing leadership role in family activities. Reportedly, his father gave him charge of operating a small water-powered sawmill erected by the family on their property. There is a story, perhaps apocryphal, that John Daniel rigged the machinery so that it would operate more slowly in order that he might read at the same time. The story goes that his father, investigating the diminished output, easily discovered the modification and gave John Daniel a sound whipping.[7]

Certainly farmwork took precedence over education, but all of the Imboden children learned to read and write well. Surviving samples of their writing show commendable handwriting, spelling, and composition. All save Jim received a higher education. Before her marriage, Kate attended the Augusta Female Seminary in Staunton (now Mary Baldwin College). George William went to the Staunton Academy, and Frank and Jake attended the Virginia Military Institute in Lexington.

There was no formal state education system in Virginia until 1869, and John Daniel went to the county school, which probably enrolled children until age fifteen or sixteen. The Staunton Academy was for the children of wealthier families and was probably beyond the means of the Imbodens when John Daniel was growing up. By the late 1840s, however, the family was apparently doing well enough financially that George William could attend there. While barely in his teens, John Daniel developed an avid interest in reading and self-education, perhaps encouraged by family attendance at the Lutheran Church.[8]

Even as a young man, John Daniel revealed the desire to elevate himself by means of education. In August 1841, at age eighteen, he enrolled as a student at Washington College (later Washington and Lee University) in Lexington, forty miles south of Staunton. Founded in 1749 by Presbyterian settlers, the school was known by 1776 as Liberty Academy. It survived thanks to a grant of stock in the James River Company, a river barge operator, given by George Washington in 1796. In gratitude for this gift, the school was then renamed Washington College. The Commonwealth of Virginia chartered the institution in 1782, and by the time Imboden enrolled there, Washington College enjoyed a fine academic reputation.

Strict regulations prohibited students from drinking, gambling, using profanity, and dancing. Tuition, room rent, and the matriculation fee came to $42 a year. Board ran $7.50 to $8.00 per month. Laundry, firewood, and candles were additional. In all, costs came to about $142 per year, not counting books and incidental expenses. The school day began with chapel services at 5:00 A.M. and lasted until dusk. Washington College offered both a four-year conventional track leading to a bachelor's degree and a two-year agricultural course "to qualify young men to become intelligent farmers."[9]

Imboden's farming background and the fact that he attended Washington College only two years and yet graduated in June 1843 suggest that he followed the agricultural curriculum. The first year's studies centered on mathematics and rhetoric; the second year addressed the physical and natural sciences. University records show that he studied chemistry, natural philosophy (physics), mathematics, ethics, French, rhetoric, and ancient history.[10]

Imboden stated later in life that he took engineering courses at the Virginia Military Institute. Founded in 1839, it was located adjacent to Washington College. As a condition of VMI's founding, the state legislature had mandated student exchanges between it and Washington College.[11]

This exchange arrangement was in fact spelled out in Washington College's catalogue, which noted that because the institutions were so close physically, the boards of the two schools had agreed that "All the classes, lectures and exercises of instruction in the one, are to be open to the students and cadets of the other, on payment of tuition fees not exceeding ten dollars per annum for each class entered."[12]

Even if Imboden took some engineering courses at VMI, he was never formally enrolled at the Institute; nor was he required to attend classes there.[13] Regardless, Imboden retained a great fondness for VMI throughout his life. In November 1863, when he was a brigadier general, he wrote VMI superintendent Francis H. Smith: "The Institute over which you have so long presided has always been an object of deep interest to me. And I have greatly regretted during the past three years that I had not enjoyed the advantages of a training within its walls. I have sons growing up, who if I live, shall not have the same cause of regret."[14]

While in Lexington, Imboden made social contacts with a number of individuals who would be important to him later in life. These included John Howard McCue, called Howard, of Fishersville; John Letcher of Lexington, who would serve as Virginia's governor at the beginning of the Civil War; VMI superintendent Smith, an influential educator in the South and lifelong friend; and John Letcher Jr., the editor of the *Valley Star* from 1839 to 1846 and a practicing lawyer in Lexington. From 1851 to 1859 the second John Letcher represented Virginia in the U.S. House of Representatives. He may also have been influential in getting Imboden to take up the practice of law.[15]

Imboden had a strong interest in engineering and may thus have met Claudius Crozet, if indeed he studied at VMI; in any case, the two became acquainted when Imboden was a young adult. Born in France and a graduate of the École Polytechnique, Crozet had taught at the United States Military Academy, West Point, for a time and in 1823 became chief engineer of the Commonwealth of Virginia. During the next forty years, he was a major influence in education and in the development of transportation in the state.[16]

Following completion of his studies, Imboden returned to Augusta County. Twenty years old in February 1843, he faced the decision of a profession. Imboden decided he would return to Staunton and settle there. Soon he obtained a teaching position at the Virginia Institute for Education of the Deaf and the Dumb and of the Blind in Staunton. Later he became a member of its governing body.[17]

Imboden did not teach long, for he decided to pursue a career in law. He loved reading, and he enjoyed improving his mental capabilities, so a career in the law must have seemed natural. There were few law schools in the United States at that time, and none was immediately available to him. In that day the majority of lawyers did not learn their profession in the classroom. Rather they "read law," usually in the office of an established attorney or at least under his supervision.

There were no law examinations. In mid-nineteenth-century America there were also relatively few legal precedents with which students had to become acquainted, and American courts relied heavily on common law.[18]

For the better part of a year, Imboden read law in Staunton. Having satisfied his mentor, possibly William Frazier, he then presented himself to the presiding judge of Augusta County and was duly admitted to the bar. In October 1844 Imboden formed a law partnership in Staunton with Frazier. Court records indicate that the firm of Frazier and Imboden was rarely involved in trial activities. The two lawyers spent most of their time in business-related matters, including debt collection, estates, and property law.[19]

In December 1844 Imboden joined the fraternal order of the Masons. His keen interest in Masonry may be seen by the fact that he was advanced to master mason after only two months, in January 1845. This suggests that Imboden had not joined the order simply as a device to attract clients to his law practice. Imboden was elected worshipful master in 1848 and again in 1849; in the latter year, also, he became district deputy grand master, a high honor in Masonry.[20]

Imboden also married. His close friendship with Col. Franklin McCue (1795–1874) led to the courtship of McCue's daughter Eliza, known as "Dice" to her family and friends. They were married on June 16, 1845. Their first child, a daughter named Jane ("Jennie") Crawford, was born on November 28, 1847.

The Imbodens purchased a lot in Staunton in December 1847 and there built a home, which they named "Ingleside Cottage." It was completed before the arrival of another daughter, Isabella ("Bel"), born on December 6, 1849. She died at two and a half on July 27, 1852. Another daughter, Martha Russel ("Russie"), was born on March 29, 1852. Their fourth child, a son named Frank Howard, was born on June 21, 1855.[21]

In May 1846 war began between the United States and Mexico, and President James K. Polk asked for fifty thousand volunteers. Although most of these came from the states closest to Mexico, Virginia contributed a regiment, to which Augusta County furnished a company. Imboden's personal reaction to the war is unknown, but his younger brother Benjamin enlisted, went to Mexico, and died there, probably of a fever.[22]

Imboden's law partnership dissolved, most probably because Frazier became increasingly interested in commercial activities, specifically the development of Rockbridge Alum Springs, a health resort seventeen miles west of Lexington. The Springs was a considerable enterprise. It extended over some two thousand acres, housed up to four hundred guests a day, and was at one point considered the most valuable piece of real estate in the South. Beginning in 1846, however, it was also the subject of a lawsuit over its rightful ownership. Frazier became more involved in the Springs, and in 1852 he and his brother John purchased it.[23]

Apparently the firm of Frazier and Imboden had done well financially as Frazier had sufficient resources to help purchase the Springs; Imboden, on his part, purchased Staunton real estate and erected houses on both North Market and West Main (today Beverly) Streets.[24] It is unclear exactly when the firm of Frazier and Imboden was dissolved, but by October 1854 Imboden was practicing as the junior law partner of John Howard McCue, his acquaintance from Washington College days and first cousin by marriage to Imboden's wife, Eliza. The partnership continued until 1860, when McCue moved to Nelson County and established his own practice there. The firm of McCue and Imboden specialized in business law, and all indications are that the practice was successful. When the firm was dissolved, Imboden went into practice by himself, building his own law office in downtown Staunton near the courthouse.[25]

The McCue family was also important to Imboden in another sense. One of John Howard McCue's cousins, John Marshall "Major" McCue, was adjutant of the 32d Virginia Militia Regiment. It is not clear who initiated the correspondence between the two men, but in 1848 Imboden wrote to McCue, asserting that he would accept appointment as an adjutant if the position were offered. In the same letter he stated that he did not have any military aspirations and indeed intended to pursue a civilian career.[26]

Imboden had also become interested in politics. Rejecting the conservative Democratic Party, he supported the more liberal Whigs. The

Whig Party had grown out of the old National Republic and Anti-Masonic Parties. Imboden found himself in agreement with their positions on improving living standards and restoring Virginia's leadership at the national level. It should not be surprising that this put him in the same political camp as his in-laws, the McCues.[27]

The Whigs had enjoyed success in Virginia, beginning with the election of Littleton W. Tazewell as governor in 1834. Three other Whig governors followed, but the party suffered a setback in 1842 when Democrat James McDowell was elected. Nationally, in the presidential election of 1844, Jacksonian Democrat James K. Polk ran against Whig standard-bearer Henry Clay, whom Imboden supported. Polk took a strong expansionist stand; he won in part because abolitionist James C. Birney of Kentucky siphoned off votes from Clay.

In the national elections of 1848 the Whigs fielded Mexican War hero Maj. Gen. Zachary Taylor as their candidate, and "Old Rough and Ready"—as Taylor was known from his military days—was easily elected. Imboden strongly supported Taylor, and was chosen as a presidential elector in 1848. The next March Imboden traveled to Washington to attend Taylor's inauguration, and on the same trip he visited Baltimore and Philadelphia.

By then Imboden had also developed an interest in promoting rail transportation, which became a lifelong passion. He was especially interested in seeing a line extended to Staunton, which lacked rail connections. Undoubtedly Imboden found much to admire in the far more developed rail nets in the North.[28]

Throughout the United States, rail transportation was expanding and costs were coming down, thanks to the durability of iron rails and the introduction of rolled iron rails, which first came into use in America in 1847. Rail lines would be very important to the economic development of the Shenandoah Valley. They could bring manufactured goods to the Valley and carry out its agricultural and mineral products. Unfortunately, the mountains to either side were a formidable barrier and, not infrequently, those traveling to the eastern part of the state from the Valley went by way of Baltimore.[29]

Securing a rail line would be extremely important to the economic development of Staunton, and in 1846 and again in 1848 the citizens of that community held meetings to try to interest the Louisa Railroad

Company in driving a tunnel through the Blue Ridge Mountains and extending its line to Covington with a stop along the way at Staunton. In May 1849 the railroad reached Shadwell, five miles east of Charlottesville, but the cost of tunneling through the Blue Ridge blocked further movement west.[30]

Imboden's growing political stature was evident not only in his selection as a presidential elector but also in his attainment of increased local authority. In 1847 he was appointed commissioner of schools in Augusta County. This involved monitoring state funds given largely for support of the Virginia Institute for Education of the Deaf and the Dumb and of the Blind at Staunton. County records indicate that Imboden continued this work until 1858.[31]

In April 1850 there was a plebiscite on the issue of calling a convention to change the Virginia State Constitution of 1830. In general, the people of the Shenandoah Valley and the western part of the state were very much behind the idea. Reformers won all five of the seats from the Valley district in the subsequent August 1850 elections. The successful candidates for the district representing Augusta, Rockbridge, and Highland Counties included Imboden's old friend John Letcher and his law partner John H. McCue. The convention duly met and drafted a new constitution, which included universal suffrage without property qualification for all white male citizens and the popular election of local officials, including judges. The constitution was ratified in 1851 in another statewide vote.[32]

Imboden, meanwhile, was elected a member of the Virginia House of Delegates. He gave his first speech to the legislature in late January 1851. In this half-hour address, he advocated extension of the Virginia Central Railroad from Richmond to the Ohio River.

Imboden clearly enjoyed politics. He wrote Eliza that he was strong politically in Augusta County but welcomed opposition because, "It has been my lot from childhood to struggle through obstacles of every kind. I have never yet undertaken anything which I have not accomplished."[33]

In March Imboden delivered another speech to the House, "of near an hour in length," in which he supported a bill to provide funding for completion of the Virginia Central line to Staunton. He noted, "Great opposition was made to it, but we were successful." He also told "Dice" that he hoped to return to Staunton soon.[34]

In March 1849 the Blue Ridge Railroad Company had been incorporated with the intent to connect the Louisa Railroad and continue westward seventeen miles toward Staunton. The Commonwealth of Virginia owned all of the company's stock, and later this line became the Virginia Central Railroad. Chief engineer of the railroad Claudius Crozet supervised the work, but the great tunnel—nearly a mile long—was some eight years in construction and not completed until April 1858.

In the meantime, track had been laid over Rockfish Gap in the Blue Ridge Mountains east of Staunton. Utilizing a series of switchbacks, that line opened in March 1854. The Shenandoah Valley was now finally tied via a direct rail line with the Tidewater and Piedmont portions of the state. In October 1854 the Orange & Alexandria and Manassas Gap Railroads connected with Front Royal at the northern end of the Blue Ridge and with Charlottesville and the Virginia Central to the south, while the Virginia & Tennessee Railroad connected Virginia to the West.[35]

As Imboden entered state office, the national political scene was becoming increasingly troubled. Southern political parties underwent great convolution during which States' Rights Whigs tended to realign themselves with the Democratic Party. In the 1852 presidential elections the Whigs again put forward a war hero, "Old Fuss and Feathers," Gen. Winfield Scott, the ranking army general who had performed so brilliantly in the war with Mexico. But with the split in the Whig Party, New Hampshire Democrat Franklin Pierce easily won election. Scott's failure to win the presidential election along with discord over the 1854 Kansas-Nebraska Act helped deepen the splinter in the North-South Whig alignment. Many southern Whigs now joined in a brief resurrection of the Know-Nothing Party or the American Party. The latter was strongly anti-Catholic; it sought a twenty-one-year residency of all foreigners as a prerequisite for full naturalization and the right to vote.[36]

All of this caused John Letcher to remark in an August 1852 letter to Imboden, "the continuing sectional crisis is exaggerating a few key differences and gradually destroying the traditional flexibility of the American political system."[37] Sectionalism was beginning to tear apart the American body politic.

This political realignment was probably responsible for Imboden's failure to win reelection as his district's representative in the 1853–1854

House of Delegates. By 1855 Imboden was strongly identified with the new American Party.[38] Its position was possible in a state where the white population was essentially homogeneous and settled. Most new immigrants settled in the North, in large part because of their inability to compete with southern slave labor.

Imboden did secure sufficient support to be elected to the House of Delegates for the 1855–1856 term. Only in his early thirties at the time, he seems to have had a considerable reputation for his excellent command of English and his public speaking ability. He was often invited to give talks to various local organizations. He also seems to have been a highly effective legislator, at least in terms of his chief project: pushing the extension of the Virginia Central Railroad to Staunton.[39]

Evidence of further sectional division occurred in the national elections of 1856. A new political body, the Republican Party, emerged. Formed by former Free-Soilers and Whigs and composed almost entirely of northerners, it was anti-slavery, at least as far as expansion of the practice into the territories was concerned. It supported industrial and commercial development and the dignity of labor. Almost immediately, the Republican Party was a force on the national scene.

The first Republican presidential standard-bearer was John C. Frémont. Known as the "Pathfinder" for his trailblazing expeditions across the Rocky Mountains and his exploration of California, Frémont had taken part in the campaign to secure California during the war with Mexico. A Free-Soiler from Missouri, he had, however, virtually no political experience. The Democrats nominated James Buchanan of Pennsylvania, known as "a northern man with southern principles," while the American Party put forward former president Millard Fillmore. Buchanan gathered significant southern support to win the election. Frémont made a strong showing, however, winning several free states. Fillmore carried only Maryland.[40]

While the national political scene was changing, Imboden experienced personal tragedy. On March 17, 1857, he and Dice had a fifth child, a second son, whom they named George William, after his uncle. Nine months later on December 23, Dice, Imboden's wife of twelve years, died following a lingering illness. Imboden found himself left to raise four children alone: Jennie, ten; Russie, five; Frank Howard, two; and George William.[41]

That same year, but before his wife's death, Imboden had run for the U.S. House of Representatives, challenging his friend and popular Democrat John Letcher Jr., who was running for a fourth congressional term. Imboden ran under the banner of the Distribution Party, a largely local collection of Whigs and Know-Nothings who were chiefly interested in the defeat of Letcher. Despite the strong endorsement of the Staunton *Spectator*, Imboden lost the election by a three-to-one margin. It is a tribute to his tenacity and principles that he was willing to take on a cause with such little chance of success.[42]

Imboden probably believed that, whatever the election outcome, the race would raise his political stature in the community. He was not through with campaigning for political office. In 1858 he ran for and was elected to a six-year term as Augusta County clerk, a post he held until 1864.[43] In 1857 Imboden was also elected as a trustee of the Augusta Female Seminary, and he continued to serve in that capacity even after the Civil War.[44]

Imboden did not remain a widower for long. No doubt the pressures of handling four young children as a politically ambitious single parent played a role, as did the need for companionship. Mary Wilson McPhail, his second wife, was ten years his junior. Born on October 31, 1833, she was from Charlotte County. Mary and Imboden were married at her family home of Mulberry Hill, in Charlotte County, on May 12, 1859.[45]

Imboden built a new family home for his new wife and children. Known as "Green Hill," it could be considered stately in the context of the time and its location. The home was situated at the top of Market Street in Staunton.

Imboden's second marriage prospered. He and his new wife had three more children. All were born at Mulberry Hill, southeast of Lynchburg. Mary loved Mulberry Hill and spent a great deal of time there with her parents, more so as her husband was away for long periods in Richmond. Especially during the Civil War years, Mary found Mulberry Hill to be a secure haven for the children. Certainly it was a much safer location than Staunton, removed as it was from the fighting to the west in the Shenandoah Valley. Because the family spent less and less time there, Imboden sold Green Hill in 1862. Unfortunately for his financial future, he invested the money realized from the sale in Confederate war bonds. In 1968 Mary Baldwin College purchased Green Hill; it was razed a year later.[46]

The Imbodens' first child, Nanine Carrington ("Nantsie"), was born on February 16, 1860. Their second child, Mary Wilson, was born on November 12, 1861, but she died only five months later, on April 28, 1862. Their third child, John Daniel Jr., was born on July 21, 1863. He died in 1877.[47]

Imboden joined the militia in 1858 as a captain in the 160th Regiment, 13th Brigade, 5th Division of the Virginia Militia. His commission, dated June 10 and signed by Gov. Henry Wise, gives his date of rank as May 22. In late August that same year Imboden was exempted from duty as a consequence of his political office, although he continued on militia rolls as an honorary contributing member with dues of five dollars a year.[48]

This was not Imboden's first time to be enrolled in the militia. In 1846 during the war with Mexico, Maj. John Marshall McCue of the 32d Regiment of Virginia Militia had asked him to become his adjutant, and Imboden had accepted.[49]

State militias had been in existence since colonial times as protection against Indian attack. All the colonies had organized them, and even Quaker Pennsylvania had a voluntary militia force. The colonists much preferred militias to a professional military. They had inherited from the mother country of Britain a strong distaste for standing armies, and, apart from the Indians, there were no real military threats that might require a professional army. During the early Republic and even to the Civil War the regular army had always been quite small.

These militias were largely untrained and, as time went on, increasingly ineffective—at least against trained, regular military formations. Although militias had successfully put down Indian uprisings and quelled civil disorders, they had an abysmal record against professional military forces, such as the regular British units they faced in the American Revolution and the War of 1812. Despite this, much of the country believed the myth that both wars had been won largely by militia contributions.

In the late 1850s national events rushed toward crisis in the widening rift over slavery and abetted the formation of militia units in the South. Two days after Buchanan's inauguration, the Supreme Court ruled in the case of *Dred Scott v. Sandford*. The decision, by a Court with a majority of southern judges, held that blacks were "beings of an inferior order" and that Dred Scott was not a citizen and thus had no right to sue in the federal courts. The Court also held that the 1820 Missouri Compromise was illegal because Congress did not have the power to ban slavery in the territories. Finally, it held that although the Scotts had been taken in and out of free territory, these moves did not affect their status. These rulings and Buchanan's endorsement of them angered many in the North. Violence increased in Kansas as both pro- and anti-slavery advocates sought to control a constitutional convention favorable to their views.

A third event that polarized North and South came in the summer and autumn of 1858 as Republican Abraham Lincoln and his Democratic opponent Stephen A. Douglas, candidates for the U.S. Senate seat from Illinois, held a series of debates that attracted national attention. Lincoln argued against the extension of slavery in the territories, while Douglas took the position that interfering in slavery was no business of the North. Douglas won the election, but Lincoln's strong stand against slavery made him a national figure and a leading candidate for the Republican presidential nomination. The possibility of a national breakup now loomed large, along with the specter of civil war.

In 1859 an event portending the now seemingly irrepressible conflict had an immediate impact in the Shenandoah Valley. On October 16 John Brown, a staunch abolitionist (who was responsible for the Pottawatomi massacre in Kansas), and eighteen followers—including five blacks—seized the federal arsenal at Harpers Ferry, Virginia. Apparently Brown hoped to establish a republic of fugitive slaves in the Appalachian Mountains and to use this as a base from which to wage war on the slave states. The raid was poorly executed, and a number of Brown's men were killed before the attackers were overrun. Charged with murder, conspiracy, and treason against Virginia, Brown rejected his counsel's suggestion of an insanity plea and was tried and hanged.

Most southerners saw John Brown's raid as an expression of true northern sentiment, even a plot on behalf of the North. Although most of the northern press and a number of the region's prominent leaders, including both Lincoln and Douglas, condemned Brown, there was widespread admiration for the man and his deed, which won praise from some ministers in their pulpits as part of a "holy" cause. Douglas, however, held that Brown's attack on Harpers Ferry was "the natural, logical, and inevitable result of the doctrines and teachings of the Republican party."[50]

Imboden's exact reaction to Brown's raid on Harpers Ferry is unknown, but the event caused much excitement and concern in the Valley, especially in Staunton. Harpers Ferry was only about one hundred miles north as the crow flies, and Staunton was now an important communications hub—with major railroad lines running both north-south and east-west—of considerable military importance. The raid certainly heightened southerners' fears about military vulnerability and led to a renewed interest in voluntary military units. In Augusta County and the surrounding area alone, twelve volunteer military companies were organizing: nine of infantry, two troops of cavalry, and one battery of artillery.[51]

Imboden took the lead in organizing the artillery battery, known as the Staunton Artillery. Elected captain on November 28, 1859, just a few days before John Brown's hanging on December 2, Imboden's reputation in the area helped him secure a full complement of officers and men. Several weeks later, on December 12, Imboden wrote to VMI superintendent Francis H. Smith telling him of his desire to secure four mountain howitzers (VMI was then also a state arsenal). It was not clear that the state even owned such weapons; failing these, Imboden requested "6-pounder brass field guns," two of which he believed were at Lexington, along with caissons and limbers. Imboden was on his way to Richmond to see Governor Wise, and he asked that Smith contact him there to let him know about the availability of the guns and suitable "artillery sabers and carbines."[52]

Wise subsequently overruled Adj. Gen. William H. Richardson and assigned two 6-pounder field guns to Imboden. In providing the guns, Wise stated: "You could not have obtained them, sir, but for the confidence I have in you and your men to keep them in perfect order—ready for service—and all I ask in return is that whenever I call for these guns, and order you and your men to come with them, you will obey the call, whether I be in or out of office or the call be private or official."[53]

Imboden responded to Wise's letter with a promise to "lacquer the guns, build them a shelter, drill his men, train his horses, and obey the call of the Governor. . . ." He also promised to provide horses and accouterments.[54]

On December 31, 1859, officers of the Augusta County volunteer companies met in the clerk's office to form a full regiment of volunteers. By that point, eight of the dozen or so companies in Augusta County had been organized, numbering 540 men. Virginia Militia Brig. Gen. William H. Harman, a veteran of the Mexican War, presided over the meeting, and Imboden was appointed secretary. A second meeting was planned for January 14, 1860, to finalize decisions and elect field-grade regimental officers.[55]

On January 17, Col. William D. Anderson, commanding the 160th Regiment of the Virginia Militia, ordered captains in his command to enroll all men eligible for duty. Boundary lines were established for this purpose, and Imboden's brother George W. Imboden, also a lawyer in Staunton and then a militia captain commanding Company A of the 1st Battalion, had the jurisdiction including all the city south of Beverly Street.[56]

On February 22, 1860, on the occasion of George Washington's birthday, Captain Imboden's Staunton Artillery of some forty-five men and the West Augusta Guard drilled before the public. Although the battery was not yet completely equipped, the men demonstrated what the Staunton *Spectator* characterized as considerable proficiency with their two field pieces, loading and firing them twenty-five to thirty times.[57]

Imboden also contracted with a Richmond flag maker for a banner for his unit. Made of silk, the flag was expensive, costing some one hundred dollars. The design consisted of Virginia's state shield against the background of the "Bonnie Blue Flag" along with the date the unit was organized: November 28, 1859. The flag was delivered in time for the annual three-day militia training period and was formally presented to the unit by General Harman.[58]

Imboden's Battery and the West Augusta Guard were also called out to greet the new governor, John Letcher Sr., when he visited Staunton from Richmond on July 5. Following a welcoming ceremony at the train depot and speeches at the nearby Virginia Hotel, the guests and militiamen moved to the homes of Lt. Thomas L. Harman of the artillery and Capt. William S.H. Baylor of the guards for refreshments. The next day Letcher and his entourage inspected the Staunton Artillery and two infantry companies. In August the artillery, guard, and a band traveled by train to nearby Fishersville for a flag presentation ceremony to the Augusta Rifles. Following a parade with some 1,500 onlookers, Imboden's men fired a salute. The Staunton *Spectator* trumpeted: "We challenge any town in the state to contrast its military companies with those of Staunton."[59] How much time Imboden spent in drill with his unit is unknown, but he requested and received three copies of *Cavalry Tactics* from U.S. Secretary of War John B. Floyd.[60]

Despite the national turmoil, Imboden continued his law practice and other duties. In early 1861 he became interested in purchasing land in another state. He considered both Florida and Louisiana, the latter having the advantage of relatives living there who could advise him on property values. For advice on property in Florida, Imboden wrote an acquaintance of Colonel McCue who was reportedly a major landowner there. In describing his situation, Imboden explained that he already owned eight hundred acres of timberland on the Cumberland River in Kentucky, an inheritance from one of his uncles, and that he engaged "20 to 30 hands at large profit in the lumber business." It is unclear whether the labor was free or slave, although Imboden did mention that he expected the property to yield at least ten thousand dollars a year in income for several years.

Clearly the national political scene troubled Imboden. Concerns that his timberland was only about twenty-four miles from Illinois may have prompted his interest in investing in southern real estate. He expected to have several thousand dollars available that year to invest in "lands somewhere in the Gulf States, with a view to their gradual improvement, and fitting them for *my home* [emphasis in original] after three or four years." Imboden wrote that he had decided "at the end of that time, if I live, to withdraw from all public employment—in which I have been a slave for 15 years—and become a private freeman." Imboden wrote that he expected to have twenty to thirty thousand dollars available to invest over the next three to four years. These plans, if indeed he was serious about them, soon fell apart with the beginning of the Civil War.[61]

Imboden cannot have been too serious about quitting his native state, because he was also involved in a number of new business interests in Virginia in early 1861. On January 23, 1861, the Virginia Assembly passed legislation incorporating the Virginia Arms Manufacturing

Company, formed to manufacture and sell "fire arms and all other implements of war" in and near Richmond. Imboden and his friend John Marshall McCue joined Joseph R. Anderson, premier southern industrialist and director of the Tredegar Iron Works in Richmond, and six other individuals as directors of the company. Also, on April 2, 1861, the Virginia Assembly passed an act incorporating the Berkeley Springs Savings Bank in the town of Bath in Morgan County. Imboden was one of nine individuals named as its directors.[62]

Events on the national scene were rapidly moving to secession and civil war. The country as a whole was in a state of excitement over the 1860 presidential elections. The Republican Party met in Chicago and nominated Abraham Lincoln as their standard-bearer. Lincoln endorsed the party plank of opposing slavery's expansion into the territories but upholding it where it then existed. Southern leaders, especially Jefferson Davis of Mississippi, played into the hands of the Republicans by splitting the Democratic Party on the issue of slavery. The Democratic Convention held in April 1860 in Charleston, South Carolina—a hotbed of secessionist sentiment—deadlocked over a ten-day period without reaching agreement on a presidential candidate, adjourned for six weeks, and met again in Baltimore, where the differences proved irreconcilable. Two separate conventions each finally nominated their own candidate. Douglas represented the northern Democrats and John C. Breckinridge, Buchanan's vice president, was the standard-bearer of southern Democrats, who favored federal protection of slavery in the territories. A new party also joined the fray: the Constitutional Union Party, formed by former southern Whigs and border-state nativists, which sought a compromise position. Their candidate was John Bell, a slaveholder from Tennessee.

Lincoln won the November 6, 1860, presidential election in a plurality of the popular vote, and thanks to the split in the Democratic Party, he took an overwhelming majority of votes (180) in the electoral college. Breckinridge carried the Deep South (72). Bell, for whom Imboden had campaigned in the Shenandoah Valley, secured the entire electoral vote of Virginia and also carried two other border states, Kentucky and Tennessee (39). Douglas carried only Missouri and part of New Jersey (12).[63]

Secession was already in the air. A year earlier, in late 1859, Senator

Robert Toombs of Georgia had pleaded, "Never permit this Federal government to pass into the traitorous hands of the black Republican party."[64]

Western Virginia was particularly torn on the issue of secession. Most of the western counties were reluctant to leave the Union. The more rural and hilly western part of the state lacked the large plantations of the Tidewater or the Piedmont, and slavery was not as central an issue there. Those slaves in the western counties were used primarily for small farming, lumbering, or building tasks or as domestic servants who tended to the house and gardens. Indeed, Imboden, who owned slaves himself, wrote from Richmond in a letter to his wife suggesting that their slaves perform garden and yard work.[65]

As evidence of strong Unionist sentiment in the Valley, on November 26, weeks after Lincoln won the election, a mass meeting was held at the Staunton courthouse to promote the cause of national preservation. Imboden used the occasion to declare his loyalty to Virginia and the South, but he also said that he did not wish to see the Union dissolved. The meeting resulted in adoption of the following resolution:

> That our senator and delegates be requested, in the discharge of the responsible duties which will soon devolve upon them, in the spirit of harmony and conciliation attempted to be expressed in these resolves, to bend all their energies to keep Virginia to her moorings as "Flag Ship of the Union," and to induce her, placed as she is between the North and the extreme South, with moderation, forbearance and wisdom worthy of her ancient renown, to exert her power and influence to preserve, on the one hand, the known and equal rights of her own people as citizens of a common country, and, on the other, the harmony of the Union and the integrity of the Constitution.[66]

Thus Staunton citizens took a stance for preservation of the Union but against coercion of the states of the Deep South.

Contrary to the impression he gave at the meeting, Imboden thought secession inevitable. He did not believe it justified by the mere election of Lincoln, however. Writing to his confidant, John H. McCue, Imboden concluded, "that the entire South will speedily have to leave the Confederacy under the present Constitution I entertain no doubt whatever—but I don't think S.C. has put the issue upon defensible ground. . . . To break up the Government for the mere loss of an election is not regarded by thousands as justifiable. It is a mere pretext on the part of disunionists per se to precipitate a revolution."[67]

On December 20, 1860, South Carolina became the first southern state to secede. During January it was followed in order by Mississippi, Florida, Alabama, Georgia, and Louisiana; Texas seceded on February 1. A week later, on February 8, 1861, delegates from these states met at Montgomery, Alabama, and formed the Confederate States of America. The next day the Confederate Congress elected Jefferson Davis as president. The seceded states proceeded to take over the federal government properties within their borders. The two notable exceptions were Fort Pickens at Pensacola, Florida, and Fort Sumter in South Carolina's Charleston harbor.

President Buchanan dithered over possible action, but so did his successor Lincoln for several weeks. Buchanan opposed secession, but he believed he lacked the constitutional powers to suppress it. Furthermore, he was reluctant to antagonize Virginia and other states that might then join the Confederacy. Several of Buchanan's cabinet members resigned in protest over his inertia.

Meanwhile, the Virginia legislature passed an act calling for the election of a special state convention to decide the matter of secession. Although the citizens of Augusta County opposed a breakup of the Union, they duly held an election on February 4, 1861, to choose representatives for the state convention. Imboden ran but was overwhelmingly defeated by Unionist candidate Alexander H. Stuart. Imboden now clearly favored secession. As he put it after the war, "I favored secession as the only 'peace measure' Virginia could then adopt, our aim being to put the state in an independent position to negotiate between the United States and the seceded Gulf and Cotton States for a new Union, to be formed on a compromise of the slavery question by a convention to be held for that purpose."[68]

Most citizens of Augusta County disagreed with this position, and they chose as their representatives only those of strong Unionist views. Indeed, of nineteen delegates selected from the Shenandoah Valley counties, only four believed that Virginia should secede. Imboden found himself in the minority: "I think Va. has turned fool," he wrote, "but my opinion is contrary to the opinion of the people and I will awate [*sic*] the arbitrement of time to prove who is right."[69]

Imboden thought the Unionists were deceiving themselves with talk that the Union might be preserved: "The Union is dissolved, and what's the use to shut our eyes to the fact, if we cannot reconstruct. Let's all go together peacefully if we can, forcibly if we must. For we have but one and the same destiny, one and the same interest. . . . What's the use to deny the true state of the case, and fool & cheat the people by singing hazanahs [*sic*] to the Union when there is no Union! I am called a fire eater disunionist . . . but I don't care what they call me. I am going to say what I think and believe, and let the consequences take care of themselves."[70]

Like Buchanan, President Lincoln was anxious to avoid antagonizing the border states and did nothing on the matter of secession for weeks. By the time of Lincoln's inauguration, only Fort Pickens off Pensacola and Fort Sumter off Charleston remained in federal hands. Sumter's situation was the more precarious. Ringed by South Carolina artillery, its garrison was almost out of provisions. The simplest course of action would be to hold on to Pickens and evacuate Sumter.

On March 30, however, Lincoln ordered a relief expedition prepared for Fort Sumter. The expedition was to be ready to sail by April 6, with Lincoln to make the final decision about Sumter at that point. The decision to try to relieve Sumter ran against the advice of a majority of his cabinet, including Secretary of State William Seward, who argued that it would probably lead to war and cause Virginia to secede; Seward proposed evacuating Sumter and holding on to Pickens. On April 6, Lincoln sent State Department Clerk Robert L. Chew to South Carolina to inform Confederate authorities there that a supply expedition was being sent to Fort Sumter, in effect leaving it up to Confederate authorities as to whether there would be war. Chew arrived on the night of April 8. Meanwhile, the relief expedition sailed on April 10.

Informed of developments, Jefferson Davis ordered Brig. Gen. Pierre G.T. Beauregard to demand Fort Sumter's surrender, and if it was refused to reduce the fort. On receiving an unsatisfactory reply from its commander, Beauregard ordered his shore batteries to open fire before the expedition could arrive. At 4:30 A.M. on April 12, the first shot of the Civil War boomed out across Charleston harbor. Fort Sumter surrendered the next day.

The shelling of Fort Sumter galvanized opinion on both sides and led to a whirlwind of patriotism in the North. On April 15, Lincoln declared the existence of an "insurrection" and called for seventy-five thousand volunteers to serve for three months.

Chapter 2

Initial Military Service

The public, both in the North and South, greeted the war with patriotic fervor. The citizenry on both sides expected a short, victorious contest. Resources available to each were quite different, however. This played a prominent role in the strategies that evolved.

The North had a vastly superior population and industrial base. The population of the sixteen northern states was some twenty-two million people, a figure that grew during the war, thanks to heavy foreign immigration. Some four hundred thousand foreign-born served in the Union Army. The North had a well-balanced economy with advanced industrial development, prosperous agriculture, and strong banking institutions. It contained 85 percent of the nation's prewar industry and 90 percent of its production. It also housed an extensive railroad net that bound the Northeast to the Mississippi and Ohio Valleys. This railroad grid would be an immense logistical advantage. The North had an extensive merchant marine and a naval supremacy that handicapped the South throughout the war. Another important and often overlooked factor was the North's development of superior managerial systems, among both soldiers and civilians. Businessmen would play prominent roles in the war, and the North enjoyed a far more effective and coordinated staff system than did the South.

The eleven seceded southern states numbered only 9 million people (with few immigrants during the war), and of this figure some 3.5 million were slaves. The South's economy was essentially agricultural, based on staples such as cotton and, to a lesser extent, tobacco, rice, sugar cane, and naval stores. Despite its abundant natural resources of iron, coal, and timber, the South's industrial resources and distribution system were stunted. This was the result of both a lack of southern banking capital (which totaled only one-third that of the North) and a shortage of technological skills and equipment. The South's railroad system was inadequate and, moreover, of different gauges. Despite expansion in the 1850s, the railroads progressively deteriorated during the war. Geographically, the Mississippi and Tennessee Rivers and the Shenandoah Valley offered easy invasion routes for Union armies, and the South's few good harbors were susceptible to blockade. Southerners had a vast and thinly populated territory to defend, and success in the war would depend in large measure on where and how the South chose to concentrate its more meager military resources. In the end, President Davis tried to hold on to it all and ended up losing all.

The South was also plagued by states' rights. States that had protested federal power were understandably reluctant to yield authority to a central government. Another problem was that the states of the Confederacy also had a much higher rate of illiteracy, and this had a pronounced effect on the Confederacy's ability to manage its war effort.

But the North could not merely sit back on its superior resources. To win the war, it would have to bring the South to heel and that meant actually invading and conquering it. The South merely had to stand on the defensive.

Seventy-five-year-old Union general-in-chief Winfield Scott was one of the few northern leaders who understood what the effort would entail. He warned Lincoln that the struggle would be hard and protracted. Scott called for a naval blockade of the South along the Atlantic and Gulf Coasts that would strangle the Confederacy while large Union armies were being trained. Once this was accomplished, the armies would be employed in conjunction with steam gunboats along the principal southern rivers—especially the Mississippi—to bisect the South. It came to be known as the "Anaconda Plan," named for the giant snake that strangles its victims to death. In the end, the North won by following the broad outlines of Scott's plan.[1]

Confederate leaders, especially given the paucity of their human and material resources, did not contemplate invading the North. They planned to remain on the defensive until the northern population grew tired of the war and forced its leaders into a negotiated settlement. In the meantime, diplomatic pressure would be applied to Britain, which consumed the bulk of the South's cotton crop. Jefferson Davis embraced a mistaken plan to suspend cotton shipments in the belief that this would bring British intervention on the side of the Confederacy. In doing so, the South wasted a splendid opportunity to rush cotton to European markets and purchase arms before the Union blockade could become effective. Most of this cotton later rotted on southern wharfs. As it worked out, northern "corn" (grain) proved more important to Britain than cotton.

Imboden was probably not much concerned with these larger issues of resources and strategy. His interests were more immediate, for with Virginia's secession Imboden left civilian life for the military. His loyalty was to his native state. The Imboden family was tight-knit, and there was never any doubt that all of its members would rally in support of Virginia once it had seceded. All five living Imboden brothers, John Daniel, George William, Francis Marion, James Adam, and Jacob Peck, as well as their brother-in-law, John Thomas Gibson, served the Confederate cause.[2]

Imboden's next younger brother, George William, had been educated at the Staunton Academy. Admitted to the bar at Staunton in 1858, he married the only daughter of Col. William Tyree, Mary Francis Tyree of Fayette County, the following year. He entered Confederate service on April 17, 1861, as first sergeant in Imboden's Battery, the Staunton Artillery. Elected a junior second lieutenant in May 1861 at Harpers Ferry, he was elected second lieutenant that November at Dumfries, Virginia. In May 1862 he was commissioned captain of Company A, 1st Regiment of the Partisan Rangers. That September he was elected major of the 62d Virginia Infantry Regiment and in December was elected colonel of the 18th Virginia Cavalry. He remained in that post until December 21, 1864, when his jaw was shattered by a minié ball in a skirmish near Gordonsville.[3]

Frank Imboden had joined the Virginia Militia in 1859 and been called out with his unit to Harpers Ferry following John Brown's Raid. He had then matriculated at the Virginia Military Institute and was a cadet there at the beginning of the war. He went with the cadets to help drill volunteer troops in Richmond during April and May 1861, but he soon resigned and by November 1861 had become a captain. He served under former Virginia governor Brig. Gen. Henry A. Wise in the "Wise Legion" for a time and was assigned to the McCullough Rangers of New Orleans. He was captured at the Battle of Roanoke Island on February 8, 1862. A letter of May 8, 1862, from Brigadier General Imboden to President Davis helped secure his exchange.[4]

Following his release, Frank Imboden returned to active service as a captain in the 18th Virginia Cavalry, which was commanded by his next older brother, George. Frank was again taken prisoner on June 5, 1864, at the Battle of Piedmont. Incarcerated at Camp Morton, Indiana, and Johnson's Island, Ohio, he was released in June 1865. He was later declared to be an honorary graduate of the Virginia Military Institute Class of 1864.[5]

Jim Imboden was seventeen when the Civil War began. Following his brothers into Confederate service, he rose to the top enlisted rank of sergeant major in his brother George William Imboden's regiment.[6]

John Daniel Imboden's youngest brother, Jake, entered VMI on March 31, 1864. Just six weeks later he was wounded in the May 15 Battle of New Market, in which the Corps of Cadets participated. Following his recuperation, Jake joined Col. John Singleton Mosby's Rangers and served with that unit until the end of the war. He, too, was declared an honorary graduate of VMI, Class of 1867.[7]

Brother-in-law John Gibson had married Kate Imboden in 1857. He joined the Confederate Army but contracted typhoid fever in 1862. Imboden secured Private Gibson's release from the Confederate hospital in Lynchburg and transported him to his home in Staunton, where he died.[8]

Even before Virginia formally seceded from the Union on April 17, John Daniel Imboden was involved in a bold plan to seize the federal arsenal at Harpers Ferry. Late on April 15 he received a telegram from Nat Tyler, editor of the *Richmond Enquirer,* calling him to Richmond for an important meeting. Imboden arrived in the state capital on the morning of April 16 and encountered former governor Henry Wise in the street. Wise was committed to securing the federal military assets in the state for the southern cause. Although no longer in office, he was

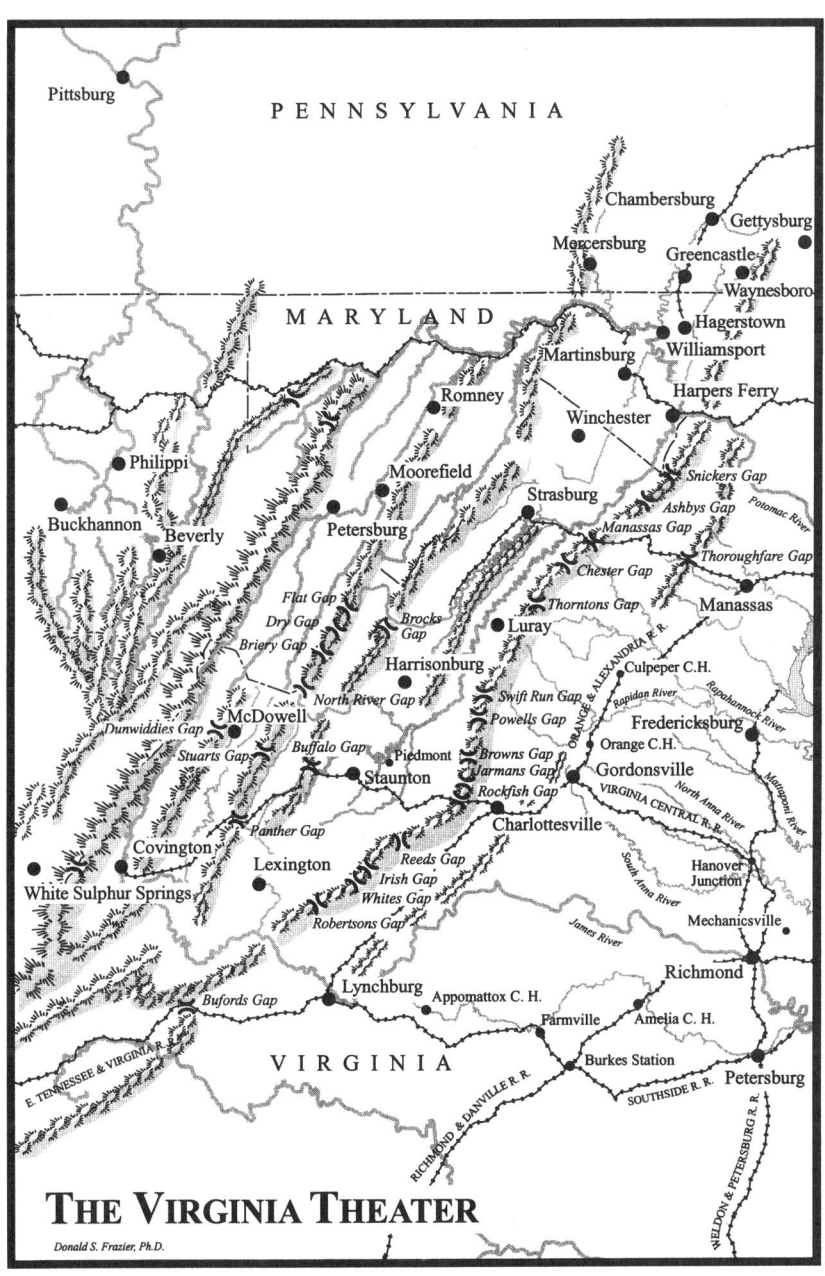

The Virginia Theater

accustomed to bold action and could call in many political favors. It is not clear whether Wise reminded Imboden of his pledge to place the Staunton Artillery at his disposal if requested,[9] but he certainly asked him to find as many officers of armed and equipped volunteer formations from the inland counties and towns as possible and invite them to a meeting the next evening at the Exchange Hotel regarding an important military matter.

Imboden located Capts. Turner Ashby and Richard Ashby of Fauquier County and Oliver R. Funsten of Clarke County, all commanders of volunteer cavalry companies; Capt. John A. Harman of Staunton; and Alfred M. Barbour, former superintendent of the arsenal and workshops at Harpers Ferry. These men joined Imboden to hear Wise's plan to seize the arsenal at Harpers Ferry the following day, on April 17, as soon as the convention had approved an act of secession. Harpers Ferry was a key military center; it was one of only two federal arsenals manufacturing and storing small arms, the other being in Springfield, Massachusetts. The plan was contingent only on securing adequate rail transportation and the support of Gov. John Letcher Sr. Time was of the essence because the arsenal was then held only by a forty-five-man federal guard. With so few defenders on hand, resolute action might secure the arsenal, its works, and weapons without firing a shot.

The plotters then sent for Col. Edmund Fontaine, president of the Virginia Central Railroad, and John S. Barbour, president of the Orange & Alexandria and Manassas Gap Railroads. They joined the deliberations around midnight and promised to make trains available for the operation, providing it had Letcher's approval. Apparently it was Imboden, promoter of rail transportation and expansion, who suggested utilizing the railroads for the operation.[10]

The group then sent some of their number, with Imboden as spokesperson, to meet with Governor Letcher. Arousing him after midnight, they asked him to authorize the seizure of all federal installations within the state. Letcher refused to authorize the raid until Virginia had formally seceded, but he did agree that planning could go forward and that he would authorize action as soon as the convention approved the ordinance of secession.

Imboden then returned to the hotel and met with the larger group. Afraid of losing the element of surprise, the men decided not to wait for the ordinance of secession. They would alert state militia units along the rail route to be ready for deployment, informing them that it was in regard to participation in the seizure of the Gosport (Norfolk) Navy Yard, a subterfuge to mask their real objective. Among those so notified was Imboden's own Staunton Artillery, ordered to assemble at 4:00 P.M. on April 17. Time became even more critical because Wise learned via telegram from his son-in-law in Washington that a one thousand–man Massachusetts regiment had been ordered to Harpers Ferry.[11]

The two Ashbys, Funston, Harman, and Imboden stayed up all night to work out the details. They secured the support of Capt. Charles Dimmock, commandant of the Virginia Armory in Richmond. A West Point graduate and a northerner by birth, Dimmock agreed to support the operation by supplying ammunition and moving it to the train station before dawn. He also provided one hundred muskets for the new volunteer company, the Martinsburg Light Infantry. Imboden signed for the weaponry and ammunition, which were then moved onto the train.

Imboden later claimed that Barbour made an unguarded remark on the train, revealing what was afoot. One of the passengers who heard it, reportedly a northern sympathizer, then wrote out a note addressed to President Lincoln and paid a black man to take it to the telegraph office. However, one of Imboden's group followed the man and took the dispatch from him. Imboden believed this action "perhaps prevented troops being sent to head us off."[12]

On the morning of April 17, as the train bearing Imboden and the others made its way west along the Virginia Central line toward Staunton, delegates to the state convention assembled for their fateful meeting in Richmond. One delegate recalled the moment:

> The scenes witnessed within the walls of that room . . . have no parallel in the annals of ancient or modern times. . . . Mr. Wise rose in his seat and drawing a large Virginia horse-pistol from his bosom, laid it before him and proceeded to harangue the body in the most violent and denunciatory manner. He concluded by taking his watch from his pocket and, with glaring eyes and bated breath, declared that events were now transpiring which caused a hush to come over his soul.[13]

Wise then told the convention about the previous evening's meeting and the plans to seize both Harpers Ferry and the Gosport (Norfolk) Navy Yard. Delegates then rose to denounce Wise and his plans. John Baldwin of Augusta County demanded to know who was involved. Wise responded that he assumed full responsibility and that the movement was already underway to "aid the people who have waited on the convention too long in vain, in seizing arms for their own defense." Wise went on to tell Baldwin that the "patriotic volunteer revolutionists" were Baldwin's own constituents, his "friends and neighbors of Staunton." Baldwin declared himself "aghast" and sat down. Another delegate, a Mr. Baylor, rushed down the aisle to Wise, grasped him by the hand and, with tears streaming down his face, said, "I don't agree with you, I don't approve of your acts, but I love you, I love you."[14]

In this emotionally charged atmosphere, convention delegates passed "An Ordinance to Repeal the Ratification of the Constitution of the United States by the State of Virginia, and to Resume all the Rights and Privileges Granted under said Constitution." This was to be ratified by a vote of the people. The convention also established a military alliance with the Confederate States of America.

Meanwhile, news of the mobilization of the Staunton Artillery and West Augusta Guard brought out a crowd of townspeople at Staunton. Because there was strong Unionist sentiment there, a number of people questioned whether Imboden had Governor Letcher's authorization. To answer this, Imboden's brother George sent a telegraph message to Imboden at the town of Gordonsville, about halfway between Richmond and Staunton, asking under whose authority he was acting. When the train arrived there, Captain Harman replied with a telegram in Imboden's name that the operation was in fact under Letcher's orders. As it was then noon, Harman assumed that the convention would have already voted the ordinance of secession and that the governor had kept his promise to send the orders.

When the train arrived at Staunton around 6:00 P.M., it was met by throngs of people as well as the Staunton Artillery and the West Augusta Guard drawn up in formation. Maj. Gen. Kenton Harper and Brig. Gen. William H. Harman of the Virginia Militia were also on hand. They met with Imboden, who informed them of the real plans. A telegram from Governor Letcher conferred command on General

Harper, informing him that full written instructions would reach him en route.

After dark, Harper left for Winchester by carriage, leaving Harman in command of the trains and additional troops that might join them on the way to Harpers Ferry. At about sunset, Imboden and his Staunton Artillery, armed with their four 6-pounder guns but without horses, embarked with Capt. William S.W. Baylor and his West Augusta Guard on a special train. They headed back east on the Virginia Central line to Charlottesville and Gordonsville. At the latter point they would proceed northeast on the Orange & Alexandria line, before switching to the Manassas Gap line to run west to Strasburg.[15]

The other officers of the Staunton Artillery were 1st Lt. Thomas L. Harman (who had attended VMI for a year), 2d Lt. Asher Waterman Garber, and 3d Lt. William L. Balthis. The battery numbered about one hundred men. Their sidearms consisted of fifty-four old-fashioned heavy artillery sabers.[16]

There was great excitement as the train pulled out of the Staunton station. Sentiments were undoubtedly not as united as the Staunton *Spectator* claimed: "There was a general feeling that the crisis was a solemn one, united with a firm and universal determination to resist the scheme set on foot by President Lincoln to subjugate the South."[17]

The train reached Charlottesville that night, and two companies from Albemarle County joined them: Capt. W.B. Mallory's Monticello Guards and Capt. R.T.W. Duke's Albermarle Rifles. At Culpepper the trains stopped again to take on board another rifle company.

As the sun rose on April 18, the train pulled into Manassas Junction. The two Ashbys and Funsten had gone on ahead by horse the day before to collect their own cavalry companies in Fauquier and Clarke Counties and also to alert Fauquier County's Black Horse Cavalry, commanded by Capts. John Scott and Welby Carter. They then crossed the Blue Ridge to join the troops moving by train at a point near Harpers Ferry. Turner Ashby also sent men to cut telegraph lines between Manassas Junction and Alexandria and to keep them inoperative for the next several days.

According to Imboden, the arrival of the train filled with troops startled the people of Manassas. General Harman immediately requisitioned the Manassas Gap train and had other trains switched so they

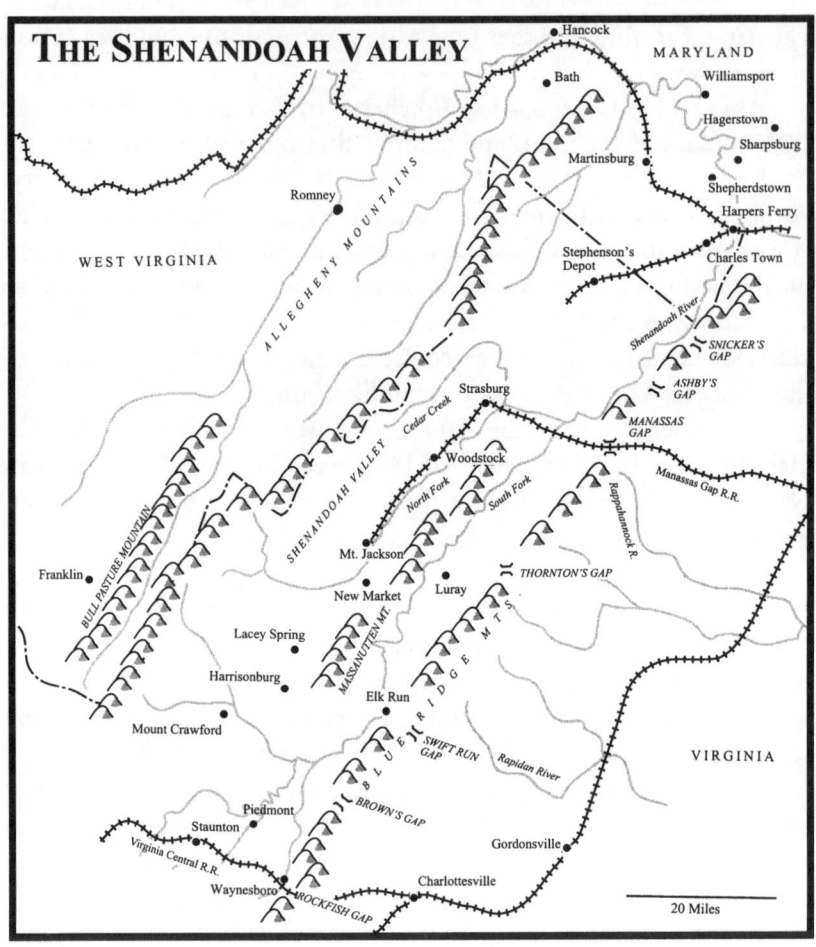

The Shenandoah Valley

could proceed west to Strasburg. He placed Imboden in command of the first train, which then set out. To his dismay, Imboden discovered the engineer was a Unionist. He let the fire go down and the train soon came to a halt on an ascending grade only about five miles from Manassas. Imboden promptly took charge and worked his way forward to confront the engineer. Imboden recalled afterward, "A cocked pistol induced him to fire up and go ahead." The train then renewed its travel toward Strasburg, this time at the fast clip of forty miles an hour.[18]

The train reached Strasburg before 10:00 A.M., and the men immediately disembarked. Soon the infantry was moving north on foot to cover the twenty miles to Winchester. Before Imboden could follow, he had to locate horses to pull his battery. He and his men approached farmers working nearby corn fields. Some agreed to loan them their horses but others refused. Because of the urgent need, Imboden and his men simply commandeered the remaining horses, despite the threat of legal action by the farmers affected. By noon Imboden's men had secured the requisite number of horses and the battery then set out to follow the infantry north down the Valley Turnpike. They reached Winchester at nightfall.

The inhabitants of Winchester were split on the issue of secession. As Imboden put it, "The people generally received us very coldly. The war spirit that bore them up through four years of trial and privation had not yet been aroused."[19]

General Harper was at Winchester and had already ordered the infantry to Charles Town, eight miles from Harpers Ferry, via the shortline Winchester & Potomac Railroad. Once this had been accomplished, the train returned to collect Imboden and his battery. The guns were unhitched and the much-relieved farmers, who had come along to watch over their horses, now got them back.

The infantry moved out of Charles Town for Harpers Ferry around midnight on April 18. Imboden and his battery, however, continued via rail to Halltown, about three miles from Harpers Ferry and twenty-eight from Winchester. There they disembarked to pull the guns by hand to Bolivar Heights, a point west of Harpers Ferry from which they could fire shells into the town if necessary. The artillerists finally got their guns into position at about 4:00 A.M.

General Harper busied himself with troop dispositions for an attack later that morning, presumably against the Massachusetts Regiment supposedly at Harpers Ferry. A little before dawn on April 19, just as Harper's troops were preparing for their assault, a bright light appeared near the confluence of the Shenandoah and Potomac Rivers. It announced the firing of the arsenal by the federal guards and their departure from that place. Harper's men then marched in and took possession of the town. Although the workshops were still intact, the arsenal was a ruin. Nearly twenty thousand rifles and pistols had been destroyed.[20]

The raiders had failed to capture the arsenal and its weapons intact, and former superintendent Barbour was responsible. After the meeting in Richmond, he had traveled to Harpers Ferry via Washington and arrived at the arsenal around noon on April 17. Collecting the workers in small groups, he told them that the arsenal would be captured by Virginia troops within twenty-four hours and urged them to remain at their posts and work for the southern cause at high wages. Most of the men agreed, but Lt. Roger Jones, who commanded the forty-five-man guard force, learned what was afoot and requested reinforcements. When none were forthcoming he decided to destroy the arsenal. He had his men run powder trains through the buildings so that they could be fired if necessary. Although the workers managed to wet these down during the night and render them harmless, Jones's troops held the arsenal building and stores. On being advised that the Confederates were approaching, he and his men set fire to the arsenal and its stores and then crossed into Maryland.

Although the raid had failed in its chief object, it was not without benefit. The Confederates now held Harpers Ferry. Bordering on Maryland and strategically important in securing the northern end of the Shenandoah Valley, it was also a transportation choke-point on the Baltimore & Ohio Railroad, a critical line of communication for the North connecting Washington with the West. The southerners also had the arsenal's workshops and machinery and the bulk of the workers, and they could utilize the gun and pistol barrels and locks that had not been destroyed. Indeed, these latter were soon sent to Richmond and Columbia, South Carolina, to be worked into firearms. The *Richmond Enquirer* reported the capture of five thousand finished muskets and parts for three thousand more. Later much of the machinery would be disassembled to be sent to Richmond and then on to Fayetteville, North Carolina.

The operation also made military history. It was the first wartime tactical deployment by rail; never before had troops and artillery moved by rail against an enemy objective.[21]

Imboden remained at Harpers Ferry following its capture. Within a week some 1,300 Virginia Militia troops arrived there to strengthen the defenses against possible Union attack. They were commanded by three brigadiers and one major general of militia. Every afternoon, weather permitting, the troops paraded in a fashion that Imboden said "would have done no discredit to the Champs Élysée." Imboden was in fact amazed at the high quality of the men in these early volunteer forces. In his battery alone there were at least a half dozen college graduates serving at the rank of corporal or below.[22]

About a week after the Confederates had occupied Harpers Ferry, General Harper announced that he had received information that the Federals were intending to try to run several trains carrying troops from the west to Washington along the B&O line at night. Determined to prevent this even at the risk of a battle, Harper positioned a number of artillery pieces, including Imboden's Battery, to command a half-mile stretch of the B&O track. These were trained during the daytime and remained loaded so they would be able to fire immediately if required. Infantry were also placed so as to be able to fire into the trains should they not stop. Pickets, placed two to three miles ahead along the track, were to fire a signal on a train's appearance.

At about one o'clock in the morning a train was heard approaching from the west. A drum roll called the men to their stations. Sentries thought they saw troops aboard and fired their guns to signal this. The batteries were poised to open fire, but Col. William S.H. Baylor, commander of the 5th Virginia Regiment, being unable to see any troops aboard, managed to signal the train to a stop only about a hundred yards from the point where the artillery would have opened up.

Baylor asked if there were troops aboard and was told there was only one older man in uniform asleep in the first car. Baylor boarded the train with some of his men and discovered that the individual in question was U.S. Army Brig. Gen. William S. Harney, who said he was on his way to Washington, resolved to resign his commission and go to Europe rather than fight in a civil war. He was taken to General Harper's headquarters, paroled to report to Richmond, and escorted to a train for Winchester. He then was allowed to proceed to Washington.[23]

Reinforcements continued to arrive daily at Harpers Ferry, and during this time Imboden struggled to get his battery into the best possible condition. He had no caissons for the guns and such harnesses as he had were insufficient. His men also had no work clothing, their uniforms being largely for dress. Imboden used his own personal credit to order harnesses from Baltimore and red flannel shirts and other clothing for his men from Richmond, expenditures for which he was later reimbursed by the state treasurer. His men also discovered in the armory some strong horse carts, and some of the men who were mechanically inclined used these axles and wheels to make caissons that served well through the First Battle of Manassas.

General Harper experienced problems in securing supplies and munitions for his command from Richmond. Because there was no telegraph line to Richmond except via Washington and mail took two days to travel between the two points, Harper decided at the end of April to send Imboden to meet personally with Governor Letcher and present him with a list of required supplies. Imboden was also to impress upon Letcher the relatively defenseless state of Harpers Ferry against a possible attack mounted by Federal troops at Chambersburg, Pennsylvania, under Maj. Gen. Robert Patterson.

When Imboden arrived in Richmond, Letcher had already given Robert E. Lee command of all Virginia forces. The convention had nullified the commissions of all field-grade militia officers above the rank of captain, granting Letcher and his military council authority to fill the vacancies thus created. Imboden observed that this would be "a disastrous blow to 'the pomp and circumstance of glorious war' at Harpers Ferry." According to Letcher's order of April 27, Col. Thomas J. Jackson took command at Harpers Ferry, with Maj. James W. Massie as his adjutant. The two men arrived there on April 29, just hours before the first combat death of the war, when Capt. John Quincy Marr, a VMI graduate, was killed at Fairfax Court House by a patrol of the U.S. 2d Cavalry.[24]

Jackson, who would become an icon of the Confederacy, was born at Clarksburg, Virginia, in 1824. An 1846 graduate of the U.S. Military Academy at West Point, he served with distinction in the Mexican War, but in 1851 he left the military to become professor of natural philosophy (physics) at the Virginia Military Institute. He commanded the artillery section of the Corps of Cadets during the hanging of John Brown at Harpers Ferry in December 1859. As a major in the Virginia Militia, he had been called to Richmond when Virginia seceded and was soon promoted to lieutenant colonel and sent to Harpers Ferry.[25]

Imboden was in Richmond only three or four days, but on his return to Harpers Ferry he found the difference under Jackson everywhere evident. Imboden recalled, "What a revolution three or four days had wrought! I could scarcely realize the change." The militia generals, including Harper, had all departed in a state of some agitation, accompanied by their considerable staffs. Jackson, who surrounded himself with VMI men, instigated rigorous training. He retained as drill instructors ten VMI cadets who had been detailed to deliver five wagon loads of powder to him.[26]

Clearly Jackson, who had been regarded by the VMI cadets as somewhat out of his element as a professor, had found himself. Once a cadet, now a junior officer, John C. Giddings, who arrived as Harpers Ferry about the same time that Imboden returned from Richmond, marveled at the change in Jackson: "[Jackson] would dispatch business in a very prompt and energetic way. He knew exactly what ought to be done and how it should be done. There was no wavering of opinion, no doubts and misgivings; his orders were clear and decisive. It occurred to us at the time that Jackson was much more in his element here, as an army officer, than when in the professor's chair at Lexington. It seemed that the sounds and sights of war had aroused his energies; his manner had become brusque and imperative."[27]

The afternoon of his return, Imboden reported to Jackson to deliver dispatches and a letter from Lee. Imboden already knew Jackson and Massie, but he was probably amused to find both men still wearing well-worn uniforms of the Virginia Military Institute. They were at work in their headquarters, a small room in a hotel near the railroad station, trying to make sense of muster rolls spread before them. To this point, Jackson had not communicated with the assembled troops, except to issue an order assuming command.

After spending perhaps a half hour with Jackson, Imboden returned to his own camp. There he discovered men of the 5th Virginia Regiment, also from Augusta County, in some agitation. They had liked the easy-going ways of their former commanders and resented their arbitrary removal. Imboden reported that the men saw this action as "an outrage on freemen and volunteers."[28]

The men of the regiment were discussing passing resolutions condemning what had happened to their officers. Seeing Imboden, they called on him for a speech. He refused because he said he did not belong to their regiment. But, undoubtedly to influence them, Imboden lined up the men of his own battery and addressed them. He told them their choice was to either enlist for twelve months or for the duration of the war, and he urged the latter. They all obliged him by shouting, "For the war! For the war!" They then signed the roll, and Imboden presented it to Jackson with the words, "There, colonel, is the roll of your first company mustered in for the war."[29]

Jackson thanked Imboden, told him he had heard of disaffection in the militia camps, and asked if he would serve as mustering officer for the other two artillery companies at Harpers Ferry, a task completed the same afternoon. The next day the remaining troops were also sworn in. A week later, Governor Letcher appointed Harper, formerly a major general, as colonel commanding the 5th Virginia Regiment. Harman, a former brigadier general, became its lieutenant colonel, and former colonel Baylor was made major. This regiment later won fame in the "Stonewall" Brigade.

Jackson's hand was felt everywhere as he set about training his command. At this point he was lenient with both officers and men, encouraging the officers to come to him regarding even the smallest military detail, believing that "it was no discredit to a civilian to be ignorant of military matters." Imboden noted of Jackson:

> He was a rigid disciplinarian, and yet as gentle and kind as a woman. He was the easiest man in our army to get along with pleasantly so long as one did his duty, but as inexorable as fate in exacting the performance of it; yet he would overlook serious faults if he saw they were the result of ignorance, and would instruct the offender in a kindly way. He was as courteous to the humblest private who sought an interview for any purpose as to the highest officer in his command. He despised superciliousness and self-assertion, and nothing angered him so quickly as to see an officer wound the feelings of those under him by irony or sarcasm.[30]

When Jackson learned that the artillery batteries did not have horses, he took action on his own, ordering Maj. John A. Harman to take some men and scour the farm communities of Loudoun County in an effort to buy and, if necessary, simply take the number required.

Harman was successful and won Jackson's confidence, continuing as his quartermaster.

Jackson was all too aware of the vulnerability of his position at Harpers Ferry, surrounded as he was by high ground. He ordered Imboden to the bridge across the Potomac River at Point of Rocks, a dozen miles below Harpers Ferry, with instructions to fortify the Virginia side. Imboden was, at the time, much concerned about an attack by Federal troops under Maj. Gen. Benjamin F. Butler. He could not have known that Butler was one of Lincoln's worst general officer political appointments; Butler proved hopelessly inept in a variety of commands throughout the war.

As a final defense against a Union foray at Point of Rocks, Imboden mined the piers of the bridge, in order to be able to destroy the structure if that proved necessary. Because he feared a night attack, Imboden adopted the practice of staying up at night and sleeping during much of the day. About a week after they had occupied the position, one of his men awakened him and pointed out two men dressed in blue uniforms riding about the camp, inspecting it. The soldier feared they might be spies. The two turned out to be Jackson and one of his staff. When Imboden came up Jackson put a finger to his lips and shook his head, signaling him to silence. In a low voice he told Imboden he approved of his dispositions and then rode away.[31]

In reporting his recollections of this time at Harpers Ferry, Imboden discussed at length a plan executed by Jackson to secure train locomotives for the Confederacy. This recollection is hard to justify, as there does not seem to be any basis for it in fact. Certainly train locomotives were in short supply in the South, which was also without facilities to build them. Jackson's supposed plan took advantage of the fact that the B&O was double tracked for some twenty-five to thirty miles from Imboden's position at Point of Rocks west to Martinsburg.[32]

To this point the Confederates had not interfered with the movement of the trains, except on that one occasion when they had stopped a train and taken General Harney. A great deal of traffic still moved along the line both day and night, including coal-filled trains moving east to the Atlantic seaboard.

At the same time that Jackson had sent Imboden to Point of Rocks, he had ordered Colonel Harper and the 5th Virginia Infantry to

Martinsburg. According to Imboden, Jackson then complained to the B&O's President Garrett that the movement of trains at night was keeping his men awake, and he demanded that the trains move only between 11:00 A.M. and 1:00 P.M. Garrett complied and the trains headed east were then duly concentrated at those hours. But the empty trains were still returning at night; Jackson again complained, insisting that they use the second track and move at the same times as the eastern-bound trains. Garrett agreed and for several days, Imboden wrote, "We then had, for two hours every day, the liveliest railroad in America."[33]

Reportedly, Jackson then sprang his trap. Imboden claimed that Jackson ordered him to take some men to the Maryland side of the river at 11:00 A.M. He was to allow all west-bound trains to pass until noon and not to allow any to proceed east. Then, at noon, he was to sabotage the line so that it would take several days to repair. The same orders went out to Harper and the 5th Virginia at Martinsburg, but in reverse as far as the movement of trains was concerned. In the process Jackson bagged all of the trains caught in the trap. These were run thirty-two miles away to Winchester on a branch line, and from there they were then moved by teams of horses, since there was no rail line between the two points, to the railroad at Strasburg. One source says that Jackson thus obtained for the South fifty-six locomotives and three hundred cars. The loss supposedly crippled the B&O for some time to come.[34]

This is all a bit bizarre since, according to Jackson biographers James Robertson and Bryon Farwell, this story has no basis in fact. Farwell wrote, "there are disturbing elements to his [Imboden's] story. Such a dramatic event ought to have stimulated many accounts, as did the later transfer of the locomotives from Martinsburg to Strasburg. If it occurred, Jackson did not report it to Lee, and that would have been most odd. It would also have been a direct violation of Jackson's orders not to disturb commerce and not to cross into Maryland unless it was absolutely necessary."[35]

Robertson is more dismissive, noting in regard to the story: "John D. Imboden manufactured it, Jackson biographer G.F.R. Henderson gave it credence, and writers over the past century have delighted in repeating it in detail."[36] Among these are Clayton Thomas, in his 1965 master's thesis on Imboden's military career; Robert Driver, who repeated it as fact in his 1988 book on Imboden's artillery battery; prominent

West Virginia historian James Callahan in 1923, and Imboden biographer Harold Woodward in 1996, under the subheading, "The Great Train Heist."[37]

It is difficult to see what motive Imboden might have had for conjuring up this story in print, especially for *Battles and Leaders of the Civil War*, but there simply is no proof of the event having transpired. Moving so many locomotives and rail cars overland to Strasburg would have been a formidable feat indeed and should have elicited numerous contemporary eyewitness accounts. As historian Robertson points out, "Not even a hint exists in official records of Jackson manipulating the B&O schedule for a massive capture of rolling stock." He notes that the B&O's master of transportation, W.P. Smith, kept detailed records and that he recorded for May 14, "Seizure of a train of cars at Harpers Ferry." Such a seizure, Robertson believes, would have been at most one locomotive and eighteen cars.[38]

While Imboden was still at Point of Rocks, James E.B. ("Jeb") Stuart arrived at Harpers Ferry and reported for orders. Born in Patrick County, Virginia, and a graduate of the U.S. Military Academy at West Point, Stuart had served in the cavalry in the West. In 1859 he had been aide to Col. Robert E. Lee briefly when the latter had been sent to Harpers Ferry to deal with John Brown's Raid. Stuart was then posted to Kansas, where he had remained until the secession of Virginia, at which point he returned to his native state and resigned his commission. Promoted captain in the U.S. Army only several weeks before, Stuart was commissioned a lieutenant colonel in the Virginia infantry. On May 24 he was promoted to colonel in the Confederate cavalry. Jackson gave him charge of the cavalry at Harpers Ferry, which totaled some three hundred men, thus beginning the 1st Virginia Cavalry.[39]

Stuart's elevation did not please Capt. Turner Ashby. The popular cavalry commander had raised a volunteer company of cavalry following John Brown's Raid in order to patrol the Virginia border and guard against another insurrection. He had also been one of those involved in the initial planning for the raid on Harpers Ferry, and had played a key role in it. Older than Stuart, he lacked his formal military experience but nonetheless believed he should have received the promotion.

When not out scouting, Ashby spent nights at Imboden's camp at the bridge. Imboden recalled years later Ashby's frustration over Jackson's order giving Stuart charge of the cavalry. Ashby felt so strongly over this that he threatened to resign. Imboden said that he urged Ashby to reconsider and indeed suggested he ride to Harpers Ferry that same evening and meet with Jackson, confident that he would remove Ashby's company from Stuart's command.

Ashby followed Imboden's advice and returned early in the morning to Point of Rocks absolutely enraptured with Jackson. According to Imboden, the real reason for Ashby's success in his meeting with Jackson was an intelligence-gathering mission Ashby had undertaken in Pennsylvania several days before that had produced much useful information.

Not only did Jackson not force Ashby to serve under Stuart, he divided the cavalry at Harpers Ferry between the two men. Jackson also promised to request Ashby's immediate promotion, thus forming the nuclei for two cavalry regiments.

If indeed Imboden's story of persuading Ashby to meet with Jackson is true—and there is no reason to doubt it—then Imboden made an important contribution to the Shenandoah Valley Campaign simply by keeping Ashby in the fold.

Promoted to lieutenant colonel of a regiment under Col. Angus MacDonald, Ashby succeeded to its command within a few months. Although Ashby's regiment had a reputation for lax discipline, it actually fought well. Ashby had a personal reputation for bravery in battle and was advanced to brigadier general in the spring of 1862, playing a key role in Jackson's Valley Campaign.[40]

Meanwhile, Virginia had formally joined the Confederacy. On May 2 Virginia adopted the Constitution of the Confederate States of America and sent representatives to the Confederate Congress. On May 20 that Congress adjourned in Montgomery to reconvene in Richmond, and President Davis arrived in his new capital on May 29. A consequence of Virginia's joining the Confederacy was that her military formations passed to Confederate command; one of the first acts of the national government was to appoint a more senior officer to take command at Harpers Ferry: Brig. Gen. Joseph E. Johnston.

Johnston was born in Farmville, Virginia, in 1807, the same year as Robert E. Lee. Both were a generation older than most Civil War generals. Johnston had graduated from West Point in 1829 and had then served in the West and in topographical expeditions in Florida, where he had fought in the Seminole War. During the 1846–1848 Mexican War he had served with distinction under Gen. Winfield Scott. After the war he returned to the Topographical Engineers. By 1855 he was a lieutenant colonel in the 1st Cavalry and in June 1860 he was quartermaster general and a brigadier general. Johnston resigned from the U.S. Army following the secession of Virginia and offered his services to his native state. On May 14 he was commissioned a brigadier general in the Confederate Army and assigned command of Harpers Ferry.[41]

On May 23, 1861, Jackson turned over his Harpers Ferry command to Johnston. By that time, several thousand Confederate troops were present, from every secession state east of the Mississippi. Johnston reorganized this command and established brigades, at which time Jackson assumed command of an all-Virginia brigade and was almost immediately promoted to brigadier general.

Well aware that Union General Patterson was moving westward with a superior force of some eight thousand to ten thousand troops, Johnston relocated his headquarters to Winchester. He left Jackson at Harpers Ferry temporarily, but on June 15 Johnston ordered him to withdraw as well and abandon that place, while at the same time maintaining position along the B&O to observe Union preparations to the north.

Imboden's Staunton Artillery was among the last units to depart. Positioned in the rear guard, it left Harpers Ferry on June 16. Imboden expected an assault by Patterson, but the Union commander moved so slowly that his troops did not cross the Potomac into Virginia until forty-eight hours later.[42]

Chapter 3

First Battle of Manassas

On withdrawing from Harpers Ferry, Johnston's Confederates moved toward Winchester. Patterson's Federals then crossed the Potomac also headed for Winchester, with a force reported at twice that of Johnston's nine thousand men. Patterson moved at a glacial pace, but battle appeared imminent. Jackson had charge of the Confederate rear guard and, wary of an attack, he drove his men hard to reach the Valley Pike and set up a blocking position there. Instead of seeking out battle, however, Johnston turned south after reaching the turnpike and proceeded to prepare defenses at Bunker Hill, a few miles north of Winchester. The Confederates remained in position there for three days, but no attack materialized and Patterson's men soon recrossed the Potomac. Imboden and his men were part of this general operation and set up camp north of the city.[1]

On June 30 Imboden's Battery had 107 officers and men. It had its four bronze, 6-pounder guns as well as the old-style heavy artillery sabers they had received when they had mustered in. Imboden reported that the men were clothed in "cadet grey uniforms" supplied by a firm in Augusta, consisting of a grey cap, a flannel shirt, gray woolen pants, and woolen socks. He had spent $298 of his own money on tents for the men. Caissons for the artillery pieces were under construction. The state had yet to provide any assistance, and the battery had been utilizing twenty-six impressed horses.[2]

On July 2 Patterson recrossed the Potomac in force; Johnston at once ordered one of his four brigades, that commanded by Lt. Col. Barnard E. Bee, to march to support Jackson at Hainesville, Virginia. Imboden's Battery accompanied Bee. A native of Charleston, South Carolina, Bee had graduated from West Point in 1845 and fought with distinction in the Mexican War, being twice brevetted for gallantry under fire. In March 1861, as a U.S. Army captain, he had resigned to accept a commission as a lieutenant colonel in the 1st South Carolina Regulars, an artillery regiment. He received the brigade command in Johnston's force on June 17.[3]

Bee halted his brigade at Darkesville, and the men formed up in line of battle, remaining in position there for three days until July 5, waiting for the Federals to come up for what Imboden assumed would be his baptism by fire. However, on July 2 Jackson intercepted a Federal brigade of 3,000 men under Patterson's son-in-law, Brig. Gen. John J. Abercrombie, headed for Martinsburg. Jackson, 380 men of the 5th Virginia Regiment, and one 6-pounder gun took up defensive positions, and a skirmish occurred near Falling Waters, a bend in the Potomac. Determining that the Federal column was much larger than his own force and obeying Johnston's orders to withdraw under such circumstances, Jackson staged a skillful retreat. He reported his losses at eleven wounded and nine missing. The Federals sustained six to ten killed, eighteen wounded, and fifty captured. Following this skirmish, the Federals again withdrew across the Potomac. Patterson claimed that he had been opposed by 3,500 men, about ten times the actual number.[4] Historian Bruce Catton's characterization of the sixty-nine-year-old Patterson as "semi-moribund . . . old and fragile and bewildered" is not off the mark.[5]

The crisis having passed, on July 5 Johnston recalled Bee's Brigade to Winchester, and Imboden's Battery resumed what its commander styled as "our arduous drilling." On July 12 the Staunton Artillery was officially assigned to Bee's Brigade.[6]

That same day, July 12, Imboden wrote home complaining about the difficulties of procuring clothing and shoes for his men. He stated that the military routine, daily drill, arrival of the caissons, new harnesses, and additional horses all improved the efficiency and appearance of the battery. In another letter, dated July 17, Imboden wrote that he expected an advance by the Federals at any time and that, in order to be prepared, the men were sleeping by the guns. He expressed his own determination: "We are resolved to die rather than let these devils drive us back to our homes."[7]

Meanwhile, events were moving toward the first great battle of the Civil War, the July 21, 1861, (First) Battle of Bull Run (Manassas). It was Imboden's first battle and one in which he would distinguish himself.

Northern leaders and newspapers had been pressing Lincoln for a quick invasion of the South. One push, they believed, would be sufficient to topple the Confederacy and end the rebellion. The pressure for an offensive intensified with news that the Confederate Congress was to assemble in its new capital of Richmond on July 20. Editorials in the northern press urged "On to Richmond." Lincoln now ignored the wise counsel of General Scott and other military advisors and succumbed to the mounting public demand for action.

Lincoln assigned the task of closing with the Confederates to Brig. Gen. Irwin McDowell, who commanded the principal Union army protecting Washington. Hailing from Columbus, Ohio, McDowell had graduated from West Point in 1838 and been an instructor of tactics there from 1841 to 1845. Up to the Civil War, he had spent most of his military career in staff assignments. In May 1861 he had been advanced to brigadier general of volunteers.[8]

McDowell's orders called on him to move west to secure Manassas Junction, the key railroad hub some thirty miles southwest of Washington. Here the north-south Orange & Alexandria Railroad that ran from the Potomac River to Lynchburg met the eastern end of the Manassas Gap Railroad, a short line of only seventy-seven miles that ran west from Manassas into the Shenandoah Valley as far as Mt. Jackson. Union possession of Manassas Junction would cut off the Valley and secure the Union right flank during the drive on Richmond. It would also provide McDowell with the best overland route south to Richmond.

McDowell had some thirty-three thousand poorly trained troops against only some twenty-two thousand Confederates in the Manassas vicinity under the hero of Fort Sumter, Gen. P.G.T. Beauregard. Major General Patterson with fifteen thousand Federals around Charles Town near Harpers Ferry was to prevent Johnston's eleven thousand Confederates in the Valley from reinforcing Beauregard.

First Battle of Manassas 47

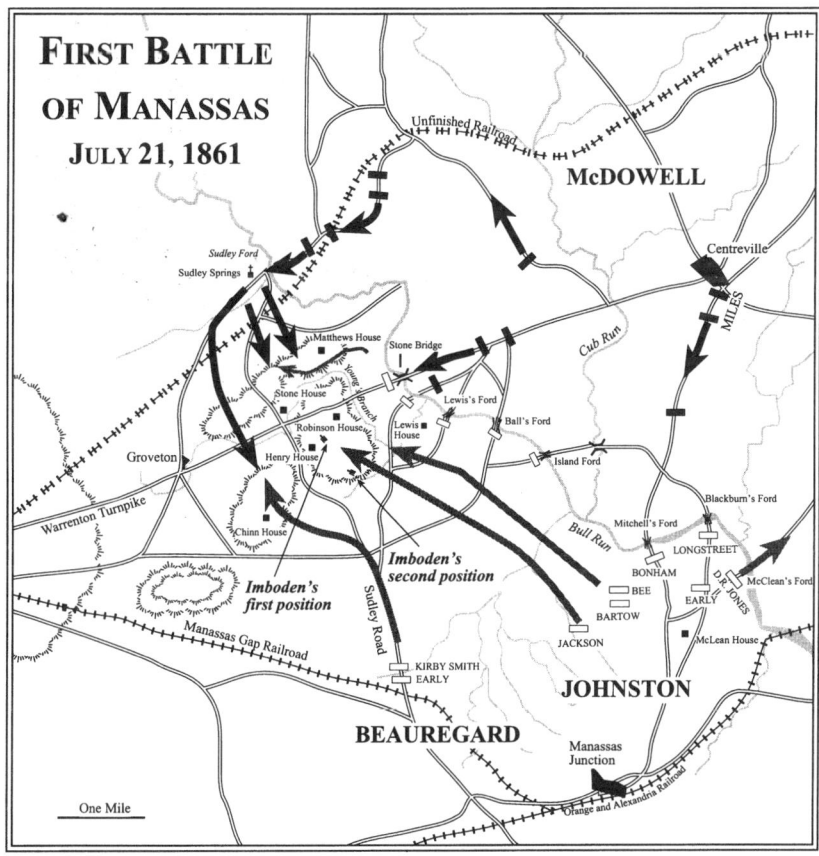

The First Battle of Manassas, July 21, 1861

On July 16 McDowell and his men set out from southwest of Washington to move the twenty-nine miles to Manassas. The Federals marched at a snail's pace, in part due to the heat and equipment, but principally because of McDowell's caution. The troops covered only five miles in the first day. On July 18 the Federals, moving along the Warrenton Turnpike, reached Centreville. Five miles farther west the meandering muddy stream known as Bull Run crossed the turnpike. It formed the only natural barrier between the two forces. Beauregard positioned his men west of Bull Run in order to guard its fords.

On his arrival at Centreville, McDowell ordered Brig. Gen. Daniel Tyler's Division to conduct a reconnaissance in force. This produced a short, sharp encounter at Blackburn's Ford on the Confederate right flank. The Confederates repulsed the Union thrust. McDowell then wasted two additional days while he brought up ammunition and supplies and developed a battle plan. Had he struck swiftly, attacking on July 19, he would have caught Beauregard before the arrival of the Confederate reinforcements, and he would most certainly have won the battle.

Spies had already informed Richmond of McDowell's movements when Beauregard appealed for reinforcements. McDowell's delay afforded the Confederates the opportunity. At 1:00 A.M. on July 18 Adj. Gen. Samuel Cooper ordered Johnston and his Army of the Shenandoah to assist. These men would be critical to the outcome of the coming battle.[9]

On receipt of the telegram, Johnston called a meeting of his senior commanders. When he was summoned, Bee sent for Imboden and the two men went to Johnston's headquarters together. Imboden remained outside during the conference of brigade commanders that lasted more than two hours, during which Johnston explained Cooper's telegram and detailed the nearly sixty-mile movement to Manassas Junction.

In the morning as Johnston's army set out to join Beauregard, the Confederates were apprehensive that Patterson might attack them en route. To be prepared for this possibility, Bee's Brigade along with Imboden's Battery acted as rear guard, while Confederate cavalry under J.E.B. Stuart and Ashby screened Johnston's movement to Manassas. They accomplished this so well, in fact, that Patterson did not learn about it until July 20, too late for him to intervene. Patterson's failure to prevent the juncture of the Valley force with Beauregard was critical to the outcome of the battle. Uninterrupted, all of Johnston's troops except one brigade were in place at Manassas by July 20. The final brigade arrived on July 21, the day of battle, and marched into the fray directly from the trains.[10]

Johnston's infantry did not get far the first day. The majority covered only fifteen miles, to the crossing point over the Shenandoah River two miles east of Millwood. There they encamped. The next morning the weary men climbed Ashby's Gap in the Blue Ridge and then passed on down to Piedmont (now Delaplane), a small village on the Manassas Gap Railroad line some twenty-three miles from Winchester. Jackson's troops were the first to arrive. Bee's Brigade, marching much of the night and the next day, did not reach Piedmont until after dark on July 19. There, trains of the Manassas Gap Railroad were waiting to carry the men the last thirty-four miles to Manassas. Jackson's vanguard arrived at Manassas on the afternoon of July 19.

While his infantry moved to Manassas by rail, Johnston ordered the artillery batteries to travel by secondary roads. He directed his chief of artillery, Col. William N. Pendleton, to form a column of his five batteries: the four brigade batteries and the one reserve. But by nightfall on July 19, only three of the five batteries had arrived at Piedmont, and Pendleton set out in the dark with these. With a rest of only two hours en route, Pendleton reached Manassas at 2:00 P.M. on July 20.[11]

Imboden's account of the movement of his battery to Manassas differs from the above. His was one of the two batteries that were delayed, although he could hardly be blamed, as his battery was the last to depart the Winchester area for Manassas, late in the afternoon of July 18. The exhausted artillerymen spent the night at Rectortown, falling asleep by their guns, oblivious to a pouring rain. Imboden said that there he received an order through Bee detailing him as senior artillery captain to collect all four artillery batteries in the column, move them to Manassas as quickly as possible by country roads where they could not be easily observed, and report to Bee immediately on his arrival.

Imboden recalled that he assembled the four artillery batteries and had them on the march early on July 20, with his own battery at the head of the column. They arrived at Salem (now Marshall) in Fauquier County around 8:00 A.M. Imboden noted their reception: "The whole population turned out to greet us. Men, women, and children brought us baskets, trays, and plates loaded with their own family breakfasts. With the improvidence of raw campaigners, we had finished the night before our three days' cooked rations; so I ordered a halt for thirty minutes to enjoy the feast. . . . I make special note of that breakfast because it was the last food any of us tasted till the first Bull Run had been fought and won, 36 hours later."[12]

The townspeople also provided forage for the horses. Imboden said that some of his men were much taken by the young daughters of Col. John Washington, "who bid them die or conquer in the fight," and that these individuals "seemed very miserable during the remainder of the march."[13]

Whatever the actual sequence of events, the artillery finally arrived at Manassas Junction shortly before midnight on July 20. Despite the hour, Imboden sought out Bee, most of whose men had arrived by train earlier in the day.

At 1:00 A.M. on July 21 Imboden arrived at the headquarters, a log cabin about a mile northeast of Manassas Junction. Bee directed him to unharness the horses and have the men bivouac in the fence corners, saying, "You will need all the rest you can get, for a great battle will begin in the morning."[14]

Both McDowell and Beauregard planned to take the offensive that day. Avoiding a frontal assault, each wanted to envelop their opponent's left flank, but confused orders delayed the Confederate advance. McDowell decided on the afternoon of July 20 to march his main force down a ten-mile road to an unguarded ford over Bull Run at Sudley.

At 2:00 A.M. on July 21 McDowell put his attack columns in motion north and west. Success depended on both speed and surprise, but his planned maneuver was too complicated for the green Union troops to execute quickly. In any case the movement was delayed as the men lost their way in the darkness. In fact, in this battle neither side was well organized or trained.

Fighting began before dawn on July 21. Union artillery east of the stream initiated the fray at about 5:30 A.M. when it fired on Confederates at Stone Bridge, the point where the Warrenton Turnpike crossed Bull Run. Here McDowell feinted his major assault along the Confederate eight-mile-long line.

Imboden's men were made immediately aware that the attack had begun. A little after daybreak they were roused by the noise of the firing of a Federal Parrott rifle two miles away across Bull Run and the sound of its thirty-pound elongated shell whizzing over the tree tops several hundred yards to their left. Despite their lack of sleep, the men were up in a flash, and in a short time they had the horses harnessed and hitched to the artillery caissons and limbers.

Bee, standing in shirtsleeves on the cabin porch, observed the artillery preparations and called Imboden over, informing him of the disposition of the Confederate forces. Bee expressed disappointment that they would in all likelihood miss the main part of the battle, for his orders called for him to relocate to Stone Bridge across Bull Run some three or four miles on the Confederate left in order to cover that part of the front. Instructed to take a battery with him, Bee selected Imboden's.

Bee asked Imboden to move at once, leaving the wagons behind. Bee and the infantry would follow immediately. When Imboden noted that his men and horses had been twenty-four hours without food, Bee said he would order supplies up, remarking: "You will probably have plenty of time to cook and eat, to the music of a battle in which we shall probably take little or no part."[15]

Imboden's Battery retraced its route of the night before to Manassas Junction and then moved west to the Sudley and New Market Road, where it turned north. Bee's infantry moved by a more direct route. After about an hour the battery gained the crest of a hill and came to the Lewis house, known as "Portici." Here they were met by a courier who reported that the entire Federal force appeared to be moving in a northwesterly direction on the other side of Bull Run. Imboden halted his battery and then rode on ahead to the top of the hill. There he could see a long column of Federal troops moving along the north side of Bull Run. In the other direction Bee's troops were marching up in the Valley. Imboden immediately rode to meet them and inform Bee of developments.

Bee directed Imboden to accompany him, and the two men then rode forward past the Lewis house, across a hollow beyond, and then up another rise through some pines. They were now directly east of the Henry house and south of the Warrenton Turnpike. After surveying the area to their front, Bee turned to Imboden, who recalled him saying, "Here is the battle-field, and we are in for it! Bring up your guns as quickly as possible, and I'll look round for a good position."[16]

About twenty minutes later, as Imboden was bringing up his guns past the Lewis house, he saw Bee emerge from the pines. The colonel stopped, put his cap on the point of his sword, and waved it frantically to signal the guns forward immediately. Imboden's Battery went at a gallop, Bee directing it to a low point about a hundred yards northeast of the Henry house, where Imboden and his men unlimbered their guns and prepared them to fire. Imboden recalled:

With his keen military eye, General Bee had chosen the best

possible position for a battery on all that field. We were almost under cover by reason of a slight swell in the ground immediately in our front, and not fifty yards away. Our shot passed not six inches above the surface of the ground on this "swell" and the recoil ran the guns back to still lower ground, where, as we loaded, only the heads of my men were visible to the enemy.

We went into position none too soon; for, by the time we had unlimbered, Captain Ricketts, appearing on the crest of the opposite hill, came beautifully and gallantly into the battery at a gallop, a short distance from the Matthews House on our side of the Sudley Road, and about fifteen hundred yards to our front.[17]

Col. Nathan G. Evans commanded the Confederate left. A native of South Carolina, he had graduated from West Point in 1848 and for a dozen years served in the West, distinguishing himself in Indian skirmishes. In February 1861 he had resigned his commission to become a major in the South Carolina forces. By the time of the Manassas battle he was a Confederate Army colonel.[18]

Evans had about 1,100 men. Believing the Federal movement to his front to be simply a demonstration, Evans was slow to appreciate the extent and direction of the Union buildup. Suddenly finding himself badly outnumbered, he worked to contain the Union advance and buy time for Beauregard to bring up reinforcements to meet McDowell's attack on something approaching equal terms.

Evans could only hope to delay the Union troops. Bee's Brigade of 2,700 men and Col. Francis S. Bartow's Brigade of Georgians arrived just in time to hold long enough to allow Jackson to come up. Fortunately for the Confederates, the Union troops had deployed three hours behind schedule, and because Confederate scouts had already informed Beauregard of the threat, the Southern reinforcements—drawn from the Confederate right that now arrived piecemeal on the battlefield—were in time.

Imboden wanted to open up on the advancing Federal troops immediately, but Bee insisted that he wait until the 4th Alabama, which he had just sent across the valley to their right front with a 6-pounder, was in position. Bee also wanted to be able to determine the type and number of the Union guns.

Soon, however, a Federal battery of six 10-pounder Parrott rifled guns opened up on their position from about 1,500 yards' range. The first several Union shots went high. Seeing this, Bee directed Imboden to fire low and ricochet his shot on the hard, smooth ground that sloped gradually down to the Warrenton Turnpike to the front of their position. "We did this," Imboden recalled, "and the effect was very destructive to the enemy."[19]

Bee then rode off to look after his troops. Federal strength continued to increase and the fighting was soon hot and heavy. Two guns of the Alexandria Artillery, commanded by a Captain Latham, were on Imboden's right but across and to the north of Young's Branch of Bull Run. Around 11:00 A.M. another battery of two 12-pounder Napoleons from the New Orleans Washington Artillery unlimbered to Imboden's right, but these departed after firing only a few rounds.[20]

Although the first Federal shells went long and burst in the Confederate rear, the Union artillerists gradually reduced the range and shortened the fuses on their shells. Fifteen minutes into the fray Imboden's Battery suffered its first casualty when a Union shell passed between two of the guns and exploded among the caissons, mangling the arm of Pvt. J.J. Points. Imboden ordered him taken to the rear. Points had barely been removed when another shell exploded in Imboden's position and killed a horse. A number of Union shells then came too low, hitting the knoll in front and ricocheting over Imboden's position; but the Union gunners soon corrected this and again began to arc their shells over the Staunton Artillery.[21]

After perhaps a half hour of battle, another Union battery of four guns, under Captain Griffin, came up to join Ricketts's Battery. It took position some four hundred to five hundred yards closer to Imboden's position in a field just to the left of the Sudley Road.[22]

Most of the damage inflicted by the Union gunners came from the smoothbores rather than the rifled pieces. As Imboden recalled after the war: "Ricketts had 6 Parrott guns, and Griffin had as many more, and, I think, 2 12-pound howitzers besides. These last hurt us more than all the rifles of both batteries, since the shot and shell of the rifles, striking the ground at any angle over 15 or 20 degrees, almost without exception bored their way in several feet and did no harm. It is no exaggeration to say that hundreds of shells from these fine rifle-guns exploded in front of and around my battery on that day, but so deep in the ground that the fragments never came out. After the action, the ground looked as though it had been rooted up by hogs."[23]

Imboden also concluded that in an open-field fight, as opposed to firing at a defensive works, smoothbore guns that fired round shot at lower velocity were preferable to rifles firing cylindo-conoidal projectiles at high velocity. The latter tended to bury themselves into sloping ground and explode harmlessly. This held true at least for ranges of up to 1,000 yards for a 6-pounder smoothbore and 1,500–1,800 yards for the 12-pounder. He believed rifled guns were superior only at longer ranges.[24]

Soon the explosion of a shell from one of Griffin's guns tore into Imboden's Battery, killing another horse and nearly cutting off one of Pvt. W.A. Siders's legs. Imboden had him removed to the rear. Then another shell wounded 2d Lt. A.W. Garber, and Imboden ordered him off the field as well. Ten Union guns were now firing on Imboden's Battery, the lone Confederate artillery replying. Imboden noted that a gun with the Alabama regiment fired perhaps three rounds. Its horses ran off with the limber, leaving the gun without ammunition.[25]

During this time the Union infantry was massing in front of the Confederate left for an attack. Imboden noted, "[They were] beyond our reach, as we could only see their bayonets over the top of the hill. Two or three times they ventured in sight when the Alabamians turned them back on their left by a well-directed fire, and we gave them a few shots and shells on their right with the same results, as they amicably dropped back over the hill when we fired at them, as almost every shot made a gap in their ranks."[26]

Bee had wanted to form a new line on Henry Hill but had reluctantly complied with Evans's entreaties, sent by a staff officer, to push his own brigade and that of Bartow across the turnpike. Against his better judgment, Bee, covered by fire from Imboden's guns, moved his troops forward to support Evans. Had Bee arrived earlier he might have formed an effective line; had he delayed but a few minutes, Evans would have been dislodged and the need for the advance gone. Thus, Bee made the best of a bad situation, purchasing some time.

The outnumbered Confederate infantry under Evans and Bee managed to hold back the Union attack for a time, but they could not do so indefinitely. Under pressure from Union divisions commanded by Brig. Gens. David Hunter and Samuel Heintzelman attacking from the front, the Confederates then came under pressure from the flank brought by Union brigades under Brig. Gen. Erasmus Keyes and Col. William T. Sherman.[27]

Around noon the Confederate infantry gave way under the heavy pressure and streamed south across Young's Branch, a tributary of Bull Run, and the Warrenton Road. Imboden's guns helped cover their retirement to Matthews Hill and then on to Henry House Hill. Imboden later claimed that for a half hour the Staunton Artillery stood "alone in its glory." He said that he maintained his position in accordance with Bee's order not to depart until ordered away, although he was surprised that no instructions to withdraw arrived.[28]

Later Wade Hampton, who would rise to lieutenant general in the Confederate forces and who commanded a cavalry detachment known as Hampton's Legion[29] in the battle that day, disputed Imboden's statement of his battery being "alone in its glory" for a half hour with no other Confederate troops present. Hampton pointed out that his six companies of infantry "supported his battery as it went into action, moved up to the turnpike, when he was forced to retire, and remained there for hours after his withdrawal."[30]

With or without some supporting infantry, Imboden's situation was precarious. Union infantry were massing near the Stone house on the turnpike less than five hundred yards from his position with the obvious intent of charging and taking it. He was almost out of ammunition and:

> My men were by this time so overcome with the intense heat and excessive labor that half of them fell upon the ground completely exhausted. The guns were so hot that it was dangerous to load them—one was temporarily spiked by the priming wire hanging in it, the vent having become foul. My teams were cut to pieces, five of the horses were killed out of a single piece [six horses constituted a normal complement for one gun], and other teams were partially destroyed, so that, alone we could not much longer have replied to the enemy's batteries as briskly as necessary.[31]

A third Union battery of four guns was also advancing into position directly in front of, and about six hundred yards from, Imboden's position. Imboden's gunners managed to disable one of the Union field pieces with a shell that cut off the trail to its carriage.

As the main Union column approached from the front of Imboden's position, his men saw another column coming down the valley from the left, perhaps four hundred yards away. Assuming them to be friendly troops, he ordered his men not to fire on them. To be certain, however, he mounted his horse and rode to the top of the hill to their left. Here he had a better view and could see two regiments. They halted about three hundred yards in front of the Union battery, wheeled, and fired a volley, apparently at the battery. Believing these to be Confederate troops, Imboden ordered his guns to fire at the Union battery in support. Not all of the gunners heard him, and some of them opened up on the infantry, who then turned and advanced on Imboden's Battery, their uniforms revealing that they were Union troops.

Imboden immediately ordered the second section of his battery to limber up and join him so that they could fire on the Union troops with canister. At this point the guns of the nearest Union battery all concentrated on Imboden. He and his horse managed to escape injury, galloping back to the battery. There he discovered that his gunners had taken his orders to mean the entire battery should limber up. Imboden then directed his men to divide up the remaining horses among the battery's guns and caissons and limber up to depart. Only later did he learn that Bee had sent Major Howard to him with an order to withdraw but that Howard had been hit on his way forward and was badly wounded.[32]

After the battle Imboden reflected that the failure of Bee's order to reach him might have been "providential," for his battery's fire had delayed the Union movement across Young's Branch. "But for that, they might have gained the Henry plateau, before Jackson and Hampton came up, and before Bee and Bartow had rallied their disorganized troops."[33]

As his battery withdrew, Imboden used both the Henry house and a ravine to mask his men and guns from the Union artillery and musket fire once Federal troops had reached the crest. Several shots from Griffin's Battery actually passed right through the Henry house, scattering debris among Imboden's men. The house itself was riddled during the battle, and old, bedridden Judith Henry was mortally wounded.

Imboden was only able to bring off three of his four guns. One of the Union rifled rounds disabled the axle of one gun, dropping its artillery tube in the field. The men saved the limber and team, however. The advancing Union infantry reached the crest of the hill in time to get off one volley at the departing Staunton Artillery, but without effect.[34]

General Beauregard noted in his subsequent report on the battle, "Imboden's battery which had been handled with great skill, but whose men were almost exhausted, withdrew when threatened by the enemy infantry on the left and front." In delaying the Federal advance, Imboden had played a major part in the outcome of the battle.[35]

Both sides now fed in reinforcements. McDowell added to his advancing right, while Beauregard sent troops to shore up his crumbling left. Among the latter was a brigade of five Virginia regiments commanded by Brigadier General Jackson.[36]

As his battery withdrew, midway between the Henry and Robinson houses, Imboden encountered Jackson moving forward with his men at double-quick step. Imboden recalled that he rode up to Jackson and expressed his displeasure at Bee's having abandoned him for so long without orders. Apparently he used some profanity, and Jackson's expression indicated his displeasure at the swearing. Jackson then directed Imboden to fall in between two of his regiments and return to the hill and fight with him. Imboden recalled Jackson as saying, "I'll support your battery. Unlimber right here."[37]

Jackson's troops, along with Imboden's Battery, now took up position on Henry Hill, some three hundred to four hundred yards from the ground it had just occupied. The Confederate troops under Bee and Bartow were in full retreat. Tradition holds that Bee, probably attempting to persuade his own troops to hold firm and seeing Jackson's Brigade firmly placed, shouted, "There stands Jackson like a stone wall! Rally behind the Virginians!" Thus, with the help of the press, Jackson's Brigade became the "Stonewall Brigade" and Jackson, "Stonewall." Although not visible to Imboden, both Beauregard and Johnston had also arrived on the hill and were in excellent position to direct the battle, encouraging the troops and positioning reinforcements.[38]

Imboden's Battery was in full view of the advancing Union troops.

The ammunition caissons were all empty, except for one. Once unlimbered, the guns opened at once but fired only slowly because there were few men to work them and the ammunition had to be brought up from a caisson two hundred to three hundred yards in the rear. Imboden recalled that "every shot here told with terrible effect, as we could see a lane opened through the enemy after almost every fire. Our first gun was worked, during this part of the action, by the Captain, First Lieutenant, and two privates. In the course of three-quarters of an hour our supply of shot and shells were exhausted—the men could no longer work—we had nothing but cannister left."[39]

Imboden believed that at this point McDowell committed his major blunder in the battle by ordering both Ricketts's and Griffin's batteries to cease fire and relocate across the turnpike to the top of Henry House Hill to take up a new position west of the house itself. The short span necessary to carry out this order allowed Beauregard time to form a line of battle on the crest of the hill southeast of the Henry and Robinson houses. Imboden stressed that if one of the Federal batteries had been left north of Young's Branch, it would have been in position to sweep the hilltop where his battery reformed and prevent it from doing so. Had his battery been forced back to the next hill, the Union troops might have turned the Confederate right flank.

When Imboden encountered Jackson and became subject to his authority, he reported that he was virtually out of ammunition and asked permission to send a caisson to the rear for resupply. Jackson insisted that he wait until other Confederate guns arrived. At that point, Imboden's Battery, which Jackson admitted had "been so torn to pieces," could retire altogether to regroup and rest.

During the lull of some twenty to thirty minutes in that part of the battlefield as both sides repositioned, Imboden's men, "black with powder, smoke, and dust," lay down to rest. Imboden and Lieutenant Harman used the interval to train one of the battery's guns on a large Federal column advancing toward the Confederate position from the left in the direction of the Chinn house. The Federals were still some 1,200–1,500 yards away.

At this point Jackson rode up and announced that, as three or four Confederate batteries were about to arrive, Imboden and his men might depart. Imboden asked if he might fire off the three remaining spherical case rounds toward the Federals and Jackson agreed. Imboden then rammed home the round himself, telling Harman to put in the primer and fire the gun. In his eagerness to observe the effects of the fire, Imboden knelt to see under the smoke, forgetting how close he was to the muzzle of the gun. When it went off, the shock of the discharge knocked him over and blood poured out of his left ear. The injury deafened him permanently in that ear. He did recover quickly enough, however, to have the satisfaction of observing the shell burst among the Federal troops.

Imboden's men then fired off the remaining rounds from the other guns and the battery limbered up. As the Staunton Artillery was departing the field, the men encountered batteries of both the Rockbridge Artillery and Loudoun Artillery coming onto the field. By the time Griffin and Ricketts had repositioned their batteries, they were opposed by as many as twenty-six Confederate guns.[40]

When the Union troops resumed their advance around 2:00 P.M., they came up against the strength of the Confederate line. The fighting was heavy and, for a time, the outcome was in doubt. Amidst the confusion, both sides mounted charges and counter-charges. Two Union batteries, mistaking a Confederate regiment for one of their own, were destroyed by a point-blank Southern volley.

Jackson ordered Imboden, as his battery departed, to go around to the new Confederate batteries and make certain that their guns were properly aimed and the shell fuses were cut to the right length. This did not take long, and Imboden returned to ask Jackson's permission to rejoin his battery. He recalled of the meeting: "The fight was just then hot enough to make him feel well. His eyes fairly blazed. He had a way of throwing up his left hand with the open palm toward the person he was addressing. And as he told me to go, he made this gesture. The air was full of flying missiles, and as he spoke he jerked down his hand, and I saw that blood was streaming from it. I exclaimed, 'General, you are wounded.' He replied, as he drew a handkerchief from his breast pocket, and began to bind it up, 'Only a scratch—a mere scratch,' and galloped away along his line."[41]

Imboden then left to find his horse. To keep it safe, he had hitched the horse in a gully some fifty yards to the rear. As he made his way in that direction he passed through an infantry formation that he claimed was Hampton's Legion, the men lying down within supporting distance of the Confederate artillery batteries, which were then all firing.[42] As Imboden was untying his horse, a Union shell exploded in the middle of Hampton's Legion, killing several men and causing fifteen to twenty others to bolt for the rear.

Imboden said that he tried to rally the deserters, but one of them, with musket in hand and bayonet fixed, had already begun to run. Imboden tried to stop him: "I threw myself in his front with drawn sword, and threatened to cut him down, whereupon he made a lunge at me. I threw up my left arm to ward off the blow, and the bayonet-point ran under the wristband of my red flannel shirt, and raked the skin of my arm from wrist to shoulder. The blow knocked me sprawling on the ground, and the fellow got away. I tore off the dangling shirt-sleeve, and was bare-armed as to my left, the remainder of the fight."[43]

Imboden overtook his own battery near the Lewis house, which was now serving as a hospital. In a field to the front he saw General Johnston and his staff mounted and under fire from Federal shells. He rode over to Johnston, reported his ammunition expended, and asked if there was any resupply nearby. Observing the battery's state, Johnston ordered Imboden to take his battery farther to the rear where it might be safe and then to return himself to see if he might be of service. Imboden took his battery back perhaps a mile, where they stopped next to a stream. Personally exhausted, he rested about an hour before returning to the front with Sgt. Joseph Shumate.[44]

Imboden's Battery had played a key role in the battle. As he noted on July 22, "We were the first battery of the left wing of the army engaged. We were in the fight till near its close, having been engaged altogether upwards of four hours. . . . No company of the army was more exposed, and none, I believe, so long a time."[45]

The Confederates, meanwhile, continued to bring up reinforcements and by late afternoon all of Johnston's troops were in place. Shortly before 4:00 P.M. fresh Southern troops charged into the Union right flank at Chinn Ridge and rolled back McDowell's men. What had earlier seemed an apparent Southern defeat now turned into a Union rout. When Imboden regained the field, the Federals had already been swept from Henry House Hill and the general Union retreat had begun.

Imboden and Shumate watched the retreating Federals for a time and then, hearing firing off between the Lewis house and Stone Bridge, rode in that direction to see what was going on. Capt. Lindsay Walker and his six-gun Parrott battery from Fredericksburg was on a hill shelling across Bull Run at Union troops fleeing in disorder into a tree line. Imboden could also see Col. J.E.B. Stuart leading his cavalry, sabers drawn, around the base of the hill to cross Bull Run and attack the Union troops. The battle was over.[46]

What had begun as an orderly Union retreat across Bull Run soon became a confused, panicky stampede back toward Washington when the retreating troops became intertwined with the carriages of congressmen and other curious bystanders who had come out from Washington to see a Union victory. A Confederate shell ripped into a wagon on Cub Run Bridge and disabled it, blocking that main escape artery and causing the Union columns to become enmeshed.

As Stuart's men disappeared in the distance to pursue the retreating Federals, Imboden and Shumate returned to their battery. Nearing the Lewis house, they saw General Johnston and his staff riding toward them, preceded by a civilian on horseback who was raising his hat to those he encountered. It was Jefferson Davis, who had arrived at the height of the battle. Imboden reported that the impulsive Shumate rode up to Davis, seized him by the hand, and cheered at the top of his voice. Davis was amused and Imboden broke into laughter. When they got close to Imboden, Shumate said, "Mr. President, there's my captain, and I want to introduce you to him." Imboden thought that Davis must have found him an odd sight indeed. He had on a battered slouch hat, a red flannel shirt with but one sleeve, corduroy trousers, and heavy cavalry boots. He was covered with burnt powder, dirt, and blood from his ear and arm. Davis shook Imboden's hand, said a few words, and then rode on.

Shumate and Imboden found their battery eating a long-overdue meal of bacon and bread. After he had something to eat, Imboden fell exhausted on a sack of oats and slept until full daylight the next day, this in spite of a drenching rain.

Imboden was awakened by a messenger asking him to go meet with General Bee. During the battle both Bee and Bartow were near the Henry house when they had come under Federal fire. Bartow had been killed outright by a musket ball and Bee had fallen mortally wounded. During the night someone had told Bee that Imboden had expressed displeasure at being abandoned without orders to withdraw, and Bee wanted to assure Imboden that he had not forgotten him and had in fact sent Major Howard to order him back. Several messengers had searched for Imboden during the night without success.

Imboden finally located Bee in the same cabin where they had met the night before. By then Bee was unconscious. A few minutes later, with Imboden holding his hand, he died. The Confederate Congress subsequently confirmed Bee's posthumous promotion to brigadier general.[47]

Davis urged that his forces pursue the defeated Federals all the way to Washington; however, the victors were exhausted and as disorganized as the vanquished. Supplies and transportation needed for this pursuit were simply not available at Manassas, and so Davis's request was impossible. By daybreak on June 23 the Union troops were back behind the defenses of Washington.

Casualties in the Battle of Manassas or Bull Run (the Confederates named their battles for the nearest town, the Union for the nearest body of water) were relatively light on both sides, at least considering the bloodletting of subsequent contests. The Confederates lost 387 killed and 1,582 wounded; Union losses were 260 killed, 1,124 wounded, and 1,312 missing.

The battle was a wake-up call for the North that the South would not be easily defeated and that the struggle would be protracted. Northerners now adopted a grim determination to see the war through to a successful conclusion, while southerners were overly optimistic that they could prevail. The battle also secured Jackson's reputation and earned him the sobriquet of "Stonewall." Less than a week after the defeat, President Lincoln replaced McDowell with Maj. Gen. George B. McClellan.[48]

Imboden must have been pleased with his own role and the recognition he received. In his lengthy official report of the battle, Beauregard mentioned Imboden and the Staunton Artillery eleven times and noted that the Staunton Artillery "had been handled with marked skill."[49] Jackson had also mentioned Imboden by name in his report. He said that he "met General Bee's forces falling back. I continued to advance, with the understanding that he would form in my rear. His battery, under its dauntless commander, Captain Imboden, reversed and advanced with my brigade."⁵⁰ Even General Johnston took note of the captain when he wrote, "Imboden rendered excellent service with his battery in this difficult operation."⁵¹

In his own report, Imboden concluded: "We were the first battery of the left wing of the army engaged. We were in the fight till near its close, having been engaged altogether upwards of four hours. We fired about 460 rounds of ball and case-shot, our whole supply, during the action."⁵²

The battery had suffered remarkably few personnel casualties: one lieutenant and two privates wounded. Of its seventy-one horses, however, ten were dead and twenty-one were either wounded or missing. The artillery piece lost in the withdrawal from Henry house hill was recovered after the battle. Perfectly fine, it was soon remounted and back in service with the battery.⁵³

Several days after the battle, Imboden learned that Jackson's wound was serious and possibly infected. He then rode to see Jackson and found him at his headquarters, a small farmhouse near Centreville. Imboden recalled that it was early in the morning but Jackson was up and out under the trees, bathing his wound with spring water. Imboden noted that although the wound was painful, Jackson "bore himself stoically." Jackson's wife, Anna, had arrived the night before and Imboden joined them for breakfast:

> I remarked in Mrs. Jackson's hearing, "General, how is it that you can keep so cool, and appear so utterly insensible to danger in such a storm of shell and bullets as rained about you when your hand was hit?" He instantly became grave and reverential in his manner, and answered in a low tone of great earnestness: "Captain, my religious belief teaches me to feel as safe in battle as in bed. God has fixed the time for my death. I do not concern myself about *that,* but to be always ready, no matter when it may overtake me." He added with a pause, looking me full in the face: "Captain this is the way all men should live, and then all would be equally brave."
>
> I felt that this last remark was intended as a rebuke for my profanity, when I had complained to him on the field of the apparent abandonment of my battery to capture, and I apolo-

gized. He heard me, and simply said, "Nothing can justify profanity."⁵⁴

There were recriminations after the Battle of Manassas over the lack of Confederate pursuit of McDowell's army. Richmond thought not enough had been done, but those on the spot knew better. Imboden himself wrote in the battery's muster roll following the battle, "the fatigue of that day together with privations and exposure to tremendous rains cause the great amount of sickness."⁵⁵

To try and resolve the matter General Johnston appointed a board of officers to investigate and report back on the condition of the forces at Manassas on July 21 and its daily conditions for two weeks following. The board consisted of three men, two of whom were former U.S. Army officers of some experience: Lt. Col. Robert B. Lee, representing the Commissary Department, and Maj. (later major general) W.L. Cabell, of the Quartermaster Department. Imboden was the third member, representing the line units.

The group organized in early August, conducted an exhaustive investigation, and produced a detailed report. It found that there was not a full day's worth of rations for the combined armies of Beauregard and Johnston at Manassas on the day of battle, and that for the two weeks afterward there was never as much as even a three-days' supply. There were insufficient wagons available to have transported three days' worth of rations, even had they been available. The commission found that in the weeks before the battle, Beauregard had made repeated appeals to the commissary services at Richmond for supplies and that commissary general Col. L.B. Northrup had not only failed to provide for an emergency situation—such as occurred when Johnston's men came up from the Valley—but had even interfered with Beauregard's commissary officers who had tried to tap the rich resources of the immediate area. Imboden noted that his group "unanimously concurred in the opinion that they proved the impossibility of a successful and rapid pursuit of the defeated army to Washington." However, Northrup and Confederate Secretary of War Judah P. Benjamin contested the board's finding, and Benjamin held that it had exceeded its authority by drawing conclusions.⁵⁶

In the weeks following the battle, Imboden's Battery was materially strengthened by receiving two captured Union guns—a howitzer and a James rifled gun—bringing it up to a total of six pieces. The increase in the size of his battery led Imboden to try to secure commissions as second lieutenants with the Staunton Artillery for his brother George and C.C. McPhail of Winchester. He wrote in justification: "Gen. Johnston has increased my Battery by the addition of two of the captured guns & directed me to enlarge my Company to 150 rank and file—Any regular officer will tell you that it is impossible to manage a six piece Battery—especially of mixed guns—rifles—smooth & Howitzers—with less than 4 Lieuts. Indeed 150 men, 110 horses & six pieces, with necessary baggage & officer's train, would well employ 5 Lieuts. in the field—but 4 are absolutely required."[57]

George Imboden received a commission and posting to the battery, but McPhail did not. George Armentrout was named an acting lieutenant but never served. Hill C. Bradford was assigned to the battery as a lieutenant, along with assistant surgeon Logan Brandt. The battery sustained a significant and unexpected loss, however, when First Lieutenant Harman, who had been with the Staunton Artillery since its inception and had played an important role in its training and operation, died of typhoid fever at Staunton in September.[58]

The battery was posted at Camp Pickens, and there its situation somewhat improved. Whereas at the end of July, Imboden had only 68 horses supporting his battery, by the end of August he had 108 horses and mules. The battery also changed its bivouac to Camp Jones at Bristoe Station.[59]

On September 18 Imboden received orders to move his battery again, this time to Dumfries, Virginia, south-southwest of Washington on the west bank of the Potomac River (just above present-day Quantico). There he would support Brig. Gen. Isaac R. Trimble's forces at Evansport.

Trimble, a native of Culpepper, Virginia, graduated from West Point in 1822. In 1832 he left the military and became chief engineer and superintendent for a number of southern railroads. Although then claiming Maryland as his state of residence, Trimble had secured a colonelcy of engineers in Virginia in May 1861. In August he became a brigadier general in the Confederate Army and secured a brigade in Maj. Gen. Richard Ewell's Division. He was wounded and taken prisoner in the Battle of Gettysburg in July 1863.[60]

Imboden did not get along with Trimble's successor, Brig. Gen.

William H.C. Whiting. A native of Biloxi, Mississippi, and a graduate of West Point in 1845, Whiting was an army engineer until February 1861, when he resigned to fight for the Confederacy. Assigned as chief engineer in the Army of the Shenandoah, he was advanced to brigadier general on his successful handling of its movement to Manassas. It is not surprising that Imboden disliked Whiting; although he was an excellent engineer, few of his brother officers cared for him.[61] Part of Imboden's dislike stemmed from the general's refusal to grant him leave. Imboden's attitude might also have been related to Whiting's undisguised dislike of "Stonewall" Jackson.[62]

Bit by bit, the battery received needed equipment, although Imboden, writing in the muster rolls on September 30, noted that the government had provided little assistance: "By recruits, increase of guns from 4 to 6 with proper caissons & harness the company is now in more prosperous & efficient condition than it has ever been since its organization on 1 November 1859. It may be proper to add . . . that this company has never received from state or Confederate governments whatever, nor blankets nor tents except, one single Yankee tent captured property nor anything except its arms, horses, harness and 100 Knapsacks & canteens."[63]

On October 17 the Staunton artillery joined other Confederate batteries located on bluffs overlooking the Potomac above Evansport in opening fire on Union ships in the river. Apparently the Union vessels were at some range, as the battery fired only its rifled gun, and that for only eight shots.[64]

From October 1861 through March 1862, the battery was located in the Evansport area and Imboden's men soon settled into a routine. For the most part, little was going on, and Imboden wrote home in early November to request shot for hunting partridges. He also sent money to buy a hundred pairs of trousers for his men. Color was not important, he said, so long as the pants were all the same and were heavy enough for cold weather.[65]

On November 7 Imboden reported: "All is quiet. The river is clear of Yankees for 5 miles, above and below the batteries. Gen. Whiting ordered me this morning to select a suitable position for another battery of 10 heavy guns some miles from the present batteries. I have found a magnificent position and will report it in the morning. I think it is probable he will put me in charge of the construction of the works.

With 400 men I can have the guns in position in a week—and do the work under cover in the day time."[66]

Imboden did have problems with soldiers who were on leave and had not returned to his unit. He wrote that he had reported their names to headquarters, and if the men did not return in a few days, "I shall be compelled to have them arrested for desertion—in which case the reward for arrest is $30—will be taken from their pay and they will be severely punished by Court Martial besides."[67]

At the end of November Imboden wrote home that he was acting as a topographical engineer for Whiting and that the situation was calm:

> Here we are perfectly quiet . . . for a while in November our generals expected an attack would be made upon these batteries, and even now Gen Whiting thinks were we to have a fight here one of these days.
>
> The mud in places for miles is to a horse's belly. God only knows how we are to get our supplies a few weeks hence. At this time it is a Herculean task. The provisions of the neighborhood are exhausted. We must be supplied by RR. It is 18 miles to Bristow—12 to Aquia. The road is next to deplorable. There are about 20000 troops in this neighborhood using about 52000 lbs of food per diem. . . . We are living hand to mouth having only 3 days ahead.[68]

The battery was then situated close to the town of Occoquan, some sixteen miles northeast of Dumfries near present-day Woodbridge. Imboden wrote home on December 7, angry at Col. Nathan G. Harman for retaining the absentees from his battery. A week later he sent an apology with the request that the absentees' names be published in the newspaper.[69]

On December 9 the Union steam gunboat and ex-Revenue Service cutter *Harriet Lane* and other vessels in the Potomac Flotilla engaged Confederate batteries at Freestone Point, Virginia. Imboden reported, "Today the Harriet Lane shelled a piquet at Freestone Point, 4 miles above us, and burnt John Fairfax's house, barn stables &c with about 400 bushels of wheat. The conflagration was visible from a hill above my camp."[70]

Ground transportation continued to be difficult. Imboden complained at the same time about problems with his horses' legs being "scalded by the mud" and noted that the battery would have to turn in twenty-five to thirty horses because of their condition. At least there was little activity from the Union side, probably in part because of the weather.[71]

The Staunton Artillery remained in the same area throughout the winter of 1861–1862. Life there was pretty much routine. The muster roll for November-December 1861 noted, "No event of interest occurred to the company during the period covered by the muster except two false alarms from Occoquan in Nov. resulting in a rapid march to the Neabsco and a slow one back each time." Imboden noted that the health of his men was "excellent."[72]

On March 8, 1862, Imboden's Staunton Artillery abandoned its position north of Dumfries and moved south, withdrawing with the rest of General Whiting's force to Fredericksburg. This was not without difficulty, undoubtedly the consequence of the poor state of the roads. Whiting reported that the Staunton Artillery had brought off "tents, ammunition, camp equipage, and battery complete, though the guns and caissons had to be brought out of Dumfries one at a time, twelve horses being required for each."[73]

On its arrival at Fredericksburg Imboden's unit was assigned to Maj. Gen. Gustavus W. Smith's Division. It did not remain near Fredericksburg long. On March 21 it was again on the move, this time for the peninsula. The poor state of the roads made this a long passage but the battery finally reached Yorktown. Imboden noted, "A part of the time the weather was extremely inclement and the roads horrible."[74]

The Staunton Artillery reorganized on its arrival at Yorktown. Imboden, who had other plans, declined reelection, as did his brother George. On April 22 the Staunton Artillery elected Lt. William L. Balthis as its new captain.[75]

Chapter 4

Forming a Partisan Command

On March 7, 1862, the day before the Staunton Artillery departed Dumfries for Fredericksburg, Imboden wrote, "I have written the President about raising a Legion for Guerrilla service in the Mountains. I will hear from him next week. If he authorizes it, I shall go home at once to raise the men in the Western Counties."[1] Soon Imboden had left the Staunton Artillery at Yorktown and returned to Staunton, where he raised two regiments, the 18th Cavalry and the 62d Virginia Infantry (Mounted), and a battery.

The reasons for Imboden's decision are not hard to discern. Ambition undoubtedly played a part. Advancement in the artillery was slow and was, in any case, limited by an abundance of West Point- and VMI-trained officers in that specialty. Imboden had seen little action since the Battle of Manassas and, while he had been recognized for his accomplishments in that action as a battery commander, he sought a more active role. There seemed to him no better place for such than in his own familiar territory of western Virginia, especially now that much of this area was passing under Union control. Imboden must have believed that if he could reverse this trend and regain the area for the Confederacy, his place in history would be assured.

The Shenandoah Valley, nestled between the Allegheny Mountains to the west and the Blue Ridge to the east, was of immense importance to the Confederacy. Its agricultural products and livestock helped feed the Army of Northern Virginia. Geographically, it could serve as an important invasion route north for Confederate forces and, conversely, had to be denied to Union forces as an invasion route south. Beyond that it could serve as a base area for raiders to carry the war into western Virginia and against the Baltimore & Ohio Railroad.

Small groups of troops who raided enemy positions during the war were known in the North and South as irregulars, independents, guerrillas, and partisans. Unionists called them bushwhackers, but that same term was often applied by southerners to northern irregular formations that raided the Shenandoah Valley. Generally speaking, bushwhackers were smaller bands, not as well organized as partisans, who operated irrespective of regular army operations. Bushwhackers were much more likely to be shot out of hand if taken by the opposing side.[2]

As one Confederate official put it, the great advantage of the partisans "is that the members are regularly in service and entitled to be treated as prisoners of war and have the benefit of exchange, which is not the case with unorganized volunteers, usually called guerrillas."[3]

Small-unit combat of this sort later came to be known simply as guerrilla warfare. The term was derived from the Spanish for "little wars" and sprang from the fighting in the Iberian Peninsula from 1807 to 1815 against French forces under Napoléon Bonaparte. Generally the side outnumbered, either in manpower or resources, was the one resorting to guerrilla warfare. It is thus not surprising that the Confederacy would adopt partisan warfare.

In June 1861 Asst. Adj. Gen. R.H. Chilton had replied favorably to an inquiry by F.A. Briscoe of Winchester regarding the establishment of partisan forces. Chilton wrote, "Such a force, when organized, armed, and equipped, will be received into service and commissions issued to the officers thereof."[4]

Such units had already appeared for defensive purposes. With few Confederate troops in the northern Shenandoah Valley, irregular companies sprang into being with the intent of protecting hearth and home. When requests for recognition of these units were received in Richmond, Governor Letcher secured authorization from the Virginia General Assembly to issue commissions for ten companies of Partisan Rangers.[5]

Then on April 21, 1862, the General Assembly regularized guerrilla warfare by passing the Partisan Ranger Act, which stated that partisan troops could be organized either as infantry or cavalry. Recruits would receive the same pay and benefits and would be subject to the same military regulations as regular soldiers. There was also one great inducement not available to regular soldiers: partisans would be paid for any arms and munitions they were able to capture and turn over to the government. Another inducement, of a negative nature, was the April 16 passage of the Conscription Act by the Confederate Congress. This provided for drafting any adult white male of military age, eighteen to thirty-five, for three year's service. Southerners owning twenty or more slaves were exempted from this first military draft in U.S. history, and there was widespread resentment to this exception. To many, therefore, joining a unit with the possibility of financial reward for plunder seemed preferable to the stigma of being drafted.[6]

Undoubtedly Imboden had learned of the partisan service early on. His brother Frank was in the partisans as a captain in Ben McCulloch's Rangers, part of Brig. Gen. Henry A. Wise's legion. Wise, an unreconstructed southerner to his death, owed his general officer's commission in the Confederate Army—as did many, North as well as South—not to military experience, for he had none, but to his political clout; Wise had been governor of Virginia from 1856 to 1860. Wise proved singularly inept as a military commander. His troops suffered defeat at the hands of Union Maj. Gen. Jacob D. Cox in the Kanawha Valley and by Maj. Gen. Ambrose E. Burnside in the defense of Roanoke Island, North Carolina, on February 8, 1862. Frank Imboden was captured in the latter engagement, and his brother then endeavored to secure his exchange, which was effected in August.[7]

What influence Frank Imboden's partisan service had in his brother's decision is unclear, but in the spring John Imboden lobbied hard to secure approval to raise a partisan unit. He probably sought General Jackson's support, for on April 29 Imboden wrote to his brother Frank requesting that he take a letter to Jackson in the Valley and offering to pay his expenses to do so. Although its content is unknown, the letter probably was related to a ranger command. In the letter to Frank, Imboden wrote: "Get his reply as soon as possible & forward it to me. . . . If the Genl. hesitates give him an earnest talk, & get John Harman to back you in it—also Ashby."[8] It is unclear what response Frank Imboden secured from Jackson, if indeed they did meet.

When Imboden left the Staunton Artillery at Yorktown it was undoubtedly with the understanding that his request for a partisan unit would be approved. Imboden received formal notification in the form of a letter of May 7 from Secretary of War George W. Randolph:

> You are authorized to raise and organize a Regiment for Partisan service in the military Department now under the command of Major General T.J. Jackson. The Companies must be enlisted of men not in the military service, and must consist, if infantry of at least 64 privates, if cavalry of at least 60, and must be regularly mustered into service for the War.
>
> As soon as the Corps is completed and reported, you will receive your commission. The other officers must be elected, and the Staff will be appointed.[9]

Imboden's was the first partisan unit to be so authorized, and he must have been pleased to be reunited with Jackson. On October 7, 1861, Jackson had been promoted to major general. Then later that month the Confederate government reorganized the Department of Northern Virginia under Johnston, subdividing it into the Valley District under Jackson, the Potomac District commanded by Beauregard, and the Aquia District under Maj. Gen. Theophilus Hunter Holmes.

The Valley District consisted of territory west of the Blue Ridge and east of the Alleghenies. On October 28 General Johnston ordered Jackson to establish his headquarters at Winchester. In early November, Richmond sent Jackson the "Stonewall" Brigade and assigned to act under his instructions some six thousand troops commanded by Brig. Gen. William W. Loring. These, together with Ashby's cavalry, brought Jackson's strength up to about ten thousand men.

The winter of 1861–1862 had been largely unproductive for Jackson and almost brought his resignation. Reinforced by four brigades commanded by R.R. Garnett, William B. Taliafero, William Gilham, and S.R. Anderson, he raided west to Romney on the South Branch of the upper Potomac at the end of December with the intention of destroying the Baltimore & Ohio Railroad and the Chesapeake & Ohio Canal. Although Jackson's troops inflicted some damage, it was only temporary.

A bitter controversy ensued, however, when Jackson ordered Loring into winter quarters at Romney. Loring wrote the Confederate War Department, charging that his men were dangerously exposed and that Jackson was showing preference to his regular command. He asked that his men be allowed to return to Winchester. Jackson was certain the remainder of his force could quickly march the thirty or so miles to Romney if need be, and he saw possession of that place as important for the resumption of campaigning in the spring of 1862. He was thus furious when Secretary of War Benjamin ordered him to recall Loring to Winchester. Jackson immediately responded to Benjamin by requesting transfer to the VMI faculty; failing that, he was resolved to resign. Jackson also wrote Governor Letcher to request his assistance in securing the VMI appointment. General Johnston then begged Jackson to reconsider, while Letcher went to Benjamin's offices and gave him a tongue lashing. Letcher then traveled to Winchester to urge Jackson to stay on. In early February Jackson agreed. Benjamin soothed Loring's feelings by promoting him to major general and assigning him to southwest Virginia.[10]

It was after this controversy that Imboden returned to the Valley and began recruiting his men. He soon circulated broadsides throughout western Virginia. These advertised in no uncertain terms and extreme language his intention to pursue a vigorous effort against Union forces: "My purpose is to wage the most active warfare against our brutal invaders and their domestic allies, to hang about their camps and shoot down every sentinel, picket, courier, and wagon driver we can find; to watch opportunities for attacking convoys and forage trains and thus render the country so unsafe that they will not dare to move except in large bodies."[11]

Imboden made clear the type of men he was seeking: "It is only *men* I want, men who will pull the trigger on a Yankee with as much alacrity as they would on a mad dog; men whose consciences won't be disturbed by the sight of vandal carcass."[12]

Imboden placed an ad in the Richmond *Dispatch*, which appeared on May 8, 1862, under the heading, "Active Service in the Mountains of Virginia," in which Imboden declared his intention to raise ten companies of "picked men" to operate west of the Blue Ridge. Declaring that his plan had "the highest military approval," he wrote: "I don't propose to rely much on military science but mainly on great celerity of movement, sleepless vigilance, good marksmanship and plenty of old-fashioned rough fighting and bushwhacking, so as to make the country too hot to permit a Yankee to show his head outside of camp."[13]

Clearly Imboden sought a particular type of person. He identified partisan service as that in which "individual prowess is not swallowed up on the mere mechanism of great masses of men."[14]

The editors of the newspaper supported Imboden's effort. They opined that partisan warfare was "beyond a doubt, the most attractive branch of the service (and would attract the attention) of all young men of daring and adventurous natures."[15] And, in fact, recruiting went well. Establishing his headquarters in Staunton, Imboden raised four full companies in less than two months. An additional four approached company strength.[16]

Several former soldiers in the Staunton Artillery wrote Imboden to ask for assistance in transferring to his new command, among them Hiram Opie. He wrote his former commander: "I will never be satisfied to remain in the Co. under the present *Officers* [emphasis in original] . . . for I have no confidence in them, and now that you are gone, I wish to go also."[17]

Losing an individual to military service often meant hardship for those who depended on his particular skill. In early July Imboden received a petition signed by twenty people in a "rough Mountain region" in Pendleton County, western Virginia. They informed him that "Jacob H. Lough who lives in our neighborhood and who is the only blacksmith we have is required to report at Staunton as a Soldier, to be mustered into the service of the Confederate States of America under your Command on the 20th day of July 1862." The citizens sought an exemption for him, for without his skills they would "not be able to put in our fall crop. The infernal Yankees have overrun our country and stripped us of nearly every thing. We had [have] to eat and starvation is just ahead if we should not be able to put in our fall crop." The exemption was granted.[18]

Meanwhile, in the spring of 1862 the war was gathering momentum; President Lincoln wanted a general Union offensive on all fronts. The naval blockade of Confederate Gulf and South Atlantic ports was daily strengthening, and the war in the West was also going well. In

February Union troops under Brig. Gen. Ulysses S. Grant and gunboats under Flag Officer Andrew H. Foote worked in tandem to secure first Fort Henry on the Tennessee River and then Fort Donelson on the Cumberland. Union troops occupied Nashville, the first former Confederate state capital to fall to Union forces, at the end of the month. These victories gave the Union armies access to middle Tennessee and some of the richest territory of the Confederacy.

In April a great bloodletting took place at Shiloh, Tennessee, when the Confederates attacked there, but Grant managed to hold and, once reinforced, pushed Confederate forces under Gen. P.G.T. Beauregard back toward Corinth, Mississippi. Then at the end of April Union naval forces under Flag Officer David Farragut ran past the batteries guarding the Southern approaches to New Orleans and took the Crescent City.

This seriousness of purpose in the western theater of operations was not matched in the East. There, all of Lincoln's entreaties to McClellan to move fell on deaf ears; finally fed up, the president removed McClellan from command of the all the Union armies in March, leaving him with the Army of the Potomac.

The Union goal in the East on land was always the capture of Richmond, capital of the Confederacy and important manufacturing center. McClellan thought he had a better plan for taking Richmond than merely driving directly south: utilizing Union naval power, he would land the Army of the Potomac on the peninsula between the York and James Rivers and advance against Richmond from the east. While approving the concept in general, Lincoln and others feared a Confederate descent on Washington while this was in progress. Lincoln ordered McClellan to leave a corps under Maj. Gen. Irwin McDowell to defend the Union capital. When McClellan was sufficiently close to Richmond, McDowell was to move south and link up with McClellan for the final assault and, they hoped, an end to the war.

On March 17 McClellan's army, ferried down the Chesapeake Bay from Alexandria, Virginia, began disembarking on the peninsula. But the advantage of this approach to Richmond from the east was largely thrown away in an advance that can only be described as glacial. Critics dubbed McClellan "the Virginia creeper."

McClellan began a siege of Yorktown in early April, but Confederate Maj. Gen. John Magruder, with only fifteen thousand men, hoodwinked the overly cautious McClellan into believing he had many times that number, and the Federals did not occupy Yorktown until early May. Finally, in mid-month, the Army of the Potomac reached the Pamunkey River only twenty miles from Richmond. Despite an overwhelming advantage in numbers, McClellan now stopped to await reinforcement by McDowell's corps.

The Confederates had quickly moved to parry the Union thrust. Gen. Joseph E. Johnston had withdrawn from Manassas in March and repositioned his forces to confront McClellan. Gen. Robert E. Lee, military advisor to President Davis, realized that Johnston was heavily outnumbered. He had only sixty thousand men against McClellan's one hundred thousand and McDowell's forty thousand at Fredericksburg. Well aware of Lincoln's concerns about the vulnerability of Washington to Confederate attack, Lee now recommended that Jackson, reinforced to nearly eighteen thousand men, demonstrate in the Shenandoah Valley and divert the largest possible Union reinforcements from McClellan. Johnston and Davis agreed.

The result was Jackson's much-praised and studied Valley Campaign of March 23–June 9, one of the finest such operations in world history, in which Jackson influenced the fighting before Richmond. In this, Jackson was indeed fortunate to come up against two Union generals who had received their commissions on the basis of political considerations: Maj. Gens. Nathaniel P. Banks and John C. Frémont.

Banks had campaigned in the Valley before, in 1861. His task now was to clear the Valley as part of the Richmond Campaign. After he defeated Jackson, he was to cover Washington, freeing McDowell's forty thousand men to advance on Richmond from the north and link up with McClellan. Frémont, who had previously commanded without distinction in the West, was new to the theater. Named in March 1862 to command the new Mountain Department, his task was to advance into the Valley from the west.

In the ensuing campaign Jackson's intelligence and communications were excellent, and his infantry marched so quickly—up to thirty miles a day—that they became known as "foot cavalry." In a series of battles, Jackson defeated the Union forces in detail, causing them to retreat across the Potomac. Jackson's successes also produced fear in Washington that he might then strike for the capital, although this was certainly beyond his means. Ultimately some twenty thousand men were detached from McDowell's command and rushed to the Valley.

With never more than 18,000 men, Jackson defeated three Union armies totaling 64,000 men in four pitched battles, six large skirmishes, and numerous other minor actions. Union losses were some 8,000 men; the Confederates sustained fewer than 2,500. Then Jackson slipped away to Richmond and the critical battles there.

Jackson's initial encounter with the Federals in the Valley Campaign did not go well. Shortly after Johnston had evacuated Manassas for Richmond on March 8–9, Jackson abandoned Winchester and moved up the Valley. Union Brig. Gen. James Shields's Division of about 9,000 men of Banks's command then occupied that place. Jackson's own forces had been whittled away for a variety of reasons, so that by early March he had perhaps only 4,200 men in his command in the Valley. He resolved, however, to do the best he could with the resources available.

Jackson was about forty miles south of Winchester when he received word that Union troops were leaving that place to move east of the mountains and cooperate with McDowell. Concentrating some 4,200 men, Jackson now moved north. On March 21 Turner Ashby reported to Jackson that a reconnaissance of Winchester indicated that the Federals had virtually abandoned the area. The information was incorrect and led Jackson into a major error. In a forced march, he moved to Kernstown, four miles south of Winchester on the Valley Pike, arriving there on March 23.

Jackson assumed that only a small Federal garrison would confront him. He planned to send Col. Jesse S. Burke's Brigade in a feint along ground near the Valley Pike while his main force of two brigades under Col. Samuel V. Fulkerson and Brig. Gen. Richard B. Garnett went to the west along Sandy Ridge to strike the Union defenders from the flank and rear. In the center, Jackson placed twenty-seven cannon to be moved as required. However, Union artillery took a commanding position on Pritchard's Hill, northwest of the pike, enabling it to engage both Confederate attacking columns. Also, two large Union brigades under Cols. Erastus B. Tyler and Nathan Kimball quickly moved onto the ridge to block the Confederate flanking attack.

The battle seesawed back and forth. The strength of the Union defense and the prolonged fighting confused the attackers. With his brigade out of ammunition, Garnett ordered it to withdraw, something that infuriated Jackson, who had issued no orders to that effect. The remainder of the Confederate attackers then followed, ending the battle. Jackson had lost one gun and three caissons, and he had 455 men killed and wounded and several hundred others taken as prisoners. However, the battle was to the Confederate strategic advantage in that the Federal withdrawal of troops from the Valley to McDowell ceased. The speed of Jackson's attack and its vigorous nature alarmed Washington, and Shields now ordered Union troops to return.[19]

The Federals in fact held an immense manpower advantage in the general area of operations. Brig. Gen. Robert Milroy, commander of the Cheat Mountain District in western Virginia, had a brigade of some 6,000 men on the Staunton-Parkersville Turnpike at McDowell, approximately forty miles west of Staunton; Brig. Gen. Robert Schenck of Frémont's command had 2,500 men at Franklin; Frémont retained another 20,000 near Franklin, fifty miles northwest of Staunton within easy supporting range of Milroy; Banks had 20,000 at Strasburg; McDowell had 37,000 men just east of the Blue Ridge; and Colonel Miles commanded 7,000 men at Harpers Ferry. After the war Imboden calculated that Jackson thus had to take into account movements by some 80,000 Federal troops located north of the Rappahannock and east of the Ohio Rivers and that not less than 65,000 of these were in some part of the Valley. Jackson's task was to keep these troops occupied so that they could not cooperate against Richmond. Were Jackson to fail in this, Imboden believed that some 100,000 Federals "would converge and move down upon Richmond as McClellan advanced from the east, and the city and its defenders would fall an easy prey to nearly, if not quite, a quarter of a million of the best-armed and best-equipped men ever put into the field by a government."[20]

If Jackson was overawed by this Union manpower advantage, he gave no indication of it. Following his repulse at Kernstown, he retreated with his force up the Valley to Swift Run Gap in the Blue Ridge Mountains, in Rockingham County. The Union commanders failed to take advantage of the situation. Taking a page from McClellan's book, Banks pursued Jackson only in fits and starts. Although the Confederates did harass his advance, it took the Union commander's 15,000 men nearly a month to reach Harrisonburg, and during that time Jackson's own numbers had dramatically increased. Jackson added to his command some 2,800 men under Brig. Gen. Edward "Allegheny" Johnson. More important, at the beginning of May he received Brig. Gen. Richard Stoddert Ewell's Division of 8,000 men.[21]

Ewell, who would be closely linked with Jackson the rest of the latter's life, was born in Washington, D.C., but had moved to Prince William County, Virginia, when he was a boy. Graduating from West Point in 1840, he received a commission in the dragoons. He had fought with distinction in the Mexican War and earned promotion to captain. He resigned his U.S. Army commission at the start of the Civil War and was initially a lieutenant colonel in the Virginia forces. He then became a colonel in the Confederate Army with command of a camp of cavalry instruction. Advanced to brigadier general in June 1861, he served with distinction in the First Battle of Manassas and in January 1862 was advanced to major general.[22]

Jackson now put together a daring plan. He would leave Ewell at Swift Run Gap to keep an eye on Banks while he slipped out of the Valley to confront Frémont's twenty thousand men moving from the west and threatening Staunton. Leaving Ashby's cavalry to demonstrate in front of Banks to keep him distracted and provide news of his movements, Jackson set out with his brigades on April 30. They marched east, past Port Republic and across the Blue Ridge through Brown's Gap and Swift Run Gap. Jackson anticipated that this movement east, which was not concealed, would confuse Banks.

Sheets of rain quickly turned the roads into seas of clay and mud, making Jackson's progress difficult at best. Jackson had ordered a sufficient number of railroad cars from Charlottesville and other points along the Virginia Central Railroad to transport his troops, and they met the trains at Mechum's Depot west of Charlottesville. To the men's relief, as many of them were from the Valley, the trains moved not east but west to Staunton, arriving there on the afternoon of May 5. Jackson's men had covered ninety-two miles in four days of marching and twenty-five miles by rail. They were met at Staunton by Brigadier General Johnson's men and the VMI cadet battalion, which Jackson had called out from Lexington for the emergency.[23]

Jackson had wanted Imboden and his Rangers with him on the operation, but Imboden was off recruiting and could not be located.

Jackson even wired Lee in an attempt to ascertain Imboden's whereabouts, to which Lee replied, "I have not seen Captain [sic] Imboden. If I can find him I will urge him to join you with such men as he can at once, as you desired."[24]

Unable to wait, Jackson moved west with his ten thousand men by means of Buffalo Gap. He had already closed off the area with a cavalry force and positioned a brigade under Brigadier General Johnson. Jackson hoped to envelop two of Milroy's regiments on Shenandoah Mountain, but the latter managed to withdraw ahead of him on the afternoon of May 7. Milroy's men retreated across the Bull Pasture River, and their commander then informed Schenck of the Confederate presence. Schenck immediately put his own troops in motion, marching them all night toward Milroy. On his arrival Schenck, the senior officer by date of commission, assumed command of the combined Union force. Outnumbered by Jackson nearly two to one, he deployed his six thousand men in defensive positions at the town of McDowell, some thirty miles west of Staunton on the Parkersburg Turnpike.

Sitlington's Hill to the east of McDowell dominated the town, and Jackson ordered his men to seize it. When Schenck saw this, he decided to withdraw his two brigades rather than be trapped.

On the afternoon of May 8, as Jackson was looking for a way to turn the Union defenses, Schenck launched a preemptive attack to purchase time for the remainder of his men to escape. The battle was hard fought and extended over several hours. Schenck finally broke off the attack and the Union forces withdrew back across the Allegheny Mountains toward Franklin to unite with Frémont. Jackson had lost 45 killed and 423 wounded, while Schenck had only 26 killed, 227 wounded, and 3 missing. Particularly grievous for the Confederates was the loss of Johnson, an excellent commander; severely wounded in the fighting, he was lost for over a year. Ultimately, though, Jackson had saved Staunton and, more important, he had prevented a juncture of forces under Frémont and Banks.[25]

Although Ashby harried the retreating Union troops and Jackson pursued them all the way to Franklin, the Confederate advance was impeded by poor roads and effective Union rear guard actions. After several days Jackson abandoned the pursuit.

Imboden finally joined Jackson on May 9, the day after the

McDowell fight. He arrived at McDowell early that morning and met Jackson at his headquarters, the home of Col. George W. Hull. Jackson asked Imboden to provide dispatch riders and to send a message to President Davis from Staunton, the nearest telegraph office, with news of the recent battle. After discarding several longer attempts, Jackson came up with a simple message. Dated "McDowell," it read simply: "Providence blessed our arms with victory at McDowell yesterday."[26]

Jackson then released the VMI cadets, who were never engaged, to return to Lexington and moved north to join Ewell at Harrisonburg. A few days later in Staunton, Imboden received a message from Jackson via courier with instructions to transmit it by telegraph to Secretary of War Benjamin in Richmond. In it Jackson signaled his intent to move against Banks but pointed out that he was prevented by orders from doing so. Less than an hour after Imboden had sent the message, a reply arrived to be sent along to Jackson, but it came from General Johnston rather than Benjamin. Johnston authorized Jackson to attack Banks if he thought he had a chance of beating him and informed him that the prohibition extended only to attacks against fortified places.

Imboden sent this message to Jackson, believing he was then at McDowell, but the courier found him only twelve miles from Staunton moving east with his army by way of the Warm Springs-Harrisonburg Turnpike. Jackson sent all of his men who were there with him, save part of Ashby's cavalry, to harry Frémont, who was then concentrating at Franklin. Two hours after receiving the message from Johnston, Jackson left for Harrisonburg, where he rejoined Ewell and gained the Valley Turnpike.

Imboden played little role in this phase of the Valley Campaign. He remained at Staunton to continue recruiting and training his men, minus those now serving as Jackson's couriers.

By forced marches, Jackson reached New Market in only two days. He was determined not to lose the initiative and the element of surprise. Jackson's movement was completely screened by cavalry, and Banks was totally unaware of what was transpiring.

Jackson, who with Ewell now had about seventeen thousand men, moved north toward an unsuspecting Banks, the only Union commander remaining in the Valley, as Brigadier General Shields had already departed with his men. Banks had his headquarters at Strasburg, where he was building strong fortifications. He had only about eight thousand men under his command, and his principal assignment remained that of containing Jackson. Yet in order to protect the area abandoned by Shields, Banks had sent some one thousand men and two guns from Strasburg to Front Royal, ten miles to the southeast on the Manassas Gap Railroad line.

Jackson feinted a strike on Strasburg, but, mindful of Johnston's prohibition, he planned to bypass the fortifications by outflanking them to the east, forcing the Union troops to abandon their positions without a fight. In order to accomplish this, he sent Ewell's Division north, paralleling his own force but on the other side of Massanutten Mountain to the east of the Valley Pike. When he himself reached New Market, Jackson turned east, moving his men over Massanutten Mountain there and joining Ewell at Luray.

On May 23, the reunited Confederate army reached the vicinity of Front Royal, where Jackson received a report from notorious Confederate spy Belle Boyd on Union strength and troop dispositions. That same afternoon Jackson sent Brigadier General Ashby and his cavalry west to hold the rail line connecting with Strasburg. Concurrently, he put his infantry in motion toward Front Royal to take and hold two bridges over the Forks of the Shenandoah River. Union troops, commanded by Col. John R. Kenly, fought a delaying action and set fire to the North Fork Bridge, but the Confederates managed to secure and save most of it. Col. Thomas S. Flournoy's 6th Virginia Cavalry then forded the river and charged after the retreating Federals, capturing most of them near Cedarville.

The May 23 Battle of Front Royal was an unqualified Confederate success. Jackson had lost only fifty men, while capturing seven hundred Federals, including twenty officers. He also negated Banks's defensive preparations, because the Union works at Strasburg faced south rather than east. More important, Jackson was between Banks and Washington, and Union positions at Harpers Ferry and Winchester were vulnerable to attack. As a result, both Jackson and Banks now hurried north to Winchester.[27]

Jackson was determined to move quickly so as not to allow Banks time to fortify the hills southwest of Winchester. At Newton on May 24, he fell on Banks from the flank and captured a number of his supply wagons, which included more than nine thousand rifles in perfect order and a considerable quantity of ammunition. Marching his men most of that night, Jackson then attacked the Union positions in the hills near Winchester the next morning.

On May 25 the Federal troops fought well, until their line at last gave way. They then bolted to the rear, retreating all the way to the Potomac, where Banks withdrew them across the river into Maryland. Following this victory at Winchester, Jackson demonstrated near Harpers Ferry, which was being held by Brig. Gen. Rufus Sexton and 7,000 men, but only long enough to allow all the captured Federal property to be shipped south to Staunton before he followed south. Jackson claimed to have captured 3,050 of Banks's men. In any case, the threat posed by Jackson now led to the decision in Washington to siphon off Shields's Division from McDowell. Ordered to return to the Luray Valley from east of the Blue Ridge in order to cooperate with Frémont, the division was thus prevented from joining McClellan above Richmond.[28]

The most immediate threat to Jackson came from Frémont in the West. Jackson knew that Frémont would immediately be informed of what had happened to Banks and would, in all likelihood, attempt to take advantage of Jackson's position in the northern part of the Valley by moving in from the west and trying to cut him off.

Jackson dispatched Ashby's cavalry to hold the town of McDowell along what he believed would be Frémont's most likely invasion route. Jackson also ordered Imboden to send as many men as possible west from Staunton to Brock's Gap—the most direct route to Harrisonburg— and to cover any other mountain passes that Frémont might be able to use to gain access to the Valley at or south of Harrisonburg. Imboden wrote after the war that he was determined to "defend the passage to the last extremity."[29]

Jackson was prescient, for on May 24, as soon as Frémont learned of Banks's defeat, he put his men in motion to try to cut Jackson off. Instead of moving through McDowell, where he knew Ashby and a Confederate force of undetermined size to be located, Frémont's force of fourteen thousand men left Franklin and made east for Brock's Gap, where Imboden had assembled some fifty men.

Imboden was familiar with Brock's Gap and selected a defile with nearly perpendicular five hundred–foot cliffs on either side. In these he concealed his men, armed with rifles. Imboden recalled after the war that he had had his men wait until the head of the Federal column was well into the gorge before opening a determined fire on the surprised Union troops, who immediately halted. A second Confederate volley and a rebel yell turned the Federals back completely.

Imboden proclaimed this little skirmish as important to Jackson's survival. He wrote that because Frémont—who had been ordered to proceed directly to Harrisonburg—did not know the strength of Imboden's force, he now detoured north to Moorefield, then on to Strasburg. As it was, his advance guard came on Jackson's rear guard two miles from Strasburg. Although a sharp skirmish took place, Jackson was able to continue on to Harrisonburg. Frémont had missed the opportunity to get in behind him.[30]

There is, however, no proof to support Imboden's claim that he prevented Frémont's passage to Harrisonburg through Brock's Gap. Frémont does not mention Imboden at all in his report, listing instead only a vague reference to "hindrances encountered." These might have included an encounter with Imboden's sharpshooters in the pass, although one would expect this to have been mentioned in some detail if it had been the cause of his turning aside in the movement to Harrisonburg.[31]

Jackson now withdrew up the Valley with two Federal columns in pursuit: Frémont from the northwest and Brigadier General Shields of McDowell's command closing from the Blue Ridge Mountains to the northeast. With their superior numbers, the Union commanders hoped to trap Jackson's force between them. Jackson sought to position himself at a point where he might be able to attack each in succession before they could combine against him.

Continuing up the Valley, Jackson ordered cavalry out to burn bridges over the Shenandoah River as far as Port Republic. The river was then up and would be impossible to ford. Reaching Harrisonburg on the Valley Turnpike, he then took the road to Port Republic. He sent a message to Imboden at Staunton to take an artillery battery and a battalion of troops to guard a key bridge over the North River at Mount Crawford in order to prevent Federal cavalry from getting in behind him. Imboden's role in the coming battle was thus a passive one. His Partisan Rangers, supported by four mountain howitzers and a rifled

Parrott gun, secured Jackson's supply trains at Port Republic against a Federal flanking attack.[32]

Frémont's force now closed on Jackson's left flank, resulting in the June 8 Battle at Cross Keys, a small village some six miles southeast of Harrisonburg and seven miles northwest of Port Republic. There on June 7 three brigades of Confederate troops under Ewell—some 5,000 men in all—prepared to meet a Union attack by 10,500 men under Frémont, coming in from the northwest along the Valley Pike through Harrisonburg.

Ewell's task was to defend Jackson's western flank. He established excellent defensive positions along a ridge facing northwest, fronted by several hundred acres of open fields with woods providing protection to both sides. Ewell positioned his artillery in the center of the line in order to secure the road to Port Republic. Brig. Gen. George Steuart's Brigade held the Confederate left and Brig. Gen. Isaac Trimble's Brigade the right. Ewell held Brig. Gen. Arnold Elzey's Brigade in reserve.

Jackson was then at Port Republic. He positioned the bulk of his force just north of that town to be able to deal with Shields's Division approaching from the northeast. Although Jackson was in supporting distance of Ewell, he expected Ewell to fight his own battle.

The Battle of Cross Keys opened at about 10:00 A.M. on June 8 with a half-hearted advance by Frémont's infantry as Brig. Gen. Louis Blenker's Division of German immigrants slowly pushed back Confederate pickets. The 15th Alabama Infantry of Trimble's Brigade held the Union troops for about a half hour, and a long-range artillery duel followed. The 44th Virginia and 1st Maryland Regiments then beat back several Union attacks.

Frémont mounted his major attack with a brigade of Blenker's Germans against Trimble's Brigade on the Confederate right. Trimble's men held their fire until the Union troops were close, then they fired a series of volleys that repulsed the assault as Confederates in the woods on the right flank exacted a heavy toll on the Union troops.

Trimble then advanced about a mile. Confident he could flank the entire Union line, he asked Ewell for reinforcements. Even though the Confederates had sustained few casualties, Ewell declined. Both Elzey and Steuart had been slightly wounded by shell fragments, and Ewell had received reports of a Union turning movement against the Confederate left.

Meanwhile, Jackson sent two brigades to Ewell under Col. John M. Patton and Brig. Gen. Richard Taylor. They arrived that afternoon and Ewell placed them in the center of his line. Later when Frémont failed to mount an attack on the Confederate left, Ewell ordered his men forward, and by nightfall they were occupying the positions that had been held by the Union troops that morning.

Trimble wanted a night attack but Ewell refused, reluctant to put too much distance between himself and Jackson. Ewell gave Trimble leave to approach Jackson on the matter, however. Jackson told him, "Consult General Ewell and be guided by him." To give his subordinate such latitude was indeed high praise from Jackson. Trimble then tried a second time to convince Ewell, who again refused. The Battle of Cross Keys was over. It was more a skirmish than a battle. Ewell had sustained 288 casualties, only 41 of them dead. Frémont, on the other hand, lost 684, nearly half of them dead or mortally wounded.

Jackson then sent orders to Ewell to leave only a holding force (Trimble's Brigade) in position facing Frémont and to march the rest of his men to join him at Port Republic to deal with Shields. Jackson hoped that once Shields was defeated, both he and Ewell could then return and complete the work of destroying Frémont. Ewell's march to reinforce Jackson at Port Republic began at dawn on June 9; the remaining Confederate troops withdrew from Cross Keys later that day on Jackson's subsequent order.[33]

The bulk of Jackson's force was just north of Port Republic at the confluence of the South River with the North River, which together combined to form the South Fork of the Shenandoah River. Jackson's position dominated the road from Conrad's Store to Port Republic, which was parallel to and south of the South Fork of the Shenandoah River—this meant that he could enfilade Shields's advance toward Port Republic.

On the evening of June 6 at Port Republic as Jackson rested his men and waited for the Union troops to arrive, he mulled over disquieting news. That afternoon Brig. Gen. Turner Ashby, his valuable cavalry commander, had been killed near Harrisonburg leading a rear guard action. Jackson was stunned by the news. According to one Jackson biographer, "it was the most shocking report of the entire valley campaign.... His grief over the passing of Ashby was deep and long lasting." Jackson wrote of Ashby, "as a Partisan officer I never knew his superior. His daring was proverbial. His powers of endurance incredible. His tone of character heroic, and his sagacity almost intuitive in divining the purposes of the enemy."[34]

Shields, meanwhile, halted at Conrad's Store to rest his division. From there he sent two brigades to probe Jackson's defenses. He also sent an appeal to Frémont for cooperation against the Confederates.

On the next morning, Sunday, June 8, Union troops reached the Confederate lines. In Port Republic Jackson had just finished telling Maj. Robert Dabney that he hoped it would be possible to conduct church service that day, when musket fire shattered the calm, and a rider came up with a report that Federal cavalry had forded the South River and were in the town. Jackson instructed the messenger to "Go back and fight." He and his staff then rode hard for the North River Bridge. Jackson got across just in time; two officers who brought up the rear were captured by Union troops. A little more vigor on the part of the Federals and Jackson himself might have been taken.

Jackson now ordered his artillery to fire into the Federals while Confederate infantry moved forward to clear them from Port Republic by the bayonet. As Jackson's men accomplished this they could hear distant artillery fire from Cross Keys where Ewell was beating back Frémont.

That night Jackson had ordered Ewell to leave only Trimble's and Patton's Brigades at Cross Keys and move the rest of his men to Port Republic. These reinforcements would give him four brigades to attack Shields. Jackson hoped to defeat Shields quickly and to turn and complete the destruction of Frémont that same morning.[35]

Jackson also sent word to Imboden via a courier to come up with his command before daybreak. Imboden got the order about 10:00 A.M. on June 8 and immediately set out. Imboden reported that this message, written in pencil on the margin of a newspaper, also contained an addendum at the bottom of the page: "Poor Ashby is dead. He fell gloriously. . . . I know you will join with me in mourning the loss of our friend, one of the noblest men and soldiers in the Confederate army." Imboden said he carried Jackson's message with him until the paper was "literally worn to tatters."[36]

Imboden and his men arrived at Port Republic an hour before daylight on June 9. Imboden recalled that he had at once gone to Jackson's headquarters but had been reluctant to disturb him at such an hour and instead sought out Lt. Alexander "Sandy" Pendleton of Jackson's staff. Inadvertently, however, Imboden awakened Jackson, who had been asleep on a bed in full uniform with sword and boots on. Imboden said that Jackson brushed aside his apology and asked that he sit down and talk. Imboden assumed Jackson was going to issue instructions for the coming battle, but instead he talked about Ashby's death and the great loss this represented for the army. Imboden said that he complimented Jackson on the victory at Cross Keys, which Jackson attributed to "God's blessing the army," and expressed the hope that it would be the case again. According to Imboden, Jackson then outlined his battle plan. Since Imboden remarked in his published account of Jackson's Valley Campaign, "I had learned never to ask him questions about his plans, for he would never answer such to any one," it is indeed strange that Jackson would describe the placement of units and his plans for the coming battle, which Imboden recalled as being the case.[37]

Imboden's brother George had raised the first company of his Partisan Rangers, and it was to this company that Imboden had assigned the four mountain howitzers and a Parrott rifled gun. Imboden recalled that Jackson now asked him to transfer the Parrott to Capt. William T. Poague's Rockbridge Artillery. Imboden's mounted men were to join the cavalry. Imboden recalled that Jackson told him he would order Brig. Gen. Charles Winder's Brigade to cross the river at daybreak and attack Shields on the Lewis farm. General Taylor, meanwhile, was to work his brigade through the woods and strike the Union right flank when the battle became general. Imboden recalled Jackson as saying, "By 10:00 we'll have them on the run."[38]

Imboden said Jackson outlined the role that his men would play in the battle as follows: "I want you in person to take your mountain howitzers to the field, in some safe position in rear of the line, keeping everything packed on the mules, ready at any moment to take to the mountain-side. Three miles below Lewis's there is a defile on the Luray road. Shields may rally and make a stand there. If he does, I can't reach him with the field-batteries on account of the woods. You can carry your 12-pounder howitzers on the mules up the mountain-side, and at some good place unpack and shell the enemy out of the defile, and the cavalry will do the rest."[39]

Although Imboden biographer Harold R. Woodward Jr. accepts Imboden's account of this meeting at face value, Jackson historians Krick and Robertson both have strongly questioned it, even going so far as to doubt that there was any conversation at all between the two men. Krick writes, "If Stonewall Jackson did encounter Imboden, it certainly was not in an intimate setting, nor did their talk include casual byplay. As one of the general's staff noted in deriding Imboden's fanciful tale, Jackson, 'spoke to and of *Sandy* [Sandie] Pendleton but to no one else in that way; he did not know how to do it.'"[40]

Imboden's account is probably not true. Other Jackson biographers have noted that Jackson consulted no one and never divulged his plans; he believed passionately in secrecy. Edward M. Alfriend wrote, "Stonewall Jackson never imparted his plans of battle or any of his military movements to any officer under him, excepting in so far as it was necessary for an officer to perform his part of the general campaign or his duty on the field of battle. Excepting to this extent he kept his plans absolutely to himself."[41]

Meeting or no, as Imboden's men obediently set out according to Jackson's instructions early that morning, Jackson moved his main body from high ground north of Port Republic, across the North River Bridge, through the town, and across the South River. As Jackson's men moved to attack Union forces to the northeast, the South Fork of the Shenandoah was to their left and the Blue Ridge to their right. Winder's Brigade led.

At 7:00 A.M. the Confederates encountered Federal pickets, and Jackson ordered the attack. Although he was not certain of Union strength, Jackson was reassured by the fact that Ewell was marching to join him. He also believed he could not delay and had to dispatch Shields's troops before Frémont discovered the weak Confederate front facing him at Cross Keys.

As Winder's Brigade advanced through wheat fields toward the Union lines, it came under heavy Federal fire. Union Brig. Gen. E.B. Tyler had only four thousand troops and sixteen guns with which to oppose the attacking Confederates, but his men were along a fence line, and Tyler had positioned six of his guns on high ground to the Union left. Their fire exacted a heavy toll.

A bottleneck had developed at the temporary bridge across the South River. The board flooring had collapsed, and Ewell's men could only cross in single file. The Stonewall Brigade now found itself virtually alone. With all chance of a dual victory lost and his situation increasingly desperate, Jackson tried to hurry his men forward. He also sent couriers to Ewell to make haste, and he ordered Trimble at Cross Keys to come up through Port Republic and burn the North River Bridge behind him so Frémont could not join the action.

Shelled to a halt, the Stonewall Brigade was barely managing to maintain its position. Brig. Gen. Richard Taylor's Brigade now arrived, marching to the sound of the guns. At this point other accounts of the battle differ with Imboden's published recollection. In contrast to Imboden's statement that Jackson had planned from the beginning to order Taylor's force around to the Union left, other authors suggest that when Taylor's lead regiment arrived, Jackson simply ordered it around to the east to take the Union battery raking the Confederate line. Jackson did not know exactly when Taylor would arrive, and thus it would have been difficult for him to have planned to use him in a pre-positioned flanking attack.[42]

Whatever the timing, the plan worked. The Louisianans forded the South River to enfilade the Union position. Meanwhile, Jackson personally rallied the Stonewall Brigade but could only hold it for a time. Out of ammunition, the brigade broke and many of its men streamed to the rear. At this critical juncture, Ewell arrived with Steuart's Brigade (temporarily commanded by Col. W.C. Scott) and blocked the Federal advance, although at some cost.

Taylor's men then struck the Federal left flank. As the Union troops attempted to wheel to engage Taylor, three more of Ewell's regiments arrived and went into action. Now outnumbered three to one, Shields's troops were soon in full retreat.

It was then 11:00 A.M. and Jackson's hopes of pursuit were dashed by the fact that Tyler's men had retreated in good order and Frémont was at his rear. Indeed, Frémont had finally come up and ordered his artillery to shell the field. Prevented by the burning of the Port Republic Bridge, he did not attempt an attack.

The Battle of Port Republic was over. Imboden and what he referred to as his "Jackass Artillery," did not play any role in it. As ordered, he had positioned his own battery several hundred yards behind the Rockbridge Artillery; during the battle, some Union shells aimed at the Rockbridge Artillery went high and landed in and around Imboden's men and their mules. Imboden recalled: "The mules became frantic. They kicked, plunged, and squealed. It was impossible to quiet them, and it took three or four men to hold one mule from breaking away. Each mule had about three hundred pounds weight on him so securely fastened that the load could not be dislodged by any of his capers. Several of them lay down and tried to wallow their loads off. The men held these down, and then suggested the idea of throwing them all on the ground and holding them there. The ravine sheltered us so that we were in no danger from the shot or shell which passed over us."[43]

Imboden recalled that while this mule "circus" was at its height, Jackson rode by on his way to rally Winder's Brigade and reportedly laughed at the predicament in which Imboden and his men found themselves. He then ordered Imboden to move the mules up the mountain and be ready to move themselves. As it was, the fight never came their way and no stand in the defile was necessary.

Union casualties in the Battle of Port Republic amounted to 1,108 men, most of them in the retreat, including 558 prisoners. Jackson had also sustained heavy losses—in excess of 800, the most he had suffered in a battle thus far. The Valley Campaign was over.

That same afternoon Jackson put his army in motion toward Brown's Gap by a path beyond the range of Frémont's guns. At the same time, authorities in Washington ordered Shields and Frémont to withdraw. Frémont was glad to go, but Shields said, "I never obeyed an order with such reluctance." Soon Jackson slipped his men out of the Valley on trains to Richmond in order to assist Gen. Robert E. Lee in the Peninsula Campaign.

Imboden left Port Republic the day after the battle to return to Staunton. There he met Brigadier General Whiting, his former commander in the Battle of Manassas, with a division of men to reinforce Jackson. Imboden entertained Whiting and his staff in his home for breakfast and then provided a guide so that he might join Jackson at Swift Run Gap. That same day Whiting returned to Staunton, complaining to Imboden about what he regarded as "outrageous" treatment by Jackson. Imboden expressed surprise at this, and Whiting explained that it was over Jackson's failure to share his plans. He had asked Jackson for orders, but the latter had ordered him back to Staunton, saying that he would send orders the next day.

Just after breakfast the next morning a courier arrived at Imboden's home with orders for Whiting to embark his men on trains and move immediately to Gordonsville, where he would receive further instructions. This order put Whiting in an even greater rage and he told Imboden, "Didn't I tell you he was a fool, and doesn't this prove it? Why, I just came through Gordonsville day before yesterday."[44]

Whiting obeyed the order, and on reaching Gordonsville he found Jackson already there and his troops not far behind. A few days afterward Jackson's combined force was at Richmond, helping to defend the capital against McClellan. Later, after the Seven Days' Battle before Richmond, Imboden ran into Whiting again, who admitted that he "did not know Jackson" when he had met Imboden earlier. He said that his plans "were worthy of Napoleon" but that he still believed Jackson should have told him of his intentions, "for if he had died [without making anyone aware of what he intended] McClellan would have captured Richmond. I wouldn't have known what he was driving at, and might have made a mess of it. But I take back all I said about his being a fool."[45]

On June 17 Jackson moved all his troops southeast, with the exception of Imboden's small force and cavalry under Brig. Gen. Beverly H. Robertson, who had been promoted on June 9 to take over Ashby's command. On June 25 Jackson was at Ashland. The relocation was accomplished so quickly and secretively that Union authorities in Washington were completely unsuspecting. Imboden wrote after the war that Jackson had told him there were two things of which a military commander must not lose sight: The first was to "mystify, mislead, and surprise" and, once an enemy had been attacked and overwhelmed, to "never let up in the pursuit as long as your men have strength to follow" for this would create panic and allow a smaller force to destroy one much larger. The second was to "never fight against heavy odds" and, if possible, maneuver so as to be able to defeat an enemy piecemeal, attacking its weakest portion first. Jackson concluded that "Such tactics will win every time, and a small army may thus destroy a large one in detail, and repeated victory will make it invincible." Although Imboden had played only an inconspicuous role in Jackson's Valley Campaign, he had learned much and must have hoped he would be able to emulate Jackson's tactics in the months and years ahead.[46]

Chapter 5

The 1st Virginia Partisan Rangers (1862–1863)

On July 3, 1862, Imboden's Company B, 1st Virginia Partisan Rangers was officially sworn into Confederate service. Imboden continued recruiting, but he was unsuccessful in his effort to add the Staunton Artillery to his command.[1]

Partisan service was appealing to many, and in early July Capt. John F. Harding requested the transfer of his entire company in the 31st Virginia Regiment to join Imboden's Rangers. Harding argued that because his men were from Pocahontas and Randolph Counties in western Virginia, they had intimate knowledge of the area in which they would be operating and would be able to enlist the support of many friends to join them.[2]

Among those joining Imboden in this period was John Hanson ("Hanse") McNeill. Born in Moorefield, Virginia, in 1815, McNeill had moved to Missouri and become involved in the cattle business. He was also active in the secessionist crisis on the Confederate side and had raised a company of mounted volunteers. Wounded in fighting to secure Missouri for the Confederacy, he was taken prisoner. He escaped in late 1861 and made his way back to Virginia with his three sons. McNeill sought approval from Richmond to raise a Partisan Ranger company in the South Branch Valley around Moorefield in Hardy County. Permission was forthcoming, but with the stipulation that he report to Imboden. Through August, McNeill raised volunteers, and on September 5 he became captain of Company E, 18th Virginia Cavalry, nominally in Imboden's command.[3]

Imboden's first major operation with his Partisan Rangers was to be a raid against the Baltimore & Ohio (B&O) Railroad. A key Union line of communication between Ohio and the East, nearly 190 miles of B&O track ran through western Virginia. Gen. Robert E. Lee, who well understood the importance of the B&O to the Union war effort, ordered Imboden to destroy the railroad bridge at Rowlesburg, some 150 miles northwest of Staunton and west of Maryland.

Lee had assumed command of the Army of Northern Virginia on June 1, 1862, when General Johnston was seriously wounded in the Battle of Seven Pines. Lee was about to begin the first major Confederate invasion of the North, an effort that would culminate in the September 17, 1862, Battle of Antietam. As Lee moved his army north, it was vital to isolate the area of operations and prevent superior Union manpower resources from being brought to bear. Immobilizing the B&O was a key part of such an effort.

The operation would be conducted in hostile territory, as western Virginia was now firmly in Union hands. In the spring of 1862 the Confederates had abandoned most of the western portions of Virginia beyond the Allegheny Mountains, and this area had immediately become occupied by Union troops. The occupation fell on fertile ground. The people in the poorer western counties of Virginia had long resented the domination of the more populous eastern part of the state. They had objected to property qualifications for suffrage and thought themselves to be underrepresented in the Virginia General Assembly. The more militant among them had long threatened secession. Indeed, in 1829 a convention had been held to address these issues, but the eastern delegates dominated it and made few concessions. The resentment continued to grow, and this alienation of many western Virginia residents from the Confederate government in Richmond worked to Union advantage.

When Virginia passed the ordinance of secession in April 1861, some of the inhabitants of the western counties refused to go along and organized a general convention to take action. Convening on June 11, 1861, at Wheeling, this convention met for two months, reorganized the state government for all Virginia, and created the new state of Kanawha with its capital at Wheeling. The delegates also authorized a new legislature, elected Francis H. Pierpont "Governor of Virginia," and approved a constitutional convention. The latter met in November and created the constitution for the state of West Virginia. In April 1862 this document was ratified by voters who had taken an oath of allegiance to the Union. The new state legislature, which met in May, then petitioned Washington for statehood, which was granted in December 1862 with the proviso that West Virginia abolish slavery. President Lincoln signed the proclamation on April 20, 1863, and West Virginia formally entered the Union on June 20, 1863.

As with all border states, however, sentiment in West Virginia was far from uniform. While many people favored the Confederacy, sentiment in the new state was overwhelmingly Unionist. Historian James Callahan has estimated that West Virginia furnished more than 30,000 men to the Union Army along with 2,300 Home Guards formed into thirty-two companies, one to each county to guard against invasion. He claims only 7,000–10,000 West Virginians fought for the Confederacy, although this number seems low.[4]

This was not the first Confederate attempt against the B&O. The Confederates had made other efforts to destroy the bridge over the Cheat River, but all had failed. In June 1861 Confederate troops under Gen. Robert S. Garnett had reached Huttonsville, but they were forced back by superior Union forces under Maj. Gen. George B. McClellan and Brig. Gen. William S. Rosecrans; Garnett was mortally wounded while directing his troops back across the Cheat River on July 13. The year 1861 was the last time the Confederates mounted a serious effort to recover the trans-Allegheny region.

In late September 1861, Col. Angus McDonald had led cavalry into western Virginia, but he only reached Romney. In January 1862 Brig. Gen. William Loring had also failed in an effort to damage the railroad. These failed efforts solidified sentiment for the Union side in the new state. Although as late as 1863 certain Confederate political leaders and generals still believed the great majority of West Virginians were loyal to their cause, it simply was not true.[5]

Imboden assembled six companies of men for the attempt. They departed Franklin, one hundred miles from the objective, on August

14, 1862. The topography was difficult, and the men often had to hack their way through heavily wooded, mountainous terrain. They managed only twelve to fifteen miles a day.[6]

Lee wrote Jefferson Davis on August 16: "I hope to hear every day of Imbodens [*sic*] success in his attempt on the B. & O. R. R. He started from Staunton sometime since with about 600 men & by his own calculations would have reached the trestle work four or five days since. We must make allowance for delays & difficulties. I hope he will be in time to arrest troops from the West."[7]

Imboden's first objective was a Union outpost manned by a company of western Virginia troops at Parson's Mill, ten miles above St. George and twenty-three miles south of Rowlesburg. After a night march on August 18–19, Imboden's men surrounded the Union camp, only to discover that the Federals had fled.[8]

The Union troops had been warned only a few hours before. A Unionist, nineteen-year-old Mary Jane Snyder, had ridden twenty-five miles to warn them. In addition, a deserter from Imboden's own force had stolen a mule and warned Federal authorities at Beverly. Learning that Union troops had reached Rowlesburg and outnumbered him five to one, Imboden wisely abandoned the raid and returned to Staunton. During the retreat George Imboden reported a sharp skirmish with a Federal picket or advance guard on the Beverly road, near Carrick's Ford. The men subsisted on meat and potatoes, "there being no flour or meal in the country." Imboden had been joined in operations in West Virginia on August 22 by Brig. Gen. Albert G. Jenkins. Imboden did not file a formal report, but his September 1 letter to C.W. Russell provides details of the raid.[9]

Meanwhile, Lee and the Army of Northern Virginia were headed north. Lee crossed the Potomac River during the first week of September, with Harrisburg as his probable ultimate objective. McClellan, restored by Lincoln to command the Army of the Potomac, proceeded with his customary caution, despite the fact that Lee's operational plan had fallen into Union hands. Incredibly, McClellan was slow to take advantage of this windfall; it took him two days to cover the ten miles to the South Mountain passes in Maryland.

Federal victories over Lee at South Mountain and Crampton's Gap on September 14 did not come in time to save Harpers Ferry, which fell to Jackson on September 15 along with its eleven thousand–man garrison and a great quantity of equipment. Nonetheless, Lee's division of forces into three major bodies spread over twenty miles provided an opportunity for the Union Army to defeat the Confederates in detail. McClellan failed to take advantage of the situation, however.

On the afternoon of September 15 the major part of the Army of the Potomac was within easy striking distance of Sharpsburg, Maryland, where Lee placed three divisions, waiting for the arrival of his remaining six divisions. On that day Lee had only eighteen thousand men. But McClellan did not attack until September 17. Meanwhile, Jackson's corps of three divisions came up from Harpers Ferry on September 16, and the three remaining divisions arrived as the battle got under way. Still, Lee was heavily outnumbered. Despite this he chose to stand and fight in excellent defensive terrain. McClellan failed to utilize his superior numbers: two entire corps totaling thirty thousand men did not see action in the battle, nor did McClellan plan a coordinated attack.

The carnage at Antietam on September 17 produced the bloodiest single day of fighting in the entire war. Union casualties were 12,410 killed or wounded (15 percent of effectives), while the Confederates lost 10,700 (26 percent). Lee now pulled back into Virginia, while McClellan postured for the press and proclaimed victory. Lincoln was furious at the lack of pursuit. The Army of Northern Virginia might have been destroyed at Antietam, and the responsibility lay with McClellan. Cautious to a fault, he had refused to risk victory.[10]

Throughout the war, Union Brig. Gen. Benjamin F. Kelley had command of Union troops guarding the vital B&O in western Virginia and Maryland. Kelley was handicapped in that, with only infantry and artillery under his command, he had no cavalry to throw against the Confederates. He could, however, shuffle his troops back and forth by train along the B&O in an attempt to stymie Confederate raiding west of Harpers Ferry.[11]

On returning from his early raid into West Virginia, Imboden gathered several hundred recruits in Highland County and then set out with about four hundred men to attack Romney. His men crossed Shenandoah Mountain at Brock's Gap, proceeded down Lost River, and made a night march on Romney. Unfortunately, the garrison there had fled. Three

Confederate soldiers, escorting several ladies to Romney under a flag of truce, had boasted that Romney would soon be taken and the Union garrison then evacuated. Imboden moved in and held Romney for two days, sending out patrols and drawing in Union forces. Anticipating Union cavalry, he laid an ambush. In the brief fight that followed, the Confederates unhorsed a number of the Union troopers, killed several—including a lieutenant—and captured two men and eight good horses. Imboden claimed he had "kept Kelley running up and down the railroad with troops for ten days." Imboden reported from his camp in Hardy County, West Virginia, on September 27 that he had nine hundred men, but just six hundred of them were armed.[12]

Imboden's efforts along the B&O did tie down several thousand Union troops during the Antietam Campaign. It is unlikely, however, that even had these Union troops been able to defeat Imboden they would have abandoned the B&O to strike at Lee's supply lines to the north.

Nonetheless, the Union side was frustrated by the seeming ability of Imboden's raiders to strike at will. One Union soldier wrote to Governor Pierpont in Wheeling, "it is a burning shame that Imboden is permitted to stalk through this country as he pleases without being even annoyed by any of our men."[13]

Kelley did receive some New York cavalry, and at the end of September he ordered these out after Imboden. Some of these men were taken prisoner by McNeill, now operating independently.

The Antietam Campaign at an end, Imboden abandoned raiding for a time in order to recruit a full regiment of ten companies. To improve recruiting, he moved operations to Hampshire and Hardy Counties, setting up his headquarters at Bloomery. By the end of the month he had recruited more than the required ten companies. His 1st Regiment, Virginia Partisan Rangers included infantry, cavalry, and artillery. Imboden spent the remainder of September and October recruiting, training, and operating in western Virginia.[14]

The North, shocked at Lee's escape from Antietam, was further dismayed by McClellan's procrastination and by a daring cavalry raid by "Jeb" Stuart into Pennsylvania around Gettysburg (October 10–12, 1862). Following the Antietam Campaign, the Army of Northern Virginia had withdrawn into camps in the northern Shenandoah Valley.

Stuart proposed to ride around that portion of the Army of the Potomac in southern Maryland. He was certain he could get around McClellan's right flank in Pennsylvania, then return to Virginia by circling around the Union Army and moving south between Washington and McClellan's left flank. Lee agreed with the plan.

In order to draw off Union resources from Stuart and ensure the success of his larger and much more risky operation, Imboden mounted another raid into West Virginia. Imboden began this operation on October 2, when he left his base camp at Capon Bridge. He headed west some seven miles to Hanging Rock near Salem, where his men ran into a scouting party of the 1st New York Cavalry. Imboden's more numerous force captured five of the New Yorkers, fourteen horses, and a quantity of small arms. Imboden then turned his command north to strike at the B&O. On reaching the railroad his men tried to destroy the railroad bridge over the Potomac. The structure was of iron, however, and they were unable to do more than temporarily disrupt traffic. They then headed east along the rail line.[15]

At daybreak on October 4, taking advantage of a dense ground fog, the Confederates charged an entrenched Federal camp manned by Company K of the 54th Pennsylvania Volunteers. This position guarded the railroad bridge at the mouth of the Little Cacapon River. Imboden's raiders took the defenders completely by surprise, killing or wounding eight and taking fifty-five prisoners. They then burned the wooden bridge, nearby railroad buildings, and some rolling stock.

Imboden then continued eastward along the line to the railroad tunnel at Paw Paw, Maryland. He sent his infantry against the Federal camp, while his cavalry crossed the Potomac into Maryland to cut off a Federal retreat. The Union troops offered only token resistance before surrendering. Imboden again netted a number of prisoners—this time ninety men of Company B, 54th Pennsylvania Volunteers. They also captured 175 Austrian rifles and 8,000 rounds of ammunition. When his scouts reported two train loads of Union reinforcements arriving from the east, Imboden ordered most of the captured stores burned and hastily withdrew southward.[16]

Imboden's three-day raid had been an unqualified success. He had temporarily disrupted traffic on the B&O and captured 150 Union troops, several hundred weapons, and other assorted supplies. All this had been accomplished at no loss to his own command. Lee was fulsome in his praise: "I have read with pleasure your report of the attack upon the enemy's cavalry at Hanging Rock and the subsequent surprise of the two companies of the enemy's infantry stationed at the mouth of the Little Capon and at Paw Paw Tunnel. The results accomplished, and the judicious arrangements which enabled you to effect them without loss of life on your part, are deserving of high commendation, the appreciation of which it gives me pleasure to express."[17]

Four days after Imboden's attack at Paw Paw, Stuart set out on his own raid, successfully circling around McClellan's army and returning safely to Virginia. Frustrated by the turn of events, on November 7 Lincoln replaced McClellan with Maj. Gen. Ambrose E. Burnside.

On his return to camp Imboden learned to his dismay, however, that Union forces had taken advantage of his absence. On October 4, while he was attacking the railroad bridge on the Little Capon River, two companies of the 1st New York Cavalry Regiment raided his base camp at Capon Bridge. Confederate Lt. Henderson Stone had only some one hundred largely unarmed men and two small mountain howitzers. The Confederates were surprised by a sudden Union charge across a covered railroad bridge into the camp. In a fight lasting only a few minutes, the partisans suffered several dozen casualties; the remainder of the men got away by precipitous flight into the nearby mountains. The Union troopers took a half dozen wagons laden with supplies, the two howitzers, and a large number of horses and mules. They also secured all of Imboden's personal papers and official records.

On their return, Imboden and his men immediately set out in pursuit of the Union cavalry. They pressed the cavalry to the point that its members abandoned the wagons and cut loose most of the horses and mules. This meant that Imboden's net loss came to about one wagon load of supplies.[18]

The revelation of the vulnerability of his camp led Imboden to relocate. In mid-month he moved it to a valley between Petersburg and Moorefield. There his men prepared for the onset of winter by building huts and laying in supplies.[19]

The war in western Virginia grew in ferocity and ruthlessness. Here in this border area, so hotly contested between Confederate and Union forces, individuals were forced to choose sides and then stick with that decision. Yet when one side dominated, it ruthlessly expropriated and destroyed property belonging to the other. As a result, in early November 1862 Union Brig. Gen. Robert Milroy, commander of the Cheat Mountain District, issued an extraordinarily harsh edict to his subordinate commanders that, in effect, assessed Confederate sympathizers for losses incurred by those supporting the Union. If they failed to pay, "their houses will be burned and themselves shot and their property all seized." Milroy called on his subordinates to "carry out this threat rigidly and show them that you are not trifling or to be trifled with." Milroy instructed his men to "inform the inhabitants for ten or fifteen miles around your camp, on all the roads approaching the town upon which the enemy may approach, that they must dash in and give you notice, and that upon failure of any one to do so their houses will be burned and the men shot."[20]

Milroy's edict reportedly gained Imboden a number of western Virginia recruits. When Job Parsons in Tucker County was informed of an assessment of $14.25, he rode to Imboden's camp and enlisted. Parsons showed Imboden this assessment as well as two others, one against his father for $300 and another on a separate relative for $700. Imboden in turn sent these to Confederate authorities in Richmond, along with sworn statements by Parsons. Imboden noted that "we have an effectual remedy for these crimes by the adoption of an inexorable rule of retaliation."[21]

Most of Imboden's recruits were in fact drawn from Augusta, Barber, Bath, Braxton, Frederick, Hampshire, Hardy, Highland, Lewis, Pendleton, Randolph, Pocahontas, Rockingham, Shenandoah, Tucker, Upshur, and Webster Counties; a number had seen prior military service with the 25th, 33d, and 52d Virginia Infantry Regiments. A study of the later 62d Virginia Infantry Regiment of Imboden's command concludes that of its known members, 75 percent were from the counties of present-day West Virginia.[22]

Imboden also wrote President Davis a defense of his own men and their conduct: "The pretext of robberies of Union men by bands of guerrillas is a falsehood. The fact is that Union men have conspired to run off each other's horses to Pennsylvania, where they are secretly sold, the new owners afterward setting up a claim for reparation on the false ground that guerrillas have robbed them. I enclose this evidence of the atrocity of General Milroy for such action as Your Excellency may deem expedient in retaliation, either as a restraint upon this savage or a punishment should this horrible threat ever be carried into execution. This is only one of a thousand barbarities practiced here in these distant mountains of which I have almost daily heard for the last four months. Oh, for a day of retribution!"[23]

Davis forwarded Imboden's letter and enclosure to Lee, instructing him to write to Union Major General Henry W. Halleck and protest Milroy's actions. Lee did so, giving Halleck ten days in which to respond. Lee also wrote to Imboden on January 10, saying: "With regard to the orders of Milroy, you must endeavor to repress his cruelties as much as possible. I will recommend to the Secretary of War that prisoners taken from his command be not exchanged, but held as hostages for the protection of our citizens."

On January 20 Lee wrote to Imboden a second time in regard to Milroy: "By the direction of the President, I have written to General Halleck on the subject of Milroy's orders. He replied that these orders are unauthorized, and if on investigation he finds them authentic, he will order Milroy to change his course. I do not think retaliation upon the Union people of the northwest would help our cause in that region."[24]

"Retribution" came a day after Imboden's letter to Davis in the form of another raid against the vital Cheat River B&O Railroad bridge. On November 7, the day after he received a supply of overcoats and blankets, Imboden set out with 310 of his best armed and mounted men. That same afternoon, with a heavy snow falling, the men rode out of their camp on the South Fork in Hardy County, heading west. Their immediate objective was St. George, a small town in Tucker County, thirty-eight miles away over the Allegheny Mountains. Imboden hoped to arrive there the next night.

The snowstorm delayed Imboden's progress. The men reached the eastern foothills of the Alleghenies at midnight and halted there until sunrise. On November 8 they followed an "obscure and rarely used cattle-path" over the mountains, the passage of which was so difficult that the men had to dismount and lead their horses. At nightfall they were forced to halt and wait for the rising of the moon. Just as they were starting out again at midnight, a county resident provided Imboden with news that a six hundred–man Union regiment had passed by that same day and was then camped eight to ten miles to Imboden's rear, while at the same time Milroy and four thousand men had gone from Beverly toward Monterey.

This news presented Imboden with a real dilemma, as he now faced the real possibility of being cut off by superior Federal forces. His own horses were too weak to retrace their steps without being fed, and Imboden decided to push on to St. George, where he would surprise and capture its Union garrison and then determine his next step.

Although the going was slow because of the snow, just after daybreak on November 9 the Confederate raiders came upon St. George. Imboden dismounted most of his force and the men surrounded the town. The Union garrison consisted of Capt. William Hall and thirty-three enlisted men of Company F of the 6th [West] Virginia Regiment. At about 7:00 A.M. Imboden sent in a demand for surrender under a flag of truce to the Union garrison in the town's new courthouse. Hall requested ten minutes to consider the demand and was allowed five. Finding every escape route blocked, Hall surrendered.

The courthouse had been barricaded, and Imboden thought it "might have given us a good deal of trouble" had Hall decided to fight. The Union company was armed with new Enfield rifles. Incapable of transporting his prisoners, Imboden paroled Hall and twenty-eight enlisted men; three others escaped notice. Those paroled agreed not to take up arms again until they were formally exchanged. Imboden took possession of the Union rifles, ammunition, rations, overcoats and blankets, and a horse. The coats and blankets were particularly welcomed since not all of Imboden's men had them.

Imboden's horses were now worn out, and all of his captains, save one, urged that they return to base. Imboden also learned that Union supporters had informed Milroy of his presence and that the Union general had left Beverly with two thousand men to search for him. Destroying what goods his men could not easily carry, Imboden ordered a retreat. He thought the only practical course was to return to the Dry Fork and then try to get behind Milroy and follow him until such point as he could get past him at night.

That same morning at 10:00 A.M. the Partisan Rangers departed St. George, retracing their steps. By 9:00 P.M. they had crossed Dry Fork below the mouth of Glade Creek and halted there until midnight, at which time they resumed their march, following a path up Glade Creek.

At 4:00 P.M. the next day the raiders made camp for the night about ten miles east of Beverly.

There Imboden learned from a civilian who had just come from Beverly that Milroy had taken the field and that his baggage train was probably at Camp Bartow on the Greenbrier River. This news brought an immediate change in plans. Imboden resolved to attack the baggage train and then escape back through Pocahontas and Bath Counties.

At dawn on November 11, Imboden set out through an unbroken forest with a skilled local guide and a compass. At about 5:00 P.M. the raiders reached a settlement at the headwaters of the Greenbrier River, eleven miles from Camp Bartow. On the morning of November 12 six of Imboden's horses were unable to go further. He left these with one man, who was to bring them in eight to ten days; their riders agreed to follow on foot. The remaining men set out that morning. It was dark and rainy and, after proceeding about four miles, the Confederates became lost, despite the guide and his compass. The men then retraced their steps back to their camp of the night before.

November 13 dawned bright and cloudless. Imboden knew he could not tarry and that it was too late to try to raid Camp Bartow, so he ordered a movement east to recross the Alleghenies. Emerging from the forest, Imboden learned from both a sympathizer and a discharged prisoner that Milroy had three columns attempting to intercept him. The Confederates halted briefly at the farm of a sympathizer and secured grain for the horses, their first in days. Not long afterward they came across a camp used by one of the Union columns of about 1,300 men; they followed in the tracks of this column toward Franklin for a time as a means of covering their own route. They then passed back through a gap in the mountains to safety. The raiders returned to Augusta Springs through North River Gap on November 14.

In his report to General Jackson, Imboden was able to report only less than satisfactory results. Still he found comfort in the fact that he and his men had gotten away at all: "Our escape, under all the circumstances without the loss of a man, is felt and acknowledged by all to be truly providential."[25]

Jackson forwarded the report to Lee, who replied that he understood the "extraordinary difficulties" that Imboden had encountered. He asked Jackson to inform Imboden "that it is my desire that he will not lose sight of this important enterprise, and that I hope on some future occasion his efforts will meet with the success they deserve."[26] Lee also summed up the raid in a communication to Secretary of War George Randolph: "I learn that Colonel Imboden was unable to destroy the bridges at Cheat River in consequence of the strength of the enemy in that quarter, and is in position on the Shenandoah Mountain. He captured one company of the enemy, paroled the men and brought off their arms and equipment."[27]

Perhaps the most important effect of Imboden's raid was that it caused Milroy to abandon his own raid on Staunton in order to pursue Imboden. Milroy noted: "It was very unfortunate that I was recalled from beyond the Allegheny to this [railroad] by causeless alarm. Had I been left alone, I would ere this had Staunton, Warm Springs, and Lewisburg."[28]

Once again, however, the Federals had taken advantage of Imboden's departure to raid his base camp. Eight hundred of Kelley's cavalrymen had swept through St. George and burned Imboden's camp. Although most of the Confederate defenders had again gotten away into the mountains, the Federals had taken fifty prisoners, a large quantity of arms, 350 hogs, and a number of horses, cattle, and wagons. Over the next weeks Imboden was preoccupied with securing supplies and replacements for the destroyed and lost equipment as his men busied themselves building cabins for the winter.[29]

The lull in Confederate raiding activity caused the Federals in western Virginia to lower their guard. As weather allowed, Imboden sent his men out in small groups, the largest being company size, to inflict what damage they could on Union outposts and Union sympathizers. Making reference to the previous August's raid, Unionist Constance Woolson of Tucker County expressed in less-than-perfect verse the general anxiety in the region over the raids:

> I was awake that morning when someone came through the pass,
> Riding like mad down the road, 'twas Farmer Snyder's Lass;
> Bareback she rode, she had no hat, she hardly stopped to say:
> "Imboden's men are coming, they're marching down this way,
> I'm out to warn the neighbors, he isn't a mile behind,
> He seizes all the horses, every horse he can find.

Imboden, Imboden the raider, and Imboden's terrible men
With Bowie knives and pistols are marching down the glen.³⁰

The war was changing in character. Initially, paroles had been common occurrence—a captured soldier would simply give his word ("parole") not to fight again. But Milroy's declaration had led Imboden to send prisoners to Richmond rather than issue paroles whenever possible. The Union side replied in kind. Moreover, there was a general Union sentiment that the Partisan Rangers were not soldiers and were in fact little more than brigands and outlaws. On occasion they were strung up and hanged upon capture. Understandably, this brought considerable correspondence between Richmond and Washington. Imboden found an ally in the Confederate government. It refused to exchange prisoners taken by the Partisan Rangers until the North agreed to the exchange of partisans captured by Union troops. The result was the aforementioned circular that extended to Partisan Rangers the status of regular prisoners eligible for parole.³¹

Other issues were not so easily resolved. Outraged when Imboden's men took a Unionist sheriff prisoner and sent him to Richmond, Union troops promptly took into custody fifteen men and women of Southern sympathy and threatened to shoot them if the sheriff was not returned within fifteen days.³²

Imboden responded with a fiery letter to Milroy. In it he provided an explanation for taking the sheriff prisoner and accused the Union general of encouraging his troops to commit atrocities, including the murder of two civilians near Philippi for failure to comply with his order that they provide warning of the approach of Confederate forces. He closed with the threat that if Milroy executed the hostages taken for the sheriff, "I will hang two of your men for each one so executed."³³

Milroy's response was that he had more Confederate prisoners than Imboden had Federals and that Imboden should thus "beware of trifling with Federal humanity."³⁴ Fortunately for the non-combatants caught in the middle, neither side carried out its threat to execute civilians as official policy.

Throughout the winter of 1862–1863 Imboden continued his policy of small-scale raids, weather permitting. Most of these were ambushes in which the Confederates would lie in wait for a target of opportunity, most often a Union wagon train. One such raid of two dozen men was led by Captain McNeill near Rodney. The Confederates hid in woods along the road, and when a Union supply train passed by, they surrounded it and ordered the Federals to throw down their weapons. Following a brief skirmish, McNeill captured 27 wagons and 106 horses and took 72 prisoners. McNeil and his men then escaped back across the South Branch of the Potomac. Imboden reported the raid to Lee, who passed along the report to President Davis with the comment, "These successes show the vigilance of the cavalry and do credit to their officers."[35]

Another raid involved Lt. Monroe Blue and fifteen men, all of Imboden's command, and Pvt. John C. Casler, who met up with them while on leave from the Stonewall Brigade. Each armed with a rifle and a pistol, the men decided on their own initiative to carry out a raid into Hampshire County. They hid themselves along the road midway between a Federal camp and the B&O Railroad, from which the Union soldiers drew their supplies. After allowing several stronger groups to pass unmolested, they captured a mail wagon and four extra horses and took three Union soldiers prisoner. Emboldened by this success, they attempted to take a wagon train the next day. Although they made prisoners of an escort, five wagons, twelve horses, and four guards, some of those in the wagon train escaped and raised the alarm. Soon the hunted became the hunter, with Union cavalry in pursuit and the raiders themselves ending up losing one man and three horses. The remainder made it back to Imboden's camp.[36]

Meanwhile, efforts were underway in Richmond to transform the Partisan Rangers into the regular army. On December 23 Adj. Gen. Samuel Cooper informed Imboden by telegram at Camp Hood in Hardy County that Secretary of War James A. Seddon "invites your cooperation" in order "to change your entire present organization from partisan rangers to a regular command for the war." He authorized Imboden to fill his command with conscripts and recruit all men that he could from counties held by the Federal forces. Cooper concluded, "From the energy and zeal you have displayed in the service, the department has no hesitation in committing you to this important undertaking."[37]

Most of Imboden's men believed they had been effective as partisans but had no real opposition to what largely seemed a paper transfer

Brigadier General John D. Imboden. (Courtesy of the Library of Congress)

to the regular army. Imboden would, after all, remain in command. Imboden spoke to the men and explained the planned transfer and then allowed all of them to decide whether they wanted to do so or not. Most went through with the transfer. The plan to incorporate his men into the Confederate Army was particularly appealing to Imboden, as Secretary of War Seddon offered the inducement of nominating him for promotion to brigadier general on January 28, 1863, contingent on his raising a brigade.[38]

Imboden must have believed that his military ambitions were being realized. In a span of only twenty months he had risen from captain to brigadier general. While rapid promotion was not unusual during the Civil War, most incidents of this involved those with a military background, which Imboden lacked. The happy news of his impending promotion was, however, offset by an unexpected tragedy: On December 12, 1862, George William, Imboden's son by his first wife, Dice, died at age five.[39]

Chapter 6

The Spring 1863 Jones-Imboden Raid into West Virginia

Imboden's hometown newspaper applauded his January 1863 promotion to brigadier general. It admitted that although the army had been "rather unsuccessful" in western Virginia, "we predict, from what we know of the man, and the material of which his command is composed, that General Imboden will accomplish whatever is possible in that section."[1]

Such action would have to wait, for in early 1863 Imboden was preoccupied with reorganizing his command and recruiting the requisite number of men for a brigade. While this was occurring, on January 2 Commander of the Valley District Brig. Gen. William E. "Grumble" Jones launched a raid into territory from which many of Imboden's men were drawn. The men set out from New Market across Great North Mountain into the South Branch Valley to secure supplies and challenge Union control of West Virginia. The raiders returned to the Shenandoah Valley after four days in the field with only five wagon loads of supplies to show for their effort; these had been garnered by the 18th Virginia, cooperating with Jones in the venture.[2]

Following this raid Lee may well have concluded that the best hope of driving Union forces from western Virginia was to use Imboden's men, many of whom had been recruited from that area. Four days after the raid, Lee wrote to still-colonel Imboden: "I am anxious for you to proceed, as rapidly as possible, in the organization and increase of your command, so that you may bring a strong brigade into the field at an early period. I wish the enemy driven out of the valley entirely, both the South Branch and the Kanawha."[3]

Imboden's Northwestern Brigade, successor to his 1st Regiment of Virginia Partisan Rangers, consisted of Col. George H. Smith's 62d Virginia Mounted Infantry Regiment, Col. George Imboden's 18th Virginia Cavalry Regiment, and Capt. John. H. McClanahan's battery of horse artillery. In addition, three independent commands, those under Lt. Col. Elijah White and Capts. Harry Gilmor and John Hanson ("Hanse") McNeill, reported to Imboden. The brigade remained unchanged in composition until the addition of the 23d Virginia Cavalry in the spring of 1864.

Imboden's men evidently regarded him as a competent commander. Private Baker of the 18th Virginia Cavalry wrote, "Our General Imboden was never surprised. He was one of the best watchers I ever saw, always posted his men well and was always on the lookout."[4]

Until Imboden's Brigade was wholly ready for active field operations and the weather would permit large military operations, small units continued to conduct limited isolated raiding activities. Imboden's first major operation as a general officer was a spectacular raid into Unionist-held western Virginia, known militarily to the Federals as the Middle Department. Lee's order to Imboden for general offensive operations in West Virginia has already been noted. Writing to General Jones on January 27, Lee stressed the need to secure beef to feed the Army of Northern Virginia: "The question of provisioning this army is becoming one of much difficulty. I have thought that the present might be a favorable time for you to send into the counties of Hampshire, Tucker, Randolph, Pendleton, and Highland, and any others you might find convenient or useful, with a view of collecting cattle or salt meat for our use."[5]

The idea for the raid originated with McNeill, then commanding a Partisan Ranger company. He proposed to lead six hundred men on a swift strike into western Virginia to destroy the vital Cheat River B&O bridge in Tucker County.[6]

On March 2 Imboden seconded this suggestion in a long letter to Lee. Imboden recommended the destruction of all bridges along the B&O from Oakland as far west as Grafton; capture of Union garrisons at Beverly, Philippi, and Buckhannon; and enlistment in the Confederate Army of "the young men of the northwest." Rather unrealistically, he expressed hope that he could "hold that section of the country long enough to overthrow the local government, of which four-fifths of the people are heartily tired, and would joyfully unite in our State elections in May."[7]

In order to accomplish these ends, Imboden proposed a major Confederate demonstration toward Winchester with General Jones also demonstrating, "real or feigned," toward Romney, New Creek, and Cumberland. Simultaneously, Imboden would send five hundred well-mounted troops from Romney to Oakland "without baggage of any kind," who by a long night march would reach Oakland by surprise, intending to destroy the wooden bridge there and deny Union forces the ability to move west over the railroad. The cavalry would then move, probably by the Northwestern Road to the Cheat River, cross it in two places, and destroy the bridges behind them.

Imboden believed that destruction of these bridges would provide ample time to burn the bridge at Rowlesburg. With all the bridges destroyed, the only danger to the raiders would be from Union garrisons to the west. These would be taken care of by sending his infantry and artillery toward Beverly two days before the cavalry departed for Oakland. Having neutralized the Union garrisons, Imboden believed he could then in a few days destroy much of the Northwestern Railroad. With reinforcements he might then operate against Charlestown later in the spring. Imboden stressed the necessity of speed: "The movement must be a dash from its commencement to its conclusion . . . it is impossible to prevent information from spreading through these mountains."[8]

Although Imboden described his own recruiting as "going forward rapidly," he told Lee that many of his new companies would "not be full in time for the early movement I propose." To carry out the plan he would need reinforcements: "I have not men enough here to move on Beverly, as proposed, after sending my cavalry to the railroad." To make up the shortfall, Imboden requested the veteran 25th and 31st Virginia Infantry Regiments. As they were drawn from "the northwest," he believed they "would fight like tigers the vandals who have so long domineered over their helpless families."[9]

In early March Imboden reported the Northwestern Brigade's aggregate strength as 1,592 officers and men: 792 in the 62d Virginia Infantry Regiment, 706 in the 18th Virginia Cavalry Regiment, and 94 men in McClanahan's Battery. Two other regiments were in process of formation.[10]

The B&O was certainly a worthy target. The shortest route from the Ohio River to the Potomac, it was the primary means of supplying Federal military operations in the trans-Allegheny and lower Shenandoah Valley. It also speeded the movement of coal and timber for the Union war effort, much of which went to sustain the Federal naval blockade. In late 1862 Governor John Letcher had declared: "The Baltimore and Ohio Railroad has been a possible nuisance to this state, from the opening of this war to the present time; and unless its management shall hereafter be in friendly hands, and the government under which it exists be a part of our Confederacy, it must be abated."[11]

Confederate leaders in Richmond, aware that Lee's Army of Northern Virginia was hard pressed for meat rations, supported the raid to secure cattle that could be driven back to the Valley to provide beef into the summer.[12] They also seem to have shared Imboden's hope that the raiders might hold much of western Virginia permanently, or at least long enough to destroy a wide swath of the railroad system west of the Alleghenies. Finally, those supporting the raid hoped that it might draw off Federal troops from the lower Shenandoah Valley around Winchester, opening that area to Confederate recruiters and quartermasters. Realizing all these goals was, however, far beyond the means of the forces committed to the operation.[13]

Imboden and Brig. Gen. "Grumble" Jones met and, after conferring with Lee, agreed on a two-pronged attack. Imboden would lead one brigade in a single column against Beverly, Philippi, and Grafton. Jones's Brigade would parallel Imboden's route to the north, advance to Moorefield, secure control of the Northwestern Turnpike, and attack the B&O at Oakland, Maryland, and Rowlesburg.

Imboden's plan called for 2,500 troops in two columns from Staunton. One would move along the Staunton-Parkersburg Turnpike and the other along the Northwestern Turnpike. The covering force under Jones, whose troops were then also located in the middle Shenandoah Valley region, would strike Romney, New Creek, and Cumberland. Imboden's cavalry units were to move through Moorefield, attack the B&O at Oakland, and destroy the important Cheat River Railroad Bridge at Rowlesburg. His infantry, artillery, and the remaining cavalry then would march to Beverly, capture Philippi, and occupy Grafton.[14]

The final stated goals for the raid were similar to those proposed by Imboden in March. The final plan called for the destruction of all bridges and trestles on the B&O between Oakland, Maryland, and Grafton. Jones and Imboden were also "to defeat and capture Union forces at Beverly, Philippi, and Buckhannon"; to topple the new Union government at Wheeling; to recruit men for the Confederate forces; and to secure needed supplies, especially horses, mules, cattle, and grain.[15]

Although there was doubt about their arriving until just before the expedition set out, Lee did ultimately grant Imboden's request for the two additional infantry regiments, sending the 25th and 31st Virginia, fteh 25th from Brig. Gen. Isaac R. Trimblee's Division and the 31st was in Brig. Gen. Jubal Early's Division. Commander of the Department of Western Virginia Maj. Gen. Samuel Jones made this possible by promising to temporarily replace the two regiments in the Army of Northern Virginia with the 50th adn 54th Virginia Regiments.[16]

The importance of the operation is shown in Lee's willingness to release two veteran regiments, even if they were quite small, when he was so badly outnumbered by Maj. Gen. Joseph Hooker's Army of the Potomac. The Battle of Chancellorsville was just weeks away.

Imboden's status was ambiguous. His men were operating in the Department of Western Virginia, commanded by Maj. Gen. Jones at Dublin in Pulaski County. Jones, a Virginian by birth who graduated from West Point in 1841, was a captain in the U.S. Army when the Civil War began. He had advanced rapidly to command the Department of East Tennessee, but in December 1862, when he had failed to provide troops that Braxton Bragg had requested for Kentucky, he lost that command and was shifted to Virginia. He assumed command of the Department of Western Virginia around December 1. Although not formally part of the Army of Northern Virginia, he nonetheless came under Lee's supervision.[17]

Samuel Jones was not a success in his new command. He complained, justifiably, about a lack of resources. He also complained of an area "cursed with intrigue and political plotters ever since the war commenced." He claimed that he found politicians among the soldiers but few soldiers among the politicians. Jones was also handicapped by the fact that many of his troops—such as those in Imboden's command—believed they had been recruited only to defend a particular district and resented orders to go elsewhere. Jones believed it was impossible for him to hold southwestern Virginia and part of east Tennessee with the few troops available to him.[18]

As planning went forward, Jones expressed concern to both Brig. Gen. William Jones and Imboden about the divided command and lack of communication between the two of them and whether McNeill was also operating independently. He wrote Imboden, "Surely there cannot be contemplated two expeditions, starting from and for the same points, and about the same time, under separate and independent commanders." He urged that Imboden communicate both with William Jones and McNeill. Maj. Gen. Samuel Jones concluded his letter to Brig. Gen. William Jones by asking, "I do not understand Imboden's position exactly. Is he under you, or does he receive orders directly from General Lee or the War Department?" At the same time, Major General Jones did what he could to assist the operation, supplying a detachment of engineers, along with tools and demolition equipment, to destroy bridges.[19]

Lee, meanwhile, kept in close contact with both Brig. Gen. William Jones and Imboden. He informed Jones that he regretted the necessity of a divided command; he told Imboden he had directed that requisite arms and ammunition be provided and requested that Jones threaten Union forces at Romney, New Creek, and Cumberland to prevent them from moving west. He also said that Maj. Gen. Samuel Jones had agreed to make a coordinated demonstration to attract Union attention to the Kanawha Valley and that he hoped he could release two regiments to assist at Beverly. He ordered Imboden to keep the "entire march a secret, even from your own men," and not to send any dispatches by telegraph relative to his movements "or they will become known." He also asked that Imboden inform him of progress and that he move "as soon as the roads and mountain streams permit."[20]

On March 28 Imboden and Major General Jones conferred at Dublin. Jones then requested that Lee release the 25th and 31st Virginia Regiments, promising one regiment of his own equal in strength to the two others combined. He thought the addition of the two regiments to Imboden's force would enhance the possibility of success and informed Lee that Imboden expected to be able to return them to Lee "in a few weeks with their ranks filled."

The replacement regiment sent by Jones to Lee turned out to be the 50th Virginia. Jones referred to the 25th and 31st Virginia sent to Imboden as "skeleton" regiments and noted that the 50th had as many or more men than the two of them combined. Referring to the raid in a letter to Confederate Secretary of War James A. Seddon, Jones also took credit for the expedition, beginning with, "I think it proper to inform you of an expedition I am now preparing."[21]

Major General Jones thought Imboden's force was too small, so he added men of his own. Col. William L. Jackson, a member of "Stonewall" Jackson's staff and former commander of the 31st Virginia, figured prominently in the raid's execution. A cousin of "Stonewall" Jackson, he earned the sobriquet of "Mudwall" in August 1863. Born in Lewis County, William Jackson was widely popular there; he had served as circuit judge of the Twenty-first Judicial District of Virginia before the war. Jones ordered Jackson to bring together different units into the 19th Virginia Cavalry Regiment, to be added to Imboden's force. He also promised Imboden he would supply Col. George S. Patton's 22d Virginia Infantry and Lt. Col. A.C. Dunn's 37th Battalion of mounted infantry.[22]

Both Imboden and W.E. Jones expressed themselves as ready to move as soon as road conditions would allow. The spring of 1863 was wet, however, and the expedition had to be put off until after April 1. While the Confederates waited for dry weather, Lee, Jones, and Imboden continued to push their own agendas for the campaign. Jones in particular sought a major role for his men, which Lee then granted.[23]

The final plan called for departure on April 15. Imboden was to move all of his force in a single column against Beverly, Philippi, and Grafton; meanwhile, Brigadier General Jones would advance to Moorefield, secure the Northwest Turnpike, and destroy the B&O bridges at Oakland and Rowlesburg. The revised plan called for simul-

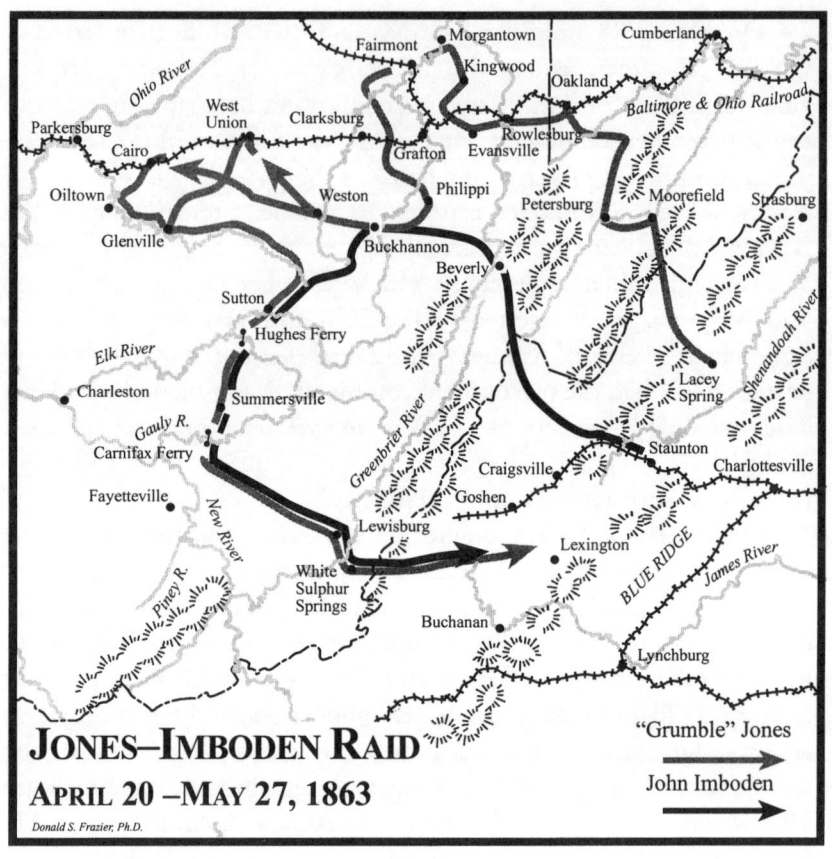

Jones-Imboden Raid, April 20–May 27, 1863

taneous attacks by the two commanders on the B&O at Oakland and Grafton.[24]

Union forces defending western Virginia were far more numerous than the Confederate raiders. On April 30 Commander of the Middle Department Maj. Gen. Robert C. Schenck had 34,297 men available for duty. His total force was even larger. As Union General-in-Chief Henry Halleck stated in a communication to Schenck on April 29, "You have 45,000 men under your command. If you cannot concentrate enough to meet the enemy, it does not argue well for your military dispositions."[25]

Brig. Gen. John R. Kenley's Maryland Brigade protected the B&O; it was strung out along that line from the Ohio River to Harpers Ferry. Defense of western Virginia fell principally to Brig. Gen. Benjamin S. Roberts's 4th Separate Brigade of VIII Corps. Substantial numbers of Union troops were located at Beverly and Buckhannon and in the Kanawha Valley. During the raid, reinforcements would be sent to Clarksburg from Maj. Gen. Robert H. Milroy's command at Winchester. Additionally, Maj. Gen. Ambrose E. Burnside ordered some troops from the Department of the Ohio by rail to Marietta and Bellaire and arranged for two gunboats to go to Parkersburg. Militia were called to active duty in western Virginia, western Pennsylvania, and eastern Ohio, and some of these men were sent to Fairmont, Grafton, and Clarksburg.[26]

Although the Union had substantially greater manpower resources, the Federals were widely dispersed, so concentrating their troops once the railroad lines were cut would be difficult. At least in the short run, Imboden's and Jones's tactics of dividing their resources, moving swiftly, and striking different targets simultaneously would serve to mask—and at the same time appear to magnify—overall inferior Confederate strength.

As Jones's command waited at New Market, a dispatch rider arrived from Lee with word that Federal cavalry under Maj. Gen. George Stoneman was moving from the Rappahannock toward a gap in the Blue Ridge, however, this threat passed the next day. On April 17 Jones issued his men sackbags, and many of the men received new clothing. On April 18 the cavalry left for Harrisonburg. All of Jones's men were now concentrated in camps between Harrisonburg and Lacey Spring.

On April 21 Jones departed Lacey Spring. His planned route of march was to proceed through Brock's Gap, to Moorefield, and then on to the B&O at Oakland. Jones had the 7th, 11th, and 12th Regiments, as well as battalions of cavalry under White, Brown, and Witcher, each with small detachments of infantry and artillery. Thus, in all, Jones had about 3,500 men. He kept the objective secret from his men until April 22, when the troops crossed over the mountain into the Lost River Valley.[27]

Heavy rains turned the roads into quagmires and delayed the advance. As a consequence, Jones did not reach Moorefield until late in the afternoon on April 23. The South Branch of the Potomac was up too high to cross, and by the next morning it was out of its banks. The prospect of a prolonged delay caused Jones to try crossing upstream. As a result, he ordered his artillery, infantry, and wagon trains, along with a three hundred–man cavalry escort, back to the Shenandoah via Franklin. This reduced his force by some one thousand men. Jones and the cavalry then detoured twelve miles upstream to Petersburg. There the Confederates finally got over the Potomac that afternoon, but not without cost: one man and several horses drowned.[28]

Meanwhile, Imboden also set out. His force included the units supplied by Maj. Gen. Samuel Jones, which were shifted east from the Greenbrier Valley, numbering in all about 1,400–1,600 men. Jones also provided about one hundred thousand dollars to purchase provisions. Jones's troops believed that they were being posted to the Shenandoah Valley, but this was merely a feint to put Federal scouts off the scent. Jones dispatched Col. George S. Patton's 22d Virginia Infantry of about 650 men from Lewisburg. It marched east to White Sulphur Springs and then turned north and passed through the eastern part of Greenbrier and Pocahontas Counties into Highland County. Troops in Pocahontas County, consisting of Colonel Jackson's 19th Virginia Cavalry (about 400 men) and Lt. Col. A.C. Dunn's 37th Battalion of mounted infantry (about 450 men), moved toward Warm Springs. After a day's march, they too turned north. These forces rendezvoused at Hightown, a point on the old Staunton and Parkersburg Road six miles west of Monterey. The troops were ignorant of their objective, but they were delighted when they joined Imboden there and learned they would be marching west on the Staunton and Parkersburg Turnpike.

Imboden and his immediate command had left Shenandoah Mountain on April 20. Originally set for April 15, their departure was delayed on the insistence of Brigadier General Jones, who had encountered some Federal cavalry in the Valley.[29]

Imboden and his staff marched at the head of his brigade, accompanied initially by fife and drum. Imboden had the 62d Virginia Mounted Infantry, the 18th Virginia Cavalry, some independent companies, and McClanahan's battery of six guns. The two regiments belatedly released by Lee also arrived in time: the 25th Virginia Infantry (led by Col. John Higginbotham) and the 31st Virginia (led by Col. John S. Huffman). Altogether Imboden had perhaps 1,825 effectives. Reportedly there were also refugees from northwest Virginia who had found out about the operation and who accompanied the raiders.

On April 21 Imboden's men joined the other force at Hightown, which consisted of the 22d Infantry Regiment (under Colonel Patton), the 19th Cavalry Regiment (under Col. William L. Jackson), and Col. Dunn's battalion. This brought Imboden's total strength up to 3,365 men, perhaps 700 of whom were mounted. One participant, however, put the total number of troops at 5,000. The raiders had but limited rations: thirteen days' worth of flour and thirty days' rations of salt. They would secure meat from the countryside.[30]

On the first night, the troops camped on the battlefield of Camp Baryow, some twenty miles west of Hightown and site of a Confederate victory on October 3, 1861. The next morning it rained and then snowed as the troops began to climb Cheat Mountain. The road over the mountain was a quagmire, and there were six inches of snow at the summit.

The troops spent the night of April 23 at Huttonsville. Imboden had marched his men seventy miles in only four days, and in these conditions, many of his poorly clad troops were suffering. The men had to endure sleet and snow, at some places as high as eighteen to twenty inches deep. By that time Imboden's men knew the broad outlines of the plan and were aware that they were operating in conjunction with forces under Jones to the north.[31]

At Huttonsville, Imboden's men passed a difficult night, largely exposed to the elements. It rained all night and through the next day until late in the afternoon. The Confederates were then within eleven miles of the entrenched town of Beverly, where Col. George Latham commanded 876 Union troops, supported by artillery. Shortly after daybreak on April 24, a morning that he described as "one of the most gloomy and inclement I ever saw," Imboden set his men in motion north toward the unsuspecting Federal garrison at Beverly.

Imboden feared the Federals had been warned of his approach. He estimated Union strength at Beverly to be two regiments of infantry, an artillery battery, and two cavalry companies: 1,500 men in all. This was nearly double their actual strength.

Imboden pushed his infantry and four guns along the east side of the Greenbrier River. The cavalry and a section of two guns, all under Col. George Imboden, went up the mail road on the west side of the river. Brigadier General Imboden instructed his brother that as soon as they were discovered, his men were to press forward and take possession of the road to Buckhannon, about thirty miles west of Beverly, cutting off any Federal retreat by that route. About five miles from Beverly the cavalry advance came upon Randolph County sheriff J.F. Phares, who immediately fled. Although shot and wounded, Phares succeeded in reaching Beverly and sounding the alarm.

On the east side of the river the Confederates encountered an unsuspecting Federal foraging party and swooped down on them without a shot being fired, capturing the men, forty-two mules, wagons, and a mounted escort of a dozen soldiers. They also passed a Federal major on horseback, who assumed the raiders were part of the foraging party and rode right past them, only to be taken by Confederate troops toward the rear. The advanced party then encountered a squad of Union cavalry who, alarmed, rode off. The Confederates pursued for a mile or two but were unable to catch them. On Imboden's orders, the advance then waited for the infantry to come up in order to have them available for the assault on the Union breastworks, located south of the town.

Imboden found the Federal defenders drawn up in line of battle in an excellent position on high ground that commanded about a mile of road. The Union troops opened up with artillery when the Confederates came within range. Fearful of a frontal assault that might result in "hundreds" of Confederate casualties, Imboden decided to try and flank the Union position by working his infantry around to the north. To fix the Federals in place, Imboden ordered one of his rifled guns to open fire on the Federal line. He also ordered his cavalry forward under Union fire to secure the Buckhannon Road west of the river and cut off any Union retreat.

The Federals at first stood firm, but became demoralized after several hours and abandoned their positions, withdrawing behind a strong line of skirmishers. A little before sunset, Imboden's men finally succeeded in getting north of the town, but not in time to cut off the Union retreat toward Philippi, thirty-one miles away.

The Philippi Road provided the easiest access to the B&O, but darkness and the poor road conditions halted the Confederate pursuit. Personnel losses on both sides were slight: three Confederates were badly wounded; Union casualties were one dead, two wounded, and thirteen captured.[32]

The fight at Beverly did yield a significant quantity of Federal supplies. About a third of the town was destroyed by fire as the Federals had attempted to destroy stores. Still, the Confederates had obtained significant stocks, including some badly needed ammunition. Imboden estimated Union supply losses at one hundred thousand dollars.[33]

The Confederate troops were exhausted, many having marched over a hundred miles from points as far away as Staunton and Harrisonburg, but they were elated at the capture of Beverly, which had been in Union hands since General McClellan had taken it in July 1861. With no other fortified Union town east of Beverly, this opened the surrounding rich farming area to Confederate exploitation.[34]

The next morning, April 25, any hope of pursuit of the Federal force was dashed when Imboden's cavalry reported that deep mud rendered the road toward Philippi impassable for artillery or wagons. Imboden was also aware that Union General Roberts and a considerable number of his troops were at Buckhannon, and he did not dare move against Philippi with them on his flank. Imboden planned to cross Rich Mountain and then either attack Buckhannon or get between it and Philippi, attacking whichever one of the two towns circumstances allowed. Imboden then sent out Maj. D.B. Lang and two companies of cavalry to try to contact Jones.[35]

Looting by his men at Beverly displeased Imboden. On April 25 he issued General Order No. 20:

> I. The Commanding General regrets that occurrences at Beverly and in the neighborhood on yesterday have developed the fact that to some extent the idea prevails or at least is acted upon that individuals in the command have the right to seize and appropriate to their own use the property of Union citizens in this part of the State of Virginia. It is now distinctly announced that any seizure or appropriation to private uses of the property of any citizen, will be treated and punished as robbery. In respect to the property of Union citizens useful & necessary for the army, impressments will be made by the proper officers in legal form, and certificates given under General Orders from the Hd.Qrs.

II. To prevent the lawlessness of a few men from bringing discredit on the fair fame of this command, it is ordered that hereafter, whenever the command enters any town or village, the Col. or other officer in command of the first Regiment arriving, shall immediately detail a company to guard every store & home in the place, and the Captain of such guard will be held responsible for the protection of all property in the place, till [*sic*] he is relieved. As a general rule it is the stragglers & skulkers, who profit by plunder, while the faithful soldier is performing his duty. This fact of itself, if there were no higher consideration, requires the suppression of all plundering—and it shall be suppressed.[36]

On the evening of April 26 Imboden's command quit Beverly. His men crossed Middle Fork and encamped between Philippi and Buckhannon, at a location about a dozen miles from each. Imboden then sent his cavalry forward to seize the bridge over the Buckhannon River. At this point Imboden heard artillery fire from the direction of Philippi. Shortly thereafter he received a report from his brother George that the Union Beverly force had instead gone to Buckhannon and that a Union brigade under Bvt. Brig. Gen. James A. Mulligan, which had been east of the Alleghenies, had arrived at Philippi by rail from New Creek. His brother asked Imboden to send two regiments of infantry and a section of artillery as reinforcements to the bridge.[37]

Imboden called a meeting of his regimental commanders to determine which regiments to send to his brother. At the conference, however, Colonel Patton announced that his men had captured a Union courier from Buckhannon with word that six Union brigades had been posted to secure the B&O. This news led Imboden to conclude that Jones had failed to cut the railroad as planned. Imboden was fearful he might be cut off, a conclusion shared by his regimental commanders. All agreed that "the safety of the command requires that we should fall back to a position where escape would be possible if we were overpowered."[38]

Imboden then recalled his cavalry from Buckhannon Bridge and ordered his entire command to fall back on Beverly. The road was so poor that it took them nine hours (from 5:00 A.M. to 2:00 P.M.) to cover two miles. That night they camped at Roaring Run. Union area commander Brigadier General Roberts, meanwhile, had gathered forces from Birch, Sutton, and Bulltown at Buckhannon. Aware of the vital position of Clarksburg, with its considerable military stores and railroad, he decided to concentrate his 2,800 troops there. After midnight a scout Imboden had sent toward Buckhannon reported that Union troops had evacuated that place, burning bridges over the Middle Fork and Buckhannon Rivers to block the Confederates from that direction.[39]

On the morning of April 28 Imboden ordered the advance resumed toward Buckhannon. The next morning he succeeded in getting a regiment to Buckhannon over the ruins of the bridge. The Confederates found most Union stores at Buckhannon burned and two cannons—which the troops had been unable to move—spiked, but they salvaged what they could.

Unable to cross his artillery and cavalry over the Buckhannon River, Imboden ordered a raft constructed. He also had his men round up horses and cattle and forage in the area. His own horses were in poor shape, with some having died under the strain of the march and lack of nourishment. Imboden decided to remain there that day and the next, resting his horses and men, and gathering supplies, food, and fodder.

The foragers did not have great success. Grain was particularly in short supply, and the Confederates sometimes secured less than a bushel per house. Imboden undoubtedly exaggerated when he noted in his official report, "I required everything to be paid for at fair prices, such as were the current rates before we arrived in the country. This gave general satisfaction in the country, and our currency was freely accepted." One has to conclude that the latter assurance is at best questionable.[40]

On April 29 Imboden had his first communication from Jones, a letter from Evansville dated April 27. Once Jones had gotten across the Potomac with his reduced force, he again made for Oakland, but the same terrible weather conditions that had delayed Imboden also held up Jones. On April 25 at Greenland Gap, a narrow pass through the Knobley Mountains, the Confederates encountered a detachment of eighty-six men and three officers of the 23d Illinois and 14th West Virginia Infantry. Jones demanded their surrender under flag of truce but the Federals refused. Fighting from within a barricaded church, the Federals then repelled three Confederate charges and inflicted considerable casualties at minimal cost to themselves, holding up Jones for four hours. Finally, the Confederates set the church afire and forced the defenders to surrender. The Union side suffered two dead, six or eight wounded, and eighty captured; the attackers lost seven killed and twenty-two wounded. The delay purchased by the Federal troops at Greenland Gap allowed Union reinforcements to be moved along the B&O against Imboden.[41]

Jones's men then continued their ascent of the Alleghenies. Marching all night, they reached the North Branch of the Potomac after daylight. Upon crossing it, Jones divided his force. He sent Col. Asher W. Harman and part of his command, consisting of the 11th Regiment, White's and Brown's Battalions, and McNeill's Partisan Rangers, north to Oakland, where they were to operate along the B&O and cut it. He ordered Harman to occupy Oakland, destroy its railroad bridges, and then proceed into Preston and Monongalia Counties.[42]

On April 24 General Roberts wired Union General-in-Chief Maj. Gen. Halleck that he was prevented from protecting the B&O because "the roads in this region are impassable." Halleck quickly fired back a scathing reply: "Collect your forces, defend the railroad, and drive the enemy back. You are strong enough to do it if you try. Do not call for reenforcements from here. You have no need of them, and we have none to give you if you had. I do not understand how the roads there are impassible to you, when, by your own account, they are passable enough to the enemy. If you cannot drive the enemy out, we will seek some one who can."[43]

Jones, meanwhile, led his main body to Rowlesburg to destroy the vital B&O bridge over the Cheat River. Jones arrived there early on Sunday afternoon, April 26. Lee recognized well the importance of the bridge. As early as 1861 Lee had written, "The rupture of the railroad at Cheat River would be worth to us an army."[44]

A Union force of 250 men of the 6th (Western) Virginia Volunteer Infantry held the Cheat River viaduct. They had established defensive positions there of logs and crossties at each end of the bridge, and they were also positioned in the hills. These strong Union positions left Jones no alternative but a frontal assault, and he ordered Lt. Col. John Shac Green's 6th Virginia Cavalry to attack dismounted and drive the Federal troops out. Assisted by sharpshooters from the 7th and 11th Regiments, Green drove forward. The Federals laid down a heavy fire, repelling the Confederate assault.[45]

Given the strength of the Union defensive positions, Jones decided not to attempt a second attack. Late that same afternoon, the Confederates withdrew to the Northwestern Turnpike. They arrived at Evansville on the afternoon of April 27 and spent the remainder of that day destroying small railroad bridges at Independence and rolling stock and stationary railroad property at Newburg. Jones also sent out patrols in an attempt to make contact with Imboden, who was a day's ride to the west, but these failed to make contact.[46]

Pennsylvania Governor Andrew G. Curtin was alarmed. He wired Secretary of War Edwin Stanton in Washington that he had heard the Confederates had taken Morgantown and held it in force. Fearing an invasion of his own state, he said he had no troops available and asked if Washington might send some. President Lincoln replied with an accurate assessment: "I do not think the people of Pennsylvania should be uneasy about an invasion. Doubtless a small force of the enemy is flourishing about in the northern part of Virginia on the 'screwhorn' principle, on purpose to divert us in another quarter. I believe it is nothing more. We think we have adequate force close after them."[47]

Although Jones had little idea of Federal troop dispositions, he ordered his men north, and they reached Kingwood after dark. After a brief stop there, the Confederates resumed their march along the Morgantown-Kingwood Turnpike. Jones halted the men at midnight to sleep, without taking defensive precautions. At 4:00 A.M. on April 28, Jones and his men were awakened by the approach of cavalry. Fortunately for them, it turned out to be Harman's men rejoining the main body.[48]

Harman had been able to carry out his orders fully. His men had cut both the railroad and telegraph at Altamont and Oakland and also demolished railroad bridges and culverts at Cranberry Summit (Terra Alta). They had narrowly missed capturing a westbound train filled with Federal officers, but they succeeded in raiding much of the area along the Pennsylvania border, destroying railroad property, and taking prisoners and horses.

At Oakland, Harman's men had achieved complete surprise. The 11th Virginia Cavalry arrived in the town about 11:00 A.M. on April 26, just as the soldiers and civilians were on their way to church. Those in uniform—fifty-seven men and two officers—the Confederates immediately captured, then paroled.[49]

Harman's force then separated into smaller detachments, raiding most of Preston County from Kingwood to the Pennsylvania border. Forewarned, the inhabitants of Morgantown did what they could to conceal their livestock or drove them into Pennsylvania. Several hundred armed civilians had thought to defend the town, but the one thousand–man strength of the attackers and assurances of proper conduct led them to abandon this idea, and they surrendered their arms at the courthouse. While some of Harman's men searched the countryside for horses and cattle, others remained at Morgantown for several hours. There was no looting, although the Confederates made a number of purchases in local stores, paying for these with inflated Confederate script. Many patronized the local bars, and not a few got drunk.

The Confederates also raided strongly pro-Union Monongalia County. During these operations, three civilians, who had been out hunting, fired on the raiders, killing a horse from underneath one of the Confederates. The raiders then rode down, captured the men, and after a brief trial executed two of them. The third escaped by falling to the ground and feigning death when the firing squad opened up.[50]

At sunset the Confederates departed, rejoining the remainder of Jones's command early on April 28. His force again reunited, Jones headed back to Morgantown, arriving there at about noon that same day. This time, the inhabitants were caught by surprise and did not have time to protect their cattle and horses. The process of the previous stay in Morgantown was repeated; some of the men raided the countryside, while many remained in town, paying for purchases in the stores with their worthless currency. This time the Confederate officers posted guards in front of the saloons to assure that the men remained sober. Before sunset, the raiders departed, crossing over the Monongahela River on the suspension bridge. They grazed their horses and then, after dark, rode off toward Fairmont.

At Fairmont, Jones captured four hundred Union soldiers and rebuffed an attacking Union force that had come down from Grafton to defend the railroad bridge. Jones and his men then went to work. Using tools and explosives brought with them for this purpose, they worked until late in the afternoon and destroyed the three spans of the nine hundred–foot-long iron B&O bridge there and blew up its piers. Jones pointed out that the bridge had taken two years to build and had cost nearly five hundred thousand dollars. The raiders looked for cattle and horses, destroyed sawmills and a gunstock factory, and burned Governor Francis H. Pierpont's library. Pierpont, an object of particular hatred, had placed a number of Confederate officers and individuals thought to be Confederate sympathizers in a chain gang, working them at hard labor until certain western Virginia civilians and officers were released by the Confederate side.[51]

At dark Jones resumed the march. From Fairmont the raiders headed south toward Clarksburg, which was well defended by Union troops. The Confederates continued their advance until they encountered the Union outposts; they then turned east to Bridgeport, where they struck the Northern Virginia Railroad. At Bridgeport on April 30 the Confederates captured a company of Union troops, destroyed a train, and burned bridges and trestles.

The next day, May 1, the Confederate cavalry moved toward Philippi. As his force approached that town, Jones decided to send back to the Shenandoah Valley the booty his men had taken thus far, including most of the cattle and horses. To escort these home, he detached Colonel Harman and part of the 6th Regiment. Jones then put the rest of the men en route to Buckhannon, where, he learned later that day, Imboden was camped. In all, Jones and his men had destroyed nine railroad bridges and captured two trains, an artillery piece, 500 prisoners, in addition to a considerable number of horses and cattle.[52]

Imboden and Jones had been unable to communicate, so each was unaware of the other's movements. Lee was also in the dark. On April 29 he informed President Davis, "I have received a dispatch from Gen. Imboden dated April 28th. . . . I have had no report from Gen. W. E. Jones."[53]

On May 1, meanwhile, Imboden sent a regiment of cavalry to Weston, but Union forces had evacuated that town and destroyed its stores. The Confederates found Union forces five miles to the north, at Jane Lew. Fearful that Jones had been cut off and would be unable to link up with him, Imboden gave orders to move early on May 2. The raft, now completed, could be used to cross the Buckhannon River and proceed toward Philippi. The Confederate troops were just underway when a courier arrived with the news that Jones and a portion of his command were about six miles away. At the same time Imboden learned that a party of Colonel Jackson's 19th Cavalry had succeeded in destroying all bridges thirty miles west of Fairmount. The bridge on the Northwestern Virginia Railroad, six miles west of Clarksburg, had also been burned.[54]

Jones was the senior general, and Imboden had told him that he would follow his orders as long as their two commands were together, which he now did. Both men were in agreement that they should attack Roberts's forces at Clarksburg, now reinforced by Brig. Gen. John R. Kenly's Maryland Brigade. Imboden recalled his raiders and Jones sent messengers to Harman to join him.

The road was in such poor condition that it was May 3 before the Confederates got to Weston, sixteen miles west of Buckhannon and twenty-three miles south of Clarksburg. At Weston Imboden sent out foragers; again little grain was to be had, although they did secure a number of cattle. Many of the Confederate troops rested, even playing ball on public grounds at a hospital for the insane. The two commands also held a parade through the town and were presented with a flag.[55]

In a report of May 3 to Brig. Gen. A.G. Jenkins, Imboden described the raid to that point as "a splendid success, especially on General Jones' part, in the destruction of the railroad." He reported they had taken perhaps 2,000 head of cattle and 1,200 "fine horses for the Government." Jones had captured five hundred Union troops, while Imboden had secured twenty to twenty-five men. Imboden said that word had reached him that Jenkins was moving on Parkersburg, and he suggested that the disparate forces unite. If this could be accomplished, he felt, "the northwest is saved."[56]

A personal matter occupied the attention of the Imboden brothers at Weston, where their elderly parents resided. Capt. Frank Imboden, who had accompanied his brothers on the raid, discovered his parents' vulnerability to Union reprisals and decided that they had to be taken from the area. As Frank put it in his diary on April 30, "They have suffered martyrdom from the accursed abolitionists."[57]

The brothers agreed that their parents should be returned to Augusta County. Frank Imboden arranged for horses and eight wagons and loaded them with all their parents' possessions, but unfortunately the wagon train encountered a Union patrol, which seized the horses and the bulk of the personal property. Frank Imboden succeeded in getting away with the one wagon in which his parents were riding, which carried only a few of their personal belongings.[58]

The united Confederate commands spent several days at Weston resting and consolidating their forces. Much of Jones's Brigade arrived from Beverly on May 5, the same day that Union troops surrounded and attacked Imboden's picket at Jane Lew. All the Confederates escaped, except for three men who were taken prisoner when their horses were shot out from under them. That same day Imboden learned from a reliable source that Union Generals Roberts and Kelley had 4,500–5,000 infantry and twelve guns at Clarksburg. The next day's reinforcements reportedly brought the force up to 6,000–8,000 men, who were throwing up entrenchments.

Jones and Imboden concluded that they could not hope to be successful against such a large force. Because of desertions, the large number of sick, and the segment detached to guard cattle sent east, Imboden had only 2,000–2,300 men, while Jones had another 1,200. Even their combined force was too weak to take a reinforced, entrenched position. The two leaders decided to separate again on the morning of May 6—Imboden to head south toward Summersville and Jones to move westward to continue assaults on the B&O.[59]

On May 6 Jones ordered Harman to break the Northwestern Virginia Railroad at West Union. Jones himself led the main body west on the Staunton and Parkersburg Pike to attack the same railroad near its western terminus at Parkersburg, on the Ohio state line.[60]

At West Union, Harman captured ninety-four members of the railroad guard and burned two nearby railroad bridges. Jones also took the railroad guard at Cairo, burned three bridges, and damaged a tunnel. A Union gunboat on the Ohio River prevented an assault on Parkersburg. At Wheeling in the far north, where a constitutional convention was meeting to form the state of West Virginia, militia were called out to defend the city. The convention adjourned, its members fleeing in disorder into Pennsylvania or Ohio.

Jones's men then marched to Oiltown to ravage the Kanawha Valley petroleum fields, the largest oil works in Virginia, which employed a thousand men. On May 9 at Oiltown the Confederates destroyed oil field equipment and set fire to 150,000 barrels of oil. In his report to General Lee, Jones described the scene: "By dark the oil from the tanks on the burning creek had reached the river, and the whole stream became a sheet of fire. A burning river, carrying destruction to our merciless enemy, was a scene of magnificence that might well carry joy to every patriotic heart."[61]

Jones then moved to Glenville, to Sutton, and finally south to Summersville, to meet up with Imboden. There, Jones wrote, "Our exhausted condition and exhausted supplies rendered homeward movement necessary."[62]

Imboden, meanwhile, again experienced bad weather, which slowed his march. He ordered his sick and stores from Buckhannon and Beverly to Monterey and put the rest of his force at Weston on the road to Summersville. By May 9 it had rained hard for fourteen days. The roads were such that his troops covered only five and a half miles the first day; and it took them three days to move fourteen miles to Summersville. To bring the artillery through, Imboden was obliged to destroy spare wheels and throw away fifty shot from each caisson. Along the way the Confederates scoured the countryside for horses, mules, and cattle, despite the pleas of their owners. The horses had little to eat, apart from grass along the road. Along the way at Bulltown, Suttonville, and Big Birch, they discovered that Union troops had destroyed stocks of supplies they had been gathering for the summer campaign. Imboden completed this work by burning a number of blockhouses and quarters.[63]

On the night of May 12 Col. George Imboden, who was twelve miles ahead of the main column, informed Imboden that Union forces were in the process of evacuating Summersville. Despite having fewer than two hundred men with him, Colonel Imboden said that he would attack, and he asked that reinforcements be rushed to him as soon as possible. When his men reached Summersville, he discovered that the Union forces had departed an hour earlier. Imboden ordered a pursuit and caught up with the mounted Union rear guard about six miles from the town. Attacking immediately, the Confederates took twenty-three prisoners and twenty-eight wagons loaded with supplies, along with 168 mules and harnesses.[64]

On learning of his brother's appeal, General Imboden immediately ordered reveille sounded. His men then got under way and, despite their tired state, covered the twenty miles to Summersville by 3:00 P.M. His brother's capture of the Federal wagon train was indeed fortunate. The horses were worn out, and the mules could aid in pulling the artillery. But the supplies were critical; as Imboden noted, his men "had only been allowed half a pound of meal per day after leaving Beverly, and our scanty supplies were exhausted."[65]

Jones rejoined Imboden at Summersville that same evening; the remainder of his command came in the next day. After discussing their options, Jones and Imboden agreed that they had accomplished their aims and that they would again separate for the return to Virginia. Imboden also divided his own command, detaching at their own request the 22d Regiment and Dunn's Battalion to proceed via Meadow Bluff to Lewisburg. The remainder of Imboden's men would travel to Gauley and then attempt to cross into Greenbrier County near Frankfort by Cold Knob Road, which was only rarely attempted by wagons. The march was successful, Imboden covering the fifty miles to Sinking Creek in Greenbrier County in only four days.[66]

Union cavalry did attack the Confederates at Fayetteville, thirty miles southwest of Summersville, but they were halted by troops under Col. John McCausland, who later worked closely with Imboden. Maj. Gen. Samuel Jones had ordered McCausland from Princeton to threaten Fayetteville and act to assist Imboden if need be. With 1,200 men, a cavalry company, and an artillery battery, the capable McCausland saved the valuable Confederate supply train.[67]

In his after-action report to Lee, William Jones was somewhat critical of Imboden. He noted that the original plan had been for the two Confederate commanders to stage "simultaneous attacks" on the B&O at Grafton and at Oakland. Thus he was surprised to receive a letter from Imboden once the raid was in progress, "stating that I would reach Oakland the day he reached Beverly, so as to cut off re-inforcements from the east. It was now too late to rearrange or halt." It had also been specified that the raiders would not employ wagons, given the difficulty of moving them over the mountain roads in early spring. He was thus surprised on meeting Imboden at Buckhannon to see that Imboden had the seventy captured Federal wagons in tow. Jones concluded: "Had our original plan been carried out, I feel confident Northwestern Virginia could have been cleared to the Ohio." Given Federal strength in the region, however, this would seem to be mere posturing on the part of Jones.[68]

Jones did claim that his men had captured nearly seven hundred Union soldiers, their small arms, and an artillery piece. They had destroyed two trains, sixteen bridges, a tunnel, a large quantity of oil field equipment, and 150,000 barrels of oil. They had also brought off 1,000 cattle and 1,200 horses, which drovers had taken to Lee's army. Reportedly Jones used many of the horses to remount his entire brigade. All this had been at a cost of ten dead, forty-two wounded, and not more than fifteen missing.[69]

In his own report, Imboden made no mention of any changes in orders, and he willingly gave Jones most of the credit: "In the horrible condition of the roads, I could not move with the celerity that was desirable, and deemed myself fortunate in being able, by pursuing an interior route, to keep the way of escape open at all times for General Jones, while he, being mounted, ventured to go much farther than I could do."[70]

Still, Imboden was proud of what his men had accomplished. They had marched more than four hundred miles through Union-held territory over thirty-seven days, themselves destroying or forcing Union troops to destroy substantial stocks of supplies. They had also burned numerous bridges. Finally, Imboden's men had brought off what he estimated at one hundred thousand dollars' worth of horses, mules, wagons, and weapons. Imboden also put the number of cattle secured at 3,100, worth at least three hundred thousand dollars. His losses had been negligible: one lieutenant and one private killed and fourteen men taken prisoner— three wounded men left at Beverly, eight sick, and three captured outright. At the same time, between 375 and 500 volunteers had been added to the Confederate ranks, although this figure was partially offset by the mass desertion of 200 men from Dunn's Battalion of mounted infantry at Beverly. The latter was a consequence of Imboden's having issued specific orders forbidding the seizing of private property. The men had objected to not being able to take horses for their own use and, frustrated by Imboden's order, had promptly deserted.[71]

In all, Imboden and Jones together had destroyed twenty-four bridges, damaged a tunnel, and cut telegraph lines. They had also burned large stocks of oil, captured one thousand small arms and an artillery piece, and destroyed Union Army supply depots. Moreover, they had inflicted as many as eight hundred Union casualties—killed, wounded, and captured—all for slight losses of their own.[72]

In forwarding Imboden's report, General Lee noted: "Although the expedition under General Imboden failed to accomplish all the results intended, it nevertheless rendered valuable service in the collection of stores and in making the enemy uneasy for his communication with the west. The men and officers deserve much credit for the fortitude and endurance exhibited under the hardships and difficulty of the march, which interfered so seriously with the success of the enterprise."[73]

Militarily, the raid was a great embarrassment to the Union. The sole Union achievement had been protecting the Cheat River Viaduct. The Confederates had held the initiative throughout, and Union commanders were never able to inflict a defeat on them. General Roberts had kept his four thousand men at Clarksville while Jones's inferior force had leisurely occupied nearby Bridgeport. Even when he had increased his strength to six thousand men and the Confederates were at Weston, Roberts had made no effort to move against them. On May 1 Roberts had estimated Imboden's and Jones's force at six thousand men, double their actual size; on May 6 he approximated Rebel cavalry strength alone at four thousand men.[74]

The raid had important political effects. In the short run, it temporarily broke up the Unionist convention at Wheeling and diverted thousands of Union troops into the area. But it also stirred up sentiment against the Confederacy. At its reconstitution on June 20, 1863, the Convention promptly voted to declare the "State of West Virginia," as part of "the United States of America." One writer has claimed that the raid "had done more to crystalize local public sentiment in favor of the separate State of West Virginia than all other agencies combined."[75]

Imboden communicated his own reaction to the raid in a general order issued at Sinking Creek, in Greenbrier County, on May 17. Because the raid was one of the most important events of Imboden's military career, it is worth quoting most of that pronouncement here.

Imboden began by telling his men of his "profound admiration" of their "patient and manly deportment under all circumstances." He then went on to sum up the raid and its effects:

Soldiers! You have nobly performed your duty. Within 28 days you have marched through rain & mud, climbed mountains and waded rivers for a distance of nearly 300 miles without one murmur of complaint that has ever reached my ears.

You formed part of an expedition that has successfully accomplished a most important work. Damage to the amount of millions of dollars had been done [to] the enemy in the form of the destruction of the Baltimore & Ohio and N.W. Va. Railroads. The destruction of these roads was one of the primary objects of your expedition. The actual damage was mainly done by the Cavalry Brigade of Gen. W. E. Jones, but is no less on that account a part of your work, because you supported and protected his operations by drawing the enemy to concentrate his largely superior forces at one point in your front, thus compelling him to abandon the whole line of the Railroad to Gen. Jones' rapid attacks.

You have enabled the agents of the Confederate Government to purchase and drive to a place of safety about 3000 head of cattle of inestimable value at this time to our great army in Virginia. You compelled the enemy to destroy large amounts of army stores at Beverly, Buchanan, Weston, Bulltown and Sutton, and captured a fine train of wagons and teams at Summerville [*sic*].

But rising above these mere property considerations, you have accomplished a work of the highest political importance to the Confederate States, and especially to Virginia, in certain national contingencies, that will probably exist in the next few weeks or months. You have proven that the pretended State of Virginia is not under the exclusive control of the Washington and Wheeling despotisms, but that we can, whenever we choose, go into and occupy almost any portion of it. In the event of foreign intervention, this fact may be of immense importance.

You had an opportunity of meeting the enemy but once—at Beverly—and there two companies of skirmishers under Maj. Land whipped him 1500 strong, with the aid of a few rounds from one gun of McClanahan's Battery, before you could reach a position of attack yourselves. The perfect coolness with which the entire command pressed forward under a somewhat annoying cannonade would have elicited the praise of an older soldier than I am.

It will be a pleasing duty in my report to our Government to bear more ample testimony to the high soldierly qualities of the officers and men, who have so faithfully followed me on this long and trying expedition. Many of us met as strangers—we part as friends and brothers. . . .

It has been my aim to act justly with the people where we have been. Many of you have your homes in N.W. Va. and your families have been victims to the atrocities of our brutal enemies and their sympathizers, the Union traitors, and you naturally felt the resentment, which is a part of human nature, but I am proud to testify that no one of this command disgraced himself and comrades by imitating the infernal practices of our enemies.

We have left N.W. Va not from fear of the enemy, but from the destitution of army supplies. This destitution will not always exist; and I promise you, whenever we can live there, no one will be more willing to return with you than I, and then, if our forbearance on this occasion has not been reciprocated, we will go as avengers, and teach the cowardly oppressors of women that brave men can inflict punishment, as well as they can bear injury with patience."[76]

Though this statement is eloquently phrased, the denial of looting is repudiated by his earlier issuing of General Order No. 20, instigated by events at Beverly. It is noteworthy that in his remarks Imboden held out hope of foreign intervention, that he makes reference to impending Confederate military action—Lee's invasion of the North that culminated at Gettysburg—and that he holds out the possibility of retribution against Union sympathizers in western Virginia.

The raid made clear to the North the need for more mobile Union forces, which did not rely solely on the railroad. As a result, cavalry became the major defensive arm in West Virginia. Also, Washington lost little time in replacing the cautious Roberts. On May 18 cavalry officer Brig. Gen. William Woods Averell was named to assume command of the 4th Separate Brigade; he reported to Weston four days later.[77]

Averell's orders called on him to establish his headquarters at Weston or Buckhannon, "or such other point as you may find it best to select south of the Baltimore and Ohio Railroad, drawing your supplies from the depot at Clarksburg." He was to have charge of all of West Virginia between the B&O and the Kanawha River and keep that area clear of Confederate troops. As much as possible, he was to make his command into a "mobile force"—capable of rapid concentration and movement—the aim being to convert his command insofar as possible into "a force of cavalry, with light artillery and with little or no infantry." He might also be called upon "in emergency" to move east across the mountains into "the Valley of Virginia."[78]

Averell, an 1855 graduate of West Point, went on to become a cavalry instructor and then gained a reputation as a capable commander in fighting Indians in New Mexico. After the start of the Civil War he commanded the 3d Pennsylvania Cavalry, and in 1862 he had distinguished himself in the Peninsula Campaign, winning promotion to brigadier general in the Army of the Potomac. He lost this command following the Battle of Chancellorsville.[79] This seemed not to have unduly diminished Averell's luster, for the news of his appointment brought an immediate improvement in morale in the 4th Separate Brigade.[80]

Averell took command of a brigade that was scattered over a dozen counties, insufficient in numbers for the task at hand, and poorly equipped and trained. As the mustering officer of the brigade, Maj. Theodore F. Lang, observed: "The master hand of discipline and drill had not been a part of their military experience."[81] Certainly there was no hope of undertaking offensive operations in the immediate future. Yet the clear intention was to build up the Union forces in West Virginia with the idea that Averell would turn the tables on the Confederates and ultimately raid into their lines to the east.

Averell immediately concentrated his brigade at three principal locations. The men were then drilled, rearmed, and reequipped, thereby transforming a three thousand–man brigade into cavalry. His success in transforming the brigade, later known as the 4th Division and then the Cavalry Division, may be seen in the fact that within three months of his taking command, it went on the offensive. In August, November, and December 1863, Averell led successive, long raids against Confederate lines of communications, often over treacherous terrain in bad weather. The last raid, during December 8–25 with 2,500 cavalry, ended in Salem, where the Union troops damaged the railroad and destroyed Confederate stores.[82]

Chapter 7

The Gettysburg Campaign

In early May 1863 Imboden's Northwestern Brigade was at Bulltown in Braxton County. Late that month, however, Lee ordered him to reposition his brigade "by easy marches" at some point down the Shenandoah Valley, preferably to Shenandoah Mountain or a similar location, where he could "keep strict watch on the movement of the enemy." On June 1 Imboden moved to Buffalo Gap near Staunton in Augusta County. There his men enjoyed a considerable improvement in their diet. During the raid into West Virginia they had made do with salt beef and a half pound of meal per man per day. Now they enjoyed fresh beef, corn, molasses, and bacon.[1]

Securing fresh mounts was a constant problem, and in Buffalo Gap Imboden was also able to replace worn-out horses as well as acquire new wagons. His men also received new uniforms. The week-long stay at Buffalo Gap was short, but it certainly rejuvenated his command. Imboden then shifted his brigade westward, to Monterey in Highland County.

Maj. Gen. Samuel Jones was increasingly agitated about Imboden's status. While he had significantly strengthened Imboden's force for the raid into West Virginia, he had sought to bring Imboden under his own control by asking that he report to him. Jones now intensified this effort. At the end of May he wrote Lee: "I do not understand the status of General Imboden and his command. Does he report directly to you? Is he to operate in the Valley, or west of his present camp? If the latter, he should report to me, and be under my orders. He captured something over 165 mules and 32 wagons at Summerville [*sic*], all of which he took with him out of my department, though I contributed to his expedition two-thirds of the men."²

Lee did not mince words in his response: "General Imboden's command was organized for service in Northwestern Virginia and the Valley, and he reports directly to me. I have instructed him to operate in the Valley and on the line toward Staunton, Huttonsville, Cheat Mountain, Monterey, and the Potomac."³

Imboden's men were not idle long, for they soon took part in General Lee's invasion of Pennsylvania that culminated in the great Battle of Gettysburg. Lee's objectives in his second invasion of the North were limited. General Hooker's Army of the Potomac, Lee believed, was rebuilding its strength for a push south to Richmond. If there had to be fighting that summer, Lee wanted it to be in the North, in conditions of his choosing. His plan was to move beyond the Blue Ridge, cross the Potomac River, and then march east, threatening Philadelphia and Baltimore. This would cut Washington's communications with the rest of the country and put pressure on Hooker to attack him. Lee also expected to bring the war home to a part of the North as a way to add to antiwar sentiment there, and, more important, secure needed cattle, horses, foodstuffs, and other supplies from the rich Cumberland Valley, as the extension of the Shenandoah was known in Pennsylvania.

To strengthen his cavalry for the invasion, Lee recalled Brig. Gen. William E. "Grumble" Jones's Cavalry Brigade of four regiments and a battalion operating in the Shenandoah Valley. To replace Jones, he ordered Brig. Gen. Albert G. Jenkins's Brigade of cavalry sent to Staunton or some other convenient location. These men were not well trained and were often referred to as mounted infantry. They were assigned to II Corps, now under Lt. Gen. Richard Ewell, who took command following "Stonewall" Jackson's death from his fatal wound at Chancellorsville. These men accompanied II Corps into Pennsylvania and proved their worth in the campaign. Lee also secured Brig. Gen. Beverly Robertson's small command of two regiments from North Carolina. Finally, Lee ordered Imboden to ready his command for the northern invasion. While some of Imboden's men were probably even more untrained and ill-disciplined than Jenkins's command, they could ride and shoot well and they could drive cattle. These skills were certainly sufficient for them to act as auxiliaries for gathering intelligence, screening Lee's forces, foraging, and protecting wagon trains.[4]

At the end of May, Lee's forces were positioned south of the Rappahannock River in and near Fredericksburg; Hooker's army lay just north of the river. Contrary to Lee's belief, Hooker was not being reinforced. In fact, he was losing strength as enlistment terms of a number of volunteer regiments expired and the men returned home. Hooker still had the advantage in terms of size and, certainly, logistical support, but the numbers were much closer than they had been or would be again: Hooker had some eighty-five thousand to ninety thousand men, while Lee had about seventy thousand.

From Buffalo Gap on June 2 Imboden communicated the loss of the 25th and 31st Regiments, as well as his own reaction to the forthcoming Confederate offensive:

> In the constantly changing vicissitudes of this great struggle for the maintenance of the rights of freemen, the heroic & faithful 25th & 31st Virginia Regiments now a part of this Brigade, are called upon for another display of that gallantry & devotion to our sacred cause which have so eminently distinguished them during the two last eventful years.
>
> In the opinion & by the order of the great Commander of our armies in Virginia, Genl Lee, the exigencies of the country require their separation from this Brigade, at least for the present. In communicating this fact to the Brigade, I would be unjust to myself if I failed to express the feeling of profound personal regret which the separation excites. A few weeks ago we met as strangers to each other but the arduous service in which, during the time we have been engaged, has made us acquainted, and has made us friends in that solid & enduring basis which has ever characterized the ties of soldiers in a common cause of right & justice. . . .
> When we were united in April it was hoped that we would not be separated again during the war. I believe however that the present separation is necessary and has been ordered for wise & controlling considerations of public policy—and I hope it will be but temporary and that in a few weeks we will be again united in our

native mountains and that when you return to the Brigade it will be with fresh laurels upon new battle fields when the genius of Lee & Southern valour will again & again prove to the world that our hated foe can never triumph.

Till we meet again God bless & protect the 25th & 31st.[5]

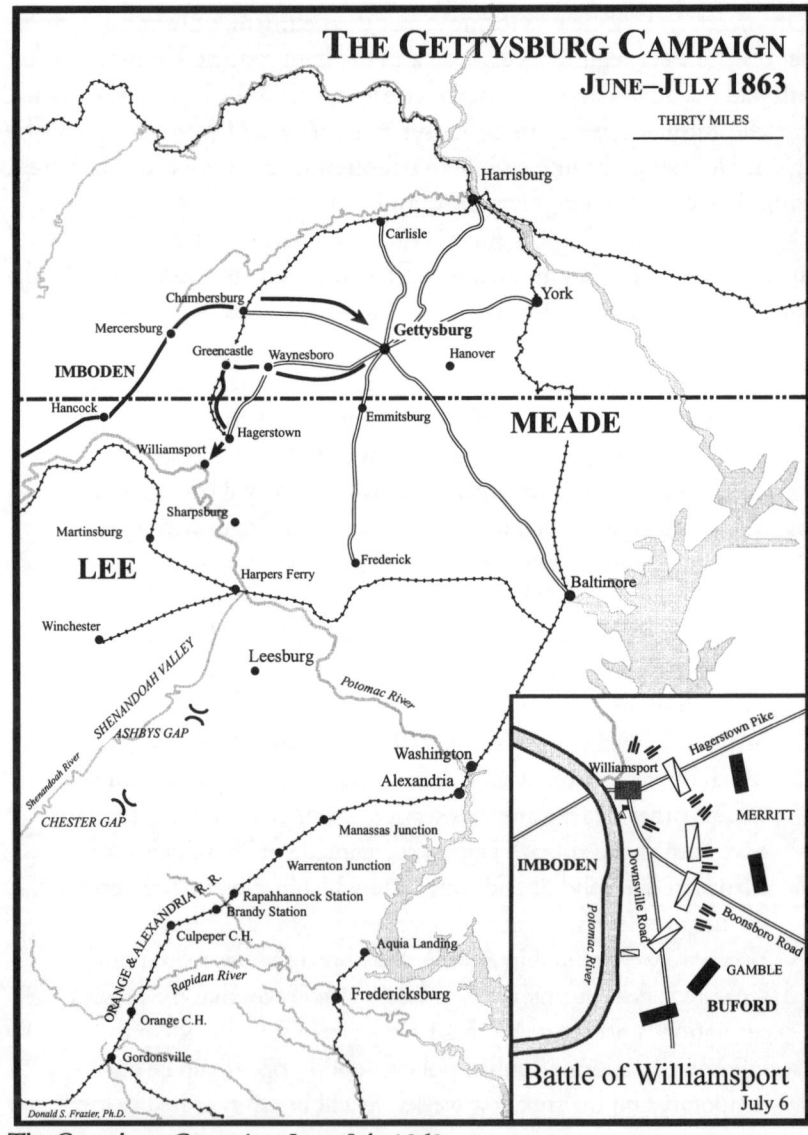

The Gettysburg Campaign, June–July 1863

On June 3 Lee set his army in motion west toward Culpepper. Hooker followed on a parallel track, keeping the Army of the Potomac between Lee's Army of Northern Virginia and Washington. The Shenandoah Valley provided Lee a secure route northward as the Blue Ridge Mountains and South Mountain in Maryland masked his forces.

On June 7 and June 10 Lee issued specific instructions to Imboden for the campaign. Imboden was to detach a "sufficient guard" on Shenandoah Mountain. Then as soon as possible he would move with the bulk of his command down the Shenandoah Valley and into the Hampshire Valley along the South Branch of the Potomac River. There, he was to distract Union forces by threatening Romney or some other convenient location. Lee hoped Imboden could create sufficient diversion to tie down a large number of Union troops as well as prevent Union reinforcements from reaching Winchester. He also called on Imboden to inflict whatever damage possible, including destruction of railroad bridges. Finally, he instructed Imboden to try to obtain cattle for the army and recruit both cavalry and infantry for his own brigade.[6]

On June 8 the Northwestern Brigade got underway. With 2,100 men and six guns, it consisted of the 18th Virginia Cavalry (led by Col. George W. Imboden), the 62d Virginia Infantry (led by Col. George H. Smith), a company of the Virginia Partisan Rangers (led by Capt. John H. McNeill), and an artillery battery (led by Capt. John H. McClanahan). As the brigade moved northwest into Hampshire County, its members rounded up cattle and horses. Thanks to the many horses thus secured, Imboden's command was soon one of the best mounted in the invading Confederate Army. As it moved north the brigade destroyed a major railroad bridge across the South Branch of the Potomac by firing solid artillery shot at the support beams. The bridge collapsed on the eleventh shot.

Lee directed that Imboden support Ewell and operate on his left flank. Ewell and his II Corps defeated General Milroy at Winchester and then prepared to invade Maryland. Imboden, meanwhile, crossed into Maryland at Hancock, then launched a series of strikes against the B&O, felling the important bridges in the vicinity. Imboden had divided his force as it advanced toward the Susquehanna, sending part of it against the Chesapeake & Ohio Canal near Cumberland, Maryland, to damage dams and locks. Imboden hoped that widely separated damage would prevent rapid repairs.[7]

Over a twelve-day span Imboden's men disrupted Federal communication with the West by driving off Federal defenders, dropping a half dozen B&O bridges from Martinsburg to Cumberland, and destroying rolling stock, depots, water tanks, and several blockhouses. He also cut the Chesapeake & Ohio Canal in two places where there was a forty-foot high embankment, removing the entire embankment for about fifty yards.[8]

Lee was pleased with Imboden's destruction of the bridges. He was especially "gratified" over Imboden's success at gathering in large numbers of cattle and horses, both of which were in short supply. These were, according to Lee, "not only important but essential, and I request that you do all in your power to obtain all you can." Lee urged Imboden to cross the Potomac "should you find an opportunity." He was to repress any "marauding," take only the supplies necessary, and give receipts to the owners for any property taken, "the valuation to be made according to the market price in the country where the article is taken." Lee also ordered that Imboden destroy all letters from him after reading them and memorizing their main points. Finally, he was always to station his forces to Ewell's left and keep all the "upper routes" open for the "return of the army, should circumstances render it necessary or convenient."[9]

At the same time, Lee ordered the commander of the Department of Western Virginia, Maj. Gen. Samuel Jones, to threaten Federal garrisons in West Virginia and, if possible, mount a real attack there. The wider the invasion front, the better. Such activity would dissipate Federal resources and provide a larger area from which to draw resources.[10]

Norval Baker, a private in Company F, 18th Virginia Cavalry, noted that in a raid into Pennsylvania his unit captured several hundred horses and that these, when added to those captured in Cumberland, were sufficient to mount the 62d Virginia Regiment.[11] Union commanders viewed this activity quite differently. Brig. Gen. Daniel Tylor reported, "Imboden has been out into Pennsylvania, stealing horses and plundering."[12]

Once Imboden's Brigade was in Pennsylvania, it was to continue as a screen for Lee and secure needed supplies for the Army of Northern

Virginia. Rejoining Lee would be up to Imboden, who apparently decided that the "opportunity" did not present itself.[13]

By the end of June Lee had all of his army north of the Potomac. While Imboden was on Lee's left flank, Major General Stuart's cavalry was to be on his right. Lee now lost touch with both Stuart and Imboden. This was an important development, as Lee relied on Stuart implicitly. An inveterate headline hunter, Stuart was also a capable cavalry commander, and Lee counted on him to provide vital intelligence on Hooker's whereabouts and strength. But Stuart had run into trouble. During the march north, Stuart discovered that Hooker's men had blocked crossings he hoped to use, and as a result he had been pushed further east. Instead of rejoining Lee in thirty-six hours as planned, it took Stuart a week. Stuart's reputation for absolute reliability led Lee to surmise that the Army of the Potomac was still in its camps in northern Virginia. From June 27 to June 28 Lee assumed that all of the mounted forces were doing their duty and that all was well, but there was concern that no information was being received about Union movements.

By June 28, however, Lee's army was dangerously dispersed over a forty-five-mile crescent. Ewell was off to the east, threatening Harrisburg and York; Lt. Gen. Ambrose P. Hill was poised to move after him; and Lt. Gen. James Longstreet was with Lee at Chambersburg. Meanwhile, on June 25 Hooker's entire army had crossed north of the Potomac unobserved by the Confederates.

Lee was thus shocked on the evening of June 28 to learn from a Confederate spy that Hooker's entire army was massing in the vicinity of Frederick, Maryland. It was in fact much closer to the separate pieces of his army than those pieces were to each other. Lee would be destroyed if he did not concentrate at once.

That night Lee sent couriers to call the army together at Cashtown, some eight miles northwest of Gettysburg, a small but important road hub. The Army of the Potomac was also hurrying toward Gettysburg. The Federal troops moving there were no longer Hooker's army. He had lost the confidence of leaders in Washington, and on June 28—with a major battle clearly in the offing—Lincoln had made the difficult decision to replace him with V Corps commander Maj. Gen. George Gordon Meade.

Meade was the fifth commander of the Army of the Potomac in ten months. Ordered to keep his forces between Washington and Lee's army, Meade came in from the south to Gettysburg while Lee came from the northwest. Sometime before July 1, Lee received news of the change in command of the Army of the Potomac. Although Lee had a higher opinion of Meade as a commander than of Hooker, it did not affect his plans. Indeed, he had to assume that the period of adjustment that inevitably followed installation of a new commander would be beneficial to him.[14]

While this was transpiring, Imboden's Northwestern Brigade was moving north. The brigade found the people of Pennsylvania decidedly unfriendly. Capt. Frank Imboden noted in his diary for June 23–24 that his men had seized many "stores" and "articles." He spent June 24 "in the disagreeable occupation of impressing horses. The people we found in Fulton Co. . . . exceedingly hostile to the . . . S. Government."[15]

Imboden subsequently took position at Hancock, and, after Longstreet and Hill arrived at Chambersburg, Lee directed that Imboden march by way of McConnellsburg, Pennsylvania, to Chambersburg to relieve Maj. Gen. George E. Pickett's Division. The reserve trains of the army were parked between Greenwood and Cashtown, and Lee ordered Imboden to secure that area, control the road from Greencastle to Greenwood, and "pay particular attention to the safety of the trains, which are for the present placed under your charge, and upon the safety of which the operations of the army depend."[16]

At McConnellsburg on June 19 the Northwestern Brigade sustained its first reverse. Company G of the 18th Virginia Cavalry, led by Capt. William D. Erwin, was surprised by Capt. Abram Jones's company of the 1st New York (Lincoln) Cavalry. Two men were killed, and Erwin, Lieutenant Jordan, and twenty-two others were taken prisoner—evidently the result of their own carelessness. Lee rebuked Imboden over this event: "I hope it will have the effect of teaching proper circumspection in future."[17]

From McConnellsburg, Imboden's Brigade moved to Mercersburg on June 30 and camped there. The absence of Stuart and the failure of Imboden and Robertson to come to Chambersburg on their own forced Lee to leave behind General Pickett's strong infantry division of three brigades to do the work of cavalry in guarding his rear area. Longstreet recalled that the loss of this division to him early in the battle of

Gettysburg had provoked Lee's wrath as did few events of the war. It made such an impression on Longstreet that he in fact mentioned it twice in his memoirs as one of the few examples of Lee's having lost his temper. Longstreet reported that this occurred on July 1 over Imboden's men at Hancock.[18]

On June 30 the Northwestern Brigade had moved from near Mercersburg to close to Greencastle. The men insisted that the citizens of Mercersburg contribute bacon and flour. On July 1 the brigade passed through Greencastle and moved to two miles south of Chambersburg.[19]

This move would release Pickett's Division for duty in the front line and establish a cavalry screen along the roads converging on the Chambersburg-Gettysburg Pike near Greenwood. But far more vexing to Lee was Stuart's continued absence. Stuart's well-trained cavalrymen were indispensable.[20]

Preliminary contact between the Army of Northern Virginia and the Army of the Potomac began at Gettysburg on June 30 between part of A.P. Hill's force and Union Brig. Gen. John Buford's cavalry division. Both sides poured men forward, though Lee was upset that his subordinate commanders had forced the battle on him by prematurely engaging Union troops. If he had to fight the entire Army of the Potomac, he wanted to do it from prepared positions at Cashtown, some eight miles northwest of Gettysburg. Instead, at Gettysburg, it was the Confederates who would be attacking strong Union defensive positions.

The two sides were actually quite evenly matched. Lee probably brought 75,000 men to Gettysburg, while Meade had about 85,500 effectives. The two sides were about equal in terms of arms and equipment, as well, although Meade had more artillery than Lee (362–374 artillery tubes in the Army of the Potomac to 272–281 guns for the Army of Northern Virginia), somewhat superior ammunition, and greater uniformity in equipment. The Federal infantry was exhausted and hungry, however, after a well-planned and executed, albeit forced, march to the battlefield. All things considered, the two armies were fairly even. Never again would Lee have such an excellent opportunity to defeat his opponent under conditions that would bring about the results he sought.[21]

The Battle of Gettysburg lasted three days. July 1 was a Confederate victory; July 2 was a draw; and July 3 went to the Union forces. On the first day the Confederates drove Union forces back through Gettysburg to strong positions on Cemetery Hill to the west and Culp's Hill to the east. The Union position, anchored on these two hills, was about three miles in length. It ran from the hills south along Cemetery Hill to Little Round Top and Round Top. Known by its shape as the Fishhook, it gave Union defenders the advantage of interior lines. The Confederates occupied Seminary Ridge, a long, partially wooded rise to the east of, running north-south, parallel to the Union position. Buford's stand on July 1 had purchased valuable time to allow Union reinforcements to come up, but this was at high cost: of eighteen thousand Federals who fought on July 1, only a third remained.

On the morning of July 2 as the Army of Northern Virginia was preparing to assault the Union lines, Imboden's Brigade arrived at Chambersburg, twenty miles to the west, to serve as rear guard for Lee's army. There Imboden's Brigade released Pickett's three Virginia brigades for immortality and the bloodbath of the last day of battle. Protecting the rear guard of the army would normally have fallen to Stuart's cavalry, but Stuart did not arrive at Lee's headquarters until later that same day.

The second day of the battle was the day of heaviest fighting, and it clearly revealed the advantage of the Union defensive position. In contrast to the Federals' interior lines, the Confederates were operating on exterior lines, extending about six miles. Meade was thus able to shift troops and supplies more quickly than Lee, and he could communicate more effectively than his Confederate counterpart.

Longstreet urged a movement around and behind the Union forces, cutting them off from the rear. Lee, however, planned a two-prong attack on the two flanks of the Union line. They were to be semi-simultaneous, but orders reached Longstreet an hour late and an additional two hours were lost maneuvering to avoid Union lookouts on Little Round Top.

The Confederate attack on the two Round Tops to the south came two to three hours before Ewell's attack on Culp's Hill on the Union right. Lee gave his corps commanders great discretion, but Ewell was no Jackson and it was the first time he had commanded a corps in battle. Longstreet drove back the Union defenders but failed to take Little Round Top, which would have enabled him to enfilade the entire Union line. Col. Joshua Chamberlain's 20th Maine Regiment, badly outnumbered on Little Round Top, anchored the left flank of the Union line and, in a desperate charge, threw back the attackers.

Meanwhile Ewell attacked Culp's Hill, but his forces were finally driven back. Early was also driven off Cemetery Hill. His attack came at 8:00 P.M., a desperate after-dark assault. The second day thus ended in a draw.

Imboden and his brigade had no role in the Battle of Gettysburg itself. Part of the brigade was close to Gettysburg in order to protect against a possible cavalry raid, and from their positions those men nearest the battlefield could see part of the action on the Little Round Top. Frank Imboden wrote in his diary for July 3, "Witnessed at a distance the great battle of Gettysburg."[22]

On the third day, July 3, having tried the flanks and failing, Lee proposed to attack the center of the Union line. Longstreet opposed this course of action. Union forces were now stronger, thanks to continuing reinforcements. Moreover, Maj. Gen. Winfield Scott Hancock—perhaps the best Union general on the field—commanded II Corps in the center of the line. Yet Lee planned a massive frontal assault with Stuart's cavalry sweeping around the Union line to the north and back in behind it from the east.

As it worked out, Stuart's cavalry was halted five miles east of the battlefield and there defeated by Union cavalry under Brig. Gens. David M. Gregg and George A. Custer. The infantry advance against the center of the Union line went forward, preceded by the greatest artillery duel in the history of North America. Pickett welcomed the glory of the attack, which included his own and two other divisions. Only a small portion of the attackers reached the Union line, where desperate hand-to-hand fighting ensued. Finally, the Confederates were driven back. The 12,000-man, nine-brigade Confederate assault force sustained about 7,500 casualties in the attempt.

Lee had made his best effort against the largest Union army and had come up short. He halfway expected and certainly hoped that Meade might then attack him. Yet the only realistic opportunity for a strike by the Union side was in the immediate aftermath of Pickett's charge, and Meade's force was then too disorganized and had suffered too many casualties itself for him to attempt it. Besides, Meade refused to oblige Lee in repaying the favor of a long charge by infantry over open ground against artillery and rifled muskets. Lee held his ground early on July 4, as both armies licked their wounds and prepared for the renewal of battle.

Lee undoubtedly hoped that Meade would repeat his own mistake of attacking prepared defensive positions across open ground. When Meade refused to attack, Lee was forced to decamp. It was either escape or be destroyed. The Battle of Gettysburg was over.

Imboden himself did not arrive in the vicinity of the battlefield until about noon on July 3. He may have been involved in an attempt early that morning to destroy the iron Mill Creek Railroad Bridge over the Juniata River near Mount Union. A report on the evening of July 2 that Imboden's men were planning to attack there had led to a strong Union reinforcement. When the Confederate cavalry appeared at 2:00 A.M. on July 3, the Union troops easily repulsed them near Bear Valley Pass about six hundred yards from the bridge defenses.[23]

In any case, at about 11:00 P.M. on July 3 a courier arrived with a summons for Imboden to report to Lee. Imboden immediately mounted and, accompanied by his aide, Lt. George W. McPhail, took the road to Gettysburg. After riding for several miles they found Lee's headquarters, located in a meadow. Inquiring after Lee, Imboden was informed that he had gone to meet with General Hill at the latter's headquarters perhaps a half mile closer to Gettysburg. Imboden then rode there, located Hill's tent, and found Lee and Hill sitting on camp stools studying a map by candlelight. He dismounted and approached the two generals but was told to return to Lee's headquarters and wait for Lee there.[24]

When Lee finally returned to his tent, riding up alone at a slow walk at about 1:00 A.M. on July 4, Imboden recalled him as being in deep thought. Years later, Imboden described the scene in these words:

> When he arrived there was not even a sentinel on duty at this tent, and no one of his staff was awake. The moon was high in the clear sky and the silent scene was unusually vivid. As he approached and saw us lying on the grass under a tree, he spoke, reined in his jaded horse, and essayed to dismount. The effort to do so betrayed so much physical exhaustion that I hurriedly rose and stepped forward to assist him, but before I reached his side he had succeeded in alighting, and threw his arm across the

saddle to rest, and fixing his eyes upon the ground leaned in silence and almost motionless upon his equally weary horse,— the two forming a striking and never-to-be-forgotten group. The moon shone full upon his massive features and revealed an expression of sadness that I had never before seen upon his face. Awed by his appearance I waited for him to speak until the silence became embarrassing.[25]

Imboden wrote that to break the silence he finally remarked to Lee, "General, this has been a hard day on you."

Lee then replied, "Yes, it has been a sad, sad day to us." He then relapsed into silence, but after a minute or two he straightened up, turned to Imboden, and remarked in a voice full of emotion:
I never saw troops behave more magnificently than Pickett's division of Virginians did to-day in that grand charge upon the enemy. And if they had been supported as they were to have been,—but for some reason not yet fully explained to me, were not,—we would have held the position and the day would have been ours.
Lee then added in an anguished tone, "Too bad, *Too bad!* OH! TOO BAD!"[26]

Imboden recalled, "I shall never forget his language, his manner, and his appearance of mental suffering." Within a few moments, Imboden wrote, Lee had suppressed his emotions but spoke movingly of several fallen officers, including Brig. Gens. Lewis Armistead, Richard Garnett, and James Kemper.

Imboden said that Lee then invited him into his tent and, when they were seated, announced, "We must now return to Virginia." He had sent for Imboden, he said, because his men and horses were fresh, and for that reason they would be assigned the vital task of protecting the supply train. "The duty," Imboden reported Lee as saying, "would be arduous, responsible, and dangerous" because of the likelihood of harassment by Union cavalry. Lee then inquired as to his numbers, which Imboden gave as 2,100 men, all of whom were well mounted. This included McClanahan's six-gun battery of horse artillery.

Lee promised as much extra artillery as Imboden needed but no additional manpower. Lee said he would need as many men as possible in order to retreat by a different and shorter route than the one Imboden would be taking. Imboden would be able to secure artillery ammunition from a supply that Lee had ordered sent from Winchester to Williamsport. Lee entrusted Imboden with the care and transportation of nearly all the Confederate wounded. Imboden was to cross South Mountain on the Chambersburg Road, then move to Williamsport by whatever route he thought best. Imboden was not to halt until he reached the Potomac, resting there only long enough to feed the animals. He would then ford the river, again marching without halt until he reached Winchester, where Lee would again communicate with him.

Imboden reported that the two men then discussed roads and the best disposition of Imboden's force to cover the vast baggage train he would be escorting. Part of the Confederate baggage train would proceed south by way of Fairfield; the remainder, guarded by Imboden, would move by way of Cashtown. Lee then ordered the chiefs of his staff departments to appear and, in Imboden's presence, informed them of the need to ready the baggage trains and ambulances that Imboden would convoy south. All wounded capable of making the journey were to be placed in ambulances and empty supply wagons.

When Imboden finally departed Lee's headquarters at about 2:00 A.M., Lee told him that he would receive general instructions in writing later that morning. As Imboden was about to mount his horse, Lee told him that he would be entrusting him with a sealed package for President Davis. Imboden was to retain the package in his personal possession until he crossed the Potomac, then give it to an officer in whom he had complete confidence, who would take it to Richmond as quickly as possible and deliver it to Davis personally. Whatever happened, the package could not fall into Union hands; if captured, Imboden had been instructed to destroy it at the first opportunity.

As promised, later that morning Imboden received Lee's written instructions as well as a large official envelope addressed to Davis. Despite Lee's hopes that the baggage train could get underway that morning, however, it was late afternoon before the wagons and wounded were collected and ready to move. Lee fulfilled his pledge of additional artillery: Imboden received eight 12-pounder Napoleons from the Washington Artillery of New Orleans under Major Eshleman, a four-gun battery under Captain Tanner, and a Whitworth rifled gun under Lieutenant Pegram. Brig. Gen. Wade Hampton had been wounded in the Battle of Gettysburg, but his cavalry brigade, then commanded by Col. P.M.B. Young and accompanied by Capt. James F. Hart's four-gun battery of horse artillery, was assigned to cover the rear of all trains moving under Imboden's command along the Chambersburg Road. Counting McClanahan's six guns, Imboden had twenty-three artillery pieces.[27]

Lee also provided additional assurance to the train by ordering Maj. Gen. J.E.B. Stuart to send brigades under Brig. Gen. Fitzhugh Lee and Col. L.S. Baker to act as a rear guard.[28]

Late on July 4, the Army of Northern Virginia decamped as Lee began his retreat. That day was a difficult one for the Army. The smell of decaying bodies hung in the hot July air as burial details worked to entomb the dead. Doctors and ambulance drivers tried to do what they could to prepare those wounded who could be transported for the hazardous journey ahead. Shortly after noon it began to rain. The water fell in blinding sheets, turning fields into quagmires and streams into raging torrents. As the rain poured down, thousands of Confederate wagons, ambulances, and artillery carriages assembled in fields along the road from Gettysburg to Cashtown. Imboden remembered it as "one confused and apparently inextricable mass."[29]

The storm raged on. The canvas of the wagons provided little protection from the rain and lashing wind; the wounded, lying on the wooden boards of the wagon beds, were soon drenched. Horses and mules, blinded by the wind and rain, were almost unmanageable.

Finally, at about 4:00 P.M. Imboden gave the order for the head of the column near Cashtown to set out, beginning the ascent of the mountain road toward Chambersburg. Luther Hopkins of the 6th Virginia Cavalry recalled that he was grazing his horse that evening when he heard "a low rumbling sound . . . resembling distant thunder, except that it was continuous. . . . a number of us rose to our feet and saw a long line of wagons with their white covers moving . . . along the Chambersburg Road. . . . The wagons going back over the same road that had brought us to Gettysburg told the story, and soon the whole army knew the fact. This was the first time Lee's army had ever met defeat."[30]

Imboden remained behind at Cashtown, giving orders and inserting artillery detachments every quarter to third of a mile or so. By dawn on July 5, when the last of the column left its positions near Gettysburg and Young's Cavalry—accompanied by Hart's Battery—began its ascent of Cashtown Gap in South Mountain near Cashtown, the entire column stretched over seventeen miles. One participant recalled, "It was the longest wagon train I ever saw, some said it was 27 to 30 miles long."[31]

Imboden ordered that there be no halt whatsoever. If a wagon became disabled, it was to be pulled off the road and abandoned. Col. George Imboden's 18th Virginia Cavalry and a section of McClanahan's Battery led the column. With them was an ambulance carrying Brig. Gens. William Pender and Alfred Scales, both determined to bear the torture of travel by wagon to Virginia rather than become prisoners. Both men survived the trip, but by the time Pender's thigh wound had received proper medical attention, massive infection had set in, forcing amputation of his leg. He did not survive the operation. Scales, however, recuperated from his wounds and returned to fight the remainder of the war.[32]

Night had fallen by the time Imboden left Cashtown and began working his way to the head of the column. He recalled:

> For four hours I hurried forward on my way to the front, and in all that time I was never out of hearing of the groans and cries of the wounded and dying. Scarcely one in a hundred had received adequate surgical aid, owing to the demands on the hardworking surgeons from still worse cases that had to be left behind. Many of the wounded in the wagons had been without food for thirty-six hours. Their torn and bloody clothing, matted and hardened, was rasping the tender, inflamed, and still oozing wounds. Very few of the wagons had even a layer of straw in them, and all were without springs. The road was rough and rocky from the heavy washings of the previous day. The jolting was enough to have killed strong men, if long exposed to it. . . .
> . . . No heed could be given to any of their appeals. Mercy and duty to the many forbade the loss of a moment in the vain effort then and there to comply with the prayers of the few. . . .

The storm continued, and the darkness was appalling. There was no time even to fill a canteen with water for a dying man; for, except the drivers and the guards, all were wounded and utterly helpless in that vast procession of misery. During this one night I realized more of the horrors of war than I had in all the previous two years.[33]

Private Baker of the 18th Virginia Cavalry wrote in his diary:

'Twas an awful night, it rained all night, one thunder storm after another. The rain fell in sheets and vivid flashes of lightning and so dark we could not see our hand an inch from our eyes when there was no lightning. The roar of the waters and heavy bursting thunder, the cries of the wounded and dying soldiers made it awful.[34]

Yet, as Imboden was well aware, darkness was the ally of the retreating Army of Northern Virginia. He and all those in the train knew that with dawn Union cavalry could be expected at any point along the column. Thus the goal was to cover as much ground as possible by first light.

Another participant, Randolph Shotwell of the 8th Virginia Infantry, described the retreat in these words:

Soon the difficulty of the road which was narrow and rocky, added to the drenching rain, and the bottomless mud, caused the trains to become crowded, and embarrassed, filling the highways and rendering the movements of the footmen, i.e., the prisoners and their guards exceedingly wearisome.

Wagons, ambulances, artillery, cavalry, stragglers, wounded soldiers, Yankees, and guards were irretrievably mixed, and the continued succession of momentary halts, to be followed by a rapid trot of a 100 yards, and then another halt, resulting from the breaking down of wagons, or difficulty in passing mud holes, were so inconceivably vexatious, and fatiguing that I have often wondered why all the prisoners did not escape for the guards became almost indifferent, especially in the confusion after dark, when the crowded trains were painfully toiling up the winding pass at Cashtown. Doubtless more of the prisoners would have escaped had they not been too near physical and mental exhaustion to have the necessary energy.

We bivouacked at the top of Cashtown Pass in a wet swampy meadow where the water arose around our bodies as we lay in the dark grass. Fire was out of the question even if there had been fuel, for the rain fell increasingly, and of food we had none. During the day I had kept up with the moving mass through energy born of despair—a kind of reckless desperation of endurance. But this night threatened to be too much straw for the camel's back.[35]

It is unclear why Shotwell would have bivouacked that night. Imboden, his brother Frank, and Private Baker all recalled the column as moving all night.[36]

The Valley Pike ran north-south through Chambersburg, but to connect with that would mean further movement north-northwest, in effect away from their goal. Thus, on crossing South Mountain, Imboden decided to avoid Chambersburg altogether. The baggage train traveled west to Greenwood, then left the main road and headed southwest on the Pine Stump Road, passing through New Guilford and New Franklin. From there it proceeded on to Marion, six miles south of Chambersburg. The column then struck south to Greencastle, which the head of the train reached by dawn on July 5. The men had covered about forty miles and were then about twelve to fifteen miles from the Potomac at Williamsport, where presumably they could cross into Virginia and safety.

At Greencastle, however, the column came under attack by civilians. After the advance guard 18th Virginia Cavalry was about a mile past the town, some thirty to forty townspeople attacked the wagons with axes, cutting the spokes of ten or twelve of them and dropping the wagons in the streets. On learning of this activity, Imboden immediately sent cavalry to apprehend as many of the guilty as possible and treat them as prisoners of war. This stopped the partisan activity, but now a more serious threat appeared, in the form of Union cavalry.[37]

Unaware of the actual conditions at Gettysburg, Lincoln was convinced that only half a battle had been won there. He wanted Lee's army cut off in the North and destroyed. If this could be done, then the war would be practically over. He applied pressure on Meade to attack and destroy Lee's retreating army, pressure that his field commander resisted.

Meade believed he had good reasons not to engage in a precipitous pursuit. His army had sustained heavy casualties at Gettysburg. He believed his men needed rest, and he was convinced that Lee could not get across the Potomac because of rising water from recent heavy rains. In any case, he was mindful of Halleck's instructions always to keep his own army between Lee's army and Washington.

It was in fact unfair of Lincoln to accuse Meade of desiring merely to maneuver Lee back out of the North without resuming the fight. Meade wanted to engage Lee, preferably in the North rather than in Virginia, but he also insisted that such an engagement occur on terms that would be favorable to him. Meade did, however, order out a reconnaissance in force under Brig. Gen. Gouverneur K. Warren and Maj. Gen. John Sedgwick to ascertain Lee's intentions. Meade planned to move only when he was certain that Lee's troops had entered the mountain passes. Learning from other sources that Lee was in full retreat, however, late on the morning of July 5 Meade ordered a general movement of the Army of the Potomac toward Maryland.[38]

On the night of July 4–5 Union cavalry under Brig. Gen. Judson Kilpatrick arrived at Fairfield. They easily swept aside Robertson's pickets but then ran into a company of the 1st Maryland Cavalry with one gun. The Marylanders' fierce resistance in the darkness threw off Kilpatrick. Finally he ordered Brig. Gen. George A. Custer to charge. The defenders were then swept away, and the attackers took some of Ewell's baggage train and captured prisoners, mostly among the wounded in the ambulances.[39]

Lee matter-of-factly noted the impossibility of guarding the long trains completely: "In passing through mountains in advance of this column, the great length of the trains exposed them to attack by the enemy's cavalry, which captured a number of wagons and ambulances, but they succeeded in reaching Williamsport without serious loss."[40]

Meanwhile, Sedgwick's and Warren's men got underway by noon on July 5. With Meade's approval they took the entire VI Corps, but the formation was not such as to produce a rapid advance. Finally late in the afternoon Brig. Gen. A.T.A. Torbert's 1st Brigade of the 1st Division ran into Ewell's rear guard near Fairfield. In the resulting skirmish the Confederates were able to hold the Union forces at bay with their pickets. The engagement did, however, cause Meade to shift his army toward Fairfield, where he now believed the bulk of Lee's forces to be located.

Early on July 6 Meade ordered Sedgwick to push forward vigorously with his entire corps. To this point, Sedgwick and Warren had chosen to interpret Meade's instructions conservatively, and they had no intention of initiating a battle. They had merely followed the retreating Confederates at a safe distance without ordering supporting units up. Even on July 6 Sedgwick had allowed a stiffening of Confederate resistance to stop the forward movement of his troops. On July 5–6, while the Confederate troops were still in motion, Sedgwick might have brought on a general engagement. A thrust against Ewell would have caused Lee to turn and strike back, for he had already told Ewell that he would do so. Instead the Union advance continued only to the top of Monterey Pass, just above the Maryland state line. The Confederates were allowed to continue down the other side unmolested. Thus Sedgwick's remark after the campaign that Meade might have pressed Lee more aggressively would appear to be mere posturing.

Indeed, Sedgwick informed Meade that he was convinced the Confederates held the passes in force and that a small Confederate force could delay any Union effort there for some time. Meade then abandoned his plan of simply following after Lee and ordered Sedgwick to proceed south on a parallel track east of Lee, to Emmitsburg. Meanwhile, Meade detached a brigade and a battery from Sedgwick's corps. Reinforced by a brigade of cavalry, these were to keep in contact with the retreating Confederates and provide constant word of their movements to Meade. The Union commander then ordered the rest of his army to resume its march to Middletown.[41]

As Meade's infantry moved south toward Maryland, elements of his cavalry ranged westward to attack the Confederate wagon train moving south toward Williamsport. Kilpatrick's raid against Ewell's baggage train early on July 5 was replicated by a foray of Col. Lewis B. Pierce's cavalry that attacked wagons belonging to Stuart's Division on the road to Greencastle in Imboden's convoy.[42]

The Union cavalry struck in small groups, coming up at crossroads or across fields. They hit different locations, trying to select points where there were few or no guards. When word reached the escorting Confederate cavalrymen, they rode to the rescue. Unable to use the road because of the congestion of the baggage train, the defending cavalry reached the attackers by using the fields on either side of the road. Imboden recalled that in one instance he had McClanahan's guns fire canister against a group of about fifty Union cavalrymen, but their numbers were such that Imboden would have been captured had not his brother George, having heard the firing, arrived on the gallop with a detachment of cavalry, surrounding and capturing the entire Union force.[43]

The Union cavalry achieved limited success. Pierce claimed ninety wagons taken along with one artillery piece and 645 soldiers—more than half of whom had been wounded at Gettysburg. General Stuart reported sixty wagons lost "while in the special charge of General Imboden," but made no mention of an artillery piece or prisoners. Maj. Gen. Darius Couch reduced Pierce's figures of wagons taken while increasing the number of prisoners. Frank Imboden noted a Union cavalry attack at about 10:00 A.M. that "carried off many waggons [*sic*], rifled 12 pr. & 100 prisoners. Pursued them & recaptured everything, with one Yank Capt. & 10 men." Captain Imboden lost three men killed and several wounded in the operation. He also reported in his diary that later one hundred wagons and more than four hundred wounded were captured by the 1st New Jersey Cavalry. Stuart was angry enough over the loss of his wagons that he demanded a court of inquiry to investigate it, but the results are unknown.[44]

Adding to his anxieties, Imboden received word that Union troops held Williamsport. Despite this, he decided to push on. Fortunately for the Confederates, the report proved unfounded. Most all of the baggage train reached Williamsport late on the afternoon of July 5. The bulk of the remainder, along with Hart's Battery, arrived early on July 6, Young having halted in order to guard the road from the west.

Williamsport is located on a horseshoe bend on the Potomac at the juncture of that river and Conococheague Creek, which empties into the Potomac from the north. These two streams enclosed the town to the south and west. Behind Williamsport there is a low range of hills a mile distant. Four roads then converged on the town: the Greencastle

Road (Valley Pike), the Hagerstown Road, the Boonsboro Road, and the River Road.

The Confederates now turned Williamsport into a vast hospital for their wounded. The surgeons who had accompanied the train immediately went to work to try to alleviate the suffering of those who had not been properly attended. Those wounded who had died in the movement from Gettysburg were buried. Imboden ordered the local families to cook for the sick and wounded, threatening those who refused with having their kitchens taken over for that purpose by his men.[45]

Imboden's men also requisitioned a quantity of flour from a nearby mill, bought some bacon from a local merchant, and secured wheat, straw, and hay for the animals.[46] Two fresh regiments had arrived, detailed to hold the river crossing: the 54th North Carolina of Brig. Gen. Robert F. Hoke's Brigade, which had come up from Staunton, and the 58th Virginia of Smith's Brigade.

The temporary halt at Williamsport was necessary because the Potomac was in flood. The heavy rains had raised the river to ten feet above fording depth, and it was impossible for the wagons to cross. On his arrival, Imboden immediately requisitioned two small ferry boats ("flats") and pressed them into service for the less seriously wounded, of whom there were a considerable number. Having been fed and their wounds dressed, they were taken across the river in these ferries. Once in Virginia they were instructed to walk to Winchester.

Because there were so many walking wounded, the ferries were kept in constant service. Operating on a wire rope, the ferries could make a crossing in about seven minutes. On their return trip the ferries brought back ammunition and supplies. Meanwhile, the wagons were jammed along the banks of the river under a bluff and in the streets of the town.

Still, the situation was difficult. Imboden estimated the baggage train included perhaps ten thousand animals, nearly all of the wagons of Lee's Army of Northern Virginia, and several thousand wounded from Gettysburg. Yet supplies were very short. Imboden had several wagons of flour in his own baggage train, a small number of cattle collected in Pennsylvania during the advance to Gettysburg, and some sugar and coffee taken at Mercersburg.[47]

Early on July 6 Imboden learned of a large number of Federal cavalry approaching from the direction of Frederick, twenty-five miles to the southeast. This was the force under Buford and Kilpatrick. For the first time in over a week Buford had all three of his brigades together, a total of some four thousand men, which Imboden mistakenly calculated at seven thousand. Buford had learned of the baggage train and sought to destroy it before it could get across the Potomac.

Buford's Division left Frederick for Williamsport at 4:00 A.M. No doubt Maj. Gen. William H. French, who had his headquarters at Frederick, had informed Buford that the Potomac was up to the point that the fords across it could not be used. Buford hoped to destroy the Confederates before they could reach safety.

Imboden recalled that on learning of the Federal advance, he positioned his artillery on the hills to cover the approach and dismounted his own men to support them. He also ordered as many of the wagoners as possible to arm themselves with weapons belonging to the wounded from Gettysburg. Wounded officers able to get about assisted Imboden in this, including Col. J.L. Black, Capt. J.F. Hart, and Col. William R. Aylett of Pickett's Division. By noon seven hundred wagoners had been organized into companies of some one hundred men each, commanded by the wounded officers and commissaries. Confederate walking wounded, commissaries, and quartermasters were also pressed into service.

Colonel Aylett had charge of about 250 of the wagoners on the right flank anchored on the Potomac, while Colonel Black had as many men on the left flank. The remaining wagoners were employed as skirmishers in front of the Confederate position. Imboden's own command held the center. Imboden said that his men well understood that if they could not hold, they would all be captured and Lee's army would lose all its transport, "which at that time could not be replaced in the Confederacy."[48]

Private Baker remembered the events differently and did not credit Imboden for the decision to arm the wagoners. Baker wrote in his diary: "The enemy had a large force of cannon and they had the air full of flying shells in a very short time and our little brigade the only organized army to fight them, but it happened that General Jones was either on the sick list or among the wounded, and came on the field. He saw how things stood and told General J.D. Imboden to do the best he could while he (Jones) went and armed the wagoners and sent them to the field. It was not long till we saw General Jones fetching out armed wagoners two and three hundred at a time and in every part of the field."[49]

The General Jones referred to could only have been Brig. Gen. John Marshall Jones, who commanded a brigade under Ewell. He had been wounded in fighting at Culp's Hill on July 2, but Imboden makes no mention of him as among the wounded in the train.

The first Federal troops arrived at about 1:30 P.M. along both the Frederick and Boonsboro Roads. The Union cavalry drove in the Confederate pickets around the town to within about a half mile of the parked baggage trains. The fight for control of the baggage trains opened around 2:00 P.M. with artillery fire on both sides; it continued until about an hour after dark. Rapid Confederate artillery fire caused hesitation in the Union ranks, but the Southern batteries soon began to run out of ammunition. This was replenished by the timely arrival from Winchester of an ammunition train. Two wagons full of ammunition were ferried across and run out onto the field; the boxes of ammunition were then tumbled out to be broken open with axes. Soon the Confederate guns were again firing rapidly.

Because most of the Confederate troops were concealed from Union view, Imboden said he employed a ruse to impress the attackers with their numbers. He had the men march up in ranks to the crests of the hills on the Hagerstown Road front fifty to one hundred yards in advance of the artillery positions. The men were then slowly withdrawn again. Imboden then shifted the dismounted 18th Virginia Cavalry and the 62d Virginia Mounted Infantry to the right in order to meet and repel Union advancing regiments, which were also dismounted. The Confederate right was soon heavily engaged. Seeing this, Captain Hart, commanding the Confederate left in Colonel Black's absence, charged the Union right flank, enfilading their line. At the same time Major Eshleman brought his eight Napoleons about four hundred yards forward, securing an enfilading position, where he poured heavy artillery fire into the Union line. The 62d Virginia and Aylett's wagoners, supported by the 18th Virginia Cavalry and Captain McNeill's Partisan Rangers, then charged the Union troops, who withdrew to their horses.[50]

As with so much of Imboden's military career, even this last is not without controversy. Private Baker credits Jones rather than Imboden with rallying the wagoners. He recalled in his diary: "We were supporting two batteries, we were all dismounted. After charging our line a few times, then they ran us on the double quick from one battery to the other till Jones got out all the wagoners. It was an awful hot sultry day and we had our side arms and sabres and all the straps, etc., a cavalry man has to carry which made it awful hard on us boys and our clothes were soaked with perspiration."[51]

Frank Imboden's diary entry for that day is quite succinct and sheds little light on events: "Command attacked by 13 regts. of Stonemans Cavalry. & 18 guns at Wmspt. Splendidly repulsed by Genl. Imboden with 2 regts. of Cav., 5 of Infantry, about 2 batteries & many organized stragglers. Even wagoners fought well."[52]

Lee, in his report to Adjutant General Cooper, did not dwell on the Union attack of July 6. He simply states that at Williamsport the Confederates "were attacked by a strong force of cavalry and artillery, which was gallantly repulsed by General Imboden."[53]

At the peak of the battle, Buford could hear Kilpatrick's guns off to the east in the direction of Hagerstown; as the sound grew louder, he sent word for Kilpatrick to reach out and connect with his right flank for mutual support.[54]

After his raid on Ewell's baggage train early on July 5, Kilpatrick had gone to Boonsboro, where he spent the night, regrouped, and turned over the prisoners and wagons to General French. On July 6, he had taken his command in the direction of Hagerstown, where he had been informed Stuart was located. Yet the Confederate force at Hagerstown was actually only two brigades, those under Col. John R. Chambliss and Brigadier General Robertson. Kilpatrick easily drove the Confederate cavalry from Hagerstown, but he then met Brig. Gen. Alfred Iverson's infantry which, in forced marches, had just arrived on the north side of the town. Iverson skillfully deployed and then drove the Union cavalry down the streets of Hagerstown. At that point, Stuart arrived on the scene with most of his men, save two brigades under Brig. Gen. Fitzhugh Lee. A part of Maj. Gen. John B. Hood's Division also came up. They drove the Union forces out and retook Hagerstown.

Kilpatrick now gave up trying to take Hagerstown and, in compliance with Buford's instructions, left a brigade under Col. Nathaniel P. Richmond to guard his rear; he then turned his command around to cooperate with Buford in attacking Imboden at Williamsport to the west. The joint attack by Buford and Kilpatrick failed, however, because of increased pressure by Stuart and the other Confederate forces at Hagerstown on Kilpatrick's rear and right flank. With Kilpatrick's men giving way, Buford's rear guard became exposed to attack. Buford then halted the attack and that night gradually withdrew his men to join Kilpatrick's command near Jones's Crossroads (Lappan) on the way to Boonsboro.[55]

With dusk approaching, word arrived from Brig. Gen. Fitzhugh Lee, urging Imboden to hold on for about a half an hour, until he could come to his aid with some three thousand men. The news was immediately conveyed to the defenders, who sent up a wild shout of excitement. The Confederates, sensing they had won the battle, then slowly advanced on the Union line. As they did so, they could hear the distant rumble of artillery to the rear of the Union lines on the right and toward Hagerstown. These were Stuart's men coming on that road. Fitzhugh Lee, meanwhile, was advancing from the north along the Greencastle Road. The Union forces then broke to their left and retreated by the Boonsboro Road. It was now about an hour after dark, and all chance of a Confederate pursuit had been lost by the time Fitzhugh Lee and his men arrived. Private Baker recalled, "We slept on the field with our guns that night, the rain came down like cloud-bursts and drenched us."[56]

Imboden estimated the losses in the Williamsburg fight to be 125 Union soldiers captured for about 125 Confederates lost. His brother Frank put Southern casualties at about 150 men killed and wounded, but assistant surgeon Isaac White of the 62d Virginia reported that his unit alone had 80 killed or wounded.[57]

Imboden particularly praised the wagoners, a number of whom were killed when they charged a farm from which Union sharpshooters were firing on Eshleman's artillery and picking off its men and horses. Imboden realized, however, that the battle could have gone either way: "A bold charge before sunset would have broken our feeble lines, and then we should all have fallen an easy prey to the Federals. The next day our army arrived from Gettysburg."[58]

Leaders on both sides in the battle claim it had been lost to superior numbers on the part of the other, but the two sides were actually fairly evenly matched, although the numbers did favor the Confederates as the fighting wore on. Imboden's force of 2,100 men—plus the 700 armed wagoners—had been augmented by two infantry regiments of Maj. Gen. Jubal A. Early's Division, some 600–700 men in all. Thus Imboden probably had something like 3,500 effectives, sufficient to deal with Buford's 4,000. Indeed, in his attack Buford had only employed two of his three brigades, holding the other in the rear in order to be able to utilize it to exploit any breakthrough or to cover a retreat if necessary. Then when Kilpatrick moved to assist, Stuart and Fitzhugh Lee were released to come to Imboden's rescue with 5,000 cavalry. In addition to this, there were 650 members of Brig. Gen. Alfred Iverson's Brigade, the vanguard of Lee's infantry, approaching Hagerstown. In his study of the Gettysburg Campaign, Edwin Coddington concludes that it should not have come as a surprise that Imboden was able to hold off Buford. "Though Imboden handled his forces well, for which achievement Stuart gave him no credit, he was not battling against the great odds he pictured so dramatically in his account."[59]

The Battle of Williamsport was Imboden's major contribution to the Gettysburg Campaign. The next evening, on July 7, the 18th Virginia Cavalry drove back Federal troops on a road to the northwest of Williamsport. Private Baker recalled, "It was our duty to look after these Yankees on this part of the line and not let them get too close to Williamsport till our wagons and infantry all passed over to the Virginia side of the river."[60]

Imboden's men remained at Williamsport for several more days and endured difficult conditions. Baker noted in his diary:

> It was an awful place, the dead horses and offal of the great number of beeves, etc., killed for the army packed around the little town made it very unpleasant for us when we returned to camp after night. The green flies were around us all the time and orders were not to unsaddle or unbridle our horses and be ready for duty all the time. Our blankets were under our saddles and soaked with water and the green flies were working under the rawhide covering of our saddles and ulcerated backs of our horses.... It was rush all the time, when we would go to camp for food and sleep, we would very likely be ordered out on the line again by the news of the outposts being attacked and drove

in, and then we would very likely spend the rest of the night looking for a fight.

This work was kept up for quite a while and quite a number of the soldiers fell with disease were sent to the Virginia side of the river with the wounded. We fed our horses on sheaf wheat and the beards made the horses' tongues sore (ulcerated). Our regiment was about a mile or so south of the river with orders to unsaddle our horses. Our horses' backs were raw with ulcers, one or two inches deep and full of maggots. The green flies had put up a big job on us, our blankets were full of maggots in them and we had to run them out with hot water and soap and it was months before the horses' backs were cured.[61]

The strain on cavalry horses in the war was considerable. Baker's horse's mouth and back were in "terrible condition," and, when she did not recover, he was forced to replace her, "which is four I have rode out of service." His former mount died a few days after he had purchased a fifth horse.[62]

Meanwhile, work of ferrying Confederate wounded and Union prisoners across the Potomac continued. It took two to three days just to get the four thousand Union prisoners across. This having been accomplished, on the morning of July 9 Lee ordered Imboden to take a single regiment, the 62d, and escort the prisoners to Staunton, from which point they would be sent on to Richmond. Lee had originally assigned Pickett's Division this task, but on Pickett's objection at being separated from the army, he reassigned it to Imboden. Lee expressed concern to Imboden that Union cavalry might cross over the Potomac at Harpers Ferry, intercept his force, and release the prisoners before they could make Winchester.[63]

Before he departed on the morning of July 9, Imboden met with Lee at his headquarters near Hagerstown. While he was there, Lee called in his quartermaster, Col. James L. Corley, and expressed his displeasure with the length of time it was taking to bridge the Potomac. Lee ordered Corley to put Maj. John Harman in charge. Harman and his men subsequently tore down a number of warehouses on the canal and used the wood to build boats, which were then floated down the river to Falling Waters, where they constructed a bridge.

Imboden recalled years later that while he was meeting with Lee in his headquarters tent, General Longstreet arrived. Imboden noted that Lee greeted him warmly with the words, "Well, my old warhorse, what news do you bring us from the front?" Imboden believed that Lee's cordial greeting of his subordinate was sufficient to put to rest stories of animosity between the two over Longstreet's alleged failure on the second day of the Gettysburg battle.

Imboden set out with his men and had already crossed the Potomac and gone several miles beyond the river when Lee's courier overtook him and ordered him to return immediately to Lee's headquarters. Imboden halted his column, recrossed the river, and overtook Lee close to Hagerstown, where he had gone with his staff on news of a major probe by Union forces against the Confederate defenses. Lee asked Imboden if he was familiar with fords across the Potomac from Williamsport to Cumberland and the roads to them. On being assured that he was, Lee called over a member of his staff to write down answers to very detailed questions he posed to Imboden regarding fords, roads, and surrounding country on both sides of the river. He also asked that Imboden send his brother George and the 18th Virginia Cavalry to act as an advance and guide should it be necessary. Although Lee did not say this in so many words, Imboden thought his situation was "precarious in the extreme."[64]

Lee subsequently sent Imboden orders from near Williamsport. Lee had learned that Union forces might be massing in the vicinity of Cherry Creek on the Virginia side of the river. He ordered Imboden to "cross the Potomac, and proceed to that vicinity, ascertain the truth of the report, do all in your power to repress the advance of the enemy, and to protect the trains passing on towards Winchester." Lee also told Imboden to coordinate with General Stuart "and let your pickets be relieved by such troops as he may designate for duty in Clear Spring Valley."[65]

Lee readied his own forces for a probable Union assault. He inspected much of the ground himself and had Jedediah Hotchkiss and others among his engineers produce detailed maps of the area. Conococheague Creek helped protect the Confederates from an attack from the west. To guard against an attack from the north and east, the Confederates threw up strong earthworks, positioned to allow frequent artillery positions capable of enfilading and frontal fire. A possible weakness was the length of the line, some six to eight miles.

Meade correctly assumed that the Army of Northern Virginia was concentrated in the area between Hagerstown and Williamsport, bounded by the Potomac. From July 9 to July 11, Meade maneuvered his forces west of South Mountain. Lee abandoned Hagerstown on the morning of July 12, and Meade cautiously moved his forces forward—probably too slowly—for fear of an engagement over which he might not have control.

Meade's men and draft animals were exhausted by their movement over rough country, made more difficult by the heavy rains. The further his forces moved west, the more removed they were from his base at Frederick, Maryland. Occupation of Hagerstown did not alleviate the problem because the railroad there from Harrisburg was not operating and would not be repaired for another five days. Some supplies for his men had to come from as far away as Gettysburg.

On the morning of July 12, just as the Confederates completed their defenses, Meade's forces came up to confront them. Up until this point, Lee had his men occupy as much territory as possible to allow for foraging and, primarily, to ensure that he had sufficient ground over which to maneuver. Lee sought only a defensive battle if he had to fight, and he probably thought that in these circumstances he might indeed be able to reverse the Gettysburg decision. Longstreet's corps was on the right, Hill's in the center, and Ewell's on the left. Stuart's cavalry was positioned on the left flank, ready to enfilade the Union right in the event of an attack.

Meade informed Halleck that he planned to attack on July 13, but when he called a meeting of his infantry corps commanders on the evening of July 12, five of the seven were unalterably opposed to an attack. Meade therefore postponed his planned "reconnaissance in force" until July 14 so that he might personally reconnoiter the position. Once he did this, he reconfirmed his plan of the day before.

Meade was later much criticized for following the advice of a council of war and not acting decisively on July 13, but these same critics would likely have been the first to accuse him of rashness had the attack gone badly. Later, after the Confederates had decamped, some of the Union commanders inspected the defenses they would have had to assault and concluded that postponing the attack prevented a Union disaster. Even had Meade's attack succeeded in piercing the Confederate line, there is no indication that Lee's Army of Northern Virginia could have been utterly defeated and the war ended at that point.[66]

As Meade was inspecting the front lines on July 13 in preparation for his assault the next day, Lee was anxiously anticipating a Federal attack that same morning. He looked forward to it, confident it would be repulsed at heavy Union cost. Skirmish firing beginning at dawn convinced Lee that an attack was imminent, and he was disappointed when the firing ended and he was informed that the Federals were digging emplacements.

Shortly thereafter Lee ordered a retreat, having been informed that Confederate engineers had finished the pontoon bridge over the Potomac and that the river had receded to the point that some fords were accessible. The retreat began at dark. Longstreet's and Hill's corps and the artillery went across the pontoon bridge at Falling Waters and Ewell's men forded at Williamsport. A pitch black night and heavy rains helped mask the army's move. By 11:00 A.M. on July 14 all the Confederates were over the river save two divisions at Falling Waters.

Meade had ordered a reconnaissance in force for 7:00 A.M., but even before that there was word of a Confederate withdrawal. As Union skirmishers pushed forward, they discovered the Confederate works deserted and Lee's army gone. Union forces pushed on to Williamsport, and Meade ordered a general pursuit at 8:30 A.M., but it was too late. They did, however, catch Lee's rear guard of Henry Heth's Division at Falling Waters, securing 719 Confederates prisoners.

The retreat was over. But Lincoln's use of the word "escape" and his appraisal that Meade's lack of initiative had produced less than might have been gained seems in retrospect to be harsh and unrealistic. Lee had achieved much. He had carried the war into the North, disrupted Union offensive plans, secured considerable quantities of provisions and supplies, brought off a number of Union prisoners, and forced a section of the North to experience the horrors of military occupation. But Lee had also paid a very high price in casualties to the Army of Northern Virginia. Although he was still the "Marble Man" and hero of the Confederacy, the myth of his invincibility was shattered and could never be recovered. Nor had the invasion of Pennsylvania drawn off a single Union soldier from the siege of Vicksburg. Indeed on July 4, as Lee was decamping from Gettysburg, Confederate Lt. Gen. John C. Pemberton was surrendering the Mississippi stronghold and over thirty thousand troops to Maj. Gen. Ulysses S. Grant's Union besiegers.

The Union had suffered heavier casualties at Gettysburg than had the Confederacy, but the Army of the Potomac had great recuperative power and the net effect of that battle was to provide confidence that had been sorely lacking. The soldiers of the Army of the Potomac had at last lived up to their promise, and they now knew what they could accomplish under a competent commander.[67]

After the four thousand Union prisoners had been ferried across the Potomac, they were kept for a few days just south of the river. Imboden's men divided their prisoners into divisions to march by columns of four. Confederate cavalry and artillery were positioned en masse between the divisions, while the Confederate infantry moved in two files, one on each side of the prisoner column. There was very little to eat on the march south, but other than that the prisoners were generally well treated. John L. Collins, of the 8th Pennsylvania Cavalry, who had earlier been relieved of his boots by one of his captors and was forced to march barefoot, recalled, "Imboden's Brigade did not seem to have had hard service, at least I thought so because their clothes were new, yet the general had a new suit of grey on, and certainly he had seen plenty of hard service. The men were as kind to us as could be expected; only one unpleasant affair came under my observation all the way. In the heat of a discussion a guard clubbed his musket and struck a wounded man on the head. I have no doubt that the latter had his tongue to blame for it; but he was a prisoner and a wounded man, and the guard was promptly placed under arrest."[68]

Collins recalled that the prisoners were well received as they passed through Martinsburg, where there were a large number of Union sympathizers who turned out to greet them. Seemingly well informed, the townspeople called out to the prisoners not to be discouraged, for they had won a great victory at Gettysburg and although they were prisoners they had been avenged by Confederate dead or prisoners left behind in Pennsylvania. Collins noted, "It must have been very galling to Imboden's command to be reviled that way by their country-women, but they bore it with down-cast heads, and made no reply. We could not have done it, I fear, had we been the guards, and in Pennsylvania."[69]

Collins reported that some of the prisoners then told the women they had not had anything to eat, whereupon the latter had rushed into their houses and returned with all sorts of food. A great commotion ensued as the prisoners tried to get to the food and their guards sought to prevent it. In the melee that followed, some of the women were pushed back and fell down, probably by accident, but the prisoners reacted to this by overpowering some of the guards and throwing them down in turn. It looked as if there might be a general fight, "which must result in the death of many prisoners and the escape of others." This was prevented by the prompt arrival of cavalry and artillery. "Then the general, or some one for him, promised the people and the prisoners that the latter would be halted outside the town to receive the contributions." This was indeed done.

As the prisoners moved farther south, the attitude of the people in the towns through which they passed changed dramatically, and there was considerable taunting, to which the prisoners responded in kind. At length they arrived at Staunton.[70]

The prisoners were not the only ones short of food. Frank Imboden recorded in his diary for July 16: "A most horrible incident committed by some members of this regt. . . . Old gentleman killed in his corn crib, without provocation, by men trying to steal his corn. Man's son's in army, one a surgeon. Board appointed to investigate & find out murderers." Capt. Imboden also reported arrests of Confederate soldiers for "stealing whiskey & other outrages. 18th regt. becoming an interesting set of *ruffians* [emphasis in original]."[71]

In his diary, Private Baker reflected on the last several months and the loss of "twenty to thirty thousand men since we first crossed the river and invaded Maryland and Pennsylvania." The war was awful, and the Southern troops claimed "it is to free the negro," to make him equal to whites and allow mixed schools and negroes to marry white women. The men were saying "they will wade in blood to their chins before such a thing shall happen to our people." Yet Baker reported that Northern prisoners said that the war was to save the Union "and if they thought it is to free the negro they would lay down their arms and go home." Baker concluded, "Well, we size it up in this way, there is [*sic*] some people making millions of dollars out of this war and don't care how many brave men fall, so they can keep this money and they will try to keep it up as long as our Southern States can keep an army in the field."[72]

Lee wrote Imboden at Staunton on July 16 that he hoped he had already reached that place. Lee ordered Imboden to dispose of the prisoners as soon as possible and then return to Winchester. Lee wrote: "Your services are much needed there against your old enemy, who has advanced from the west along the Baltimore and Ohio Railroad, and relaid the track as far as Cherry Run." Lee ordered Imboden to use Col. George Imboden's cavalry to ascertain the strength and disposition of Union forces. In the meantime, Imboden was to collect all available men, leaving only the "feeble" to guard Shenandoah Mountain, have his horses shod, and prepare to resume active operations.[73]

Gettysburg cast a pall. Frank Imboden noted at the end of July:

Another month has passed and the results are perhaps more disastrous than even Feby. '62. Vicksburg, Port Hudson & Gettysburg have been fought and leave a gloom on the country.
Unless unchanging success attends the Confederate arms, fits of despondency at once overhang every community. Even the army grows despondent, and evidences of demoralization are visible. More desertions than usual are occurring. Rumors of renewed difficulties in the South are circulating.[74]

General Imboden's views on the above are unknown, but on July 21 Imboden received an important reward when Lee gave him command of the Valley District. It comprised all territory west of the Blue Ridge Mountains to the Alleghenies, south of the Potomac, and north of the James River in Botetourt County. Imboden must have been pleased, as he was well aware that the district had been created in 1861 expressly for "Stonewall" Jackson.

In conducting military operations in the Valley, Lee urged Imboden to use "great energy and watchfulness." He instructed him to keep himself well informed regarding enemy dispositions, to "seize every opportunity of striking him a blow, and annoy him all in your power." Imboden would hold his new command until almost the end of the war.[75]

Chapter 8

Imboden's Second West Virginia Raid

Following the Gettysburg Campaign, Lee rested his army in northern Virginia. At the end of July, however, he moved the army east of the Blue Ridge to the area of the upper Rappahannock River near Culpepper. Meade's Army of the Potomac deployed north of that river.

Meanwhile, Imboden held the Valley. Initially his new command counted some three thousand men: his own Northwestern Brigade of cavalry and mounted infantry (the 62d Virginia Mounted Infantry), Brig. Gen. Gabriel C. Wharton's Infantry Brigade, Captain McClanahan's six-gun battery, Captain McNeill's Rangers, and two small battalions of cavalry commanded by Majs. Harry Gilmor and Sturgis Davis of Maryland.

For three months following the Gettysburg Campaign there was a lull in the eastern fighting as Lee's Army of Northern Virginia and Meade's Army of the Potomac regrouped. Imboden's area of operations was also quiet. The few Federal troops in the vicinity were those guarding the B&O, and they rarely ventured more than a few miles from it. The Valley was so tranquil that Lee, who needed all possible resources to resist an inevitable thrust south by Meade's Army of the Potomac, ordered Wharton's Brigade to join him east of the Blue Ridge along the Rappahannock. This was a serious blow to Imboden's force.[1]

Imboden reported to Lee the presence in the Valley of large numbers of Confederate deserters, who were able to hide successfully from the small squads of men sent to arrest them. Lee noted in a letter to Jefferson Davis on August 17, "Many cross the James River near Balcony falls en route for the south along the mountain ridges. Night before last thirty went from one regiment and eighteen from another. Great dissatisfaction is reported among the good men in the Army at the apparent impunity of deserters."[2]

In August 1863, Brig. Gen. William Averell mounted an attack with more than four thousand men from Moorefield, West Virginia, into Hardy, Pendleton, Highland, Bath, Greenbrier, and Pocahontas Counties. Averell employed a mixed force of cavalry, mounted infantry, and artillery; in a series of skirmishes he drove Confederate forces out of Pocahontas County and over Warm Springs Mountain. They destroyed a saltpeter works and burned Camp Northwest and a substantial number of Confederate supplies, equipment, and arms. They then fought a tough, two-day battle at the end of August at Rocky Gap, about one and a half miles from White Sulphur Springs, in Greenbrier County. The principal Confederate force engaged there was Col. George S. Patton's 1st Brigade, under the overall command of Maj. Gen. Samuel Jones, commanding the Department of Western Virginia.

The battle was fought from 9 A.M. until 7 P.M. on August 28 and then again on the morning of August 29, when Averell's forces made two additional attacks. Confederate reinforcements and a shortage of ammunition then induced Averell to withdraw. Although the Confederates pursued, the Union movement was accomplished in good order. In the entire operation, the Federals estimated that they had killed and wounded some 200 Confederates; they also took one artillery piece and 150 prisoners. Union losses in killed, wounded, and missing came to 130 men. Imboden was not close enough to support Jones, so he did not participate. Once Averell had retreated, Imboden moved from Monterey with the intention of reaching Huntersville and blocking the Federal retreat, but he was too late.[3]

Lee was not pleased. He wrote Imboden, "I regret exceedingly that the enemy escaped with so little damage to himself." Lee urged greater effort in the future: "It seems to me the command of Averell should have been more seriously punished. Unless we are active in inflicting all the loss we can upon the parties sent on these expeditions, and in using every opportunity of cutting them off, they will continue to be sent out, will desolate the country, and bring great distress upon the people. I hope you will be more successful in the future."[4]

Lee continued to press Imboden to mount raids against Grafton, New Creek, and Piedmont. Lee corresponded regularly with Imboden, directing him to carry out small raids with the "dual purpose of distracting the enemy and gathering supplies." The Confederacy could use whatever Imboden could bring in.[5]

Skirmishes between Imboden's men and Federal troops continued sporadically throughout this period. On September 7 three officers and twenty-six men of Gilmor's Battalion, a number of whom had been recruiting in Winchester, attacked a Union camp at Bath before dawn. The defenders, two companies of Col. John Wynkoop's Pennsylvania Cavalry, had fifteen minutes' warning of the Confederate approach. The fight was short and hard and held at close quarters. The Confederates sustained only two men wounded. Imboden set Union losses at eight to ten men killed—including a captain—and a number wounded. The Confederates captured twenty-three Union soldiers and one African-American, along with fifty horses and a number of pistols and sabers.[6]

Lee wanted such operations continued. Locally raised troops raiding the Union-held western counties would have a better chance of raising recruits for Confederate forces. When Lee learned that Gilmor's troops had run into bands of Confederate stragglers and deserters, he also ordered Imboden to use every possible means to capture or kill them.[7]

Inadequate equipment and mounts remained a problem. In early September, Imboden noted that he was two hundred horses short of the number needed for his command, and that none could be had "unless captured from the Yankees."[8]

Capt. Frank Imboden, in charge of a detachment of four companies of the 18th Regiment in Hardy, also engaged the Federals. On September 7 part of his and Capt. McNary Hobson's command clashed in Patterson's Creek Valley with a superior Union force on its way to reoccupy Petersburg. The resulting engagement was inconclusive. One Confederate soldier was killed, and reportedly Frank Imboden shot and mortally wounded a Federal captain. The Confederates turned back the

Federal force and learned the location of their camp near Moorefield. On this news, Imboden ordered eighty cavalrymen under Capt. John McNeill to leave Imboden's own camp near Brock's Gap and join his brother.

Meanwhile, six companies numbering some three hundred men of the 1st [West] Virginia Infantry and a company of cavalry of Col. James A. Mulligan's 5th Brigade arrived at the Union camp near Moorefield from Petersburg. McNeill, Hobson, and Frank Imboden decided to attack the Union camp before daybreak the next day, September 11. They set out from their own camp, four miles from Moorefield, posting a few men at Brock's Gap.

The Federals were entrenched and had pickets out as well as about fifty men as skirmishers. They had also sent out two companies to strike the Confederate camp. The attacking Confederates managed to flank the Union pickets and get between the skirmishers and the Union camp. They even captured a Union patrol without alerting the sleeping Federals. The Confederates then charged the camp at dawn, yelling and firing into the tents. Surprise was complete. The Union troops put up resistance, but the fight was of short duration. Frank Imboden reported the raiders had killed or wounded twenty-five to thirty Federals and brought off fourteen prisoners—including eight officers—and all useful camp property. The raiders then had to fight two Union detachments near Moorefield sent to capture them, losing a dozen horses in the process. In the two engagements the Virginians also lost a lieutenant and three soldiers wounded.[9]

J. Marshall McCue noted the arrival of the Union prisoners in Staunton on their way thence to Richmond: "Captains McNeill, Imboden and Hobson made their appearance in our midst Tuesday last with 147 prisoners captured by their companies near Moorefield, Henry County, a few days since. . . . Captain McNeill received a slight scratch and Captain Hobson had his hat shot off his head."[10]

Such small scale engagements continued throughout the fall and winter of 1863–1864. Imboden recalled that the Confederates "frequently raided the railroad [B&O], destroying bridges and trains as we could, and capturing some small detachments posted and fortified on the railroad or found scouting too far from it."[11]

Many of Imboden's men were dismounted; some were always detailed or on sick leave. He believed he had to have more men if he was going to conduct effective offensive operations, but his frequent appeals to Lee, who was hard pressed himself and faced the principal Union strength, met with no success. The only reinforcement Lee could offer came in the form of a small company of dismounted Missouri cavalrymen, recently exchanged prisoners.[12]

In mid-September 1863 Imboden sent Maj. D.B. Lang and one hundred men of the 62d Virginia Infantry on foot across the Allegheny Mountains toward Barbour County. At midnight on September 24, Lang and his men attacked Company A of the 2d [West] Virginia Infantry of Averell's command, who were camped for the night some nine miles northeast of Beverly, where the Seneca Trace crossed the Cheat River and near what was called Burnt House. Lang and his men captured a lieutenant and thirty-six soldiers, all their weapons, and thirty-eight horses. This was the entire Union force, save two men who were badly wounded and one who drowned in the river attempting to escape. Lang's command then withdrew without loss.[13]

The Harrisonburg newspaper commented on this successful action the following week when the Federal prisoners were moved through the town: "General Imboden, it will be seen, is affording the abolitionists of the Northeast the best facilities he can command to enable them to get quickly and safely on to Richmond."[14]

In late September, Imboden sent his 18th Cavalry Regiment on a reconnaissance into Frederick, Jefferson, and Clark Counties. They spent most of three days below Winchester, hoping without success to draw some of the Federals out from Martinsburg and Harpers Ferry. Their only accomplishment was to gain a sense of Federal strength. Imboden reported about 1,000 Federal troops at Martinsburg, 1,200 to 1,500 at Harpers Ferry, and a small force in the fortified jail at Charles Town. The B&O was heavily defended along its entire length.

At the end of the month Averell had 3,000 mounted men at Beverly and was apparently preparing for a raid, probably toward Lewisburg. Imboden had an outpost at the base of the Allegheny Mountains with couriers positioned to carry word back sixty miles to his camp. He hoped for sufficient warning to be able to meet Averell at Shenandoah Mountain, the pass through which had been fortified.[15]

Imboden dispatched Lt. Col. D.E. Beall and 250 men of the 18th

Cavalry into Hampshire to try to destroy the rail line there. He also sent a smaller force under Gilmor to attempt the same in the vicinity of Martinsburg. Imboden had little confidence of success, however, as Union troops strongly defended the major bridges, and damages elsewhere on the line could soon be repaired. With considerable numbers of Union troops at Romney, Martinsburg, and Petersburg, any attacking Confederate force would find retreat difficult.[16]

On October 2 Imboden mounted another raid on the B&O, but it reached only as far as Wardensville. Heavy rains, unfordable streams, and roads that were quagmires all forced an early end to the mission. On October 7 Imboden received orders from Lee to move his command from Rockingham County, where it had been camped, to Berryville in the northern Shenandoah Valley in order to join up with forces there under General Stuart. They were to cooperate in a second raid into West Virginia. The goal was to attack both Harpers Ferry and Charles Town and, if possible, take them. This was in fact projected as part of a much larger operation. Imboden would serve as the far left flank guard of the Army of Northern Virginia as it moved north on the eastern side of the Blue Ridge Mountains in what became known as the Bristoe Station Campaign.[17]

Both Lee and Meade were detaching troops for service elsewhere. In September Lee sent Longstreet and two divisions west to join Gen. Braxton Bragg's Army of Tennessee at Chickamauga. When Meade learned of this, he advanced on Culpeper, and Lee then withdrew behind the Rapidan River. But Meade was unable to capitalize on the situation, for in early October he lost his XI and XII Corps, sent west to Chattanooga.

The Bristoe Station Campaign resulted from Lee's attempt to take advantage of Meade's temporary weakness by advancing north on Washington. On October 9, screened by Stuart's cavalry on the left flank, Lt. Gens. Ambrose Hill and Richard Ewell put their two corps in motion northwest toward the Army of the Potomac at Culpeper. For two days the two sides skirmished as Meade withdrew and Lee advanced. The Confederates took Culpeper on October 11. Lee then sent Hill on a wide sweep to the west while Ewell pushed the Federals back along the line of the Orange & Alexandria Railroad. Fighting continued through October 12–13 as Meade, while outnumbering Lee, conducted a skillful withdrawal.

Early on October 14, as his leading elements approached New Baltimore, five miles north of Warrenton, Hill learned that the Federals were withdrawing to the east almost parallel to his own force. He then turned eastward toward the railroad stop of Bristoe Station, and without reconnoitering fell on the Federal column. Hill walked into a trap set by Maj. Gen. Gouverneur Warren and his II Corps, concealed behind the railroad track embankment to protect the Union withdrawal. This battle was the major one of the campaign, and it saw Hill repulsed and Meade able to consolidate his lines around Centreville near Manassas. Lee had pushed the Federals back forty miles but there the advance halted. For two days Lee probed the Federal entrenchments without success and then began his own withdrawal on October 17.

The roles then were reversed as the retreating Confederates found themselves pursued by the Federals. By October 20, most of Lee's army was again back across the Rappahannock. The campaign had been one of wasted opportunities on both sides. Lee had sustained 1,381 casualties, 1,300 of which occurred at Bristoe Station. Meade put his own losses at 2,292. The Bristoe Campaign was without strategic significance in the war.

Imboden's role in the Bristoe Campaign was, as mentioned, to protect the far left Confederate flank, guard the mountain passes on Lee's left, draw off Union resources, and prevent reinforcements from reaching Meade. When the campaign opened, Harpers Ferry was held by General Sullivan's Brigade. The 9th Maryland Regiment of Infantry and a squadron of cavalry was at Charles Town, eight miles from that place. Col. Benjamin L. Simpson, a Baltimore businessman with little military experience, had command.

At the time Imboden received Lee's orders he had less than one thousand men. Much of his brigade was spread out guarding the mountain passes from Beverly to Harpers Ferry. His brigade consisted of the 62d Virginia Mounted Infantry Regiment, commanded by VMI graduate Col. George H. Smith; the 18th Virginia Cavalry Regiment, commanded by the general's brother, Col. George W. Imboden; White's Battalion, under Maj. Robert White; the Maryland Battalion, led by Maj. Thomas Sturgis Davis of Baltimore; Gilmor's 2d Maryland Battalion, under Maj. Harry Gilmor of Baltimore; McNeill's Rangers, commanded by Capt. John H. McNeill; and McClanahan's Battery, commanded by Texan Capt. John H. McClanahan.[18]

Imboden's men took the Valley Turnpike as far as Strasburg. They then marched through Front Royal and on to Berryville. Late on the evening of October 17, the Confederate advance guard reached Berryville and drove Union scouts from the town. Private Baker recorded in his diary: "They made a general run for it and the 18th regiment after them. We rode down quite a number of them and got more guns than we got prisoners. The road was dotted with hats, guns, canteens, etc. Indeed, they cut loose everything to lighten their horses."[19]

Unfortunately for the Confederates, Stuart's men were not present, as high water had prevented them from crossing the Shenandoah River. Imboden decided to proceed alone if the odds would allow. Major Davis volunteered to carry out a reconnaissance, and Imboden agreed. Davis knew two Southern sympathizers in the area and roused one of them around midnight, demanding the information. The individual told Davis that his brother was an official in the West Virginia state government and that he was then in the town. Many of the townspeople were upset with his brother, and he was afraid that he would be treated roughly if captured. He agreed to provide the information on condition that he be allowed to get his brother out safely. Davis agreed with this condition, and the man told him what he knew. Davis then returned to Imboden's headquarters in time to allow the Confederates to get to Charles Town and mount an attack there by daybreak.

At 2:00 A.M. on October 18 Imboden's force set out from Berryville. Surprise was complete, and his men soon had Charles Town surrounded. As the Confederates came up the Berryville Pike, the Valley was partly obscured in fog. Imboden's plan was to drive in the Union pickets, then quickly push his artillery to the courthouse, jail, and some other adjacent buildings where the bulk of the Union forces were quartered. These had been altered with holes for firing muskets, and the courthouse yard was also enclosed by a wall of oak timber.

Imboden divided his force. He sent the 18th Regiment and Gilmor's Battalion to block the Harpers Ferry Road. Imboden himself then led the 62d Regiment and McClanahan's Battery against the town itself. After his men were in position, he sent in Captain McNeill and his own adjutant, Capt. Frank B. Berkeley, under a flag of truce to demand an immediate and unconditional surrender. Colonel Simpson, who had assumed he could hold the town, asked for an hour to consider the request. Imboden, who well understood the necessity of acting swiftly given Union forces at Harpers Ferry, granted him five minutes. Simpson's reply at the end of the time limit was, "Take us if you can."[20]

The Confederates then sent in an artillery piece, and a young boy directed it to the courthouse. Imboden is reported to have said, "Boys, unlimber that piece of artillery, and I'll take them out." The men unlimbered the gun in the street, less than two hundred yards from the building. Union troops standing in the building's large windows fired a volley at them, but the shots went wild. According to one of the artillerymen involved, Imboden dismounted and did actually sight the gun himself. Its discharge immediately obscured the courthouse in smoke. Reportedly the first shot tore through the door of the courthouse. Other shots were then directed against the wall to the left of the door, then the wall on its right. Imboden reported that about a half dozen rounds were fired in all. The Union troops then halted fire and the Confederates followed suit. When the smoke cleared, the Confederates could see that the Union troops had fled. Only one man, a Union lieutenant, had been hit. He was lying on the courthouse steps, a hip shattered.

The Union troops who had attempted to flee toward Harpers Ferry were soon overtaken at the edge of town by Col. George Imboden's 18th Cavalry Regiment and Gilmor's Battalion; they then surrendered. Despite a Confederate pursuit, Colonel Simpson, his lieutenant colonel, and three others—all of whom were mounted—broke through the Confederate lines and reached Harpers Ferry and safety. In his report to Lee, Imboden said they had "fled at the first fire."[21]

A Union major had high praise for Imboden's conduct of the operation: "The Johnnies had some pretty damned smart officers during the war, and some of them that did the most effective work were the least heard of. Imboden was one of them. Imboden with a half dozen shells and a volley or two of carbine and pistol shots and considerable dash has scooped in pretty nearly as many as his own force."[22]

Imboden's men had captured most of the 9th Maryland Regiment and three companies of cavalry, in all 434 men. They also secured horses, mules, wagons, and supplies, including clothing, blankets, medicines, and food. Much to the subsequent chagrin of one of the artillery lieutenants, who had instructed his men to use a captured wagon to remove what supplies—particularly knapsacks and blankets—they could from the courthouse, his men showed up with thirteen drums of various sizes. Subsequently, Colonel Smith used them to organize a drum corps in the 62d.[23]

The Confederates could not stay long at Charles Town; less than two hours after Imboden had attacked, a Federal force of infantry, cavalry, and artillery arrived there from Harpers Ferry. Imboden had expected this, and as the Federals arrived, Capt. Frank Imboden and a Confederate detail led the prisoners back through the town at double quick.

As the Confederates exited from one side of town, the Federals entered the other. Crowds of townspeople were out in the streets. According to one Confederate officer, the civilians were begging the Confederates to stay. Nonetheless, the crowd in the streets precluded the retreating Southerners from firing canister from their guns against the advancing Federals.

From 10:00 A.M. until about sunset, the Union troops pursued Imboden's force as far as Berryville. During that time, the Federals made several unsuccessful attempts to attack the Confederate column and rescue their comrades. According to Lt. Carter Berkeley of McClanahan's Battery, the Confederates kept the Union troops at bay by firing their artillery *en echelon*. Some of the guns would fire while others withdrew to a new position to cover the first guns; then they in turn departed. At one point, Union troops were within a few feet of some of the Confederate guns before they could be turned about, but the artillerymen were saved by a cavalry charge led by Major Gilmor. The Confederates also successfully ambushed advancing Union troops on several occasions.[24]

As one of the horse artillerymen remembered it: "Before our horses were through eating the Federals came up from Harper's Ferry and attacked our rear guard. When we heard the firing of shots, we pulled stakes and moved on, taking position and beating the enemy back from every hilltop for a distance of twelve miles; but we came out safely with prisoners and provisions which we had captured in little old Charles Town. When night came on, we were well-nigh spent, and our prisoners, in the language of the today, were simply 'all in!'"[25]

The Union major who participated in the pursuit noted: "The whole day was a stern chase, but occasionally when Imboden was pressed too closely and in need of time to keep the prisoners and plunder ahead out of the way, he stopped long enough to give us a sharp taste of fighting that showed the mettle that was in him."[26]

Imboden's losses were slight. He reported three men killed, three to four mortally wounded, and another fifteen to twenty wounded. He also lost perhaps fifteen to twenty stragglers, taken by Union forces during the withdrawal.[27]

The Confederates marched nearly the entire night and reached the Forks of the Shenandoah River near Front Royal by daybreak on October 19. Although the river was up that day, they managed to get across the North Fork, where Imboden believed they would be safe from further pursuit. The men were exhausted; part of his command had just marched sixty miles, and the other forty-eight miles. Finally, once between the North and South Forks of the Shenandoah they could rest easy; there, Imboden wrote to Lee.

In addition to reporting the results of the raid, Imboden informed Lee that he had learned that there were substantial Union forces nearby: four regiments of infantry and four of cavalry at Martinsburg, and two brigades at Harpers Ferry. Because these forces were so much larger than his own and forage was in short supply, Imboden said he intended to retire up the Valley to Shenandoah County. Although he was also concerned about a report of five thousand Union troops under Averell near Hightown, Imboden expressed confidence that if Lee could spare a division of cavalry to operate with his own force, within a week they could take all the Federal outposts from Harpers Ferry to New Creek and again destroy the railroad and canal.[28]

Lee responded with warm praise for Imboden's accomplishments: "This duty was well performed by that officer [Imboden] and on the 18th instant he marched upon Charlestown and succeeded, by a well concerted plan, in surrounding that place and capturing nearly the whole force stationed there."[29]

Of 2,436 Union prisoners captured in October 1863, Lee noted that Imboden's Brigade claimed credit for 434. Lee did not, however, follow up on Imboden's suggestion for an offensive against Union outposts in the lower Valley.[30]

Historian James Callahan notes in his *History of West Virginia* that the raid failed to have a positive impact for the Confederacy in West Virginia. It found few West Virginians willing to "grasp the opportunity to enter Confederate service," and for the first time Confederate authorities understood the true sentiment of West Virginia regarding the war.[31]

With the Shenandoah River in flood and unfordable, Imboden's force remained in defensive positions near Front Royal until October 25. The weather turned bad, however, pouring rain and sleet. Lt. Julian Pratt of the 18th Virginia Cavalry voiced the wishes of many when he wrote, "I hope we shall have no more very active duty this winter."[32]

Lee urged Imboden to continue his raids against the B&O Railroad. Imboden responded with a request for reinforcements, claiming that he then had too few men to accomplish anything significant. Nothing came of this request, however.[33]

Meanwhile, Union Brigadier General Averell again raided from West Virginia into western Virginia. On November 1, 1863, he left Beverly with a sizeable force of more than five thousand infantry, mounted infantry, cavalry, and artillery, most of them West Virginia volunteer units. Pushing in a southerly direction, Averell intended to raid toward Lewisburg. The Union troops marched along the Staunton-Parkersburg Turnpike to Greenbrier Bridge and thence by Camp Bartow and Green Bank to Huntersville, driving in Confederate pickets and capturing or dispersing partisans. They reached Huntersville around noon on November 4.

Imboden was encamped some four miles from Bridgewater near Harrisonburg when he received reports from Lt. John T. Byrd at Hightown in Highland County of five thousand Union troops having arrived at Camp Bartow and then moving off toward Huntersville. At daybreak on November 5 Imboden broke camp and moved to Buffalo Gap, where he again encamped. He ordered six days' of hard bread and bacon rations sent by train to Goshen Depot, and on November 6 he left Buffalo Gap headed west with six hundred cavalry and a section of artillery. After a halt at Goshen to draw provisions, the men then moved on, camping that night at Bratton's in Bath County.

At dawn on November 7 Imboden's force broke camp and resumed its westerly movement. His men passed Warm Springs at 1:00 P.M. There Imboden learned of a battle fought the previous afternoon on Droop Mountain between Averell's force and Brig. Gen. John Echols's 1st Brigade of the Army of Southwestern Virginia, which had come up to assist Confederate troops in Pocahontas County under Col. William Jackson. In all, the Confederates had only about 1,700 men.

Hoping to get in behind the Union force and cut it off, Imboden pushed ahead. When he and his men reached Back Creek Mountain, however, another courier arrived with news that Echols had been badly defeated on November 6 in the Battle of Droop Mountain, which took place just north of Lewisburg, with a heavy loss in killed, wounded, and prisoners.

Following an artillery duel, Averell used his infantry to turn the Confederate left and then mounted a frontal assault by four regiments of dismounted troops. Confederate casualties were not as great as was thought initially, as many of the men had simply scattered and later straggled back in. In all, the Confederates lost perhaps 175 men, killed, wounded, and captured. Although Echols claimed many more Union troops had been casualties, in truth, Averell's force had suffered 6 killed, 112 wounded, and one missing, for a total of 119 lost.

The defeated Confederates had subsequently withdrawn through Lewisburg toward Monroe. The courier informed Imboden that a large pursuing Union column had arrived at Lewisburg, and he erroneously reported total Union strength at upwards of fifteen thousand men.[34]

Maj. Gen. Samuel Jones, meanwhile, called on Richmond for reinforcements and mobilized his resources. Echols estimated the Federals at ten thousand men, but Jones more realistically put Averell's strength at seven thousand. Although no Confederate reinforcements were available, Averell did not press his advantage.[35]

Meanwhile, news of Echols's defeat at Droop Mountain led Imboden to change his plans; he now withdrew southwest along the Jackson River toward Covington. Meanwhile, at 7:00 P.M. on November 6, news had reached Lexington of Averell's raid. The next day some eight hundred of the Rockbridge Home Guards and the VMI Corps of Cadets, along with two 6-pounder guns, set out to come to Imboden's assistance. By November 7 they were at Millborough, and Imboden sent word for them to proceed to Clifton Forge.

When Imboden's men arrived at Covington they discovered one hundred stragglers from Jackson's command. Another hundred men came in that night. Imboden's pickets there also came under Union attack on November 8.

At dawn on November 9 some four hundred Union cavalry arrived at Callaghan's and attacked Imboden's pickets, which slowly withdrew back on the main body. About a mile and a half west of Covington, Imboden took position on a crest to give battle. When the head of the Union column came in view at about 1,200 yards, Imboden ordered his artillery to open up. Imboden reported that their fire scattered the Union troops, whereupon he sent two companies of his cavalry against them. The cavalry drove the Union force back in confusion to Callaghan's, where it joined the main Union column of some three thousand men. The whole Union force then moved off on the Warm Springs Road. Imboden had rearmed the nearly two hundred stragglers from Jackson's command with Virginia state weapons discovered at Covington and then formed the men into two companies. Most of these men ran away, however, when the artillery fire commenced.

Aware of the Union movement and having been informed that the Federals had seven artillery pieces, Imboden feared being cut off by means of a county road. To prevent this he withdrew to a strong hill position about a mile east of Covington, where he intended to give battle. He put out a cavalry screen under his brother Col. George Imboden about four to five miles in advance of his position. At the same time, he sent a dispatch to the Rockbridge Home Guards and the VMI cadets, now relocated at Clifton Forge thirteen miles away, and urged them to join him as soon as possible.

Early in the afternoon, Imboden was informed that General Averell's force had left the Warm Springs Road and was moving toward Huntersville. Imboden feared a ruse in which he might be cut off and decided to move by way of Clifton Forge to Goshen. He set out at once, and his men reached Goshen, forty miles away, in slightly more than twenty-four hours. He then dismissed the Rockbridge County men and the cadets.

Scouts informed Imboden that Averell was moving rapidly up Black Creek, toward Monterey. On November 11 Imboden was at Buffalo Gap, where he learned that troops under Colonel Mulligan would join Averell that evening at Monterey. Fearing a Union attack on Staunton, Imboden that night ordered 150 of his men to the top of Shenandoah Mountain, sixteen miles away. In the morning he sent up an additional 750 men, along with four pieces of artillery, and he called out the Augusta County Home Guards.

Although Mulligan and Averell did join forces, with about four thousand men, they made no effort toward Staunton and instead moved off toward Hardy County and established a camp near Petersburg. Imboden at once sent small forces to harry their withdrawal.

Although Imboden had not inflicted any appreciable casualties on the Union forces, he reported that the column he had repulsed at Covington had been on a mission down the Jackson River in order to destroy bridges, depots, and furnaces and then withdraw back on the main body. Imboden was confident he had saved the iron furnaces in western Rockbridge and Botetourt Counties, six to eight of which were then in full blast.

Averell's November 1863 raid was only a limited Federal success. The Union troops did take several hundred Confederate prisoners, 150 horses, and several hundred cattle. Imboden reported to Lee that he expected Averell and Mulligan to winter at Moorefield but that their combined force of four thousand men was too large for him to expel.[36]

In his own report to his headquarters, Averell was, however, dismissive of Imboden's efforts and leadership during the raid:

> Near Covington, General Imboden was observed with a command upon my right. Not regarding his force of sufficient importance to delay the march of my column, two squadrons of the Eighth [West] Virginia Mounted Infantry were sent against him, which drove his forces away from my line of march.
>
> A lieutenant and 20 men of his command were captured. His apparent intention and readiness to avoid me rendered it inexpedient to endeavor to capture him. I have brought with me about 150 captured horses. Several hundred cattle were captured in the course of the march.[37]

Both sides continued to conduct small-scale raids against the other's territory, and on November 16 a Federal force commanded by Col. William Boyd, raiding from Martinsburg and Harpers Ferry, attacked a reinforced battalion of Imboden's Brigade, commanded by Maj. Robert White, at Mount Jackson in the Valley. Imboden estimated Federal strength at seven hundred men. It included Boyd's 21st Pennsylvania and the 1st New York Cavalry, along with a section of artillery.

After a sharp fight White repulsed the Federals, sending them in retreat. White dispatched Capt. Thomas S. Davis and sixty of his men after the Federals, who then camped below Woodstock. Davis and his men fired into the Federal camp during the night and forced the Union troops again to retreat, but not before the Federals had shot some of their own lame horses to prevent them from falling into Confederate hands. White estimated Union casualties at eight killed and eighteen wounded; he also captured eleven men and some horses. Confederate losses were a lieutenant and eight men captured while on picket duty, and one man wounded; three horses were also killed. During the fight a Blakely 12-pounder gun, which Imboden said was defective when he had received it, burst. Imboden was pleased to report that the Federals had obtained no Confederate government horses, cattle, or property in their raid.

Imboden, meanwhile, was having his men carry out a series of raids against Federal supply trains and sending out detachments with "torpedoes" (mines) to blow up Union rail trains.

On November 16, the same day as Colonel White's raid, Captain McNeill of Imboden's command, leading some one hundred men within his own company and a detachment under Lt. M.N. Moorman from the 62d Infantry, struck a Federal supply train near Burlington in Hampshire County. The Union train of eighty-five wagons loaded with supplies had set out the day before from New Creek, bound for Averell's camp near Petersburg. Approximately one hundred Union infantry guarded the mile-long train, which made only thirteen miles the first day before stopping for the night near Burlington.

The Union supply train set out again early on November 16, unaware that McNeill and Moorman were monitoring their movements. When the wagon train passed a seemingly abandoned house midway between Burlington and Williamsport, Confederate soldiers, who had hidden in it, opened fire on the advance guard. This was the signal for the men of the 62d to attack the front of the train while McNeill's men struck it from the rear. After a sharp fight, the Union troops broke and sought safety in the nearby forest.

The Confederates brought off 43 drovers and some 300 horses, complete with their harnesses. They set fire to the wagons, but could not complete the job because they had to depart in some haste to escape a large Federal cavalry force, estimated at 600 men. In the Confederates' haste to get away, some of the captured horses were lost, so McNeill ended up with only 245 new mounts. McNeill's men took to the mountains, pursued by the much larger force, but managed to escape. Confederate casualties were one mortally wounded and five others badly wounded, one of whom had been left behind and was presumed dead.[38]

In late November Imboden had to answer a complaint brought by the city fathers of Winchester. Some men, allegedly members of his command, had carried out an armed robbery there, and the town council requested that Imboden arrest and bring the men to justice. They also wanted him to station troops there to prevent such outrages from occurring in the future.

Imboden informed the council that if the men involved could "be arrested & identified I will *order* them to be hung immediately without further trial than to be satisfied of their identity." It was not certain, however, that they were indeed his men and he feared that, in any case, "they are beyond my reach." Imboden said he did not have the resources to station troops at Winchester and wondered why a town of several thousand people could not create its own police force for the security of the inhabitants.[39]

Imboden's forces were indeed stretched thin. As one soldier of the 62d put it in a letter home, "I doubt very much whether we shall see any winter quarters this winter as we have a very extensive country to protect. In fact it is more than Gen. Imboden can do. We ought to have more troops."[40]

More troops were on the way, but not until Averell had carried out another operation. On December 8 he undertook a long raid with about four thousand cavalry from New Creek through the Alleghenies south to the Virginia & Tennessee Railroad. His orders were to destroy the railroad either at Bonsack or at Salem in Roanoke County.

Averell's raid again caused Imboden to call out the Home Guards and the VMI Corps of Cadets. On December 13 he wrote to Col. James W. Massie, commander of the Rockbridge Home Guard, informing him that Averell was on the move with four thousand men. That same afternoon he had fought a skirmish with Averell's advance guard at McDowell. Imboden told Massie that he expected an attack the next day, which he hoped to rebuff, causing Averell to attempt to reach the

Shenandoah Valley via Warm Springs. In view of these developments, Imboden requested that Massie call out his men and move them to Goshen or Millboro where he would receive further instructions. He also asked that VMI superintendent Francis H. Smith lend his support. Imboden informed Massie that he had asked other forces to fall back in that direction as well so that the Confederates might concentrate their resources.[41]

After the war Imboden noted the "daring" nature of Averell's attack but claimed that his men "prevented his getting into the Shenandoah Valley to strike at Staunton." Averell, however, swept around behind the North Mountain Range to strike the Virginia & Tennessee Railroad at Salem. Arriving there on December 16, in just six hours Averell's troops destroyed three depots filled with commissary and quartermaster supplies intended for Longstreet in Tennessee. They also fired the water tower, railroad turntable, and three rail cars, and they destroyed several miles of track and five bridges.[42]

Road conditions were terrible as a result of freezing rain, and a number of the VMI cadets were without shoes. The cadets went into bivouac at Goshen until December 18. Imboden put them, his own engineers, and Jackson's small force to work building fortifications on the Cowpasture River seven miles from Goshen at Buffalo and Jennings Gaps, and at other potential approaches from the mountains to the west.[43]

It was almost impossible to defend against that type of quick raid. Margaret Preston of Lexington was not impressed with the appearance of Imboden's men when they marched through that place on December 18: "At 11 o'clock, Imboden's cavalry and artillery passed through. It is the first time I have ever seen an army. Poor fellows! With their broken down horses muddy up to the eyes, and their muddy wallets and blankets, they looked like an army of tatterdemalions; the horses looked starved."[44]

Despite the appearance of Imboden's men, the people of Rockbridge County gladly shared with Imboden what little they had in the way of provisions. Later Imboden wrote to thank James D. Davidson, commissariat in Lexington.[45]

On learning of the raid and in order to reinforce Imboden, Lee sent Maj. Gen. Jubal Early to the Shenandoah Valley with instructions to intercept Averell as he withdrew. The Confederates now outnumbered their opponent. Along with his own infantry and Imboden's small force, Early could draw on two brigades of cavalry under Maj. Gen. Fitzhugh Lee, Brigadier General Echols's Brigade from Gen. Samuel Jones's Department of Southwestern Virginia, and a detachment of dismounted cavalry commanded by Col. William L. Jackson.

Early's problem lay not in numbers but in locating Averell in time, fixing his force, and bringing his own superior numbers into play. Although Early hurried to Staunton and acted forcefully enough, heavy rains delayed the transit of his troops and he guessed incorrectly as to the route Averell would utilize in his withdrawal. Colonel Jackson's troops on the Virginia Central Railroad at Jackson River Depot were in position to block Averell there if he should decide to return by the same route. But Averell believed Covington to the west was only lightly held, and he decided to withdraw via that place and New Castle back to his base at Petersburg. To cover his retreat he sent a small detachment in a feint against Buchanan, having previously put out erroneous information that this would be his route of advance.

This deception worked. Imboden was at Collierstown, west of Lexington, on his way to Covington to cover the bridges and crossings there; high water and the rain had forced him to take a roundabout route. Early also sent Fitzhugh Lee's troopers to Covington to join Imboden. Lee and Imboden then conferred and came to the conclusion that Averell would pass by way of Buchanan, and they set off in that direction. Averell then slipped in behind them, crossing the Jackson River at Covington and gaining a two-day march on his pursuers. Jackson's five hundred men tried to stop Averell but were swept aside, and the Union force escaped largely unscathed. The VMI cadets, ordered on December 18 to attempt to block Averell at Buchanan, were then countermarched to link up with Colonel Jackson's force. As infantry they were quite unable to pursue the Federal cavalry, and the 21st were ordered to return to Lexington.[46]

Gen. R.E. Lee directed that Early remain in the Valley at least temporarily. He expressed the hope that Early would be able to secure supplies from the West Virginia counties along the South Branch of the Potomac.[47]

On December 16, 1863, Imboden reported to Col. W.L. Jackson at Warm Springs that Union troops under Averell and Mulligan had camped at Monterey the night before and that he expected an imminent attack. While he was confident he could defeat them, he expected that this would cause the Union troops to try and turn his flank by way of Williamsville or Warm Springs, and that it would thus be best if he and Jackson could combine forces.[48]

After extensive preparations, on the last day of the year, Early mounted a raid of his own. For this operation he temporarily split Imboden's Northwestern Brigade, sending McNeill's and Gilmor's units with Maj. Gen Fitzhugh Lee from Mount Jackson into the South Branch Valley toward Moorefield and Petersburg in Hardy County, West Virginia. Imboden and the remainder of the brigade went with Early in a diversionary tactic, down the Shenandoah Valley toward Strasburg.

Terrible winter conditions sharply limited what Lee could accomplish; the ice-covered steep mountain roads were impassable for vehicles and almost so for horses. Although Lee had to leave behind his artillery and wagons, on January 3 he did capture a forty-wagon Union supply train near Moorefield. It contained only artillery ammunition and raw beef hides. Lee then detached part of his force to accompany the captured wagons back to the Shenandoah Valley, while he pressed on with the remainder. He then defeated small Union detachments at Burlington, Williamsport, and McLemar's Church. The raid came to an end in a major hailstorm on January 6, and Lee and his men returned to Shenandoah County the next day.[49]

Early was disappointed that Fitzhugh Lee had not been able to accomplish more, but he believed his men had done the best they could under the circumstances. His own diversionary attacks had not been very successful, much of the time being spent engaging Union troops in the vicinity of Middletown and Strasburg.

The war and his military command apparently did not dampen Imboden's desire for political office. In the fall of 1863 he paired with gubernatorial candidate Thomas S. Flournoy to run for lieutenant governor of Virginia on the Whig ticket. Although Imboden won the military vote for his office, the election went to Democrats William "Extra Billy" Smith and Samuel Price.[50]

That Christmas Frank Imboden wrote in his war diary: "Dec. 25— Xmas. George, Jim, Jake, Ma, Pa and myself are all at home, only the General absent. Will we meet on another X-Mas?"[51]

Chapter 9

The 1864 Shenandoah Valley Campaign

Following Fitzhugh Lee's raid in the first week of January 1864, Imboden's Northwestern Brigade had reunited and gone into winter quarters near Mount Crawford. It spent the next six weeks resting and replenishing. In early 1864 clothing and shoes were in short supply, but medical supplies were apparently adequate, despite an outbreak of chicken pox.[1]

During this period Imboden was away from the brigade, tending to personal matters in Staunton. In his absence, Col. George Smith of the 62d Virginia Mounted Infantry commanded the brigade. Although Smith did his best, the men had been too long in the same area under less than strict discipline, and friction soon developed with Maj. Gen. Jubal Early—which would probably have been the case even had Imboden not been away.

Early always had a low opinion of "irregular" cavalrymen who believed they had enlisted only for limited service in the areas near their homes. Indeed, Early developed a strong prejudice against Imboden's troops. In any case, Early complained that he was much inconvenienced, and that in Imboden's absence his cavalry failed even to carry out proper reconnaissance. Matters came to a head when a lieutenant in Imboden's

Brigade killed a sergeant in the streets of Staunton. Early exploded in a complaint both to Smith and Fitzhugh Lee.[2]

Historian Douglas Southall Freeman has noted that it was typical of Early neither to forget nor forgive. Early continued to complain frequently and with some vehemence in private conversations that the greater part of Imboden's Brigade was inefficient, disorganized, poorly disciplined, and unreliable. He also stated that he believed many of its members had deserted from other Confederate units.

Freeman concluded that Early's two great failings as a general were, first, his tendency, as Robert E. Lee had noted, to fight battles by division instead of throwing his entire force into battle and, second, his "singular ineptitude" at handling his cavalry, which Freeman traced to Early's assignment in the Valley. Indeed, this experience seems to have soured Early toward all cavalry in general. As Freeman observed, "he made no effort to acquaint himself with that arm or to study its place in tactical co-ordination. For this neglect, whatever its origin, he was doomed to pay."[3] Freeman noted that Early:

> devoted more energy to criticizing than to disciplining them. A military student who reviews Early's limited correspondence on the subject is left in doubt whether the faults the General attributed to most of his cavalry were or were not alleged to cover Early's own lack of skill in handling mounted troops.[4]
>
> ... "Old Jube," in short, acquired a violent dislike of the troopers who garrisoned the Valley and probably, without being aware of it, became prejudiced against cavalry in general.[5]

Lee himself was not happy with discipline in Imboden's command. In September 1863 he wrote Imboden: "Prominent citizens of the valley have made serious complaints of the conduct of Captain Shearer's company of Gilmor's battalion. I wish you would see to it. If they cannot be brought under proper discipline, and continue to harass our own citizens by their bad conduct, they had much better be disbanded."[6]

In any case, when Imboden returned, he was incensed to learn of Early's attitude and the complaint to Smith. Although Early had not raised the matter in Imboden's presence or made it a personal issue, on February 12 Imboden protested Early's charges in a formal, dignified, and well-reasoned letter to Lee, in which he noted: "the fact that [General Early] is my commanding officer justifies me in the effort I now make to defend myself and command against sneers unofficially and publicly made which are calculated, if true, to bring me and my command into disrepute and contempt. I hope to be able to prove that Gen. Early has done me and my command gross injustice by yielding to the promptings of prejudice rather than reason."[7]

Imboden demanded that a court of inquiry look into the matter and that its findings, adverse or positive, be published in the Valley.[8]

Early stated that reports of his remarks had been "very greatly exaggerated." He did, however, reiterate his opinion that Imboden's command was in fact very poorly disciplined and that, as a result, he would be reluctant "to have to rely on it in an emergency." Referring to the recent murder, Early said that he had not insulted the brigade, because there was a general belief that the cavalrymen were "inefficient and undisciplined." Early recommended the court of inquiry be held and hoped that it would result in an improvement of Imboden's command.[9]

Lee realized there was much more to be lost than gained in a court of inquiry, and so he refused to authorize it. Instead, he notified Imboden that he did not think a court "advantageous." There the situation remained. Freeman concluded that although Early had "sneered privately" from the beginning of the war, "now he was careless, if not loud, in his condemnation of those he did not approve. It was not a change of character that would improve leadership in the Second Corps."[10]

Undoubtedly Lee agreed with much of Early's impressions. He found Imboden's command structure inefficient and in need of a thorough reorganization, and he was not impressed with Imboden's men. He wrote President Davis:

> My own opportunities of observation have not impressed me favorably with regard to the discipline and efficiency of General Imboden's troops....
>
> He [Early] says he can get no information about the enemy because he could make no reconnaissances with those troops. I have been disappointed in my expectations of the service of General Sam. Jones' command also. I think a reorganization of these troops necessary, and a change of commanders desirable.

The department requires a man of judgment and energy, whose discretion can be depended upon without always awaiting orders. . . . We can afford to lose nothing by want of discipline and efficiency among the troops.

Lee suggested to Davis that no new men be allowed to enter Jones's and Imboden's Brigades "beyond the number required to fill up existing organizations in those commands." Lee did note, however, that the situation in the Valley was also true in other states. His solution was to channel new recruits into the "more important and active armies."[11]

Imboden's Brigade was not long without activity. On January 16 Early ordered Imboden and his command northward. Early intended to mount another raid into the South Branch Valley, which he would lead in person. As with the last raid, Early divided Imboden's forces. Gilmor's and McNeill's troops and McClanahan's mountain howitzers accompanied Early's troops into Hardy County. Imboden and his remaining men were left behind.[12]

This second raid was much more successful. Early and his men took a sizeable Federal supply train of 93 wagons and also destroyed bridges over Patterson's Creek and the Potomac. When the raiders returned to their camp near New Market on February 5, they brought with them 1,700 head of cattle and sheep and 50 wagons full of supplies.[13]

Following the raid, Imboden removed his brigade to Rockbridge County. His command broke up into smaller detachments for scouting, tending to picket duty, searching for deserters, and collecting supplies.[14]

At this time, another instance of friction occurred between one of Early's commanders and one of Imboden's men. Captain McNeill criticized Brig. Gen. Thomas Rosser over his treatment of horses. Rosser was incensed that a low-ranking partisan officer would criticize a West Point–trained general officer, and he complained to both Fitzhugh Lee and Stuart concerning the Partisan Rangers. Rosser found sympathetic support from both of the regular cavalry commanders, who supported a plan to do away with the partisans entirely—a plan that gained momentum when Richmond repealed the Partisan Ranger Act. The secretary of war had authority to grant exception, however, if a company was serving behind Union lines. McNeill thus secured reprieve, although under heightened scrutiny.[15]

In February a change of command occurred that directly affected Imboden. Lee had been unhappy during the Gettysburg Campaign with what he perceived to be a lack of support from Department of Western Virginia commander Maj. Gen. Samuel Jones. His area of responsibility was a vast one, comprising all of southwestern Virginia, eastern Tennessee, and parts of Kentucky, as well as the area that had become West Virginia.

Lee's displeasure was compounded by Jones's failure to halt Federal raids into southwest Virginia and his apparent reluctance to seize the initiative. Discontented lawmakers in the region demanded more adequate protection. Finally, Jones's panicky report regarding the small November 1863 engagement near Droop Mountain did not sit well with Richmond. Largely at Lee's insistence, authorities in Richmond decided in February 1864 to relieve Jones. He accepted his reassignment with good grace and in April resurfaced as head of the Department of South Carolina, Georgia, and Florida.[16]

When it was suggested that Jones's successor might come from the Army of Northern Virginia, Lee appraised a number of his lieutenants, but President Davis settled on Maj. Gen. John C. Breckinridge, former U.S. vice president (1857–1861) and electoral runner-up to Abraham Lincoln in the 1860 presidential election. It turned out to be a wise choice. Following an early fiasco in February 1862, during which the Kentuckian escaped from Fort Donelson rather than take the onus of defeat, Breckinridge proved to be both a capable and aggressive commander. Promoted major general in April 1862, he commanded a corps in the Battle of Shiloh, led an attack on Baton Rouge in August, and played a major role at Stone's River in December. He later fought at Jackson, Mississippi, in the Battle of Chickamauga and commanded a corps at Missionary Ridge.[17]

At the end of February Early left the Valley to rejoin the Army of Northern Virginia as senior division commander in Ewell's II Corps. Breckinridge would need all his military acumen, as he would soon be called upon to hold the Valley against a major Federal thrust, in which Imboden would also play a key role.

Imboden's command, now the only major Confederate force in the Valley, relocated to Rockingham County and camped for two months at Bridgewater, where it would be well placed to meet a threat either from the west or north. There were few encounters with Union troops during this period, and the brigade spent March and April in relative inactivity.[18]

During this time a problem emerged, however, in the form of the Swamp Dragoons. This pro-Union group of bushwhackers operated against civilians in western Virginia with the support of the U.S. Army. In April McNeill carried out a well-organized raid on the Swamp Dragoons' camp that inflicted some casualties.[19]

Among his other duties, Imboden had to oversee courts-martial and the administration of military justice. At least one civilian had been arrested, and he became the object of admonishment by Gen. Robert E. Lee, a stickler for civilian control of the military, who wrote Imboden as follows:

> I have been informed that you have in arrest a citizen of Hardy County named Michael Yoakum, who is charged with outrages committed upon the person and property of some of our citizens of that county, and that you proposed trying him before a court-martial. I am also informed that a writ of *habeas corpus* has been sued out by Yoakum, to which you have made return claiming jurisdiction over the case. You have the power to afford immediate protection to our citizens against threatened or attempted violence, but where an offense has been committed by one not in the military service of the United States or our own you have no jurisdiction to try the offenders by a court-martial. You can arrest and deliver him to the civil authorities, who alone are competent to try him. If the facts of the case be such as I have represented them above, I desire that you will surrender the accused to the civil authorities, in obedience to the writ to be dispersed of by the court of jurisdiction.[20]

Presumably Imboden released Yoakum. Other cases did fall under Imboden's jurisdiction, and most of these involved soldiers who had left their units. Usually the more serious charge of desertion was reduced to absence without leave. The usual sentence for the latter was confinement to the guardhouse and extra duty. An exception to this was the case involving Pvt. John Mick of the 62d Virginia Mounted Infantry.

Mick had not only deserted his unit, but also joined the Swamp Dragoons. Captured, he was found guilty of desertion, sentenced to death, and executed before the assembled brigade on March 18, near the regiment's camp in Rockingham County.[21]

In considering possible Union threats to the Valley, Imboden initially concentrated on a Federal thrust from the west. On March 10 he predicted to Lee that there would be a "big raid some time this month." To counter this, Imboden began construction of fortifications in the mountains, but he feared they would not be completed in time. He warned Lee that if Averell attacked with five thousand to six thousand men and threatened two or three places at once, "say Staunton, Lexington, and the Virginia and Tennessee Railroad, we shall be sorely put to meet him unless these works are finished and other troops sent to the district." Imboden also urged that Breckinridge undertake a similar project.[22]

By the end of March, routine duties faded as Union forces again became active. On March 23 Imboden reported to Lee regular heavy movements of Union troops west along the B&O during the previous week. Lee believed these reinforcement were destined for the Union Army of the Tennessee and that their movement probably presaged a Union push against troops under General Johnston or possibly forces under General Longstreet. He thought that for the moment, at least, a Union push was more likely there than in Virginia: "The condition of the weather and the roads will probably be more favorable for active operations at an early day in the south than in Va. where it will be uncertain for more than a month."[23]

In mid-April Lee warned that Averell would probably attempt an attack on the Virginia & Tennessee Railroad or Staunton from a "point beyond North Mountain." He hoped that Imboden and Breckinridge might beat Averell back, for "I shall be so occupied, in all probability, that I shall be unable to aid you." He also added, "I see no indications of a movement up the Valley."[24]

At least regarding the latter, Lee was mistaken. Imboden was at Mount Carmel in Rockingham County when he learned of the presence of newly appointed commander of the Department of West Virginia Maj. Gen. Franz Sigel at Winchester and the probability that he would soon be advancing up the Valley. Sigel arrived in Martinsburg from Cumberland on April 25. The next day he shifted command responsibilities. Maj. Gen. Julius Stahel, who had commanded the department's cavalry, now took command at Martinsburg of his own 1st Cavalry Division and Brig. Gen. Jeremiah C. Sullivan's 1st Infantry Division.

On April 29 Sigel's troops left Martinsburg and marched to Bunker Hill; on May 1 they reached Winchester. Sigel sent his cavalry on to Cedar Creek and Strasburg to scout for the Confederates. In the process, he learned that his only opposition in the Valley was from Imboden's cavalry and mounted infantry, estimated at about three thousand men.[25]

Sigel's advance was part of Union general-in-chief Lt. Gen. Ulysses S. Grant's grand strategic plan for a multipronged simultaneous Union offensive. In the western theater Maj. Gen. William T. Sherman was to drive into Georgia with the goal of destroying Johnston's army. At the same time, Maj. Gen. Nathaniel Banks would try to take Mobile.

Simultaneously, a major Union effort would be mounted in the eastern theater in the form of a multifaceted operation in Virginia. Grant would accompany Maj. Gen. George Meade's one hundred thousand–man Army of the Potomac, assembling at Culpeper for a drive south to Richmond. At the same time, Maj. Gen. Benjamin Butler's thirty-six thousand–man Army of the James was to march up the south bank of the James and cut Lee and Confederate forces off from the lower south. In the western part of the state, Averell would lead some two thousand cavalry east from West Virginia via Lewisburg to Saltville in Wythe County to destroy the valuable saltworks at that place. Brig. Gen. George Crook would take his three brigades of more than six thousand men across the Alleghenies and Blue Ridge to attack the Virginia & Tennessee Railroad and destroy vital Confederate stores at Dublin Depot. Colonel Harris would also make a demonstration from Beverly. Finally, there was Sigel's thrust up the Shenandoah Valley. If all went well, Sigel would join up with Crook and Averell in the vicinity of Staunton or even Lynchburg.

With only a weak Confederate force confronting him, Sigel expected to be able to reach Staunton and draw off Confederate resources facing Crook and Averell. Sigel's force consisted chiefly of the 1st Infantry and 1st Cavalry Divisions and five artillery batteries.[26]

With Averell already on the move, Lee assumed that Averell and

Sigel would be operating together against the Virginia & Tennessee Railroad or Staunton. On May 1 he telegraphed Breckinridge and urged the Department of Western Virginia commander to work "in concert" with Imboden against them. He warned Breckinridge that he would be operating alone, as "it will be impossible to send any reinforcements to the Valley from this army." Lee assumed the Union objective to be Staunton.[27]

On May 4 Lee assigned Breckinridge "general direction of affairs" beyond the Blue Ridge. He instructed him to "use General Imboden's force as you think best." Lee ended his dispatch with, "I trust you will drive the enemy back."[28]

Imboden was confident enough. On May 2 he reported to Lee a raid by a unit of the 62d Regiment against the Swamp Dragoons at Pendleton and the securing of 130 cattle. Imboden also said that he was "perplexed" regarding Union intentions to the west. Although he pointed out that his own force was too small to divide, he boasted, "My knowledge of the country is so perfect that I believe I can beat back an invading party five times my own numbers."[29]

Imboden gave his strength on May 2, the day he broke camp at Mount Crawford some seventy miles south of Winchester, at 1,492 effectives, along with about 100 men employed as scouts both in front and behind Sigel's force. Gen. William Harman's militia numbered at best 1,000 men. Untrained, they were armed with a variety of muskets and shotguns. Writing well after the war, Imboden described his own force as "in splendid condition for hard service."[30] The exact size of Imboden's actual force is hard to pin down; in June he reported to Lee that he had 3,000 men, but this figure undoubtedly included reserves.[31]

Imboden's command consisted of Col. George H. Smith's 62d Virginia Mounted Infantry, Col. Robert White's 41st Battalion of Virginia Cavalry, Col. George Imboden's 18th Virginia Cavalry, and Capt. Hanse McNeill's Partisan Rangers. He also had Brig. Gen. Gabriel C. Wharton's Infantry Brigade, Capt. John McClanahan's Battery of Horse Artillery, Maj. Harry Gilmor's Battalion of Maryland Cavalry, Maj. Sturgis Davis's Battalion of Maryland Cavalry, and Capt. J.H. Bartlett's Valley District Signal Corps. If the need arose, Imboden could also call upon the reserves, consisting of able-bodied men between the ages of eighteen and forty-five and boys between the ages of sixteen and eighteen. Imboden feared that use of the reserves would indeed be necessary, and he sent a message to General Harman at Staunton to alert reserves in Rockingham and Augusta Counties, as well as "detailed men" working at shops and furnaces, to be ready to move on a moment's notice. He also notified VMI superintendent Major General Smith regarding calling out the cadets, although he told Smith that he hoped to delay "placing the entire force in the field if practicable till the Spring Crops are fairly under way."[32]

On May 3 Imboden reported Union troops at Kernstown. Substantial Union artillery was located there and at Winchester. Imboden reported Union strength at three thousand men. The next day he was at Mount Jackson with his entire command; Sigel was then at Front Royal. Imboden reported Sigel's strength at seven thousand men and concluded that the Union troops would head east across the Blue Ridge. Imboden informed Breckinridge that he believed Sigel "is doubtless going to Grant via Chester Gap." On May 5 Imboden was at New Market, where he suggested that he immediately move against Cumberland with Breckinridge threatening Grafton. One of the telegraph operators did not have the correct cipher, for Breckinridge replied from Dublin that he could not make out Imboden's message but had four thousand men en route for Jackson River Depot, there to entrain north. On May 7 Imboden reported Averell had arrived at Winchester two days before with three thousand cavalry and that Sigel was also there with four thousand infantry. For the moment at least, the Union forces were not moving.[33]

That same day, May 7, Lee ordered Breckinridge to move north: "The movements proposed in the Valley, if made, must be made at once." Breckinridge's men covered the 145 miles in three days, reaching Staunton on the evening of May 9.[34]

At this point Imboden's plan was to drive into Hampshire County and attack the B&O. He believed that such a move would force Sigel to quit Winchester and fall back to protect the railroad. Imboden was confident that when Breckinridge joined him, their combined force would be sufficient to "clear this border in five days, destroy railroad, canal, and coal mines from New Creek to Martinsburg."[35]

Actually Imboden had already ordered Captain McNeill and his Rangers on another raid against the B&O. McNeill set out with sixty men on the evening of May 3. The second night they crossed over a ford on the South Branch of the Potomac and into Maryland; they then moved east to Bloomington on the B&O. By dawn on May 5 they had taken the town and commandeered an eastbound freight train. McNeill's men rode the train nearly two miles to Piedmont Station, the location of considerable railroad stores and machine shops. On arrival they detached the locomotive, which two of the Rangers rode into the town under a flag of truce. The others followed on horseback. The small Union detachment at Piedmont quickly surrendered, and McNeill's men then set about the task of destroying the shops and supplies. Within an hour, they had destroyed property estimated to be worth more than one million dollars, including 7 machine shops, 9 locomotives, and more than 150 loaded freight cars. The raiders ran six other locomotives, steam up, into nearby New Creek and then burned the railroad bridge across the North Branch of the Potomac leading to Cumberland.[36]

At the same time another smaller ranger detachment under Capt. John T. Pearce acted against the rail line itself. The men wrecked two loaded Union freight trains and boldly demanded surrender of a third train with passenger cars containing Union troops. The Union commander surrendered his one hundred men to only eleven Confederates, without a shot being fired. Pearce then withdrew with the prisoners and rejoined McNeill.[37]

On the afternoon of May 8, Confederate signalers from atop Massanutten Mountain reported two groups of Union cavalry on the move, each estimated at about one thousand men. The actual forces involved were much smaller than reported. Sigel had ordered Col. Jacob Higgins with some five hundred men of the 23d Pennsylvania Cavalry west to Wardensburg to protect his right flank. The Confederates spotted this force as it moved west across North Mountain on the road to Moorefield.

At the same time Sigel also sent Col. William H. Boyd and three hundred Union cavalry into the Luray Valley to cover his left flank. The Confederates picked up this force as it moved east through Port Royal, passing by that town and then traveling on the road through Chester Gap in the Blue Ridge Mountains. Imboden recalled years later that these Union movements demonstrated that Sigel wanted to determine, before moving south with his infantry, whether there were Confederate forces to his flanks. Imboden recalled that his own intention was to defeat one or both of these cavalry screens before they could rejoin the main Union body. Aware that Union sympathizers in the area would soon report his movements to Sigel, Imboden let it be known that he was moving the bulk of his command to North Mountain to secure better grazing land for his horses.

Leaving Col. George Smith in command with only some 510 men of the 62d Regiment at Woodstock, at about 4:00 P.M. on May 9 Imboden departed with the 18th and 23d Virginia Cavalry Regiments and two guns in an effort to join McNeill and overtake the Union cavalry that had ridden toward Moorefield. Imboden had been reporting increasing Union strength to his front, with indications of movement in a day or two.

Imboden's report to Breckinridge on his intentions differs, however, from what he recalled years later. His dispatch to Breckinridge on May 9 merely informed his superior that 1,300 Union cavalry were trying to intercept McNeill and that he was leaving with two regiments of cavalry and an artillery section to assist McNeill and help bring in his prisoners. He informed Breckinridge that he expected to return in four to five days.

With a Union advance in the offing, the intention that Imboden recalled after the fact of cutting off one or more of the Union cavalry pincers would make more sense than attempting to rescue McNeill and sixty men. Probably Imboden's primary task was to secure the return of McNeill and the prisoners, while at the same time—if the situation proved favorable—he would seek to destroy part of the Union cavalry screen.[38]

Heading west and traveling all night, Imboden crossed North Mountain by way of Devil's Hole Pass. He and his cavalry arrived at Lost River in Hardy County, West Virginia, before dawn on May 10. They linked up with McNeill north of Wardensville and learned that the Federals had spent the night at Moorefield. Enjoying a two-to-one numerical superiority, the Confederates decided to lay an ambush for Higgins's five hundred Federals, made up of the 15th New York and 22d Pennsylvania.

The Federals had earlier surprised McNeill at Moorefield, although McNeill had been warned just in time for most of his men to escape. Some, however, had been captured. Now the tables would be turned, for Imboden had about eight hundred men. McNeill's men skirmished with the Federal cavalry at the entrance to Lost River Gap and then fell back, drawing the Union troopers into the gap where Imboden's cavalry lay in wait. Battle was joined and the Federals soon fled in confusion. One of the members of the 18th Virginia Cavalry noted, "We got them on a stampede and run them all day." Imboden's men pursued the Federals over some sixty miles, all the way across the Potomac River at Oldtown, Maryland.

Imboden claimed his men had killed five Union soldiers, captured twelve new supply wagons, an ambulance, and thirteen prisoners. The Confederates took more than twenty horses, and the Union troopers killed others to prevent their capture. Imboden's men then returned to Lost River.

In reporting his success to Breckinridge, Imboden announced, "I thrashed part of three regiments cavalry in Hardy yesterday." The loss of five hundred members of his cavalry at the very onset of the campaign was a serious blow to Sigel and reinforced his already pronounced caution.[39]

Meanwhile, Crook was making progress to the south, despite bad weather. He had pushed his more than 6,000 men across the Alleghenies and into southwestern Virginia toward his objective of the Virginia & Tennessee Railroad. On May 9, however, Crook ran into a patchwork Confederate force commanded by Brig. Gen. Albert G. Jenkins. With only about 2,400 men and 10 guns, Jenkins had selected a defensive position on high, wooded bluffs some five miles north of Dublin Depot in Pulaski County, Crook's principal objective.

In the Battle of Cloyd's Mountain (or Cloyd's Farm) on May 9, superior Union resources carried the day. Crook dismounted and personally led Union troops in the fight. Although repulsed on the Confederate right, Col. Rutherford B. Hayes and his 1st Brigade struck the Confederate center and, in vicious fighting, drove it back. Jenkins, wounded, was taken prisoner, and his injury required the amputation of his arm. He had begun to recover when an attendant knocked off a ligature, leaving Jenkins to bleed to death before a surgeon could be called. Col. John McCausland, commander of the 26th Virginia Regiment, succeeded Jenkins.

Although the Union suffered 688 casualties, the Confederate tally of 538 was twice that of the Federals in percentage of force. There on May 10, twelve Federal artillery pieces engaged in a prolonged artillery duel with fourteen Confederate guns. The Southerners turned back repeated Union attempts to destroy the bridge, but shortly after noon, their ammunition exhausted, they were forced to withdraw. Crook then went on to burn the New River Railroad Bridge, a major objective. McCausland withdrew his command east to Christiansburg, where it rested for several hours, before going on to Big Hill near Salem, where McCausland intended a stand on the Staunton River. Crook camped at Blacksburg. The Federals, short of supplies in any case, withdrew beginning on May 12, when Crook learned through some false telegrams that Grant had been defeated in the Battle of the Wilderness and was retreating. McCausland was subsequently promoted brigadier general of cavalry and took over Jenkins's brigade on a permanent basis.[40]

Meanwhile, Sigel had begun his drive south up the Valley on May 8. He moved south at a glacial pace, which was indeed fortunate for Breckinridge, who needed all the time he could secure for his own defensive efforts. On May 9 the Union troops marched fifteen miles to Stone House, some three miles north of Strasburg. They remained there until May 11, when they broke camp early, arriving at Woodstock by 4:00 P.M.[41]

That day, Colonel Smith reported to Breckinridge in Imboden's absence that Union strength was not over six thousand men. He estimated it at perhaps four thousand infantry and the remainder in cavalry. The Union troops were now advancing, and he had received no word from Imboden.[42]

Imboden rejoined Colonel Smith at Mount Jackson on May 11. That same day, Sigel's troops drove back Davis's Maryland Battalion and entered Woodstock. The Federals captured the telegraph office before its records could be destroyed and there learned that Breckinridge was advancing to support Imboden. This led Sigel to hesitate, allowing the Confederates an opportunity to consolidate. Indeed, Sigel informed Washington that while his intention had been to threaten Staunton, divide Breckinridge's forces, and assist General Crook (from whom he had not heard word since May 6): "My own forces are insufficient for offensive operations in this country, where the enemy is continuously on my flanks and rear. My intention, therefore, is not to advance further than this place with my main force." Skirmishing was going on, and, he wrote, "If Breckinridge should advance against us I will resist him at some convenient position."[43]

Imboden, meanwhile, placed Sigel's strength at some 11,000 men: over 8,000 infantry, 2,500 cavalry, and three to four artillery batteries. From the west signalers reported another Union force of 7,000 men at Lewisburg, little more than one hundred miles from Staunton, apparently awaiting Sigel's progress south before they themselves moved. Imboden communicated these figures—which turned out to be exaggerated—by telegraph from New Market to Richmond, appealing to Lee to send immediate reinforcements.

At Mount Jackson, Smith informed Imboden that he had withdrawn before Sigel's advance. He had in place a mounted picket at Fisher's Hill, behind which there were stations of couriers ready to relay word of further Union movement. Imboden also conferred with Major Gilmor, who he had sent to Luray to learn about the progress of the second detachment of Union cavalry under Colonel Boyd. Atop the Blue Ridge, Gilmor had learned from fleeing Rappahannock County residents that the Federal cavalrymen were looting and in no particular hurry. They told inhabitants that they would rejoin Sigel at New Market.

Imboden then moved to the vicinity of Rude's Hill, four miles north of New Market, where he was informed of the arrival of the second of Sigel's cavalry columns that had departed the Union camp on May 8. Acting on this information, Imboden prepared a trap for the Union force, which was sprung on May 13.[44]

After leaving Sigel, Colonel Boyd's 1st New York Cavalry of three hundred men and two mountain howitzers had moved across the Blue Ridge into the Luray Valley and then headed south, the best means of approaching New Market without detection. By the morning of May 13 they were headed west back across the Blue Ridge through Luray, where they discovered and destroyed a considerable quantity of Confederate commissary supplies. Men of the 18th Virginia Cavalry spotted the Union troopers as they issued through Luray Gap east of New Market. Imboden immediately called upon his 18th and 23d Virginia Cavalry Regiments. He sent the 23d to the bridge over Smith's Creek to meet the Union troopers head on and fix them in place while the 18th and two of McClanahan's artillery pieces worked around behind the Federals and cut off their retreat.

Outnumbered two to one, the defeat of Boyd's regiment was inevitable. Part of the Federal force broke free, but the Confederates took seventy-five prisoners and killed and wounded many others. Elon Henkel of New Market recorded the Confederate pursuit as "neck and neck, the horses hoofs hammering the pike, the scabbards of the sabres rattling, and the cavalrymen giving the rebel yell."[45] Capt. James H. Stevenson of the 1st New York wrote, "Our men were seen running in all directions on foot.... their horses having given out or got fast among the rocks; while some of the horses rushed along wildly without riders, the saddles under their bellies."[46]

Those Federal troopers who got away scattered into Massanutten Mountain. Lt. James M. Potts of Company G of the 18th noted, "[We] drove them into Massanutten Mountains, capturing nearly the entire detachment. We sent the prisoners up the Valley, but kept their splendid horses to take the place of our badly jaded stock."[47] Sigel more accurately put the Union loss at 125 men and 200 horses. In his later published account of the Battle of New Market, Imboden claimed his men captured 464 Federals, many more than the actual number in Boyd's force.[48]

Regardless of Imboden's inflated figure, in a short span he had inflicted several hundred casualties on two divided Union cavalry and scattered many more who would not be available for the coming battle. He claimed, correctly, that his two defeats of Sigel's flanking cavalry "secured us the all important few days' respite from his dreaded advance, and enabled General John C. Breckinridge, from south-western Virginia, to reach the valley with something over 2500 of his best veteran troops to be united with mine for a battle with Sigel wherever we might chance to meet him."[49]

General Lee recognized the accomplishment in his General Order No. 41: "A part of the enemy's force threatening the Valley of Virginia has been routed by Genl. Imboden, and driven back to the Potomac, with the loss of their train and a number of prisoners."[50]

At the same time, with resources stretched thin and facing pressure by the Army of the Potomac, Lee replied that he would need all his own forces, at least for several days. He urged Imboden to do what he could to retard Sigel's advance in every way possible, while at the same time avoiding being surrounded and captured. Indeed, Lee wired Breckinridge that if he could defeat Sigel, "it would be very desirable for you to join me with your whole force."[51]

At Breckinridge's direction, the VMI cadets and a section of artillery moved north from Lexington on the morning of May 11. Some of the men were as young as fifteen. The 229 cadets were armed with Austrian muskets; each carried 40 rounds of ammunition. Among them was Jacob "Jake" Peck Imboden, aged seventeen, General Imboden's youngest brother.[52]

Sigel's slow advance up the Valley resumed on May 13. Imboden had his pickets at Rude's Hill and announced to Breckinridge that he intended a stand there against Sigel's cavalry. If Sigel reinforced with infantry and artillery, Imboden undoubtedly would have to retire to Lacey Spring. On May 14 poor weather conditions prevented Confederate signalers on Massanutten Mountain from ascertaining Federal movements, but Imboden believed falsely "that enemy has fallen back."[53]

On May 12 Breckinridge reached Staunton, where he allowed his men a day of rest while awaiting the arrival of the VMI cadets. The men then cooked two days' worth of rations. Once united with Imboden, Breckinridge would have some 5,300 men and eighteen guns to oppose Sigel's much larger Federal force. Breckinridge had about 4,200 infantry, the bulk of which was in the 1st Brigade under John Echols and the 2d Brigade under Wharton. The latter included Col. George H. Smith's 62d Virginia Mounted Infantry (448 men), which Breckinridge detached from Imboden's command to fight dismounted as infantry. Other commands included an engineer company, the 23d Virginia Cavalry (which also fought as infantry), reserves from Augusta and Rockingham Counties, and the Virginia Military Institute Corps of Cadets. Breckinridge could call on 735 cavalry, the bulk of which—615 men—came from Imboden's 18th Virginia Cavalry under his brother Col. George Imboden. It also included units under Maj. Harry Gilmor and Capt. John McNeill. In addition there were 341 men in artillery units, with a total of 18 guns. This force included Capt. John McClanahan's Battery of 93 men with four 3-inch ordnance rifles and two howitzers.[54]

The assumption was that Breckinridge would wait for the Federals at Staunton and throw up breastworks there to help offset the larger Federal numbers. But Breckinridge was determined to attack rather than wait to be attacked, and he resumed the march north on May 13. Despite a driving rain, the Confederates covered twenty miles that day, and they reached Lacey Spring on May 14.[55]

In order to ascertain Imboden's strength, on the morning of May 14

Sigel sent Col. Augustus Moor on a reconnaissance in force. Moor was to proceed from Woodstock to Mount Jackson with two infantry regiments, some six hundred cavalry, and two sections of artillery. Mount Jackson, terminus of the Massanutten Gap Railroad, was seven miles north of the farming community of New Market. At Edinburg, Colonel Moor's force was joined by three hundred cavalry of Col. John E. Wynkoop's 2d Brigade and another regiment of Moor's 1st Brigade. Maj. Harry Gilmor and his 2d Maryland Battalion defended before Mount Jackson, but his small force of forty men could only delay the Union advance of some 2,350 men.[56]

As Moor moved up at 3:00 P.M., heavy firing could be heard to the front. Some six hundred men of the 1st New York Cavalry Regiment under Maj. Timothy Quinn were already engaged. Moor collected units as he advanced along the Pike. The Union cavalry pushed the Confederates back and seized the bridge over the North Fork of the Shenandoah, two miles south of Mount Jackson. There they came under fire from one of Imboden's batteries some distance beyond the bridge. The two sides then exchanged long-range artillery fire. Sigel delayed a crossing until his infantry could come up the next day.

On May 14 Imboden's infantry were deployed in line across the pike at Rude's Hill, about a mile south of the bridge over the North Fork of the Shenandoah and four miles north of New Market. With the situation apparently calm and having been informed by courier that Breckinridge would be in Lacey Spring, ten miles south of New Market, by noon, Imboden left Smith in charge and rode south to confer there with Breckinridge.

Imboden was at Lacey Spring discussing strategy with Breckinridge over dinner when a courier arrived from Smith to report some 2,500 Union cavalry at Rude's Hill and desperate fighting there as Union forces pushed Col. George Imboden's 18th Cavalry Regiment back. Smith had formed a line of battle to the south to cover the 18th's retreat.

Imboden immediately left his meeting with Breckinridge and rode to rally his men. Artillery fire audible in the distance underscored the serious nature of the fighting. Imboden remembered Breckinridge's orders as "to hold New Market at all hazards till dark, and then fall back four miles... where he would join me during the night with his troops."[57]

In 1864 New Market was a small farming community of some one

The 1864 Shenandoah Valley Campaign   211

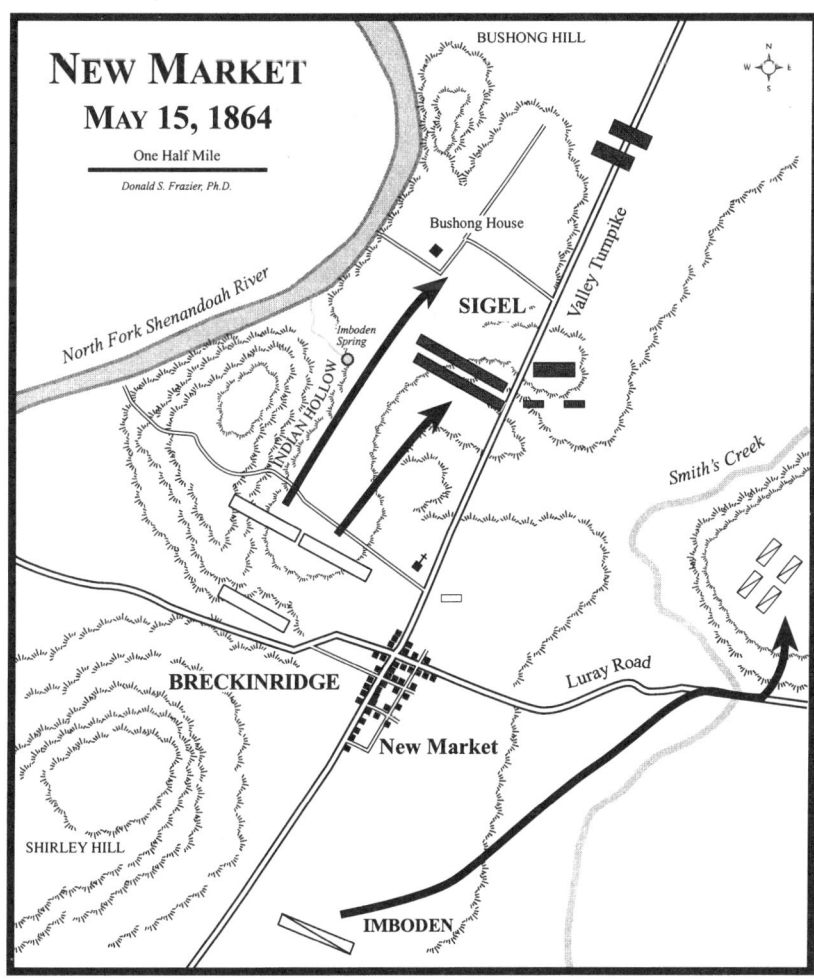

New Market, May 15, 1864

thousand people, nestled in the Valley between the Blue Ridge Mountains to the east and rolling hills to the west. The north-south Valley Turnpike, New Market's main street, lay at the foot of the hills, which were largely cleared and in cultivation on the side facing the town. The town is bounded by two streams. Beyond the hills to the west of New Market lies the south-north North Fork of the Shenandoah River, while about a mile east of the town at the foot of Massanutten Mountain is Smith's Creek. Despite its small size, in 1864 New Market was an important transportation crossroads. From the Valley Pike an important road ran east to Luray through the gap in Massanutten Mountain.

After an hour's ride, Imboden arrived at New Market to find that Smith had deployed the brigade in line formation across the pike. The men were single ranks and spread out more than usual so as to give the impression of a larger force. The Confederate line ran from about half the way up the hills west of the town of New Market east across the pike toward Smith's Creek, the right wing being concealed by woods to its front. McClanahan's Battery occupied a hill at the extreme left of the Confederate line, which gave it a commanding view of the town and terrain to the front as well as an advantage over the Union guns, which were at a lower elevation.

From McClanahan's position, Imboden surveyed the battlefield. The Union line was as yet unformed, and the only forces in view were some cavalry and a few guns. Imboden concluded that the Confederates would be able to hold their positions that evening and that any fighting would be limited to artillery fire. There was no serious damage inflicted by this to either side and at nightfall firing ceased.[58]

It rained the night of May 14–15, and as a consequence it was pitch black. During the night Colonel Moor adjusted his battle line near the Shenandoah River, occupying a plateau northwest of New Market. Union campfires betrayed the exact position.

Imboden fell asleep sometime after midnight by the road near the center of his line, but he was awakened a few hours before daybreak by a camp guard shining a lantern in his face. Breckinridge had arrived. He informed Imboden that his men would be in position by sunrise.

As daylight broke, Breckinridge's wet, bedraggled, and tired troops came up. As the men halted to rest, Breckinridge surveyed the ground and selected his line of battle. He deployed his forces into line about a mile south of New Market near Shirley's Hill, between the Pike and the Shenandoah River to the west, where he expected to meet an attack by Sigel.[59]

Meanwhile, at 4:00 A.M. on May 15, although he did not believe there was a substantial number of Confederates on hand, Sigel ordered his aide, Major Theodore S. Lang, to take a dozen orderlies and proceed to the front lines to ascertain the size of the Confederate force opposing Moor. Moor reported to Lang that while Imboden had left the Union front at about midnight, Quinn's cavalry had captured a Confederate deserter who reported that Breckinridge had arrived with reinforcements and was then about four miles south of New Market. Lang immediately urged Sigel to bring up his entire force. A battle would soon occur.[60]

At the same time Breckinridge was explaining his plans to Imboden. He had brought with him to New Market approximately 3,000 men: Echols's and Wharton's Brigades, a six-gun battery, a section of the VMI cadet battery temporarily attached to McLaughlin, and the VMI cadets formed into four companies under command of Col. Scott Shipp. Although they had been called up, the reserves from Augusta and Rockingham Counties had yet to form and were thus not present. Imboden had not more than 1,600 troops, the largest unit being his 62d Virginia with 550 men.[61]

Breckinridge ordered the 62d to fight as dismounted infantry. He planned to place them and the Corps of Cadets on the flank of either Wharton's or Echols's Brigades in the center of the Confederate defensive line. The remainder of Imboden's command—the 18th Virginia Cavalry and McClanahan's battery horse artillery—would form on the other side of the Valley Pike on the extremity of the Confederate right flank, near Smith's Creek. This was marshy ground and poor terrain for infantry, but it could be held by a thinly dispersed cavalry line.

But after daylight upon studying the terrain and with Sigel not advancing, Breckinridge decided to advance. Imboden recalled him as announcing, "We can attack and whip them here, and I'll do it."[62]

Breckinridge sent orders for his infantry to advance immediately. He instructed McLaughlin not to wait for the infantry but immediately to bring his eight guns up to the hill where Breckinridge and Imboden had been surveying the field. As soon as the artillery and infantry had come up, Imboden, as previously planned, was to form up on the right extremity of the Confederate line along with McClanahan's Battery. Perhaps 2,500 Confederates were in line west of the Pike, with another 1,000 to its east.

A terrific artillery duel now opened, with gunners on both sides firing as fast as possible. The town of New Market lay between the two sides, but because the artillery was on higher ground to the Confederate left and Union right, the shells passed over it. For about an hour the battle was limited to artillery fire alone.

Meanwhile, Lang sent one of the orderlies to Sigel with the news of the Confederate movement north, and shortly thereafter he sent another orderly with information that the Confederates were deploying a skirmish line across the Valley. Lang thought a Confederate attack imminent and urged Sigel to bring up his entire command on the double quick. Shortly after this, Lang could see the Confederates deploying into line for an attack. Soon a second line appeared, indicating a sizeable force. In all Lang sent four messages back to Sigel. Soon the skirmishers had opened fire, and a Confederate gun fired on Lang's orderlies, who were standing in an exposed position.

Having received no word from Sigel, Lang now sent a fifth messenger to spell out in no uncertain words the precarious Union position and tell Sigel that he must bring up his entire force. Lang suggested that the artillery and cavalry be positioned in the road and the infantry in the fields on either side. Lang also informed Sigel that, if he delayed, it would be too late.

Sigel had in fact resumed his march south from Woodstock at about 5:00 A.M. on May 15, crossing the North Fork of the Shenandoah River and then halting about a mile north of New Market astride the Valley Pike. Union cavalry were the first to arrive, and then Sigel rode up and met with Lang. Sigel at first was of a mind to dismiss Lang's reports as alarmist and accuse him of being "excited," until Lang pointed out the two long lines of Confederate troops before them.

When his own infantry was in position, at about 11:00 A.M., Breckinridge sent them forward. The Confederate line was anchored by Breckinridge's two brigades; between them was the 62d Virginia, now fighting on foot. The VMI cadets were in reserve in the center just behind the 62d.

The Confederate line advanced in good order, notwithstanding Union artillery fire, an occasional shell or shot from which blew a gap in the advancing line. The men would quickly reform and the advance continue.

As the Confederate infantry reached the edge of New Market, Imboden rode into the woods on the right flank to see what Union force Sigel might have deployed there and with the intention of trying to get in behind the Federals and destroy the bridge over the Shenandoah. If the Confederate advance continued, he would also be moving forward in that area. Imboden's way was blocked, however; he soon discovered the bulk of Sigel's cavalry massed to his front in fields just beyond the woods. Guns in one of their batteries had earlier lobbed a few shells over the woods in Imboden's general direction.

Imboden ordered his cavalry forward at "trot march," down Smith's Creek to the bridge on the Luray Road. McClanahan's Battery followed. Moving down the east side of the creek, Imboden's men reached a small hill less than a thousand yards from the Union cavalry, enfilading and slightly behind the Union line. McClanahan's artillerymen were able to unlimber their guns before they were discovered. The Union cavalry were massed in column, squadron front formation, and, as Imboden noted later, this close formation provided his gunners "a target of whole acres of men and horses."[63]

As the gunners fired as rapidly as possible, Imboden's cavalrymen begin working their way slowly down the creek as if they planned to take the Union cavalry from the rear. As the Confederate shells crashed among them, the Union cavalrymen, unaware that the woods to their front were held only by a skirmish line, wheeled to their right and rapidly retired. This uncovered one of their batteries, which then changed position and exchanged a few rounds with McClanahan's guns. Imboden later claimed this as a turning point in the battle: "But the rapid retrograde movement of the discomfited cavalry and our flank fire was observed by General Breckinridge, who immediately pushed forward his infantry with great energy under cover of the excellent service of McLaughlin's guns, aided by McClanahan, whose shot and shell, now that the cavalry were out of the way, began to fall upon Sigel's infantry flank. Thus pressed in front, and harassed in flank, General Sigel retired his whole line to a new position half a mile further back."[64]

At about noon the Confederates pressed north through New Market to the cheers of the townspeople. Shortly thereafter McClanahan occupied the positions on which the Union artillery had been sited the day before. Apart from some skirmishing, there was in fact little fighting along Imboden's portion of the line during the battle.[65]

Sigel formed his own line of battle on the slope of Bushong's Hill about a mile north of New Market. It was anchored by eighteen guns in three batteries on the forward sloping crest of the hill.

Despite having left troops behind to protect his supply lines, Sigel still had some 6,500 infantry and cavalry and 28 guns. The Union deployment of infantry and artillery was far too leisurely and consequently was not completed by the time the Confederates struck.

Breckinridge's infantry, meanwhile, had pushed through New Market, following McLaughlin's six guns, which occupied the position previously held by the Union batteries. There was now an exchange of artillery fire for about an hour. Much of the damage inflicted on both sides in the resulting battle was from this artillery fire. The center of the Confederate line took an especial pounding, particularly the 62d Virginia and the cadets to the rear, as some of the Union guns were firing high.

Just beyond the Bushong farmhouse, the Confederate line came under heavy Union infantry and artillery fire. On the Confederate left heavy Union fire halted Lt. Col. John P. Wolfe's 51st Virginia Infantry of Wharton's 2d Brigade. In advance of the other Confederate units, the unsupported 62d stopped to reform. Capt. Charles H. Woodson's Company A of the 1st Missouri Cavalry was fighting with the 62d as infantry, and Woodson now ordered his marksmen to take aim on the Union gunners. The Missourians managed to silence some of the Union guns temporarily, but at high cost: forty of the sixty Missouri troops were either killed or wounded, the highest percentage losses of any unit in the battle.

As the fighting intensified, one six-gun battery in particular wreaked havoc on the Confederate center, and Breckinridge ordered the 62d Virginia and VMI cadets to take it. Breckinridge had hoped to keep the cadets in reserve and avoid what Jefferson Davis had referred to as "grinding the seed corn of the nation," but at this critical moment he believed he had no choice. He ordered Colonels Smith and Shipp to "Put the boys in." The 62d also took part in the charge, but its veterans did not advance as quickly as the ardent cadets, who moved forward to fill a gap in the line and immediately attacked, despite furious Union canister and grape shot. It had been raining all day and many of the cadets were shoeless, the consequence of a muddy depression, later dubbed the "Field of Lost Shoes." Under furious Union fire, the cadets kept their formation until they received the order to charge. The cadets swept over the

Union guns and took two of them; a great yell went up when one of the cadets mounted a caisson and waved the flag over it.[66]

In all, the cadets suffered fifty-seven casualties: five killed, four mortally wounded, and forty-eight others wounded. Among the casualties that day was young Jake Imboden, knocked down and temporarily disabled by canister. Next to the Missourians, the cadets suffered the highest percentage casualty rate of any Confederate unit: 24 percent. In the process, however, the cadets took two Union guns. Although Sigel himself displayed great personal bravery and the Union troops fought well, they were not completely prepared for the concentrated Confederate attack.[67]

At the same time the cadets and 62d moved forward, the remaining Confederate infantry under Echols and Wharton charged the entire Union line, which, after a brief stand, gave way. McLaughlin, his guns loaded with canister, rumbled through New Market on its macadamized main street. It was a good thing his guns were ready to fire, for the Union cavalry made one last charge. Met by McLaughlin's guns and also under fire from McClanahan's Battery across Smith Creek, they soon retired.

At about 3:00 P.M. the battle was over. Intermittent long-range firing continued over the next several hours as Sigel skillfully redeployed in a more or less orderly withdrawal. Soon he decided in favor of a general retirement down the Valley to Cedar Creek, covered by Capt. Henry A. Du Pont's battery. Sigel reported, "Our troops were overpowered by superior numbers. I, therefore, withdrew them gradually from the battle-field and recrossed the Shenandoah."[68]

Imboden's role in the battle has been debated. Edward R. Turner, a leading authority on the battle, praised Imboden for his actions leading up to New Market: "The Confederate triumph was owing to the superb and brilliant movements of Imboden and Breckinridge, who showed themselves no unworthy successors of Stonewall Jackson."[69]

As has been noted, Imboden later claimed that his work in pushing back the Union cavalry massing on the Confederate right was the turning point in the battle. Turner, however, questioned this: "The truth, however, seems to be that this movement was almost entirely a mistake. Imboden merely took the Confederate cavalry and a portion of the artillery where they could not be used against the enemy. McClanahan's guns did indeed send some well directed shots into Stahel's midst, but this fire simply caused the Federal horsemen to move out of range, and did not prevent them a little later from making a vigorous attack upon Derrick and the Confederate right."[70]

Historian William Couper reached much the same conclusion: "the Confederate cavalry and four guns of McClanahan's Battery were effectively eliminated from the battle."[71] Union Captain Du Pont also noted that the four guns with Imboden's cavalry "cut but very little figure in the engagement."[72]

Two other military historians have credited Imboden with the Confederate victory, claiming that his cavalry turned Sigel's left flank and brought about his retreat.[73] It seems clear, however, that Imboden's men on the right flank were but little engaged. One casualty report on the battle lists Imboden's cavalry as having only one man wounded.[74]

Later Imboden was criticized by some for Sigel's escape after the battle. Had he been able to get behind Sigel and destroy the bridge over the Shenandoah, the escape route would have been cut off and the Battle of New Market would have had repercussions well beyond the Valley. Historian Roger Delauter is not among these critics, however. He points out that Imboden had under his direct command only a maximum of 625 men in the 18th Virginia Cavalry and McClanahan's Battery. Also, Imboden was following Breckinridge's specific orders that he guard the Confederate right flank and get in the Union rear only if that was possible. But the Union left flank stretched all the way to the west bank of Smith's Creek. Thus the only way that Imboden could turn its flank would be from the left bank of that creek. Imboden makes no mention in his account of the battle of an effort to ford the creek. Contemporary accounts note the swollen condition of the creek that day, the consequence of previous heavy rains, and in all probability it was simply impossible for Imboden to have gotten across it and then back across in any strength.

It is also important to remember in assessing Imboden's role in the battle that his constant harassment of the Union advance delayed it sufficiently to allow Breckinridge to come up and achieve the victory. Sigel later wrote that it was the lack of cavalry to guard his flanks that had led him to withdraw, and it was Imboden who had destroyed much of Sigel's cavalry over the previous week.[75]

Sigel, summing up the battle years later, praised Imboden's role: "The battle was well fought by the Southern troops, especially as to the timely and skillful maneuver of Imboden, by which he gained a position with his battery, which enfiladed our line on the left, without a chance for our side, on account of the intervening creek, to attack or dislodge."[76]

At about 5:00 P.M., with Sigel having been driven back about three miles, the Union commander halted his batteries on the crest of Rude's Hill and began shelling the Confederates. Breckinridge, his infantry then largely out of ammunition, ordered a halt. He positioned his artillery in an orchard on the right side of the Pike to return fire and at the same time ordered ammunition wagons forward.

Imboden had not met with Breckinridge since the beginning of the battle, and he now rode to locate him. The two generals met together near the front lines before Rude's Hill. As the Confederate infantrymen replenished their cartridge boxes, Breckinridge, who was covered with mud up to the waist, discussed the battle with Imboden and ordered him to bring his cavalry and McClanahan's Battery around to the left and push north along the Valley Pike.

As the Confederates prepared to resume their advance, Sigel decamped again and disappeared from view on Rude's Hill into Meem's Bottom. McClanahan's Battery had a shorter distance to travel than had the cavalry, which also had to negotiate thick mud. The battery thus reached the hill first and remained there for some time unsupported. Sigel's rear guard was then just crossing the bridge over the North Fork of the Shenandoah River. McClanahan fired a few rounds in their direction, but it was getting dark and so it was hard to tell their effect. Shortly thereafter the Confederates saw flames as the Union troops fired the bridge after they had withdrawn over it. With the bridge destroyed, the Confederate pursuit was halted for the night.[77]

Sigel's forces reached Mount Jackson at about 7:00 P.M. After a short rest there, they pressed on, reaching Edinburg around 7:00 A.M. on May 16. Following another short halt, the Union troops resumed their march north. They gained Strasburg that day at 5:00 P.M. The next morning the Federals crossed Cedar Creek and moved to the heights north of the creek, into the same camps they had occupied at the beginning of the campaign.

In the retreat the Union troops abandoned eight or ten wagons and burned others. On May 18 and 20 Sigel sent medical supplies under a flag of truce through the Confederate lines to assist Union wounded at New Market. The next day Imboden ordered the VMI Corps of Cadets to Staunton. Union forces remained in camp at Stone House until May 26.[78]

The Battle of New Market resulted in 841 Union casualties: 96 killed, 520 wounded, and 225 missing. This represents a loss of force engaged of 13.4 percent. Sigel also lost five guns. Confederate losses are a bit more difficult to determine but were no less than 43 killed, 474 wounded, and 3 missing, for at least 520 casualties, or a loss rate of about 13 percent. The two dismounted regiments of Imboden's Northwestern Brigade, the 23d Virginia Cavalry and 62d Virginia Mounted Infantry, paid a heavy price. Together they sustained a quarter of the Confederate casualties. The 62d bore the brunt of the fighting that day; only 10 percent of the total Confederate force, it accounted for 20 percent of the Southern casualties.[79]

The Confederate victory at New Market, while important, was hardly decisive, but it did hearten Confederate defenders elsewhere. It bought just enough time for the Valley wheat crop to be harvested, and it protected the western terminus of the Virginia Central Railroad. Losing that supply line might have forced Lee to send part of the Army of Northern Virginia to the Valley at the very time when pressure on him by the Union Army of the Potomac at Spotsylvania Court House was the heaviest.[80]

Following the victory, Lee ordered Breckinridge to leave the Valley and come east with Echols's and Wharton's Brigades in order to reinforce his own Army of Northern Virginia, now locked in struggle with Meade's Army of the Potomac. Despite Imboden's strong opposition, Breckinridge took with him what remained of the "grand old" 62d Virginia, keeping it attached to Wharton's Brigade. Imboden said his brigade's largest regiment, the 62d, was "commanded by the bravest man, I sometimes thought, I ever saw, Col. George H. Smith."

This decision left Imboden only the 18th Virginia Cavalry (under Col. George Imboden), the 23d Virginia Cavalry (under Col. Robert White), Maj. Harry Gilmor's Maryland Battalion, Maj. Sturges Davis's Maryland Battalion, Captain McNeill's Company of Partisan Rangers,

McClanahan's battery of six guns, and a few hundred reserves of old men and boys. Imboden now had barely one thousand men and six guns with which to defend the Valley, a totally inadequate force. For the time being Imboden set up camp at Rude's Hill, although he regularly sent scouting parties north, even beyond Strasburg.[81]

Breckinridge's decision was a heavy blow for Imboden, but Lee needed all the men he could secure. Grant and Meade were relentlessly driving south toward Richmond, despite suffering heavy casualties, first in the Battle of the Wilderness (May 5–6) and then at Spotsylvania Court House (May 8–12). The VMI cadets also accompanied Breckinridge as far as Richmond, returning to the Institute on June 9 after an absence of nearly a month.[82]

Chapter 10

Destruction of the Valley

Following the Battle of New Market, Breckinridge and Lee assumed the threat to the Valley had disappeared for the time being, but the respite purchased was brief. On May 19 Sigel was relieved of command; two days later Maj. Gen. David Hunter replaced him. The more determined Hunter soon again led his command south up the Valley.

Born in the District of Columbia, Hunter was the child of a Presbyterian minister. Following his 1822 graduation from West Point, he had a checkered military career, holding minor positions in the Northwest. Promoted to colonel of the 3d Cavalry in May 1861 and brigadier general that same month, he commanded the 2d Division under General McDowell. Badly wounded in the July 21 First Battle of Manassas (Bull Run), Hunter was promoted to major general that August. He then commanded a division under Maj. Gen. John C. Frémont in Missouri and succeeded the latter in command of the Western Department.

In 1862 Hunter commanded the Department of the South and took Fort Pulaski, Georgia. He had issued a proclamation freeing the slaves in his department, which Lincoln promptly repudiated. Hunter then raised the first regiment of African American soldiers in the U.S. Army, the 1st South Carolina. Hunter failed in an effort to take Charleston in June 1862 and was temporarily suspended from duty. Restored to favor, Hunter now received command of the Department of West Virginia.[1]

Known as "Black Dave," Hunter dyed his mustache black and wore a dark wig. This staunch abolitionist yearned both to restore his military reputation and to punish white southerners for their role in the war. Imboden had only contempt for Hunter; after the war he referred to him as "a human hyena."[2]

Grant sought to tie down as many Confederate forces as possible; he ordered Hunter to move on Staunton and the Virginia Central Railroad and take Gordonsville or Charlottesville, if possible, with the ultimate objective of the Confederate railhead at Lynchburg. Having destroyed Lynchburg and Confederate stores there, he was then to join Maj. Gen. Philip H. Sheridan, and the two Union generals would move east to link up with Grant, who proposed to move his army south of the James River and attack Lee at and south of Petersburg.

Grant hoped Hunter could secure Lynchburg, even for a day. On the way there Hunter planned to destroy part of the Orange & Alexandria Railroad between Lynchburg and Charlottesville. At Lynchburg he would burn key bridges and sections of the Virginia & Tennessee track. This line was Lee's principal east-west communication link and a major source of supplies from Tennessee and the southwest for the Army of Northern Virginia. In addition to being a major railhead and transshipment point for army supplies, Lynchburg was a major medical center with many of the South's scant medical supplies and a number of hospitals caring for Confederate wounded and sick.[3]

Hunter assigned Sigel command of the Reserve Division and ordered him to guard the Baltimore & Ohio Railroad and protect the supply route. Hunter then prepared to move south with the bulk of his command. On May 26 Hunter left his headquarters at Martinsburg to join his troops at Cedar Creek, where they had remained encamped following the Battle of New Market.[4]

Only Imboden's pitifully small force of some one thousand men stood in Hunter's way. Other Confederate cavalry units under Brig. Gens. John McCausland and William L. "Mudwall" Jackson were in the mountains to the west trying to contain Union forces in West Virginia under Brig. Gen. George Crook. Imboden did have the Partisan Rangers of McNeill, Gilmor, and Mosby, but these small units were only capable of gathering intelligence, nibbling on the Union flanks, and raiding to take prisoners and some supplies.[5]

Imboden came to work closely with the twenty-seven-year-old McCausland, who had graduated at the head of his class from the Virginia Military Institute in 1857 and then studied an additional year at the University of Virginia before returning to VMI as an assistant professor of mathematics. On the outbreak of the war he had organized and become the colonel of the 36th Virginia Infantry Regiment. It saw service in its home area of West Virginia and at Fort Donelson in Tennessee in February 1862, where it was one of the few units to escape capture. McCausland had thereafter performed well in southwestern Virginia, taking over command on May 9, 1864, following the wounding and capture of Brig. Gen. Albert G. Jenkins in an engagement with General Crook's three brigades at Cloyd's Mountain. McCausland was commissioned a brigadier general nine days later.[6]

Imboden tried to make such defensive preparations as possible to protect against the threatened invasion. Beginning on May 16 he detached about one hundred men to rebuild the bridge over the Shenandoah River at Meem's Bottom north of Rude's Hill. With the assistance of a professional bridge builder, the men were able to complete the work in a few days. Imboden then set off to try and locate the Union forces and determine their intentions.[7]

On May 19 Imboden appealed to Breckinridge for the return of his 62d Regiment to the Valley. "That regiment is small now," he wrote, "and will be of little value to you, but inestimable to me as a nucleus to form the reserves upon."[8] Compounding Imboden's manpower problems was the fact that he could not call upon the VMI cadets; they were in Richmond and would not return to VMI until June 9.[9]

Hunter stripped his army down to its bare essentials, sending excess baggage and equipment back to Martinsburg. He limited the amount each soldier was to carry and the number of wagons allotted. Despite Grant's orders to Sigel to avoid "indiscriminate marauding" and to take only those supplies "absolutely necessary for the troops," Hunter expected to resolve his supply problems by living off the land where possible. Indeed, from the beginning, Hunter's men foraged liberally at the expense of the Valley residents, and this at a time when forage and grain in the Valley were both in short supply.[10]

On May 22 Hunter issued marching orders to his troops. Their advance south toward Woodstock began four days later. Hunter had in all some 8,500 men and twenty-one guns. Brig. Gen. Jeremiah Sullivan had charge of the infantry; the cavalry were under former Hungarian nobleman Maj. Gen. Julius Stahel; Capt. Henry A. Du Pont had change of the artillery.[11]

At the time, Imboden had his headquarters at New Market with an advance position north at Woodstock. Outnumbered ten to one and with another Union force of like size in West Virginia, Imboden appealed to Lee for reinforcements. Lee, then locked in combat with Grant and Meade, had no men to spare, not even Imboden's 62d Virginia. Lee suggested that Imboden call out the local reserves to resist Hunter's advance up the Valley and then in turn confront Crook and Averell.[12]

Imboden's scouts kept tabs on Union preparations, and Imboden passed this information along to Lee. Lee in turn alerted McCausland at Christiansburg and suggested that he move his cavalry to Millboro and the Cow Pasture River Bridge to keep watch there.[13]

Reporting to Richmond that Union troops were advancing in strength from Strasburg on May 26, Imboden informed Confederate Adj. Gen. Samuel Cooper that he had no horses for a reserve battery at Staunton, which was then ready to take the field. Capt. Randolph Turk, quartermaster at Staunton, had horses available but was refusing to release them. Imboden appealed to Cooper, "Can I have them a few days? Am preparing for the best fight my means can afford."[14] This appeal at least bore fruit, as Imboden secured the horses he needed.

As Hunter advanced south, small groups of reserves from Augusta, Rockingham, Page, and Rockbridge Counties joined Imboden. These men had been called into service before, in August and December 1863 and again in January 1864. They were armed with only shotguns and hunting weapons, but a number were mounted and they were all determined. Among these troops were four companies of cavalry and the artillery battery from Staunton. Altogether they numbered 1,200–1,500 men. Imboden appointed Col. Edwin G. Lee, who had command of the Valley's reserve forces and was recovering from wounds received at Staunton in late May, as enrollment officer and issued an order calling up all males in the Valley ages seventeen to fifty.[15]

On May 27 the Staunton *Vindicator* ran the following announcement: "It is deemed unnecessary to make an appeal to Virginians to step forward, without coercion, and lend their aid to the noble armies that are now winning, at such costly sacrifice, our independence; our bleeding Country points to her wounds in appeal stronger than words."[16]

Colonel Lee, meanwhile, mobilized support personnel—quartermaster and commissary troops, shopmen, and telegraphers—as well as all furloughed personnel. Meanwhile Imboden recalled small detachments he had put out to watch the mountain passes, although he did leave William Jackson's force on the Jackson River near Covington, in order to keep watch on a large Federal force in Greenbrier County.[17]

Imboden wired General Lee that Hunter was advancing from Strasburg to Maurertown with eight days' rations and a supply train that included canvas pontoons. There was little he could do to stop Hunter's advance: "His cavalry outnumbers ours two to one; his infantry four to one; his artillery four to one. He is moving on my flank, and will compel me to fall back. There is no point this side of Mount Crawford where I can successfully resist him, and there it is very doubtful, though I will do my best."[18]

Imboden's only advantages were superior intelligence gathering, complete familiarity with the area, and the active sympathy of the vast majority of its inhabitants—coupled with the fact that his men were fighting to defend their homes.

Imboden's troops first encountered Union infantry in the vicinity of Woodstock. These were small engagements with Confederate actions directed at the points of least Federal resistance. At Newtown (present-day Stephen's City), Major Gilmor led an attack on a Union supply train of sixteen wagons escorted by some eighty men of the 15th and 21st New York Cavalry. The Confederate attack caught the Union troopers completely by surprise. Gilmor's men burned the wagons, inflicted some casualties, and took a few prisoners.[19]

Hunter responded by ordering Maj. Timothy Quinn and two hundred of his men to burn Newtown, sparing only the churches and the home of an elderly doctor said to be sympathetic to the Union cause. Gilmor found out about these plans and threatened to hang four Union prisoners if Newtown were burnt. Hunter refused to countermand the order, but his own officers refused to carry it out.[20]

Hunter spent May 26, the first night of his advance, at Woodstock.

Imboden's men did what they could to harass the Union flanks. Hunter sent out foragers to gather food and ordered his scouts to burn any houses in the area that might have been used by Confederate guerrillas. With the citizenry less than forthcoming with information, no homes were burned, a fact that reportedly angered the Union commander, who believed that such activities were necessary not only in reprisal for guerrilla operations but as an act of justified punishment against slaveholding southerners. At Woodstock Hunter received word from General Halleck that Grant wanted him, if possible, to push as far south as Charlottesville and Lynchburg, destroying the railroads and the James River & Kanawha Canal. Accomplishing this, he could then either return to the lower Shenandoah Valley or join Grant by way of Gordonsville.[21]

On May 29 the Federals reached Edinburg and there destroyed a large quantity of salt. They then continued south through Mount Jackson and established their headquarters at Rude's Hill.[22]

It was impossible for Imboden to do more than delay the Union advance. As he put it later, "It was vital to preserve my devoted men from capture, as a nucleus for the reinforcements hoped for, & therefore I could offer little resistance to Hunter's Army in the open Valley, for Stahl's [sic] 2500 Cavalry were ever present & ready to flank & envelope my little band of followers. Occasionally we could & did make a stand & check them, till flanked, when there was no help for it, but to fall back rapidly."[23]

Two small cavalry units did arrive to assist. These revealed the paucity of reserves available. The first was Capt. Henry Harnsberger's company of men over the age of fifty-five, and the other was Capt. George Chrisman's company of boys. These two units were armed with hunting rifles or shotguns and were assigned to Capt. Thomas Sturgis Davis's command of some fifty Baltimoreans.[24]

Imboden repeatedly appealed to Lee, who continued to reply that for the moment he could spare no one. Imboden would have to do with what he had, although Lee did promise to order Brig. Gen. William E. "Grumble" Jones in southwestern Virginia to join Imboden with as many men as possible. On May 29 Imboden telegraphed Jones from Lacey Spring: "Enemy, 7,000 strong, advancing from Mount Jackson.... Is it possible for you to aid me?"[25]

Jones was at Glade Springs near Bristol on May 30 when he received a message from Lee ordering him to Staunton with as many men as possible. The next morning Jones started out by train with the 36th, 45th, and 60th Virginia Regiments and the 45th Virginia Battalion, along with Capt. Thomas A. Bryan's six-gun battery. On June 1 Imboden telegraphed Capt. James F. Jones of the Niter and Mining Corps in southwestern Virginia to bring his men to Staunton. Within two days, Jones had 130 men at Staunton. Imboden also traveled to Staunton to enlist as many individuals as possible who were not yet in the army.[26]

The desperate nature of this effort is reflected in a broadside issued on May 31 by Maj. Beverly Randolph, commandant at Staunton: "The Genl. Commanding this District has this moment notified me, that 'every man who can fire a Gun is urgently required at Mt. Crawford'— He says: 'I see no reason why Magistrates and Constables should not *fight for their homes* in a pinch like this.' 'A man should be ashamed to claim such a *pitiful* exemption.' 'If it becomes necessary to *make them fight*, I will DECLARE MARTIAL LAW in this District until the danger is over and MAKE every man shoulder his musket.' 'A man who will deliberately refuse to defend his home, wife and children for a few days ought to be forced into the ranks. IF KILLED THE LOSS IS TRIFLING.'"[27]

Often the men who did report were commanded by officers, such as Robert Doyle, who had retired because of age. Doyle had been a lieutenant colonel of the 62d Virginia but, far beyond military age, had left the service. He returned as captain commanding Company B, only to be killed in the coming battle. There were also those recuperating at home from wounds or sickness, such as Capt. Monroe Blue of Company D and Capt. John N. Opie of Company E of the Augusta Reserves.[28]

While Imboden was desperately trying to secure men, Hunter's relentless drive south continued. On June 1 his forces drove the Confederates from New Market. Imboden then retreated to Lacey Spring, where there was a large skirmish. McNeill's men attacked Hunter's rear, causing some consternation among the Union troops. Imboden, meanwhile, was conducting a disinformation campaign, trying to mask his weakness.

On June 2 the Confederate defenders fell back to Harrisonburg with the Federals in pursuit. When the Union artillery lobbed some rounds into the town, Imboden ordered a skirmish line flung up north of the city, causing the Union troops to pause to deploy. The defending force consisted only of some 160 reserves and a small number of cavalrymen.

The Union cavalry then charged the Confederate far right, while at the same time advancing Union infantry attacked all along the Confederate line. The Confederates counterattacked and briefly drove the Union troops back, but the odds were such that the line could not long be held. When the Confederates pulled back, Hunter's men entered Harrisonburg. Soon the Union troops were looting food, livestock, horses, and private property. Union officers tried to halt this activity, but Hunter's noticeable lack of leadership in the matter stymied their efforts.

Imboden, meanwhile, had withdrawn all his men save the 18th Virginia Cavalry across the North River to Mount Crawford on the Valley Pike, eight miles from Harrisonburg and seventeen miles from Staunton. There he ordered his men to fortify the south bank of the rain-swollen North River. The men cut down trees to disrupt access to fords in either direction from Mount Crawford. Imboden also prepared artillery and infantry defensive positions in the hills that commanded the bridge over the river. His line was anchored at the bridge by Marquis's Boys Battery, manned by sixteen-to eighteen-year-olds. It had two guns: a 24-pounder howitzer and a 3.67-inch (20-pounder) Parrott rifle. But Imboden's resources were stretched over a seven-mile front, from Rockland Mills on his right to Bridgewater on his left.[29]

Imboden established his headquarters at the home of Mrs. Robert Gratton, whom he described as "that matron who as well as her three daughters would have done honor to Rome in its Palmiest days." There Augusta reserves and some men from Rockingham County joined him. He also received a telegram from General Jones with the welcome news that he was at Lynchburg and on his way north by train with three thousand men.[30]

Imboden continued to appeal to Lee, telegraphing, "Is it possible for you to give additional aid to the Valley?" Lee endorsed this request to the War Department on June 3, noting: "General W. E. Jones is, I hope, by this time with his troops in Staunton."[31]

Indeed that same day of June 3, as Hunter rested most of his troops at Harrisonburg and sent out only scouting parties of cavalry, some of Jones's men began to reach Imboden, covering on foot the seventeen miles from Staunton. Imboden and his adjutant, Capt. Frank Berkeley, spent the day and worked until about 10:00 P.M. that night organizing the new arrivals into two small brigades. The bulk of Jones's troops formed the first brigade, under command of Col. Beuhring H. Jones of the 60th Virginia Volunteer Infantry Regiment. It had three regiments: Jones's 60th, the 36th Virginia Volunteer Infantry Regiment, and a regiment of convalescents and detailed men. The second brigade, commanded by Col. W.H. Browne of the 45th Virginia Volunteer Infantry Regiment, consisted of the 45th Virginia, Lt. Col. H.M. Berkley's 45th Battalion of Virginia Volunteer Infantry, and two regiments of reserves. Lt. Col. Charles Robertson commanded a reserve division of some seven hundred men drawn from a variety of sources. Artillery support totaled fourteen guns: McClanahan's six, Bryan's six, and the two in Marquis's Battery. Thirty Maryland artillerymen, released from the defenses of Charleston, South Carolina, joined the force.[32]

Early on June 4 Jones and his staff arrived. That same morning Brig. Gen. John C. Vaughn came up with a brigade, variously given at between five hundred and eight hundred Tennessee mounted infantry, in fact a mixed formation of cavalry and infantry. Among the five hundred to six hundred men who reported were Capt. James F. Jones and 130 miners from the Nitre and Mining Corps, formed into two companies. Armed with only smoothbore muskets at Staunton, they lacked cartridge boxes and bayonets. Bryan's Battery arrived by train at Staunton, but without their horses which had been sent by road from Bristol. The horses were impressed locally and fitted with harnesses, and soon were on their way north.[33]

In his own recollection of events, Imboden stated his dismay to learn that Jones had only 2,200 men, that only Vaughn's Brigade was actually complete, and that no large organized body of troops was among the reinforcements. Aside from Vaughn's, there was no unit above a battalion, and most of the men were in companies or portions of companies. Jones had "cleaned out the hospitals from Lynchburg to Bristol of convalescents, & gathered them together with the depot guards along the railroad."[34]

Nonetheless, Imboden was impressed with what had been accomplished. He later wrote:

> Perhaps at no time during the war were such heterogeneous

materials brought together so suddenly, & compacted into harmonious and obedient bodies of troops. I have often thought this incident proved most strikingly the devoted patriotism of our Confederate Soldiers. Here, without acquaintance with each other, in the face of the enemy, and a desperate battle impending at any moment, with overwhelming odds, some 2200 men & officers without a murmur of objection accepted the situation, and with alacrity stepped into ranks and 'touched elbows' with strangers, and obeyed orders from, to them unknown and unfamiliar lips. It was an instance of sublime devotion to their Country, unsurpassed so far as I know during the war, and deserving to be held in everlasting remembrance by us, as a personal honor to each and every one of the officers and men, who thus behaved, in the face of an enemy ready to fall upon them, the next day, in the proportion of three to one.[35]

Before sunrise on June 4 "Grumble" Jones and his staff joined Imboden at his Gratton home headquarters. Because Jones was senior to Imboden in rank by a year, he took command. While he would not be in command, obviously Imboden would have a major say in troop dispositions, given his own intimate acquaintance with the area. Over breakfast Imboden briefed Jones on his organization of the Confederate infantry, and Jones confirmed what had been accomplished. Jones informed Imboden that Vaughn was coming up from Staunton with his men to join them.[36]

As finally constituted, Confederate strength consisted of a rag-tag collection of small units totaling between 4,500 and 5,000 men—some 1,000 of them mounted—and fourteen guns. These faced a much better organized and equipped and far more cohesive Union force of 11,500 men and twenty-two guns.[37]

A courier arrived from Col. George Imboden while the Confederate generals were conferring. His 18th Virginia Cavalry and two reserve cavalry companies had remained on the north side of the North River to ascertain Union intentions. While the Confederate pickets were encountering increasing numbers of Union troops, they also reported that Hunter was moving in three columns from Harrisonburg toward Port Republic by way of Cross Keys on the East Road. This route ran more north-south than east-west, along the base of the Blue Ridge. It then forked, with one road leading to Staunton and the other to Waynesboro. Colonel Imboden assumed Hunter was endeavoring to flank the Confederate positions.[38]

Indeed, on June 3 Hunter had learned from his scouts about Imboden's defensive preparations. Wisely declining to mount a frontal assault against prepared Confederate positions that would do much to offset the obvious Southern numerical disadvantage, he planned to slide to the east, moving southeast by road to Port Republic. There he would cross the South Fork of the Shenandoah and head south to Waynesboro, just east of his objective of Staunton. The Union troops began this movement at 5:00 A.M. on June 4. Hunter's cavalry led, followed by three columns of infantry. That night the Union troops bivouacked about a mile south of Port Republic.[39]

On learning of the Union activity, Jones, who was largely unacquainted with the area, deferred to Imboden, who suggested probable routes of Union advance and drew Jones a rough map showing the roads, rivers, and approximate distances involved. In discussing a blocking position where they would meet and engage the advancing Federals, Imboden proposed land belonging to George W. Mowry some three miles above New Hope on Long Meadow Run and eight miles northeast of Staunton. He urged that the Confederates position their troops on Mowry's Hill west of the stream, "with such advantages in our favor as to fully compensate for the disparity in our numbers, and insure us a complete victory at small loss of life on our side."[40]

With Jones having concurred with his suggestion on the location for the Confederate stand, Imboden then proposed "with my brigade alone, to place myself in Hunter's front that night, at or near Port Republic, and to so retard his march next morning, as to give Jones ample time to move all his infantry, and the two infantry brigades along with Vaughan's [sic] jaded command to Mowry's Hill, & occupy it long enough before the enemy appeared in his front, to throw up some light works and rest his men before action."[41]

Jones agreed with this plan, and Imboden provided guides from the Augusta County reserves to lead Jones's men to Mowry's Hill by the shortest possible route. As his brother George's 18th Virginia Cavalry continued to scout northward, General Imboden led the remainder of the cavalry eastward to harry the Federal flanks and delay Hunter as long as possible.

Upon leaving the Gratton home, Imboden and Jones rode together for a mile or two along the Valley Pike. Just before parting, General Vaughn rode up. Jones introduced the two men, who then compared their date of rank. Vaughn was senior to Imboden by about ten days, which entitled him to command all the cavalry. Vaughn "generously proposed" to remain with Jones, allowing Imboden to proceed. The three generals then parted, Jones and Vaughn and most of the Confederate forces bound for Mowry's Hill, while Imboden rode on to Mount McKinley.

Imboden recalled his brother from the north side of the North River, shifting his regiment east of the Middle River, and he threw up pickets to watch all the North River fords. That evening, Imboden learned that Hunter had crossed the river and was encamped near Port Republic.

Placing about twenty men at the forks of the road leading to Weyer's Cave on Col. Alexander Given's farm, Imboden bivouacked the bulk of his command on Col. Samuel Cranford's farm about a mile south of Mount Meridian with orders that they be ready to ride at dawn. The remaining cavalry were a few miles away near New Hope.

At about 6:00 A.M. on June 5, just as the men of the 18th Virginia Regiment were saddling their horses, they heard gunfire from the direction of the pickets. The Union troops, who had resumed their advance early, were preceded by a cavalry screen, which ran into the Confederate pickets. The bulk of Hunter's troops were slowed by the inexperience of engineers bridging the swollen North River at Port Republic. However, while the rest of the men waited for the bridge to be completed, the 1st New York and Du Pont's artillery crossed over the river by means of a ford a mile west of Port Republic.

The men of the 18th Regiment quickly finished saddling their horses and then rode to the sound of the guns. Recalling Jones's parting admonition to him to harass and delay Hunter only and in no circumstances to become so engaged in a fight that he could not extricate his forces, Imboden accompanied his brother's 18th Regiment. As the regiment rode through Mount Meridian, Imboden directed his brother to have the men take down a fence so that they could reach a hill that overlooked the road.

The 18th then formed up in line of battle. It had scarcely accomplished this when Union forces charged the Confederate pickets and drove them back across the hill. The 18th Virginia then in turn forced the Union troops back, but too far. Unknown to the men of the 18th, a substantial body of Stahel's 2,500 Union cavalry was just beyond the forks of the road. As Imboden recalled, the situation then became "very serious."[42]

The 21st New York immediately came to the relief of the 1st New York. Other Union cavalry units also came up: the 1st Maryland, 14th Pennsylvania, 25th New York, and the 20th and 22d Pennsylvania. For the Confederates, the situation immediately turned grave. Imboden described what happened next: "We were driven back and in turn pursued with great vigor. Capt. Frank M. Imboden commanding one of the best companys [sic] in the regiment was wholly cut off and surrounded, when he and about 40 men fell into the enemy's hands as prisoners. With very great difficulty the rest of the regiment was saved. I being cut off and pursued alone by an entire company owed my escape to the speed and great power of my horse, a gift stallion from my command, who carried me at a bound over a post and rail fence into the river road below the village, where no one could follow."[43]

Imboden rejoined the 18th at Bonnie Doon, just above Mount Meridian, where a running fight was in progress that would have destroyed the regiment entirely had it not been for timely arrival of reinforcements. The 18th received assistance in the form of Davis's Maryland Battalion and Captains Harnsburger's and Chrisman's companies, which arrived from the south. Several miles to the south Col. Robert White's 23d Virginia Cavalry heard the fighting and also rode north.

Captains Opie and Peck and their men joined the 23d en route. As they approached the scene of battle, Opie took charge of Peck's company and ordered them to dismount, leading them forward on foot. As was standard procedure, every fourth man was left behind to handle the horses.[44]

The Confederates formed behind a rail fence on the edge of a thicket. Fire from Opie's men, a charge led by Harnsberger and Chrisman, and then an assault by the 23d halted and then drove back the Union advance. This enabled the 18th Virginia to extricate itself from the lane in front of Colonel Cranford's house, where it had become wedged in with Union troops firing on them from three sides.

The Confederates broke up several Federal charges, until the attackers began moving on their right flank. The defenders then fell back to a new position on high ground that overlooked cleared land for more than a mile in front. Imboden recalled that his intention in occupying the hill was to force Hunter to deploy. Once he had done so, Imboden planned to withdraw his men through New Hope. He hoped to delay Hunter's advance by several hours as the Union commander would have to first deploy in line and then redeploy in column to resume his march.

Thus Imboden intended the hill position as merely a temporary location, the occupation of which would permit Jones additional time to prepare defensive positions at Mowry's Hill, three miles to the rear. The position Imboden held, however, was in fact the site of the main battle a few hours later.

Union assaults continued and grew in strength. Imboden held the Union cavalry for a time but then Moor's Brigade of infantry and artillery began arriving. These and an increasing number of Du Pont's guns probably were what forced Imboden to call up artillery. In his own recollections of that day, Imboden does not mention Union pressure on his position as forcing that decision. Rather he wrote that he saw Confederate artillery fire as helping to bring about Hunter's desired deployment.[45]

Not having heard from Jones, Imboden assumed he was at Mowry's Hill, as they had agreed. He thus sent a messenger back to Jones requesting a section of McClanahan's Battery and five hundred infantry. He believed that with these he could prevent Hunter from reaching Mowry's Hill until afternoon. Imboden's courier was not yet out of sight when he encountered Jones and his staff riding up.[46]

The day before Jones had halted at Mount Sidney but sent two companies across the Middle River toward Piedmont. Jones's men had spent the night camped along the Valley Pike. The horses for Bryan's artillery came up, but rather than attempt to change out the harnesses and gear of the caissons, it was decided to keep the impressed horses at the guns with the regular horses held in reserve. This turned out well for the Confederates, providing extra horses to replace those subsequently killed in the battle and allowing the Southerners to bring off guns that otherwise would have been abandoned.

During the night a courier arrived with a message for Jones from

General Lee informing him that he could not expect any reinforcements for at least a week and ordering him to fight Hunter—before the latter could link up with Crook and Averell—then turn and drive the latter two forces out of the Valley. After he read the note, Jones stuffed it in his pocket without sharing its contents. An hour before dawn on June 5, Jones had his men up and on the march; soon they were fording Middle River.[47]

Jones's infantry continued on to the village of Piedmont, two miles north of New Hope and seven miles southwest of Port Republic, beyond the agreed-upon position at Mowry's Hill. At Piedmont, Jones put his men to work preparing defensive positions.

Piedmont was a village of nine or ten houses. The area owed its livelihood to farming, with grain and cattle its chief products. The terrain was heavily timbered and marked by rolling hills. Now this bucolic setting would be racked by warfare.[48]

After Jones joined Imboden, the two generals then conferred privately on horseback. As Jones was killed in the subsequent battle, we have only Imboden's account of what transpired. Imboden reported that Jones promptly agreed to his request for artillery and infantry. Imboden then provided information on the morning's events and told his commander that he had been able to get one of his men into the Union encampment at Port Republic. The spy had reported Hunter's strength at 9,000 infantry, 2,500 cavalry, and 31 guns. The Confederates had but 2,200 infantry, 1,800 cavalry, 200 reserves, and 14 guns.[49]

Imboden was astonished when Jones told him that the artillery would soon be up as his lines were only several hundred yards to the rear. Imboden recalled that he exclaimed to Jones, "My God General! You are not going to fight here, and lose all the advantage of position we shall have at Mowry's Hill?"

Jones replied that he did indeed intend to fight Hunter there. Furthermore, if Hunter did not attack, Jones would move against him. Imboden protested, "We have no advantage of ground here, and he out numbers [sic] us nearly three to one, & will beat us." This angered Jones who replied with an oath, "I don't want any advantage of ground, for I can whip Hunter anywhere." Imboden, now also animated, said that he responded: "General! I will not say you cannot whip him here, but I will say, with the knowledge I have of his strength, that if you do it will be at the expense of a fearful loss of life on our side, and believing we have no right to sacrifice the lives of our men where it is possible to avoid it, as it is now if you will even yet fall back to Mowry's hill, I enter my solemn protest against fighting here today."

This angered Jones even more and he turned on Imboden to say, "By G———d Sir! I believe I am in command here today." Imboden then recalled that he replied with, "You are Sir! and I now ask your orders and will carry them out as best I can; but if I live, I will see that the responsibility for the day's work is fixed where I think it belongs."[50]

Meanwhile Lt. Carter Berkeley rode up. When Berkeley's two-gun section of McClanahan's Battery had rumbled through Piedmont, women stood on their porches and cheered the artillerymen forward. Berkeley asked for orders, halting the conversation between the two generals. Imboden then directed Berkeley to open fire on the Union cavalry, massing some 1,200–1,500 yards to the Confederate front. In short order Berkeley had opened fire, driving the cavalry back out of range. Imboden noted that the fire of the guns calmed Jones down immediately, "for he was brave to a fault, and I believe enjoyed the roar of the battle field."[51]

Jones now positioned his forces. He placed the infantry facing north about a half mile north of the crossroad that ran northwest to the Valley Pike. His left rested on a loop of the Middle River bounded by cliff-like banks; his right flank was on the East Road. The infantry formed behind a barrier of felled trees and fence rails. Colonel Browne commanded the left wing of the Confederate infantry, consisting of his 45th Virginia Regiment and Lt. Col. H.M. Berkley's 45th Virginia Battalion. Col. B.H. Jones had charge of the Confederate right, consisting of his 60th Virginia Regiment and Major Fife's 36th Virginia Regiment. Open fields of clover in front of the Confederate position afforded clear fire, but Imboden believed the position Jones had selected offered very little advantage for the defenders, and with the battle now about to be joined, there was little possibility of reforming the Confederate line.[52]

Jones then asked Imboden to ride with him alone between the road and the river toward the Samuel B. Finley house. Before departing, Jones ordered his staff to remain until he returned, joking, "Gentlemen, I don't want any of you killed, and I don't want to be killed myself."[53]

The two generals rode some five hundred yards along the Confed-

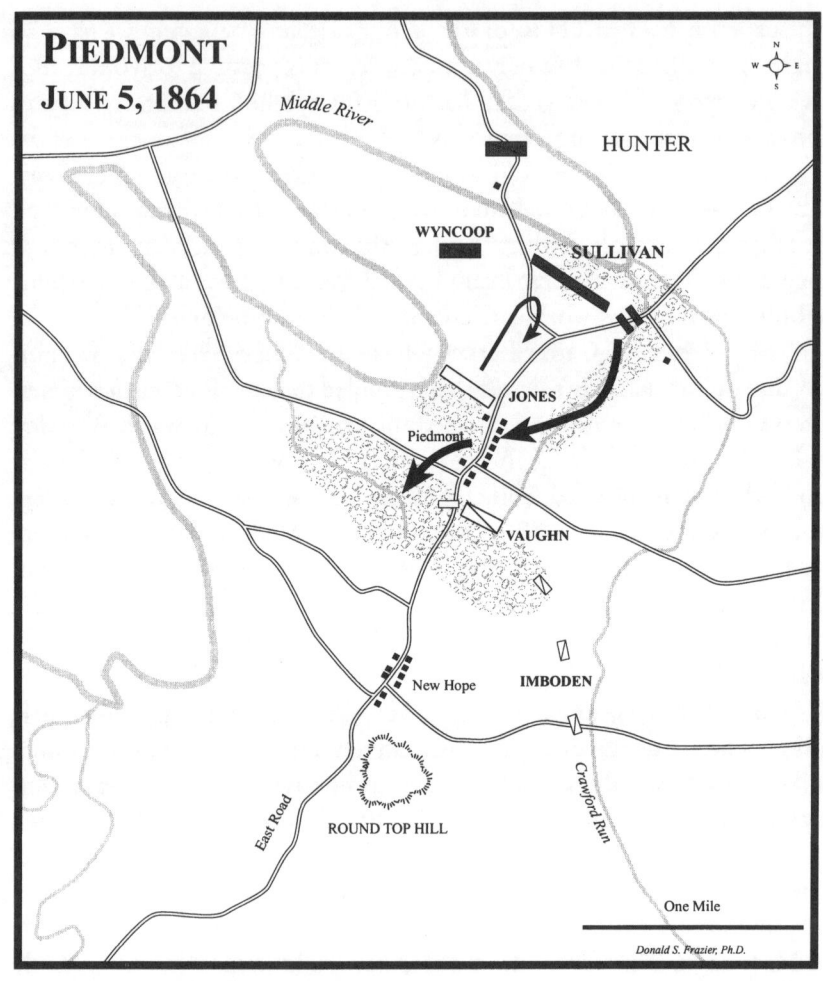

Piedmont, June 5, 1864

erate line. When they emerged from some woods, Federal rifled guns opened up on them, and one shot came within ten feet. The two generals then rapidly retired to their lines. Jones and Imboden next inspected the Confederate left. The infantry were all on line, and Imboden reported them as in "high spirits," cheering the generals as they rode along their front. Along part of their front, the Confederates had torn down fences to form breastworks of the rails. Jones stopped often in front of his men, repeatedly telling them to make each shot count and to make certain they identified their targets before firing. Because they would be firing downhill, Jones told them to "aim low" and try to hit their targets "below the belt."⁵⁴

By the time Imboden and Jones returned to the road, Union artillery fire had greatly increased. Imboden's skirmish line had been driven in to the point where Union musket fire could reach the Confederate line. Informed that Berkeley's horses would soon be killed and his guns thus unable to be withdrawn, Jones ordered the section to retire.⁵⁵

One section of Bryan's Battery, located on the Confederate left near the river, was firing on targets of opportunity, and the Union infantry were being held at bay by the two small companies of miners operating in support of the battery. A charge by Union forces drove the miners back behind a rail fence to a point left of the 36th Virginia. All of the Confederates forces were now in line.

Jones and Imboden then rode up to the top of the hill where they could see the whole of Hunter's army forming to attack. Imboden's Brigade was in a field south of the road. The men were much exposed there and not in position to be of much use. When Imboden asked for orders, Jones told him to move his men back behind Piedmont, where he would find Vaughn's men dismounted. Imboden was to dismount his men also and take up position to Vaughn's right, throwing out flankers as far as the foot of a hill. Imboden recalled Jones as saying, "Hunter will try to turn my position there, and if you can prevent that, it is all I shall ask of you. I'll attend to the rest of the field." Imboden saluted with a touch of his hat and rode off. It was the last time he saw Jones.⁵⁶

As Imboden discovered when he rode through Piedmont to reach his own men, Vaughn's dismounted men were on the north edge of a woods that ran east from the East Road just south of Piedmont and along the south side of an open field. Their horses were tethered in the woods. Vaughn's position extended for about a half mile, but there was a gap of about a quarter mile between the right flank of Jones's infantry on the north side of the road and Vaughn's left flank on the south side. As Imboden observed later, the gap was "a most dangerous, and as the result showed, fatal mistake in the formation of our lines."⁵⁷

Imboden's own line to Vaughn's right curved first south and then west, ending at Round Top Hill east of New Hope. Jones attempted to cover the gap between his infantry and cavalry with artillery: Marquis's Boys Battery supported the 60th Virginia, and to their right were Bryan's two short-range guns. McClanahan's Battery was farther right, and then near the extreme right of Imboden's position were Bryan's four-long range guns.

Some other troops were acting as scouts, pickets, and snipers. Jones placed his reserves behind, spread out along the crossroads leading from Piedmont to the Valley Turnpike. They were called up only late in the battle. Save for the gap between the cavalry and infantry, the Confederate position was strong, but Jones faced a far-superior Union force.[58]

Arriving in front of the main Confederate line, Hunter's men formed up to the right of the East Road. Colonel Moor's 1st Brigade of Sullivan's Infantry was on the Union right. To its left, Joseph Thoburn's 2d Brigade occupied the high ground to the East Road. Stahel's cavalry, which took no active role in the battle, massed behind and to the right of Moor. A light rain was falling at 10:00 A.M. as the 18th Connecticut moved across Crawford Run in an effort to flank the Confederate left. The attackers bunched up against the stream, however; and Southern snipers began to pick them off. Meanwhile, Union artillery had opened up and a shell destroyed a house next to McClanahan's Battery, forcing the guns to relocate south of the village. To the north smoke rose from a mill the Union troops had burned at Mount Meridian.[59]

The rain stopped just before noon. By that point in the battle, the attackers had driven in the Confederate skirmishers and were moving against the rail fence and main defensive line. At about 1:00 P.M. Moor attacked the main Confederate line at the fence but was repulsed with significant losses. The Confederates attempted to pursue, the defenders climbing over the fence and charging down the hill with shouts of "New Market."

At first the Confederates made headway. But Du Pont's twenty-two guns opened up an enfilading fire at comparatively short range, blowing gaps in the Confederate lines. Employing concentrated fire, he also forced back the two guns of Marquis's Battery and the two short-range pieces of Bryan's Battery that had gone forward with the infantry. The Union infantry then reformed and resumed the offensive.

Colonel Thoburn now detached from his 2d Brigade the 34th Massachusetts and 54th Pennsylvania Regiments in order to flank the Confederate left wing of infantry by moving up a ravine on the defender's right. This fell in the unprotected area between the Confederate infantry and cavalry. The regiments moved at a run through some cleared places in the woods. The farthest advanced of these men were within musket range of Imboden but concealed by timber. The two Federal regiments were then held up by Confederate artillery fire.

Although Vaughn and Imboden commanded twice the number of Federals in front of them, they did not interfere. Both generals later insisted that Jones had ordered them to hold their position until they received further orders from him and that none arrived.[60]

At about 1:30 P.M. the Federals launched another, more determined attack. The Confederates repulsed it so successfully that many on the Confederate side believed they had won the battle. This Confederate stand may have led Jones to reverse his original plan, which he had announced earlier to some artillerymen, to withdraw his infantry to woods southward of the crossroads with the hope of catching the advancing Federals in an artillery crossfire.[61]

Imboden believed this was the "crisis point" in the battle. He wrote later that Hunter had his wagon trains in the rear turned about ready to withdraw. "If Vaughan [sic] and I had then been ordered forward the day would undoubtedly have been won. Our joint commands, 1,600 to 1,800 strong, had not fired a shot, for there was no enemy in our front."[62]

There was then a lull in the battle of two to three hours, in which there was little fighting save for Federal artillery fire, which, however, exacted a toll among the Confederate infantry. Du Pont also turned his guns on Bryan's four long-range guns at the far Confederate right, disabling one of them, a 20-pounder Parrott.[63]

Hunter at length discovered the fatal gap in the Confederate lines and advanced his fresh troops as Du Pont's guns continued to shell the Confederates along the rail fence. Utilizing the copse of woods in front of Vaughn and Imboden as cover, Thoburn's men then fell on the exposed right flank of the Confederate infantry. At the same time Moor's infantry and Wynkoop's cavalry also attacked, hitting the main Confederate line from the front.

This Union attack caught Jones by surprise. He committed all available troops and, too late, sent an order by courier to Imboden and Vaughn to charge. Apparently the message never reached them. Imboden wrote, "Even then if Vaughan [sic] and I had had orders, or permission discretion to move, a rapid charge on the left flank of this flanking brigade of the enemy would have at least checked it, & given Jones time to change front to the right and repel it. But Vaughan's [sic] orders like mine, as he informed me that night, were peremptory, to take the position assigned to him, and hold, *till further orders*."[64]

Milton Humphreys, who took part in the battle, noted in his history of the Lynchburg Campaign, which was published after Imboden's death, "If . . . Vaughn and Imboden had struck the flank of the two regiments as they advanced, which they outnumbered nearly two to one, these would have been forced to wheel, and would have shielded the Confederates from the Federal artillery."[65]

Humphreys is sharply critical of Imboden's own account of the battle, both for what be believes to be serious errors and misrepresentations but also false attribution of blame. He believes that Jones chose to fight the battle ahead of the position selected by Imboden simply because of Lee's dispatch, which he had not shared with others and which had ordered him to strike Hunter before he could link up with Averell and Crook. Humphreys writes that the problem was not the position Jones had selected to fight the battle, which "happened to be an excellent one," but rather "the unforeseen and almost unparalleled efficiency of Du Pont's artillery." In summing up reasons for the Confederate defeat, Humphreys wrote, "The battle was won through the efficiency of Du Pont and was lost through the inactivity, however caused, of Vaughn and Imboden."[66]

There is no reason to doubt Imboden's statement that he and Vaughn had been ordered to hold their positions and that they had received no orders to the contrary. Undoubtedly Jones planned to use his cavalry as the situation warranted. Years later, Humphreys maintained that word was sent to Imboden and Vaughn to order them to reinforce the infantry. One such courier, Robert Tanner, maintained as late as 1902 that he was sent but had been unable to find the two cavalry commanders before it was too late. Humphreys also concluded that if Imboden's plan to fight at Mowry's Hill had been adopted, "Hunter would have crossed over to the macadamized road (5 miles) and marched straight for

Staunton, as he was avoiding a battle until Crook's arrival, and there would have been no battle at Mowry's Hill."[67]

Despite the lack of word from Jones, the two generals might have taken the initiative at the most critical juncture of the battle. As Imboden wrote years later, "The moment Jones was struck in the flank I saw the day was lost, and ordered my men to regain their horses and mount so as to be ready to cover the retreating infantry."[68]

Given the gravity of the Union move, Imboden might have seized the initiative, even if it meant disobeying orders. Piedmont was probably Imboden's least effective battle. In any case, the Union troops broke through. The attackers emerged from the wood and fell on Jones's flank. Desperate fighting ensued. Although the Confederate reserves fought bravely, in about half an hour the Confederate line collapsed.[69]

Jones did not concede defeat. Riding up and down the line, he tried to rally his men. While rushing troops forward to stem the retreat, Jones was hit in the forehead in a volley delivered by the 34th Massachusetts; he died instantly.

Union cavalry jumped the rail fence, and the Confederate infantry fled in panic. Doubling the Confederate line, the Union forces drove those they did not kill, wound, or capture back toward Middle River and then across it. Some Confederates managed to escape through the woods toward New Hope. Subsequently, Confederate prisoners identified Jones's body and the message on it from Lee was discovered.[70]

Estimates vary of Confederate casualties in the Battle of Piedmont, but they were probably about 600 killed and wounded and an additional 1,000 taken prisoner; most of the casualties were inflicted in the wild retreat. Some 1,000 small arms were taken, but no artillery pieces. Because the artillery was a bit farther back than the infantry, it escaped the full fury of the Union assault and was able to withdraw in good order up the road to New Hope. Federal losses were perhaps 150 killed, 650 wounded, and 75 missing. Stahel was among the wounded.[71]

Despite their heavy losses, the Battle of Piedmont did bring several advantages to the Confederates. It purchased time while Lee met and defeated Grant at Cold Harbor; it caused Hunter to expend much of his ammunition supply, already low because Colonel Mosby had attacked and taken some of his supply train; and most important, it won time for the Confederates to strengthen their defenses at Lynchburg.[72]

Vaughn and Imboden briefly conferred immediately after the battle. Vaughn, the senior officer, took command. He and Imboden agreed that the cavalry should do everything possible to cover the infantry in its desperate retreat. Imboden suggested that they fall back on Mowry's Hill, but Vaughn believed that it was then impossible to organize an effective resistance. Because Imboden was familiar with the area, Vaughn left the route of the retreat up to him.

With Imboden's men covering them, what remained of the Confederate force withdrew to near New Hope, where McClanahan selected a position for his six guns that enabled him to cover the road. Imboden ordered him to double-shot the guns with canister. Maj. W.W. Stringfellow's battalion of some eighty Tennessee riflemen also arrived and took up position there. Shortly thereafter they could hear the approach of Stahel's cavalry. In short order the Union troopers appeared at a gallop in close column. McClanahan let loose a salvo from his six guns, and the Tennesseans fired a single volley from their rifles. The lead ranks of the Union cavalry went down at once "in a groaning mass of men and horses." This one volley halted the Union cavalry, and a second one compelled their retreat.

Stahel's cavalry then reformed and again charged. When the attackers reached the same spot, McClanahan's guns and the Tennesseans repeated the process. This time the Union cavalry broke and retreated. Imboden's own cavalry was now in position, but he judged a pursuit too hazardous.

When, after a half hour, the Union cavalry did not again appear, Imboden ordered McClanahan's Battery to retire by sections, leapfrogging. The trailing section would withdraw four hundred yards past the last position. In this fashion he moved both the artillery and infantry some two miles past New Hope.[73]

Vaughn was pessimistic about the situation. They had at best 2,500 men. He told Imboden that Jones had received a telegram from Lee the night before, but Jones had not shared its contents. Having stuffed it in his pocket, it must now be assumed to be in the hands of Hunter and its contents known to the Union side. Union Generals Crook and Averell were also within one or two days' march of Staunton.

Given these circumstances, Vaughn decided to leave for Fishersville near Staunton to try to open telegraphic communication with Lee in an attempt to learn the contents of his earlier message to Jones and ascertain what effect it might have on Hunter's movements. Meanwhile, Imboden was to oversee the removal of the army to Fishersville. If no reinforcements were on the way from Lee, they would retreat to Rockfish Gap.[74]

Vaughn had already informed Lee of the defeat, stating, "I will try to protect Staunton, but unless reinforcements come at once, I cannot do it." Vaughn also learned that Lee had told Jones that he could spare no reinforcements for at least a week. Hunter must now know this and would undoubtedly attempt to take Staunton. They had no choice, Vaughn told Imboden, but to retreat to Rockfish Gap and await developments.[75]

Vaughn established his headquarters at the Schmucker house in Fishersville between Waynesboro and Staunton and sent a message to Colonel Lee, commanding at Staunton, informing him of the Piedmont defeat. At 10:00 P.M. on June 5 Vaughn reported to Confederate Secretary of War James Seddon: "Artillery and wagon trains safe. My command is much scattered. The enemy is pursuing. I fear I will be forced to leave the Valley. Staunton cannot be held. Crook is said to be advancing from the west, some twenty miles distant."[76]

That same night Seddon relayed this news to Gen. Braxton Bragg and said he would send it to Lee by courier, but he also noted, "I am surprised that Imboden is not in command. Can anything be done to avert the advancing enemy?" Bragg responded that nothing could be done.[77]

Imboden arrived at Vaughn's headquarters at about 11:00 P.M. Throughout the night Confederate soldiers straggled into Fishersville, bivouacking along the Staunton-Waynesboro Road. Ultimately there were something less than three thousand men. With no Confederate reinforcements available, Vaughn decided to carry out his plan to retreat east through Waynesboro to Rockfish Gap, west of Charlottesville.

That night Vaughn charged Lt. Col. Charles O'Ferrall with carrying a note to Hunter requesting the return of the bodies of Jones and other Confederate officers. O'Ferrall rode back toward Piedmont with an ambulance and three soldiers. At Mowry's Hill they encountered some Union cavalry. Under a white flag O'Ferrall conferred with their commander, Maj. Charles Otis. He refused O'Ferrall's request to deliver the message to Hunter in person, but sent a courier with the message. An hour and a half later, a curt note arrived from Hunter, rejecting the request. O'Ferrall insisted and Otis sent off another message. After a similar delay, a message arrived from Hunter that all "rebel" dead had already been buried and that the wounded were being cared for. O'Ferrall then returned to Fishersville before dawn. Jones had indeed been buried where he had fallen. After the war his remains were dug up and reburied beside those of his wife at Olde Glade Springs Church in Washington County.[78]

Meanwhile, with no troops to defend Staunton, Colonel Lee struggled that night to save what he could. He ordered supplies, war materials, official records, and valuables aboard wagons to be sent south to Lexington and dispatched railroad cars to Lynchburg.

On the afternoon of June 6, Union troops entered Imboden's hometown of Staunton for the first time in the war. As the Federal troops arrived, they fired shots into the air and shouted and cheered. A military band played "Hail, Columbia." Hunter and his staff met with the city fathers at the Virginia Hotel, where Hunter announced that he would seize or destroy all military supplies and burn all factories, shops, and storehouses. "Some disorder," he said, could be expected.[79]

The next day, June 7, Hunter's men set about the destruction. Among the places burned by the Union troops were the Crawford and Young woolen factory, the Staunton Steam Mill, the distillery, government workshops, stables, the railroad depot, twenty-six rail cars, the stage depot, the flour mill, the building housing the *Staunton Spectator*, and the shoe factory. Even the fire fighting equipment was destroyed. There was also a good deal of illegal looting of stores and destruction of private property. The troops confiscated private firearms, destroying more than a thousand of them. They tore up track of the Virginia Central Railroad both east and west of the town (west as far as Goshen), and they destroyed numerous bridges, including those at Christian's Creek and Fishersville. They also took stocks of food from private homes and killed livestock. Reportedly Hunter sought out Imboden's residence for destruction, but spared it when he discovered it had recently been purchased by a Union sympathizer. Hunter ordered prisoners released from jail, including common prisoners, who soon added to the orgy of destruction, as did gangs of freed slaves.[80]

On June 9 Hunter dispatched Colonel Moor and eight hundred men, including Moor's own 28th Ohio Regiment, whose enlistments were about to expire, to Beverly, West Virginia, by way of Buffalo Gap. They escorted the one thousand Confederate prisoners taken at Piedmont. George D. Wells then assumed command of Moor's 1st Brigade.[81]

Meanwhile Crook and Averell arrived at Staunton at about noon on June 8. Crook's 2d Infantry Division had departed Meadow Bluff on May 31 and Averell's 2d Cavalry Division left Bunger's Mills near Lewisburg on June 3. These two divisions had been ordered from West Virginia to come in behind Imboden and rendezvous with Hunter at Staunton. Confederate irregulars and brigades under McCausland harassed the Union advance but were unable to delay it. Crook and Averell moved to Staunton by way of Warm Springs, Goshen, Pond Gap, and Middlebrook. Their forces brought Hunter's strength up to eighteen thousand men and thirty guns.[82]

Crook and Averell conferred with Hunter, and the three generals agreed that they would next move on Lynchburg by way of Lexington. The day before, June 7, General Grant had ordered Maj. Gen. Philip H. Sheridan with two cavalry divisions to raid the Virginia Central Railroad. Grant instructed Sheridan to join Hunter at Charlottesville, where their two commands were to destroy the rail line to Hanover Junction. On June 11 and 12, however, Sheridan ran into Confederate Maj. Gen. Wade Hampton's cavalry at and west of Trevilian Station. Unable to join Hunter, Sheridan returned to the Army of the Potomac.[83]

While Hunter was busy destroying much of Staunton, Imboden and Vaughn led their men to Waynesboro, eleven miles east. They also occupied nearby Rockfish Gap, where the Virginia Central Railroad passed through the Blue Ridge Tunnel.[84]

Defense of Lynchburg was now a pressing concern. On June 6, the same day that Hunter took Staunton, Lee, who was unaware of the defeat at Piedmont, wrote President Davis that he had hoped Jones and Imboden might by then have combined their eight thousand men and defeated Hunter.

In his letter Lee urged that Davis send "some good officer . . . into the Valley at once to take command there and collect all the forces regulars, locals & reserves, & endeavor to drive the enemy out." Lee could offer little in the way of reinforcements, apart from releasing Wharton's and Echols's Brigades—all together 2,100 men—under Breckinridge. Wharton's Brigade included Imboden's 62d Virginia Infantry Regiment. These troops were then in reserve when on June 7 Lee ordered them provisioned for two days and returned to the Valley. Lee understood, however, that defending Richmond was the priority: "It is apparent that if Grant cannot be successfully resisted here we cannot hold the Valley—If he is defeated it can be recovered—But unless a sufficient force can be had in that country to restrain the movements of the enemy, he will do us great evil & in that event I think it would be better to restore to Gen. Breckinridge the troops drawn from him."[85]

Following the Battle of New Market, Breckinridge and the two brigades had left the Shenandoah Valley to reinforce the Army of Northern Virginia. On June 3 at Cold Harbor, Breckinridge was injured in a fall from his horse and taken to Richmond. He had recovered sufficiently to arrive on June 8 at Rockfish Gap with the troops released by Lee. Breckinridge now assumed overall command of Confederate forces in the Valley, including those under Imboden.

Hunter, meanwhile, was informed that the Confederates held Rockfish Gap in some strength, in effect barring the way to Charlottesville. Hunter also had received reports that Confederate reinforcements were on their way to the Valley. This information now led Hunter to proceed to Lynchburg, not by way of Charlottesville, but by continuing up the Valley. He planned to cross the Blue Ridge over the Peaks of Otter and attack Lynchburg from the west.

The combined Union force left Staunton early on June 10, heading up the Valley for Lexington. On June 12 the Confederates reoccupied Staunton, but the destruction there was such that never again in the war did it recover its former prominence.

Crook, Averell, and Sullivan proceeded south on different lines of advance along the western base of the Blue Ridge Mountains. Brig. Gen. Alfred N. Duffié's 1st Cavalry Division was the far left flank of the Union advance. Duffié had assumed command of the division on June 9, following Stahel's wounding in the Battle of Piedmont. Hunter instructed Duffié to move along the western base of the Blue Ridge, "making demonstrations" at the passes and sending out raiding parties to destroy portions of the Orange & Alexandria Railroad between

Charlottesville and Lynchburg. Reaching White's Gap, about seven miles east of Lexington, he would move through it to Amherst Court House and there destroy Confederate military supplies. He would then destroy the railroad to Lynchburg and rejoin Hunter and the main Union force west of the city.

Leaving Staunton at 3:00 A.M. on June 9, Duffié's men moved east on the Waynesboro Pike toward the Tye River Gap. Duffié sent two cavalry squadrons to demonstrate against Confederate troops under Imboden and Vaughn at Waynesboro, fixing them there while the remainder of the division proceeded east. For four hours the Confederates expected an attack, allowing the bulk of the Union cavalry to move twenty-five miles that day and reach Tye River Gap by nightfall without difficulty. Duffié decided not to continue south to White's Gap. The next morning, June 11, he moved his division over the Blue Ridge at the Tye River Gap. His men destroyed an iron furnace, and they also captured a Confederate wagon train conveying supplies from Staunton. Duffié took about forty prisoners, including seven officers, along with horses and a considerable quantity of stores. His men also burned several hundred thousand dollars' worth of Confederate bonds and currency.[86]

Duffié then ordered a small force to destroy the rail depot at Arrington between Charlottesville and Lynchburg. These men ran into a force under Confederate Capt. Henry C. Douthat, commander of the Botetourt Artillery Battery of six guns. Douthat and his one hundred men had been operating in southwestern Virginia when they were ordered to the Valley via Lynchburg. They were in that city when, despite reports of Federal raiders, on June 11 they were ordered north aboard a train of the Orange & Alexandria Railroad. At New Glasgow Station the conductor received word that a large Union party was ahead at Arrington Depot on the same line. Smoke indicated destruction by Union raiders of buildings there. Douthat now pressed ahead in an effort to protect a key railroad bridge over the Tye River.

Fortunately for Douthat, one of the train cars contained a large number of muskets and ammunition, which he had issued to his men en route. Duffié had sent only a sergeant and ten men to destroy the railroad depot at Arrington, and this small force indeed burned the depot there. Duffié claimed the men had "brilliantly executed" their mission, destroying "a large quantity of boots, shoes, and other quartermaster stores," as well as four small bridges and three to four miles in length. Undoubtedly this toll is exaggerated.[87]

Duffié made no mention of this in his official report, but his raiders then encountered Douthat's defenders, whom they assumed to be a heavy infantry picket. There was a brief skirmish before the Union cavalrymen withdrew. Had Duffié reversed the dispositions and sent the regiment guarding the pass instead, the railroad bridge over the Tye River west of Arrington might have been destroyed.

Had that happened, forces under Jubal Early would not have been able to reach Lynchburg in time to prevent its capture. Also, because of damage inflicted by the Union raiders earlier, Douthat's Battery was unable to reach its destination and retired back the way it had come, to Lynchburg, where it subsequently played an active role in the defense of that place.[88]

Imboden's command was now down to only four hundred badly armed and poorly mounted men. Imboden informed VMI superintendent Francis Smith that, based on news of Union movements, he was "resolved to cross at Bethel tonight and make for Forest Depot as rapidly as possible." Imboden realized this decision would make it important for Smith and the Corps of Cadets to go on toward Lynchburg. "Of this you are the best judge. There is no enemy on this side [of] the river." Heavily outnumbered and outgunned, Imboden did what he could to harass Duffié's movements, provoking numerous small skirmishes en route to Lynchburg but not seriously delaying the Union advance.[89]

Breckinridge was also on the move. He ordered Brigadier General McCausland's cavalry to keep in front of Hunter and try to delay his advance as much as possible. McCausland, aided by Col. William E. Peters and the 21st Virginia Cavalry, played a key role in the campaign. With not more than 1,600 men, McCausland harried Hunter and delayed his advance. One writer, Charles Blackford, believes this was critical in the saving of Lynchburg: "McCausland and his command were the real saviors of the city."[90]

Breckinridge charged Vaughn and Wharton, meanwhile, to oversee movement of the remaining forces to Lynchburg. On June 9, prior to departure from Rockfish Gap, Breckinridge delivered an impassioned speech to his men.[91]

McCausland, left alone to defend against Hunter's advance south to

Lexington, could do little but skirmish with the Union forces and attempt to delay the inevitable. When the Union troops camped for the night on June 10, they were within ten miles of Lexington. The next day as the Union troops approached the town, skirmishing occurred north of Lexington. After getting his own men across, McCausland then burned the bridge over the North River (today the Maury) to slow the Union advance. Confederate artillery positioned on the south side of the river also shelled the Union troops as they came up on the other side, and sharpshooters fired on the Union troops from the cliffs along the river. But such activity could only delay, not halt, the overwhelming Union strength. That afternoon McCausland and the VMI cadets abandoned Lexington, and Union troops entered the town at about 4:00 P.M.

Hunter's troops remained in Lexington for three days, June 11–13. Hunter promptly ordered the destruction of the Virginia Military Institute, and all was put to the torch, save the superintendent's quarters, which alone was spared because the superintendent's daughter was upstairs with a two-day-old baby. Hunter then made the building his headquarters. Federal troops also burned the home of former governor John Letcher. Hunter intended to burn Washington College adjoining VMI as well. Although he yielded to pleas not to do so, he allowed destruction of all scientific apparatuses, libraries, and furniture. Union troops also destroyed several iron works in the area, as well as storehouses, granaries, and farm tools and implements. Hunter's troops also damaged the branch of the James River & Kanawha Canal on the North River below Lexington in addition to looting the area. The Lexington newspaper estimated losses in Rockbridge County, including Lexington, at between two million and three million dollars.[92]

Duffié, meanwhile, moved on toward Amherst Court House north of Lynchburg, intending to tear up sections of the Virginia & Tennessee Railroad and destroy the Southside Railroad bridge over the James River eight miles east of Lynchburg. In the city, meanwhile, Confederate Brig. Gen. Francis T. Nicholls, who had lost both his left arm and his left foot in previous battles, was struggling to put together a scratch defense composed principally of local militia.

Duffié got to a point about five miles from Amherst Court House. There he received an order from a worried Hunter to rejoin him "by the most practical route and with as little delay as possible." Obedient to this order, a major mistake on Hunter's part, Duffié changed direction toward White's Gap and Lexington.⁹³

On June 12 some three hundred of Imboden's men sought to block Duffié's way at the point where the road crossed the Piney River. Duffié ordered a charge by two squadrons of the 20th Pennsylvania Cavalry of Wynkoop's Brigade. They drove the Confederates back and took some forty prisoners, including ten officers. Pushing the Confederates beyond the river and within three miles of Amherst Court House, Duffié then moved up the Piney River. He learned from the prisoners that Imboden had arrived only the night before from Rockfish Gap on his way to Lynchburg.

Duffié's men then moved to White's Gap. Near there he took another small Confederate wagon train. The troopers spent the night at White's Gap, then covered the remaining fifteen miles the next morning, arriving in Lexington at noon on June 13, along with one hundred prisoners and three hundred horses. Hunter's orders probably prevented him from capturing Lynchburg.⁹⁴

On the morning of June 13, making no mention of the skirmish with Duffié's men, Imboden alerted Nicholls of the presence of Union forces: "About 4,000 of the enemy's cavalry moved up last evening from Potter's Mill, via Mount Moriah Church, toward Amherst Court-House, and another column of 2,000, with a train of over fifty wagons, was reported as moving over White Gaps [*sic*] road. I will reach Lynchburg with my division this evening. You are in no danger of attack, except by cavalry, for a day or two."⁹⁵

On the morning of June 14 Hunter's army left Lexington for Buchanan. There the Federals burned the plantation belonging to Col. John L. Anderson, and—on Hunter's express orders—its mansion. A member of the Confederate Congress, Anderson was the older brother of Joseph R. Anderson, who managed the family-owned Tredegar Iron Works in Richmond.

The next day the Union troops crossed the Blue Ridge Mountains by way of the Peaks of Otter Road. That same day Breckinridge arrived in Lynchburg with some of his men. The strain of the trip was too much for him. Not fully recovered from his injury, Breckinridge was forced to bed on his arrival. He turned over command of the army to the ranking brigadier general, Vaughn. This move did not inspire confidence, given the latter's less-than-distinguished role in the Battle of Piedmont. The next day, more men and two hundred cadets from VMI arrived. The reinforcements were well received. One resident noted, "it was a reassuring sight, and never were a lot of bronzed and dirty looking veterans, many of them bare-footed, more heartily welcomed."[96]

On June 16, meanwhile, Hunter's troops moved through Liberty (present-day Bedford) on the Virginia & Tennessee Railroad, twenty-four miles west of Lynchburg. At the same time Crook's troops advanced along that line, destroying track, while Averell's men moved toward Lynchburg along the Bedford Turnpike (Salem Turnpike). On June 17 Crook reached New London, only about eight miles from the city.

As Union forces converged on Lynchburg, substantial Confederate reinforcements were also on their way there. Authorities in Richmond, annoyed over Hunter's raid up the Shenandoah Valley and his descent on Lexington, assumed that he would then move east of the Blue Ridge Mountains. While there was reluctance to detach men confronting Grant for a western campaign against Hunter, Confederate leaders in Richmond decided that the Federal threat from the west was such that this risk had to be undertaken. Once the decision was made, the plan was to carry it out in sufficient strength to insure that it would be effective.

Indeed, there were hopes in Richmond that a substantial force could not only defeat Hunter and sweep him from the Valley but that it might also threaten Washington and thus draw of some of the Army of the Potomac from its relentless drive on Richmond. Such an operation would require an entire corps. Jubal Early's II Corps of about eight thousand men, then at Gaines's Mill near Richmond, was selected.

With Ewell incapacitated and unfit to resume his duties as commander of II Corps in the midst of the savage summer's fighting, Lee had arranged for the promotion of Early to temporary lieutenant general, effective May 31. Sending Early to the Valley was natural enough, as many of the units in his corps had been identified with military successes there. As Freeman observed, "The old 'Army of the Valley' belonged to the Second Corps: its presence on the Shenandoah would be reassuring. Furthermore, Early was a man of independent mind, entirely self-reliant and with an aptitude for strategy. He was not a Jackson nor even a Longstreet, but he had some knowledge of the Valley and he appeared to be the most available man."[97]

Early had Maj. Gen. Stephen D. Ramseur's Division and a brigade of Maj. Gen. John B. Gordon's Division. Both units had been in the line for the previous forty days and had seen heavy fighting and sustained heavy casualties in the Battles of the Wilderness, Spotsylvania Courthouse, Gaines Mill, and Cold Harbor. Early received his orders on June 12. There was no time for reorganization, and his men were on the move before dawn on June 13.[98]

On June 16 Early's men were four miles east of Charlottesville, having marched eighty miles in four days. Early rode on ahead to Charlottesville, where he received a dispatch from Breckinridge with news that Hunter was at Liberty. Once Early grasped the situation, he requisitioned all available rolling stock on the Orange & Alexandria Railroad to move as many of his men as quickly as possible by rail to Lynchburg. He wired Breckinridge from Charlottesville five times on June 16, calling on him to do all he could to get the maximum number of cars in service. In the first dispatch he ordered, "Send off at once all engines and cars of Orange and Alexandria Railroad to this place, including everything at its disposal. I will send troops as soon as I get cars. . . . Hold on and you will be amply supported."[99]

Confederate authorities bent every effort to hurry repairs to the Orange & Alexandria Railroad to enable Early's men to move by rail to Lynchburg. Fortunately for Early, the damage was such that it could be repaired in one or two days; beginning at sunrise on June 17, Early embarked the first troops by rail to Lynchburg. Other troops set out on foot on a road paralleling the track to meet the train when it returned. Artillery and wagon trains went entirely by road.

At Lynchburg Breckinridge had only the small infantry force of Echols's and Wharton's Brigades, Vaughn's cavalry, some reserves, and the VMI Corps of Cadets. Screening these were Imboden's and McCausland's small cavalry forces, both of which were poorly armed and badly mounted and had been unable to do much to arrest the Union advance.[100]

By this point, despite his best efforts, Imboden's cavalry was in very poor shape. Breckinridge was not pleased with this or with Imboden's leadership. He reported to Braxton Bragg: "The cavalry under Imboden

Destruction of the Valley 255

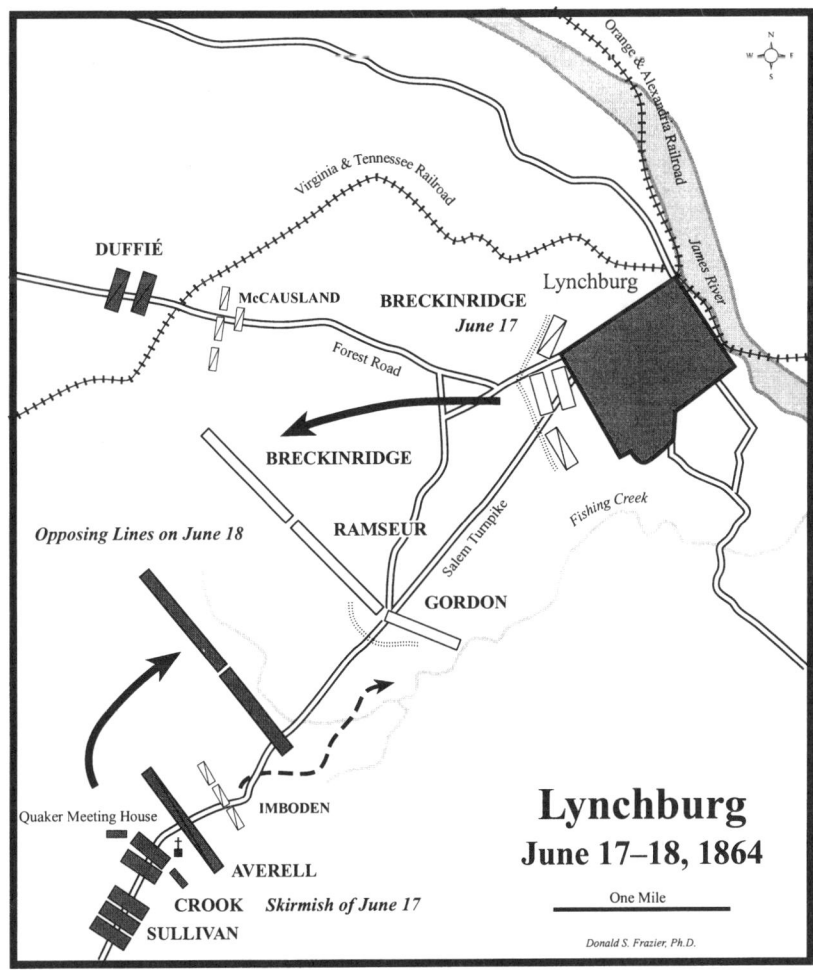

Lynchburg, June 17–18, 1864

[are] doing less than nothing. If a good officer cannot be sent for them at once they will go to ruin."[101]

Richmond had already ordered Maj. Gen. Robert Ransom to take command of all the cavalry in the Department of Western Virginia, reporting to Breckinridge. But the issue was now one of numbers rather than commanders; the numerical odds Breckinridge faced seemed insurmountable.[102]

Having gained Liberty, Hunter's army divided. On June 17 Duffié and the cavalry took the Forest Road; Crook and most of the infantry followed the Virginia & Tennessee Railroad line, tearing up track as they went; and the remaining Union troops under Averell proceeded along the Salem Turnpike.

It was 1:00 P.M. on June 17 before Early and "sufficient troops to make all safe" reached Lynchburg. He found Breckinridge still unable to ride. Early asked that Lt. Gen. Daniel H. Hill be assigned to temporary command of Breckinridge's corps.[103]

Unable even to inspect Lynchburg's defenses and displeased with Vaughn, Breckinridge had asked General Hill, then in Lynchburg convalescing, to throw up earthworks to protect the city. Hill had sited these on the west so that the much smaller Confederate force might more easily defend against the much larger Union army. The defensive works were centered on College Hill in order to cover Salem Turnpike and Forest Road. On June 17 a large number of defenders were at work on trenches and redoubts for the artillery. The works were then occupied by the remnants of the Confederate force defeated at Piedmont, the VMI cadets, and the invalid corps.[104]

Early immediately went with Hill to survey the defensive works and decided that they were too close to Lynchburg to protect it from Federal artillery fire. Early was "determined to meet the enemy with my [Early's] troops in front" in order to prevent a Union bombardment of the city.[105]

Early ordered a more advanced line some two miles west of the city, to be held by his own troops. Although Early was anxious to engage Hunter, his greatly inferior numbers then precluded offensive action. Early sought out Imboden, locating him near an old Quaker meeting house on a hill on the Salem Turnpike four miles southwest of the city. There Imboden was directing a spirited Confederate defense against Averell's attacking troops. Observers on College Hill could clearly see Union shells exploding over the Confederate positions.

Imboden, the senior Confederate brigadier general outside the city, had command not only of his own men but those under McCausland. Despite their precarious position, the peculiarities of the terrain suited the defense and the Confederates, supported by a section of artillery, were holding their own. Half of Imboden's command was dismounted and much of the rest was still disorganized after the Battle of Piedmont, yet the remnants fought well. This was an important achievement—essential to saving Lynchburg—and Imboden is too little credited for it.

With the arrival of Union reinforcements under Crook, however, the Confederates were slowly being forced to yield ground. Early saw that Union forces threatened to break through Imboden's defenders and break the entire Confederate line, and he immediately sent an aide back to Lynchburg to bring up Ramseur's Division, which had just arrived, as soon as possible. He also ordered back an artillery section into new positions.

The situation was precarious and elements of Ramseur's Division advanced on the double quick to Imboden's aid. Early, impatient, rode down the road to meet Ramseur's men in person, as he did so ordering the defenders to disengage and withdraw. Ramseur's Brigades, supported by the artillery section that Early had sent back, then took up a new defensive position some two miles from the city and a mile and a half from College Hill.[106]

Once the advancing Union troops had come up, they found Ramseur's men established in a good defensive position. The Confederates then rebuffed a Union effort to flank their position. The arrival of an additional brigade and part of Gordon's Division then allowed Early to mount a counterattack that drove Crook's men back. Darkness ended this engagement on Salem Road for the day.

That same afternoon a lesser skirmish occurred on the Forest Road north of Imboden's position on the Salem Turnpike. Imboden had sent McCausland's Brigade and a section of artillery there to check Duffié's cavalry. Proceeding along the narrow road at about 1:30 P.M., Duffié's men ran into McCausland's force, which had taken up position in the woods on either side. Conditions not being suitable for deployment of cavalry, Duffié's men then dismounted and engaged the Confederates on foot for two hours, at the end of which they had driven McCausland's men back some distance. Duffié halted at Clays Mill (now Graves Mill) for the night.[107]

That night, while Hunter rested at Sandusky, the family home of retired U.S. Army paymaster Maj. George Hutter, Early was hard at work. His situation was at best tenuous, with his line from Forest Road to Salem Pike quite thin. Half his force had yet to arrive, and he was yet short much of his artillery and wagons. By June 18 he had only some seven thousand troops and perhaps twenty guns to confront a Federal force numbering close to sixteen thousand men and thirty-six guns. Until he was stronger, Early would invite the Federals to attack him, hoping that McCausland could contain Duffié and that the main Union thrust would come against Ramseur.

That night while his men worked to strengthen their defenses and throw up earthworks, Early arranged a deception to improve his chances. He ordered one unit to march and countermarch all night to beating drums and loud cheers. Early also had a yard engine and several cars run in and out of the city on the railroad, making as much noise as possible as they did so. All this implied the arrival of significant Confederate reinforcements, which Early hoped would give Hunter pause.[108]

The deception had an impact. The theatrics unsettled the Union troops in the line and served to convince Hunter that all Confederate forces in the Valley were now concentrated in front of his lines. Hunter reported the force facing him "at from 10,000 to 15,000 men, well supplied with artillery, and protected by strong works." Deep in Confederate territory and far from his own base, with ammunition and supplies both low, he was much more cautious on June 18, despite his overwhelming superiority. Hunter thus threw away an excellent chance for victory. Of course, had he arrived before Lynchburg a day earlier, the city would definitely have been his.[109]

Early hoped to have all his men in Lynchburg by dawn on June 18, when he expected Hunter to attack. As it was, the Confederate reinforcements continued to arrive slowly by rail from Charlottesville throughout the day, obliging Early to continue on the defensive.

Early at last took the initiative with artillery, opening up against the Union lines at dawn on June 18 from positions on Salem Pike. He had only ten guns there to oppose twenty-eight Union artillery pieces. Yet instead of launching a full-scale attack as Early feared, Hunter merely returned the Confederate artillery fire and advanced skirmishers to test the Confederate lines and determine their strength. Hunter placed his two infantry divisions in the center of the Union line, along with Du Pont's artillery. He believed the Confederate redoubts were too strong to take by assault, and he resolved to first locate a weak spot in the Confederate line.[110]

Hunter ordered Crook toward Campbell Court House Road on the Union extreme right to create a diversion in the form of a series of probing attacks. Crook concluded it was impracticable to turn the Confederate left flank there, and was withdrawing around noon when he encountered several regiments of Averell's cavalry in the same area. The Union cavalrymen said they had run into a superior force of Confederate cavalry, undoubtedly Imboden's men, and had withdrawn from them.

Duffié also attacked on the extreme Union left (Confederate right) at about 12:30 P.M., driving McCausland and Wharton back to positions beyond Blackwater Creek along the Forest Road behind four hundred yards of open ground over which the Union troops would have to move. McCausland then repulsed two Federal charges there. Duffié became convinced he was facing a greater number of troops than his own, when his force was actually twice that of his opponent. Had he pressed the attack, Union forces could have burned the railroad bridges.

At about 2:30 P.M. Sullivan's Division probed Early's center. The engagement became fairly general and was, for a time, intense. The Confederates then counterattacked, driving back Sullivan's infantry until Crook came to its aid, forcing the Confederate troops back. At the same time, Breckinridge tried to turn the left flank of the Union infantry, but he too was also driven back into the Confederate works. A Confederate attack on the Union right flank was also rebuffed. The Union troops occupied a new line about a hundred yards back, and the battle ended for the night. Throughout these actions the Confederate artillery had played a key role. Imboden claimed his men suffered more than a hundred men killed and wounded that day alone.[111]

Finally, by evening the remainder of Early's men were in place. Maj. Gen. Arnold Elzey also arrived from Richmond, superseding Vaughn in command of Breckinridge's infantry and dismounted cavalry. At the same time Major General Ransom took command of the cavalry from Imboden. These changes were formally announced on June 20 at Liberty. Later Ransom reorganized the separate cavalry brigades of Imboden, McCausland, Jackson, and Bradley T. Johnson into a single cavalry division.[112]

With his men all in place, Early prepared for a general attack of Hunter's positions at dawn on June 19. Hunter, however, decided to abandon his effort to take Lynchburg. From prisoners taken during the day's fighting, he learned that Early's entire corps was at Lynchburg. Early learned after midnight that Hunter was shifting positions. He could not immediately pursue his adversary, however, until it was clear that he was withdrawing. It was possible that Hunter would attempt to attack Lynchburg again from the south or that he might be planning to join Grant south of the James.

At dawn, as soon as it was clear Hunter was indeed retreating west on the Salem Turnpike toward Liberty, twenty-five miles west of Lynchburg, Early ordered a pursuit, pushing his men as hard as he could. The Confederates skirmished with the Federal rear guard at Liberty in an infantry fight, with Ramsur's Division pushing the Federals out of that town.

This was as much as Early could do, and here the pursuit ended. The Confederate artillery could not be gotten up in time, and no cavalry were present. A message to Imboden ordering up his troopers had not reached him in time, and McCausland had taken the wrong road. Early had halted the Federal diversion and saved Lynchburg with its vital railroads, but he not been able to destroy Hunter.[113]

Believing that Hunter would withdraw over the same route that had brought him to Lynchburg, Early sent Ransom and most of his cavalry across the Peaks of Otter with instructions to try to intercept Hunter at Buchanan or Fincastle. Marching all night, the Confederates learned on their arrival at Liberty that Hunter was retiring in a more westerly direction, through Salem, thence to Buford's Gap.

The pursuing Confederates got in front of Hunter at Hanging Rock. Infantry support was not available, and for an hour or two the Confederate cavalrymen simply watched the Federals pass through the gap. Lieutenant Berkeley of McClanahan's Battery and McCausland urged Ransom to attack. Finally, without orders, Berkeley ran out a gun and opened fire. McCausland then charged the rear of the Union column, taking eleven Union guns, four of which were fully equipped.[114]

Imboden, too, pursued Hunter as far as Covington, trying to cut off the Federals before he could cross the Alleghenies. Halted at Covington on Early's orders, he and his men rejoined Early at Staunton.[115]

Hunter then moved by the Catawba Valley to White Sulfur Springs and Lewisburg, arriving at Charleston on June 29. Early gave up the pursuit altogether on June 23. Early and Lee were both disappointed that Hunter had been so little punished.[116]

Early allowed his men to rest for a day and then moved them north by way of Lexington, where he briefly diverted the men. While the band of the leading regiment played a dirge, thousands of the men who had fought under "Stonewall" Jackson marched in review past his grave site. Early then moved on to Staunton, where he rearmed and reequipped his exhausted men. The Valley was now clear of Northern troops.

Chapter 11

Final Confederate Service

At Staunton Early reorganized his command. With Hunter's army now to the west beyond the Alleghenies, Washington was temporarily exposed. Early hoped to take advantage of this in a thrust northward. Although heavily outnumbered by Union forces that were, moreover, able to concentrate quickly, Early hoped to assist Lee by forcing Grant to detach some troops from the Army of the Potomac—which was then pressuring Richmond—in order to defend Washington.

In the reorganization of his forces, Early brought Ransom and the cavalry, which had been reporting to Breckinridge, under his own direct authority. Bradley Johnson formally took command of "Grumble" Jones's Brigade. To compensate Breckinridge for the loss of Ransom and to give him resources in keeping with his abilities, Early assigned him Maj. Gen. John Gordon's Division. Maj. Gen. Arnold Elzey, who had gone to Lynchburg to take over temporarily from Breckinridge and assist Early there, was physically incapable of a hard campaign and asked to be relieved. Brig. Gen J.C. Vaughn replaced him temporarily, followed on July 7 by Brig. Gen. John Echols. VMI graduate and former professor at the Institute Maj. Gen. Robert E. Rodes and West Point graduate Maj. Gen. Stephen D. Ramseur continued in command, providing not only effective leadership but close cooperation based on mutual trust and admiration.[1]

During the reorganization at Staunton, the 62d Virginia Infantry was remounted and returned to Imboden's Northwestern Brigade. Reportedly Breckinridge was much impressed with this regiment when it had served under him and tried to retain it in his command.[2]

Early had altogether fourteen thousand men: some ten thousand infantry and perhaps four thousand cavalry and artillery. Effective employment of cavalry was always Early's weak point, artillery his strength. For the most part, the infantry was in excellent spirits, especially the divisions under Rodes and Ramseur. There were problems in Gordon's Division, but not of his making. The issues stemmed from its consolidation and officers' commanding men unknown to them. Breckinridge had a similar problem, with many of his regiments containing men who had no desire to fight for anything save their own homes. They would fight well in defense of their own territory, but in fighting on strange soil they would often disappear, only to reappear weeks later at home.[3]

Logistic problems also plagued Early's men. A major one was the lack of shoes; many of Early's men were barefoot. Early, however, chose to press on with his plans. He would hope to secure shoes from Richmond while on the march.[4]

On June 28 Early set out north from Staunton. By June 30 his army was at New Market, and by July 2 at Winchester. It was only that day that Siegel, now at Martinsburg, learned the Confederates were advancing in force down the Valley. The next day, July 3, Early's men ran into Sigel's advance guard, which they pushed back to Harpers Ferry. Confederate troops could not take that place, however, because Sigel's forces held Maryland Heights in strength.

Imboden's Northwestern Brigade had departed at the same time as Early. It had the important mission of destroying the key B&O bridge over the South Branch of the Potomac. This would prevent Federal troops and supplies from being shifted quickly east to oppose Early. Imboden led his brigade north from Valley Mills through Bridgewater and then on through Dayton. The brigade reached the head of Lost River on June 29, then marched across the mountains through Brock's Gap. They were at the designated B&O bridge on July 3.

The Confederates were chagrined to find the bridge heavily defended. Following its destruction the previous summer, the Federals had rebuilt the bridge and reinforced and repositioned the defenses—including a blockhouse—so as to prevent an attacker from getting within effective artillery range. An armored railroad car was also in place there.

Imboden's men spent a day testing the defenders. Concentrating their artillery fire on the armored railroad car, they managed to get a lucky shot through one of its ports. The shell ignited ammunition inside, causing the car to blow up.[5]

Despite this spectacular success, the attackers were unable to take the bridge. Imboden then broke off the attack, leading the brigade along the south side of the Potomac. The Northwestern Brigade rejoined Early on July 9, just south of Frederick, Maryland.

Imboden was not with his men. On July 5 he had become seriously ill with typhoid fever. Two days later he turned over command to Colonel Smith of the 62d and went to Winchester to recover. Imboden nearly died from the typhoid, which reached epidemic proportions among Confederate troops in Virginia during the war. By the summer of 1864 it was responsible for a quarter of all deaths from disease.[6]

Early, meanwhile, had led II Corps toward Martinsburg, West Virginia. On July 6, the Confederate Army of the Shenandoah Valley was encamped across the Potomac River in Maryland. This was its third such advance; the first had culminated at Antietam (Sharpsburg) and the second at Gettysburg. Although the Confederate bands played "Maryland, My Maryland," this time there were no welcoming crowds and no enthusiastic response from Marylanders for the Confederate troops.[7]

Shoes arrived and were distributed by the night of July 7. On July 8, Early's men crossed South Mountain and moved eastward. On July 9, the day that the Northwestern Brigade came up, Early's advanced elements were moving through Frederick, northwest of Washington.

East of Frederick, at about 8:00 A.M. on July 9, the advance approached the Monocacy River and reported Northern troops on the eastern side. The Union troops turned out to be a brigade of the VIII Corps and a small force of cavalry, all under Maj. Gen. Lew Wallace, Eastern Department commander. Union artillery commanded both the bridge on the road to Washington and the B&O bridge to Baltimore, about a quarter mile to the south. Two miles north of the railroad bridge, other Union troops were west of the river in advance of another bridge on the Baltimore Road, as if they meant to prevent the Confederates from crossing.

Early, not familiar with the ground, halted and deployed skirmishers. At about noon, as Early was reconnoitering, he was startled to see McCausland's Brigade ford the river about a mile below the railroad bridge, dismount, and then engage Union troops. Although McCausland's men captured a Union battery, they were not strong enough to carry the entire Union position and were forced to fall back.

McCausland's success in getting across the river, however, caused Early to push Gordon's Division across the river at that same point. The Union position was not an easy one to assault, but the Confederates charged and took a number of prisoners. Union losses during the day were about 1,300 men, with Early's losses fewer than 700.

Still, the Union troops stubbornly held up the Confederates for most of one day, repulsing five assaults before withdrawing late in the day. Early, however, had shown his failure at higher command by failing to employ his divisions as part of a wider scheme. He had committed his command piecemeal; only Gordon's Division had actively assaulted the Union line.[8]

Wallace had also been reinforced, by Brig. Gen. James Rickett's 3d Division of the Army of the Potomac's VI Corps. This was both good and bad news for Early. It was good news in that he had indeed accomplished one of the primary goals of his raid: drawing off units of the Army of the Potomac from the Richmond-Petersburg area and lessening pressure on Lee and the Army of Northern Virginia. The bad news was that—despite his success in the Battle of the Monocacy—it forced caution on Early. Uncertain of the size of the Union force facing him, he was unwilling to risk his own destruction.

Chances of success for Early were further diminished by new orders from Lee that he detach a cavalry brigade toward Baltimore in order to cut Federal lines of communication and assist in an effort to free eighteen thousand Confederate prisoners at Point Lookout, Maryland. Early complied with this by sending Bradley Johnson and his cavalry brigade.[9]

It was thus a more cautious Early who resumed the march toward Washington on July 10. Still, he pushed his men hard. That day the infantry covered thirty miles, with the Northwestern Brigade leading the advance. The Confederates, now feeling the effects of dust and intense summer heat, passed through Rockville, Maryland, and then advanced through Silver Spring in the direction of Fort Stevens, the northernmost of sixty-eight forts and batteries surrounding the Federal capital. The Confederates arrived there on the afternoon of July 11, the closest Confederate advance to Washington in the entire war. In the winter of 1861–1862, Confederate outposts north of Manassas could make out the buildings of Washington in the distance, but the Potomac River separated them from the Union capital. Now there was no river between the Confederates and their prize. Indeed, it seemed as if they might sweep into the city. As Freeman wrote, "After the war, men said that that charge on the third day at Gettysburg marked the 'high-water mark' of the Confederacy, and in the just determination of military values, they were correct; but if proximity to White House, to Capitol and to Treasury be considered strategically the greatest advance, then the honor of it fell a year and week after Pickett's charge to that strange, bitter, and devoted man, Jubal A. Early."[10]

On July 11 Early promised his men that he would lead them into Washington that very day. However, the heat had exhausted the men; many of his soldiers, even veterans who had experienced some of the most difficult marches of II Corps, had fallen out. When the advance element of Rodes's troops came within sight of the Washington fortifications, Early had to admit that there was no possibility of an immediate attack.

While he studied the Union defenses, Early deployed skirmishers and waited for the rest of his men to come up. He could only have high praise for the work of the Union engineers, who had constructed a complicated system of interlocking forts with artillery, along with breastworks, palisades, and abatis. Investment was impossible and any assault was bound to be costly.

As the skirmishers moved forward, the heavy Union siege guns, which easily outranged the Confederate horse artillery, opened up. They were manned by a variety of Union personnel, including pensioners and convalescents from the city hospitals. President Abraham Lincoln was among the observers.

Early now met with his subordinate commanders, informing them that not just one division but the whole of the Army of the Potomac's VI Corps was on the Washington front. Any attack would have to be made in short order; delay would give Union forces an opportunity to cut off II Corps by seizing the South Mountain passes and fords over the Potomac. Early and his commanders then decided to attack at dawn on July 12 unless new information was received that would change the assessment.

New information arrived that night in the form of a message from Bradley Johnson near Baltimore. He informed Early that Grant had sent not one but two corps to reinforce Washington and that it was indeed probable that the entire Army of the Potomac was on the way north to Washington. Early now hesitated, sending orders to delay the attack until daylight could reveal the extent to which the defenses were manned.

The next morning Early surveyed the defenses before him with binoculars, concluding that even if an assault were successful, it would be so costly that few of his men would be able to withdraw. If he were not successful, he would most certainly lose his entire force. Either way, it would have a depressing effect on Southern morale. His odds were simply too low; he would have to withdraw. After demonstrating in front of Fort Stevens later that day and beating back three advances by Union troops to test the strength of the force facing them, II Corps began its withdrawal on July 12.

Although Early had to leave behind four hundred wounded from the Battle of Monocacy, he brought back all Union prisoners and a substantial amount of supplies and booty. The Confederate coffers were also $220,000 richer, thanks to fines Early had levied on Hagerstown and Frederick. His cavalry had destroyed many railroad and highway bridges. On top of that the Confederates eluded Union pursuit. Although he had failed to enter Washington and the scheme to free the Confederate prisoners had also failed, Early had certainly fulfilled Lee's desire of reducing Grant's pressure on positions at Petersburg.[11]

Early's force reached Rockville early on July 13 and arrived at Poolville around midnight. It then crossed over the Potomac at White's Ford early on July 14. During the withdrawal, the Northwestern Brigade served as a rear guard. It secured White's Ford as the infantry waded across to Virginia, fighting a last skirmish with the pursuing Federals on Maryland soil.

After crossing the river, Early's men rested for a day, then started south to Leesburg. There they turned west, through Hamilton and Purcellville on their way to the Valley. Imboden's Brigade served as rear guard, McCausland's Brigade guarded the Confederate left, and Johnson's

Brigade was on the right. On July 16 as the wagon train was moving through Purcellville, it was attacked by a Union force from Harpers Ferry that broke through Johnson's men. The Union troopers took more than sixty wagons, including all those belonging to Imboden's Northwestern Brigade. In a letter to his wife, Col. George Imboden reported that it was Johnson's men who had given way, not the Northwestern Brigade: "I make this explanation because the People of the Valley are disposed to put every-thing of sensure [sic] on our Brig. that may occur in the Army."[12]

On July 16 Early reached Snicker's Gap in the Blue Ridge. Beyond this lay the Shenandoah Valley. Two days later, on July 18, at Castleman's Ferry on the Shenandoah River, a part of Crook's command attacked the Confederates but was repulsed with heavy loss. The next day the 18th and 62d Regiments were attacked at Berry's Ferry where the road from Ashby's Gap crossed the Shenandoah River. Colonel Imboden described the action in a letter to his wife: "We had one of the most gallant fights of the war at Ashby's Gap a part of the 62 and 18th fought all day two Brigades of Yankees, and six pieces of Artillery. We had one gun, the Yanks crossed the River twice at Berry's Ferry, but we drove them back and held the Ferry, we fought at least ten to one, our loss was about 15 the Federals 158."[13]

On July 20 the Northwestern Brigade reached Front Royal; the next day it was at Strasburg. There General Imboden resumed command.[14]

Although Early's cavalry commanders, such as Imboden, Harry Gilmor, and Bradley Johnson, had accomplished much in the destruction of bridges and McCausland had carried out several fine actions, the campaign had revealed a wide variance in quality of the cavalry. At this point in the war it was depleted and exhausted. It was also poorly disciplined and ill clothed and equipped. Early continued to bemoan the fact that he did not have a strong, dependable leader who could discipline and mold his calvary into a strongly united force, such as the Union cavalry led by Philip Sheridan. Early remarked, "all my operations had been impeded for the want of an efficient and energetic cavalry commander."[15] Part of this was Early's own fault, for he made no effort himself to improve his cavalry. Ransom, whom he had counted upon to do this, was ill and so nothing was accomplished.

Early's men enjoyed only a few days of rest. The raid on Washington had embarrassed Federal authorities and they were determined to exact revenge. Union forces under Hunter, Sigel, Averell, and Crook now all prepared to attack Early's II Corps.

A series of small battles followed. Near Stephenson's Depot north of Winchester on July 20 Averell attacked Maj. Gen. Stephen Ramseur's Division. Part of the Confederate force broke and ran, spreading panic and leading to the capture of 267 unwounded officers and men. Four days later on July 24 Ramseur secured partial redemption in the Second Battle of Kernstown, in which Imboden's Northwestern Brigade participated. To protect the lower Valley, Brig. Gen. George Crook's Army of West Virginia of 7,000 infantry and 1,500 cavalry occupied Winchester and set up camp a mile south of the town. Crook then sent Averell's cavalry division south on July 23. At Kernstown, Averell's horsemen ran into Early's advanced cavalry guard, leading to a day-long battle before the two sides disengaged in the afternoon. Union pickets remained at Kernstown, however.

Early, then at Strasburg twenty miles south of Winchester, decided to attack Crook at Kernstown on July 24. The Confederates set out at dawn, marching north along the Valley Pike. Cavalry skirmishing between the two sides began at about 7:30 A.M. and Crook soon learned of the Confederate advance. By noon he had most of three infantry divisions in line north of a small stream, Hogg Run.

Early then deployed Maj. Gen. John B. Gordon's leading division against the Federals. Its probing attack opened the battle. At the same time, Breckinridge, leading Echols's Brigade, swung wide to the right and then struck Crook's exposed flank. Breckinridge and Crook then charged each other. Fighting was heavy and the Union line held until the flank crumbled. The Union retreat turned into a rout, and Confederate cavalry attacked the Union wagon train, taking or burning seventy-two wagons and twelve caissons. In all, the Union suffered 1,185 casualties, including 479 prisoners. Confederate losses are unknown. This defeat convinced Union authorities that a change of leadership was necessary. Two weeks later Maj. Gen. Philip H. Sheridan assumed command of the new Middle Division—comprising the Departments of Washington, the Middle, the Susquehanna, and Western Virginia—to oppose Early.[16]

Early continued to raid to the north and west. He sent cavalry to the Potomac, and on July 27–28 they destroyed sections of B&O track at Martinsburg.[17]

At this time Early learned that during his advance on Washington Federal troops had burned homes of a number of prominent individuals associated with the Southern cause within the area of his command. He wrote later that he believed "it was time to open the eyes of the people of the North to this enormity, by an example in the way of retaliation."[18]

Early selected Chambersburg, Pennsylvania, as the object of reprisal and on July 29 sent McCausland's and Bradley Johnson's Brigades, along with a battery of artillery, to that place. Early instructed his commanders to demand either one hundred thousand dollars in gold or five hundred thousand dollars in cash as indemnity for the Southern property destroyed by Union forces. If the reparations were not forthcoming, they were to burn the town.

The Confederate cavalry arrived at Chambersburg early on July 30, and the town leaders were assembled to be informed of the demand. They rejected the ultimatum, claiming Federal forces were close by. McCausland waited until 9:00 A.M. and then ordered the town burnt. Some of his own officers and men, including Col. William Peters of the 21st Virginia Cavalry, refused to obey the order and make war on "women and children." McCausland showed them Early's instructions, but Peters still refused. McCausland placed him under arrest, releasing him only after the town had been put to the torch and the Confederates had withdrawn. Even late in life, Early never expressed regret over the destruction.[19]

McCausland also raided Cumberland, Maryland. He and Johnson then retired to Moorefield, where, believing they were secure, they let down their guard. On August 7 Averell carried out a surprise attack before daylight against Johnson's camp, routing the brigade. On the other side of the Potomac, McCausland was also forced to flee. Averell reported the capture of 420 prisoners, more than 400 horses, and 4 artillery pieces. Johnson was among those captured, but he managed to escape. In the aftermath of this fiasco, Johnson made a written attack on McCausland, denouncing his superior. He contrasted the strict orders McCausland had issued about the Chambersburg raid with his complete failure to maintain discipline over his men during it. He said

McCausland's men had been guilty, even on Virginia soil, of every imaginable crime, except murder and rape. Principally this was theft, taking the watches and wallets of civilians along the route.[20]

Pvt. Norval Baker in the 18th Virginia Cavalry also contrasted McCausland with Imboden: "Our General Imboden was never surprised. He was one of the best watchers I ever saw, always posted his men well and was always on the lookout."[21]

Although this was his responsibility, Early did nothing to resolve these problems and improve discipline. Freeman notes: "Although the responsibility was his as head of the forces in the Valley, he seemed powerless to control or to reorganize his cavalry."[22] What Early failed to realize was that the failure to act merely led to more behavior issues and further deterioration in discipline.

At this time Imboden's Brigade was conducting scouting operations for Early in Berkeley and Jefferson Counties. On August 9 Imboden reported to Early the presence of a large Federal concentration at Harpers Ferry. Imboden noted that the Union IV and IX Corps, as well as troops under Crook, were assembling there under Sheridan.[23]

Both sides, in fact, had upped the ante in the Valley. Lee sent reinforcements west in the form of Maj. Gen. Joseph B. Kershaw's infantry division and Maj. Gen. Fitzhugh Lee's cavalry. These troops were to operate east of the Blue Ridge under Lt. Gen. Richard "Fighting Dick" Anderson but in support of Early. Then on news of Sheridan's assumption of command, Lee ordered Maj. Gen. Wade Hampton to proceed to Northern Virginia with his division and also gave him command of the cavalry. But pressure from Maj. Gen. David Gregg on the James River then forced Lee to recall Hampton. Lee also had to find a replacement for Ransom, whose poor health had prevented him from retaking command in the field. On August 10 Lee ordered Ransom to Richmond, replacing him with one of Fitzhugh Lee's former brigadiers, Lunsford Lomax, now promoted to temporary major general.

Ransom claimed that a major reorganization of the Valley's cavalry forces was necessary in order to bring Early's cavalry "to anything like a state of efficiency." Among his recommendations were the transfer of Imboden's command to Wickham's Brigade and the relief of Imboden.[24]

Ransom's suggestions went to Early through Bragg, who directed that Breckinridge be consulted. Bragg himself noted in his letter to Early:

"It is feared that too radical a change may produce dissatisfaction in those commands raised mostly in the country now held by the enemy and cause many desertions. At the same time it is felt that some stringent measures are necessary to secure discipline and prevent disaster."[25]

For some unknown reason, Early neither answered Bragg's letter nor took steps to carry out Ransom's recommendations. Thus Imboden remained in his command. Although he complained frequently about his cavalry, Early thus failed to do anything about it.[26]

During the next month there was a fair amount of skirmishing as Early and Sheridan measured each other. Early developed a low opinion of his adversary, simply because the Union commander failed to capitalize on numerous opportunities to attack. This led Early to become overconfident, a dangerous state of affairs when an opponent is as yet untested in battle. Actually, Grant had ordered Sheridan to remain on the defensive until Early's strength could be determined with some accuracy.[27]

On August 11 Imboden tangled with Union forces at Double Tollgate, southeast of Winchester. There Imboden and Vaughn ran into a superior Union force, managing to drive it back toward Charles Town. Imboden reported to Early a considerable increase in the number of Union cavalry. As Private Baker put it, "the enemy had about ten to fifteen men to one of us."[28]

As Sheridan was receiving heavy cavalry reinforcement, Early lost his infantry reinforcement when Lee ordered Kershaw's troops back to the Army of Northern Virginia. The division departed in mid-September. Sheridan then had about 48,000 men, while Early's total was only 11,500, most of it infantry but also including cavalry and three battalions of artillery.[29]

In mid-August, meanwhile, Imboden "came down with fever" while at New Market and went to Staunton for treatment. In a letter to his brother Frank, dated September 22, Imboden said he had been at Rockbridge Alum Springs the past two weeks and expected to return to duty "in a few days."[30]

Imboden's Northwestern Brigade now formed part of Lomax's cavalry division, which also included the brigades of Jackson, Johnson, McCausland, and Vaughn. Their numbers had fallen off sharply, and Lomax's total strength was fewer than 1,700 men. Located at Front Royal, the division formed the extreme right flank of Early's forces.[31]

Sheridan, meanwhile, had launched a scorched-earth campaign in the Shenandoah Valley. Grant had instructed him: "Give the enemy no rest, and if it is possible to follow to the Virginia Central road, follow that far. Do all the damage to railroads and crops you can. Carry off stock of all descriptions, and negroes, so as to prevent further planting. If the war is to last another year, we want the Shenandoah Valley to remain a barren waste."[32]

In the first two weeks of September, skirmishes occurred almost daily between Sheridan's forces and the Northwestern Brigade. On September 17 Grant met with Sheridan and approved his plan to attack. Early learned of their meeting and assumed correctly that this meant a Union offensive was imminent.

Shortly after dawn on September 19, Early learned that Sheridan was advancing on Winchester. That very day, Union cavalry forded Opequon Creek, pushing through Berryville to the outskirts of Winchester. This initiated the Battle of the Opequon or Third Battle of Winchester. During the Union advance Imboden's Brigade was located at Stephenson's Depot, just north of Winchester. Here it came under attack by Averell's Division. Heavily outnumbered, Imboden's men were driven steadily back, but they made the attackers pay for their advance.

After a delayed start, Sheridan's late afternoon cavalry charge down the Martinsburg Road sent Confederate troops streaming south through Winchester on the Valley Pike to establish a new line the next day at Fisher's Hill, twenty miles distant. Rodes was killed while directing the Confederate counterattack that allowed Early's beaten army to retreat to safety. The September 19 Battle of Winchester cost Sheridan about five thousand casualties, a tenth of his command, while Early lost four thousand, or nearly a third of his forces.

The Northwestern Brigade now took up position as part of Lomax's Division on the left flank of the Confederate line, which was stretched thin over a four-mile front. To its left, separated from the division by a small valley, was Little North Mountain. Sheridan sent Crook and the VIII Corps of two divisions and artillery to flank the Confederate left. Moving his men to Little North Mountain, Crook attacked out of the woods at the base of the mountain. Outnumbered five to one, Lomax's Division gave way. The remainder of Early's force was also forced to retreat.

Another rout, the September 22 Battle of Fisher's Hill, cost Early more than 1,300 additional men, most of whom were prisoners, and 11 guns. Union losses were only about 400 men. Early continued up the Valley, stopping for the night at Woodstock. Imboden's Brigade spent much of the night trying to round up horses that had run off at the beginning of the day's battle.[33]

Early's corps departed Woodstock early on September 23, as the Northwestern Brigade protected the Confederate right flank. It moved along the Middle Road, paralleling the retreat of the Confederate infantry along the Valley Pike. Late that day, Imboden's men held off a large force of Union cavalry on Bowman's Ridge between Forestville and Timberville, allowing Early to get his wagon train safely across the North Fork of the Shenandoah River.[34]

Withdrawing another thirty miles up the Valley, by September 25 Early's force was near Cross Keys. Sheridan then moved to nearby Harrisonburg to the northwest. He remained there ten days while his cavalry raided into Rockingham and Augusta Counties. The Confederates were so outnumbered that any retaliation was limited to an occasional attack on an isolated Federal unit.[35]

Sheridan's men then fanned out the breadth of the Valley. On October 6 they started withdrawing north, continuing to carry out Grant's directive to destroy the Valley's crops. Sheridan sent one column east of Massanutten Mountain to lay waste to the Page Valley. The Northwestern Brigade, still the right flank of Early's forces, sought to prevent the destruction, but it was not strong enough to do anything apart from follow in the wake of the destruction and hope to catch an isolated part of the Federal rear guard. The men of the brigade could only watch helplessly as the Federals torched the Page Valley. The Northwestern Brigade then established itself at Milford and took up defensive positions to guard the eastern entrance to the Luray Gap. In all the Federals destroyed 400 square miles of prime farmland. In a long list of property either captured or destroyed during the period between August 10 and November 16, Sheridan included 1,200 barns, 71 grain mills, 435,802 bushels of wheat, 10,918 cattle, 12,000 sheep, and 15,000 hogs.[36]

Sheridan's depredations were such that one diarist reported that Richmond was "rapidly approaching a state of famine." Food prices soared. Bacon reached $20 a pound; flour, $1,200 a barrel; butter, $25 a pound; and wood, $200 a cord.[37]

Sheridan stopped south of Middletown on the north bank of Cedar Creek, with Early at Fisher's Hill. Not one to wait on the defensive for the next Federal foray, Early launched a spoiling attack on October 19, in which Imboden's Northwestern Brigade had a role. Maj. Gen. John B. Gordon and Maj. Jedediah Hotchkiss developed the plan. As part of it, Early ordered Imboden to move his command to the northeast beyond Front Royal, to the rear of Sheridan's army. There he was to assume a blocking position on the Valley Pike near Newtown (today, Stephen's City).[38]

On October 19 Early struck before dawn in what became known as the Battle of Cedar Creek. Taking advantage of a thick fog, Early's five infantry divisions drove on the Federal encampment at Cedar Creek and caught the Union troops there asleep. Within two hours, the Confederates had wrecked two of Sheridan's three corps and sent the Federals scurrying north toward Winchester.

Maj. Gen. Horatio G. Wright commanded the army in the absence of Sheridan, who had gone to Washington with several of his staff for a strategy conference with Army Chief of Staff Gen. Henry Halleck and Secretary of War Edwin Stanton. Only Wright's VI Corps and the Union cavalry retained unit integrity. All the Federals retreated north, some three miles beyond their camps.

There is controversy over what happened next. Many of Early's soldiers, hungry and exhausted from the strain of an all-night march, stopped to loot the Union camps. In any case, Early needed to regroup, and he halted the pursuit. This provided just enough time for the more numerous Federals to regroup.

Sheridan was not yet with his army when the attack began. On the morning of October 19 he was at Winchester preparing to rejoin the army when he received reports of firing from the direction of Cedar Creek. He left Winchester at 9:00 A.M., arriving at the Union positions around 10:30 A.M. during a lull in the fighting. Sheridan quickly assessed the situation and reformed the Union lines. After first riding the Union line to rally his men, around 4:00 P.M. Sheridan counterattacked. Union cavalry turned the Confederate left and crushed the Confederates. By 5:30 P.M. the battle was over. The defeated Confederates were sent streaming back through Strasburg.

The 62d Regiment of Imboden's Northwestern Brigade had easily reached its assigned position east of Newtown, and there they waited throughout the entire day of October 19 with no orders. It was not until evening that a Confederate courier arrived with news of the defeat. Imboden then led his dispirited men in a long ride back down the Page Valley to a blocking position near Luray astride the road leading through the New Market Gap into the Shenandoah Valley. Although Union casualties of 5,764 men (20 percent of the force) in the Battle of Cedar Creek were heavier, the Confederates had lost 3,060 (18 percent) and 23 guns. In one month Sheridan had won three major battles, earned the rank of permanent major general, and gained national fame.[39]

The Northwestern Brigade remained in position near Luray for five days after the battle until it returned to Milford on October 24 to engage a large Federal cavalry raid commanded by Col. William H. Powell. For the next two days both the 18th Virginia Cavalry and the 62d Virginia Mounted Infantry sparred with the Federals. Finally, late on October 26, Powell ordered his command back to Front Royal. This initiated a period of relative tranquility for the men of the Northwestern Brigade, who nonetheless remained in the Page Valley.[40]

Imboden now had an opportunity to try to remount his brigade. The heavy demands of the constant campaigning over the previous six months had taken a heavy toll, and the Northwestern Brigade was critically short of horses. According to one of its members, a full three-quarters of the mounts of the 23d Virginia Cavalry were unserviceable. Unlike the Union Army, the Confederates had no system for their replacement. Confederate cavalrymen were largely responsible for securing their own mounts, and without them were likely to be reassigned as infantry.[41]

As a consequence Imboden had no choice but to order out a sizable part of his command to procure replacement horses. He assigned the task to Capt. Hannibal Hill of Company E of the 62d. In late October, Hill led 380 men, drawn from all three of Imboden's regiments, across into Highland County.

When this effort failed to turn up the requisite number of mounts, Hill led the men on a quick raid against the Union garrison at Beverly, in Randolph County, West Virginia. Realizing that the countryside was heavily Unionist, and not wanting to give the alarm, Hill avoided the roads and moved his men cross country. Just before dark on October 28 the Confederates arrived about a mile from the Federal camp, but because of the lateness of their arrival they were forced to spend a cold night without benefit of fires. Early on October 29 the Confederates woke to a Union bugle sounding reveille in the Federal camp. Not long afterward the Confederates attacked, shouting the Rebel yell as they charged.

Pushed back into their cabins, the Union troops were able to pick off many of the attackers, who found themselves silhouetted in the dawn light. Realizing that the Confederates were but few, the Union troops rallied, and the Confederates found themselves fighting to avoid encirclement and endeavoring to get away.

When the fight ended, a third of the attacking Confederates were prisoners and another fifty were either dead or wounded. The 62d Virginia alone lost eight dead, ten wounded, and twenty-eight captured. This was a higher casualty rate than in most of the larger battles in which the regiment had been engaged.

The survivors of the ill-fated raid then joined the rest of the Northwestern Brigade to support Early's advance north down the Valley from New Market. The brigade reformed at Newtown, awaiting a Federal attack which failed to materialize.[42]

In November Sheridan sent cavalry into Fauquier and Loudoun Counties on a raid of destruction. In four days the men inflicted more than one million dollars' worth of damage. Sheridan then retired to winter quarters at Winchester. On November 14 Early also went into winter quarters at New Market, while the Northwestern Brigade resumed its position in the Page Valley. Throughout the remainder of November and December there were numerous small skirmishes involving the brigade and Sheridan's cavalry.

As bad weather made campaigning in the Valley less likely, Lee recalled troops from Early. On November 15 Kershaw's Division departed, followed on December 9 by Gordon's and Brig. Gen. John Pegram's men. Early then withdrew farther up the Valley to Staunton.[43]

That winter in the Page Valley the Northwestern Brigade suffered terribly, not only from the weather but from a shortage of fodder for the horses. Clothing and even blankets were in short supply, and the brigade received none of these. To add insult to injury, while the infantry were paid, the cavalry were not. The men were forced to barter tobacco for food. Clearly Early, whose dislike of the cavalry was well known, favored the infantry. By early December the situation had deteriorated to the point that Imboden thought the brigade would have to be disbanded until spring. Despite these difficult circumstances, Imboden wrote to his wife on December 4: "You hardly ever hear a murmur from the men. I have never seen such men as we have."[44]

Imboden had never really recovered from the effects of his bout with typhoid the summer before. As he recalled years later, "it so impaired my physical condition that I was incapable of performing efficiently the arduous duties of my position as a cavalry officer on active service in the mountains of Virginia, and therefore I applied to the Confederate War Office for assignment to some light duty farther south till the milder weather of the ensuing spring would enable me to take my place at the head of the brave and hardy mountaineers of the Valley and western counties of Virginia I had the honor to command."[45]

In his November 17 letter to General Cooper to request a transfer, Imboden, however, gives his wife's health as the key reason:

> It is with great pain and reluctance I request this favor at the hands of the government. . . . Nothing therefore but the most overwhelming personal considerations—purely private and domestic could compel me to this step.
>
> My wife for the last 18 months has been suffering from a painful and alarming pulmonary affliction. . . . In the opinion of her physician . . . a change . . . of climate [is] necessary to the preservation of her life.[46]

On December 6, 1864, orders from Richmond relieved Imboden of duty in the Valley District and ordered him to report to Brig. Gen. John H. Winder at Camp Lawton, near Millen, Georgia, on prisoner of war duty. The men of the brigade regarded this as a chance for their commander to recover his health in a warmer climate and expected him to return in the spring. In the meantime Col. George Imboden assumed command of the brigade, which then consisted of the 18th, 23d, 25th, and 62d Virginia Regiments.[47]

Meanwhile, Sheridan made one last effort in the Valley at the end of the year. On December 19 he sent six thousand Union cavalry under

Brig. Gen. Alfred Torbert across the mountains at Chester Gap toward Gordonsville in an effort to destroy the Virginia Central Railroad there. As a diversion to distract the Confederate cavalry, Brig. Gen. George A. Custer with three thousand cavalry moved up the Valley toward Staunton. Surprised in his camp near Lacey Spring on the night of December 20, Custer then withdrew.

Meanwhile, Torbert's main body reached Madison Court House on December 21, where it engaged Jackson's cavalry brigade. Torbert's men pushed back the Confederates and proceeded toward Liberty Mills, seven miles from Gordonsville, on the Rapidan River. As the Union cavalry approached the bridge over the Rapidan, the Confederates withdrew across it and then blew up the bridge. When the Union troopers came up to the river on December 22, they immediately came under fire from Confederates in rifle pits on the other side. This action forced the Union cavalry to deploy into two columns to locate fords to either side of the Confederate position. After stopping to rest for the night, the next morning the Union troopers got across the river and moved on Gordonsville, where Confederate reinforcements halted the advance. Torbert then broke off contact and withdrew.

At least part of the Northwestern Brigade was engaged in the fighting at Gordonsville, as it was here that Col. George Imboden was badly wounded, bringing to a close his Civil War service.[48] Pvt. Isaac Baker of Company F of the 18th Virginia Cavalry recorded: "A large ball had passed through the side of his face, tearing away his cheek."[49]

Late in December Brigadier General Imboden left the Valley, traveling by road to south of Richmond. There he rode on the Piedmont Railroad, a subsidiary of the Richmond & Danville line. On January 4, 1865, Imboden wrote General Lee from Columbia, South Carolina, that it was "the worst managed railroad on earth." It had taken almost fourteen hours to travel the forty-eight mile stretch of line from Danville to Greensboro, North Carolina, despite the fact that there were no reasons for delay. The problem seemed to be difficulty in finding anything but wet, green wood to fuel the locomotive. At one point the men tore down fence posts in order to secure fuel for its steam boiler.[50]

On January 6, 1865, Imboden reported to Brigadier General Winder in Columbia, South Carolina. A Maryland native, Winder had been a major in the U.S. Army artillery when the Civil War began but resigned at the end of April 1861 to accept a commission as a Confederate brigadier general. He was then made provost marshal and given charge of Union prisoners at Richmond, Virginia. In June 1864 Winder received orders placing him in command of Andersonville Prison in Georgia. The next month he took charge of all Confederate prisoner of war camps in Georgia and Alabama, and, in November, of all Union prisoners of war east of the Mississippi River. On January 2 Winder in turn gave Imboden charge of all Union prisoners west of the Savannah River, the area including Georgia, Alabama, and Mississippi. Imboden would have his headquarters at Augusta, Georgia. Winder did not have long to live; worn out by the strain of his duties, he died of a heart attack a month later, on February 6, 1865, at Florence, South Carolina.[51]

Although Imboden had been ordered south ostensibly to recover his health in easier circumstances, this assignment must have been a strain. In the best of circumstances, the Confederate transportation and supply system was chaotic and uneven, and in early 1865 it was at its worst. Railroads were in collapse, supplies were scarce, medicines were virtually nonexistent, and even food was in short supply. What food there was could not be moved efficiently because of the state of the railroad system. If this was the situation for the Confederate Army, it was often worse for civilians and Union prisoners, the latter having the lowest priority.

The Confederate prison system was also overcrowded, largely as a consequence of the spring 1864 Union decision to end prisoner exchanges on a rank-for-rank basis and to terminate paroles. This came about because the Confederacy illegally released Vicksburg prisoners from parole without exchange and because it refused to exchange black Union soldiers.[52]

The Union decision to halt prisoner exchanges led to a rapid infusion of Union prisoners into the already inadequate Confederate prison system, and the net result was near chaos and great suffering. Lack of facilities, overcrowding, poor diets, lack of medical treatment, and rampant disease now all took their toll. Conditions were also chaotic in the North, but the lot of prisoners was much better there, thanks to superior Union supply and administrative systems.[53]

Imboden had charge of six prisoner of war camps. These were Andersonville and Eufaula in Georgia, Florence and Columbia in South Carolina, Salisbury in North Carolina, and Cahala in Alabama.[54]

Andersonville was the worst of the Civil War prison camps. Officially known as Camp Sumter and located in Sumter County, its pine trunk walls and guard towers surrounded a camp totally bereft of trees and a yard overflowing with makeshift shelters rigged of clothing on sticks. Exposure to summer heat and winter cold compounded the misery for the prisoners, and one stream provided both drinking water and served as a latrine. Circumstances were made worse by prisoners who preyed on their weaker fellows. Life in almost all the camps was difficult, but in Andersonville conditions were hellish.

Maj. Heinrich Wirz, a native of Zurich, Switzerland, was the commandant. He claimed to be a physician, but he had no medical training. Wirz had emigrated to the United States in 1849. He had been a doctor's assistant in Kentucky but failed in efforts to set up his own practice. He had then traveled to Louisiana, where he was employed on a plantation as "Dr. Wirz." He had enlisted early in the war and, as a sergeant, was badly wounded in the May 1862 Battle of Seven Pines, losing use of his right arm. Promoted to captain, he had been assigned to Winder's staff in Richmond.

In March 1864 Wirz had assumed command at Andersonville. A harsh authoritarian in the best of circumstances, he nonetheless inherited a situation that was virtually unmanageable—an overcrowded and poorly provisioned prison that lacked proper facilities.[55]

After spending several days with Winder in Columbia, Imboden traveled to Augusta, Georgia. There Imboden set up an office and installed Lt. George W. McPhail in charge of communications with the prisons under his command. Imboden then returned to Aiken, where he established his headquarters. Imboden sent Lieutenant Colonel Bondurant on an inspection tour of the camps of his command, instructing him to report fully on conditions in each.

Shortly thereafter, Imboden was forced to quit Aiken in a hurry, a few hours before arrival there of Brig. Gen. Hugh Judson Kilpatrick's cavalry division of Maj. Gen. William T. Sherman's command. Imboden then relocated his headquarters in Augusta. He established his own residence a few miles out of town at Berzelia on the Georgia Railroad.

On the basis of Bondurant's report, Imboden decided to shut down the other camps and consolidate operations at Andersonville and Eufaula. This was prompted by reason of economics: he believed it would be easier to supply two larger camps than a number of smaller widely scattered ones. At the time he had not more than 8,000–9,000 total prisoners, with the vast majority of them—some 7,500 men—at Andersonville.[56]

Then on February 6 Winder died at Florence. With no direct superior, Imboden reported directly to the secretary of war, but, with Sherman moving through Georgia, all efforts to establish contact with Richmond were unsuccessful. Although he learned through a newspaper account that Brig. Gen. Gideon Pillow, then at Macon, had been appointed to replace Winder, Imboden never received formal notification: "I having none, could not, and did not, recognize him [Pillow] as entitled to command me, but cheerfully . . . consulted him in regard to all important matters of administration."[57]

Colonel Bondurant's report on Andersonville, along with communications from Wirz, convinced Imboden that he should visit Andersonville himself to determine conditions. The nearest railroad connection to that place was more than seventy miles away, but, before he could depart, Imboden learned from Capt. H.A.M. Henderson, commanding the Cahala Camp, of a mutiny there on January 20.[58]

At Cahala, Union prisoners had rushed and disarmed the guards, then held them in the latrines. Two of the guards at the main gate had managed to escape, and reinforcements to include an artillery piece were brought up. The threat of artillery fire had ended the riot, but the guards then withheld rations until the riot's ringleaders could be brought to justice. Imboden ordered a trial for the principal conspirator, George Shellar, alias Captain Hanchett. Imboden also ordered that any prisoner in his camps who was engaged in mutiny or an attempt to escape should be fired on and that any armed prisoner would be shot out of hand.[59]

In late February Imboden finally traveled to Andersonville, arriving unannounced and making an immediate inspection of all its facilities. Brig. Gen. Lucius J. Gartell commanded the guard force at the camp, which consisted of a brigade of Georgia reserves. A Colonel Gibbs, a former U.S. Army officer, commanded the post at Andersonville, while Wirz had charge of the prison camp.

In his inspection of the camp Imboden also went into the stockade and met there with a number of the Union prisoners. He professed himself displeased by what he discovered: "I found the prison and its inmates in a bad condition; not as bad as our enemies have represented, yet unfortunately bad. The location of the stockade was good, and had been judiciously chosen for healthfulness. It occupied two gently sloping hillsides, with a clear flowing brook dividing them. and being in the sandy portion of the pine woods of Georgia, it was free from local malaria, and had the benefit of a genial and healthy climate. It is of sufficient capacity for from 8,000 to 9,000 prisoners, without uncomfortable crowding. The great mortality of the previous year, I have no doubt, resulted in part from an excess of prisoners over the fair capacity of the stockade, and from the lack of sufficient shelter from the sun and rain."[60]

Before Imboden's arrival at Andersonville, Wirz had already informed him about the lack of sufficient shelter in the stockade and asked for means to redress it. He had made the same request of Winder, but no decision had been made before the latter's death. Many of the prisoners had dug caves in the hillsides to seek protection from the weather, but these were not properly ventilated. Clothing and food were also in short supply. Medicines were virtually non-existent. For this lack, Imboden blamed the Federal blockade: "I have no doubt thousands died at Andersonville in 1864, who would be living to-day if the United States had not declared medicines contraband of war, and by their close blockade of our coasts deprived us of an adequate supply of those remedial agents."[61]

Conditions were also difficult for the guard force, as guards and prisoners alike received the same rations. Many of the guards were in rags and barefoot. Provisions consisted chiefly of cornmeal and a little bacon. The daily ration was a third to half pound of bacon and one to one and a half pints of cornmeal, with salt. Occasionally there was wheat flour or a few potatoes, but no other vegetables.[62]

Imboden did not find the diet unacceptable: "General Lee's army in Virginia lived but little if any better. The food was sound and wholesome, but meagre in quality, and not such in kind and variety as Federal soldiers had been accustomed to draw from their abundant commissariat. Our soldiers did very well on 'hog and hominy,' and rarely complained. The Federals thought it horrible to have nothing else, and but a scanty supply of this simple food."[63]

Much of the violence at Andersonville was actually the result of prisoners taking advantage of their fellows. The so-called Raiders preyed on the weaker prisoners, stealing their food and then selling it. The so-called Regulators sought to defend those too weak or infirm to do so themselves. While Imboden was there, Regulators at Anderson detained six of the Raiders for taking advantage of other prisoners. Imboden allowed them to be brought to trial. Found guilty of stealing and cheating fellow prisoners, they were sentenced and hanged inside the stockade by the other prisoners. This led to a change in issuing of rations, precluding trafficking in stolen food.

A number of the prisoners approached Imboden about possible exchanges, and Imboden explained to the men efforts by the Confederate government to effect an exchange. A U.S. Army captain then learned that Imboden's brother Frank of the same rank was being held prisoner in the north, "where he was in a fair way to die from harsh treatment and a lack of food." He told Imboden that he had influence in Washington and that, if Imboden paroled him, he could effect his exchange for Imboden's brother, and perhaps even influence a decision on the general matter of prisoner exchanges. He promised that, if released, he would return within thirty days if he was not successful. Imboden agreed and with some difficulty got him through the lines, but thirty days later the captain returned, unsuccessful.[64]

Imboden agreed to Wirz's recommendation that more shelters be constructed for the prisoners. Under his direction a hundred or more paroled prisoners daily cut trees from the forest in order to construct huts with floors and chimneys. On their completion, some 1,200–1,500 of the weakest prisoners moved into the new shelters. On being informed by Wirz that a number of the prisoners were shoemakers by profession, Imboden authorized construction of a tannery. Thousands of hides were available at Andersonville from animals butchered the previous year, and within weeks many of the formerly barefooted prisoners had been supplied with rough but serviceable shoes. On medical staff advice, Imboden also authorized the brewing of corn beer, "by no means unpalatable, and very wholesome," to help treat prisoners with "scorbutic taint."[65]

Despite these efforts, the prisoners faced a grim situation. There was in fact little Imboden could do to improve their diet. The area around the prison was largely given over to the production of cotton, and no wheat, corn, or vegetables were readily available. There was also little livestock. Given these conditions, the only way to improve the situation was to repatriate the prisoners.

From Andersonville Imboden traveled to Macon to confer with Maj. Gen. Howell Cobb, overall commander of the District of Georgia and Florida, and with Pillow, who had been designated to replace Winder but was still awaiting orders from Richmond. The three discussed the serious situation facing the Union prisoners under their control, who were without adequate food or clothing. With the Federal government opposing all prisoner exchanges, retaining captured Union soldiers was no longer of any possible advantage to the Confederates. "Indeed it was manifest that they looked upon it as an advantage to them and an injury to us to leave their prisoners in our hands to eat our little remaining substance."[66]

The three generals agreed, despite the lack of authorization from Richmond, to parole the prisoners under their command without reciprocity, if the Federals would accept it. They planned to send the prisoners to the nearest accessible Federal military post.

As soon as arrangements could be made, Imboden sent some 1,500 prisoners to Jackson, Mississippi. Confederate Lt. Gen. Richard Taylor then commanded the Departments of Alabama, Mississippi, and Eastern Louisiana, through which territory the prisoners had to pass. He was to deliver them to Federal authorities, but Taylor protested and demanded that no more be sent that way. Taylor did not want any additional Federal prisoners and feared that, in transit to a Federal reception point, the prisoners might learn valuable military information that would later be detrimental to the Confederacy.

Because Sherman's forces had destroyed the Federal rail line to Savannah during the Union march to the sea, the only other Federal post accessible from Andersonville was St. Augustine, Florida. To reach there, the prisoners would have to move by rail to Chattahoochie, then by river to Quincy, Florida, thence by rail to Jacksonville. From that point, they would have to walk overland to St. Augustine. Imboden planned that when the prisoners were a day's march from St. Augustine, they would open communications with the Federal commander.

In mid-March Imboden sent an aide, Captain Rutherford, on ahead to Florida. Rutherford arranged with Federal authorities at St. Augustine to receive them, responding in a few days to Imboden with the telegraph message of "Send on the prisoners." Acting without authority from Richmond, Imboden ordered three days' worth of cooked rations prepared for the more than six thousand Federal prisoners who would make the difficult journey, and the men then set out. When the prisoners reached their destination, however, the Federal commander refused to accept them, claiming he could do so only on official authorization from General Grant. The only Federal route of communication from Florida to Grant at Petersburg was by sea and it would take two or three weeks to get a message back and forth.

Imboden was unwilling to let go the prisoners "without some official acknowledgement of their delivery to the United States," and he believed he now had no choice but to halt the effort. "It being impossible to subsist our men and the prisoners at Jacksonville, I could pursue but one course. I ordered their return to Andersonville, directing that the reason for this unexpected result should be fully explained to them." Imboden ordered rations hastily collected and sent on for them, and the men returned to Andersonville, embittered over the failure of their own government to come to their aid. Imboden continued well after the war to blame the Federal government for the continued suffering of the Union prisoners: "The Policy in Washington was to let Federal prisoners starve, if the process involved the Confederates in a similar catastrophe—and 'fired the Northern heart.'"[67]

The war was now rapidly coming to a close. Before Petersburg, Grant had built up his strength to 115,000 men; Lee had only 54,000. With Union forces systematically battering the Confederate lines, on March 25 Lee attempted a last desperate offensive east of the city to capture Union Fort Stedman. By nightfall 4,000 Confederates were casualties, against only 1,500 Union losses. On April 1 Lee engaged the Confederates at Five Forks near Petersburg, trying to counter Sheridan's movement against his lines of communication. Sheridan was victorious, and some 5,200 Confederates were taken prisoner.

The next day, April 2, Lee evacuated Petersburg and Richmond. He hoped to get to Lynchburg and then move from there by rail to North Carolina and join forces with Gen. Joseph Johnston. The Confederate government also fled Richmond, setting up in Danville, Virginia.

With Grant in pursuit, at Appomattox Lee found his movement south and west blocked by Union forces under Sheridan. Lee's forces had shrunk to less than thirty thousand men, with few rations remaining. On April 7 Grant requested that Lee surrender, and Lee asked for terms. On April 9 the two men met in a private residence at Appomattox Court House and quickly came to terms. Lee's soldiers were paroled to return home. The officers were permitted to retain their side arms, and all soldiers were allowed to keep private horses and mules. All equipment was to be surrendered. The Union Army issued rations to the hungry Confederate troops.

Meanwhile, Union cavalry under Bvt. Maj. Gen. James H. Wilson closed on Andersonville from the west. After conferring with Generals Cobb and Pillow, Imboden realized that they were powerless to prevent Wilson from taking Andersonville, releasing the prisoners, and capturing all the Confederate forces there. Thus, he again sent off all the Federal prisoners who could travel to Jacksonville. The Confederates abandoned Andersonville, releasing the Georgia troops there to General Cobb at Macon.[68]

Shortly thereafter, on April 18 at Durham Station, North Carolina, General Johnston surrendered his thirty-seven thousand–man Army of Tennessee and all that portion of the Confederacy to Sherman. The Confederate prison system then ceased to exist. By late April Imboden was himself a prisoner at Augusta, Georgia. It is doubtful that he ever surrendered in person, but a military pass of May 3, 1865, allowing him to return to his home refers to "John D. Imboden, a Brig. Genl. P.A.C.S." (Provisional Army Confederate States) as "a Paroled Prisoner of the Army commanded by Gen. R. E. Lee." Despite this document, Col. George W. Imboden steadfastly maintained that Imboden had never been paroled. On May 5 Imboden was ordered to parole all Federal prisoners of war under his jurisdiction.[69]

A few days later Imboden was sent with other paroled prisoners to Hilton Head, South Carolina. There he met about two thousand of the former Andersonville prisoners, who were awaiting shipment north. Imboden noted "their condition was much improved. Many of them were glad to see me." Four days later, Imboden embarked with several hundred of the former Andersonville prisoners on the steam transport *Thetis* for Fortress Monroe.[70]

Imboden's war was over. After his parole, he made his way north from Georgia to join his family and regain his health from the recurring fever at the home of his father-in-law in Charlotte County. Soon after Imboden's arrival there, Frank Imboden arrived from Augusta County with a horse for his brother, in the event he was forced to flee from Union arrest. Imboden spent several months at Mulberry Hill trying to regain his health.[71]

Chapter 12

Post–Civil War Career

The Civil War was over. Chaos reigned in the South, which was prostrate and in ruins. More than 10 percent of its adult male population lay dead. The economy was in shambles. Railroads were in terrible shape. With many mills and factories burned or otherwise destroyed, industry was at a standstill. Agricultural production was well off prewar levels, and much of the livestock, especially in Imboden's beloved Shenandoah Valley, has been killed or driven off. Federal troops and northern carpetbaggers occupied the South.

President Lincoln, who had hoped to ease the path of the former Confederate States back into the Union, was shot by an assassin on April 14, 1865, and died the next day. His successor, Andrew Johnson of Tennessee, tried to implement Lincoln's policies but was unable to stand up to northern radical Republicans led by vindictive Representative Thaddeus Stevens of Pennsylvania.

Joseph Waddell of the Virginia Historical Society provided this picture of the postwar scene in Augusta County, Virginia: "For many days afterwards all the roads in the State were full of weary men wending their ways homeward. Many homes were devastated and poverty-stricken. The army of the Confederate States had wasted away, and . . . the people were impoverished. Some food was left in the county—more indeed than was generally known of a few weeks before—and the pressing need was for articles of clothing. Railroads had been torn up, factories destroyed, farms laid waste, towns wrecked, the banks were all broken, and there was literally no currency in the country. Farmers set to work to do what they could, and a few other people found employment. Most white people were idle from necessity, and the negroes asserted and proved their newly found freedom by leaving the farms and flocking to town."[1]

Imboden's military career was over. At age forty-two, he could nonetheless anticipate that much of his useful life still lay ahead of him, but, as with all defeated southerners, Imboden approached the future with uncertainty. He did at least enjoy an advantage over most of his fellows in that he was recognized as a prominent individual.

Indeed, the "general," as Imboden would be known the remainder of his life, enjoyed notoriety for his role in the war. He had impressed many people and made useful connections, and he was determined not only to be successful but to assist his native state in its postwar economic recovery.

In August Imboden received a subpoena to testify in Washington, D.C., at the trial of Maj. Henry Wirz, his subordinate at Andersonville. Instead of being paroled at the end of the war, Wirz had been imprisoned, and in late August a military commission convened to try him for the mistreatment of Federal prisoners at Andersonville. Imboden was among those called for the defense. Although Imboden arrived to testify, he was not allowed to do so and Wirz was found guilty and hanged in November.

Wirz was undoubtedly more a victim of wartime hysteria and the search for scapegoats than deserving of his punishment for any crimes he may have ordered committed. Imboden wrote years afterward, "He may have committed grave offenses, but if so, I never knew it and do not believe it." Imboden attributed Wirz's trial and execution to the fact that "he was a foreigner and comparatively friendless."[2]

The joy of Imboden's family over his safe return from the war was short lived. His wife, Mary, died of consumption on September 21.[3] For the second time Imboden had lost his wife, and his children their mother. Imboden had little time to grieve Mary's death, as he had to find some means of providing for his family. He considered reopening his law practice in Staunton but decided in favor of Richmond. He had already concluded that he would use his knowledge of the law only as an adjunct to his plans for economic development, and the state capital would be the best place to realize the latter.

In September 1865 Imboden received an invitation from an old friend, Michael Harman, to participate in the establishment of a business to meet shipping needs in the South. Supported by Richmond bankers Charles W. Purcell and L.W. Glazebrook, Harmon extended an invitation to join the firm to a number of former Confederate officers seeking employment.

On October 31 Imboden's former commander, Joseph E. Johnston, became president of this firm, the National Express Transportation Company, with headquarters in Richmond. Johnston needed a trusted subordinate and in mid-November Imboden assumed the post of company general superintendent.[4] The board of directors included Harmon, Purcell, Glazebrook, John Echols of Staunton, and New York businessman Benjamin Hart. Imboden's old friend James L. Kemper became the treasurer.[5] The company was officially incorporated in Virginia on December 12. The charter listed the firm's business as "an express and general transportation business, by land and water, for the conveyance of persons and property of every kind throughout or beyond the limits of Virginia."[6] From this point on, Imboden considered himself a businessman and promoter of economic development rather than a lawyer.

In November Imboden had written Gen. Robert E. Lee at Lexington concerning an individual being considered by the board of directors for a post with the company. He ended by expressing his great pleasure that Lee would be president of his alma mater: "The venerable old College is doubly dear to me now."[7]

The National Express Transportation Company prospered and its line came to extend from New York to St. Louis in the West via Cincinnati and as far south as Columbia and Charleston, South Carolina. With nine million dollars in subscribed capital, it was a major corporation in the South in the early postwar years. As general superintendent, Imboden traveled to various cities of the nation. In January 1866 he shifted jobs within the company, giving up the post of superintendent to become general attorney, a position he held for nearly two years.[8]

Imboden also remarried. Either before the war or perhaps soon after the death of his wife, he met in Richmond Edna Paulding Porter (1841–1870), the daughter of Commodore N.D. Porter and his wife

Elizabeth Beale and a granddaughter of Commodore David C. Porter. They were married in Richmond on October 2, 1866, and established their home there. Imboden's third marriage produced no children.[9]

Postwar Virginia politics were turbulent and, for some time, dominated by outsiders. In December 1867 Imboden accompanied his long-time friend John H. McCue to a convention to organize a new conservative party in the state with the plan of ultimately ousting the Radicals then in power. Imboden was perhaps too busy with development projects to be actively involved in politics.[10]

In 1867 Imboden left the National Express Transportation Company to work for Virginia's state Domestic Agency of Immigration, Office of Virginia Lands. That agency was created to encourage settlement in Virginia. Imboden was appointed "domestic state agent of immigration" with his main office in Richmond and a branch office in New York City. At the same time he retained his private business capacity as a "general land agent."[11]

In September 1869 the name of the agency was changed to Virginia Land and Aid Immigration Company, and six months later it became the Virginia Lands and Southern Real Estate Generally. The changes in title reflected a shift in emphasis from increasing the population in Virginia to promoting land development and the investment of capital.[12]

In correspondence Imboden noted the large number of inquiries from northerners about purchasing land in the state. He experienced difficulty, however, in interesting them in lands not close to railroads. He wrote in September 1869, "Northern people are so accustomed to Railroads that it is almost useless to talk to them about lands remote from such facilities."[13]

Undoubtedly Imboden's involvement in land promotion prompted his renewed interest in railroad construction, especially in central Virginia. He recognized the important role railroads would play in rebuilding the state and in developing its natural resources. Among other such efforts, Imboden wrote to the *New York Tribune* to promote a rail line in Buckingham County, which lacked even canal transportation.[14]

In March 1870 Edna Imboden died unexpectedly. That same August, while working on promoting railroad construction in Boydton, in Mecklenberg County, Imboden met Annie Harper Lockett (1851–1888). Aged nineteen, she was the daughter of Howard and Augusta Lockett.

Imboden, nearly thirty years older, was immediately smitten. He wrote to Annie expressing his devotion and asking that she reply without delay to his Virginia Lands office in New York City. He told her he hoped she would soon be his wife. On December 30, 1870, he wrote Annie from New York: "I am tired to death of this great crowded city. I do long for a few weeks back in old Virginia—not in Richmond—but in the depth of the Wilderness of Mecklenburg. You make it an Eden."[15]

Imboden's efforts met with success, and he and Annie Lockett were married on March 15, 1871, at her parents' home of Lombardy Grove in Boydton. They had one child, a daughter, Helen Maguire. Born on May 5, 1874, she lived into adulthood.

Virginia was readmitted to the Union on January 26, 1870. At last the conservatives were able to oust Governor Gilbert Carlton Walker, a Carpetbagger from New York, and replace him with Confederate war hero and former major general James Lawson Kemper. With the end of the war, Kemper had urged his fellow Virginians to accept the inevitable and rebuild their state. Governor from 1874 to 1877, Kemper's tenure was turbulent and marked by strife between "Debt-payers" and "Readjusters" over the matter of the debt incurred by the state during the war.

State leaders in Virginia recognized the need to restore the railroads as soon as possible. In order to promote private capital for the development, the state liquidated its own extensive railroad interests. On March 28, 1872, the Virginia General Assembly approved the sale of all railroad stock held by the state. Almost all these securities, with a face value of some fifteen million dollars, were sold at public auction on February 5, 1872.[16]

Imboden's interest in development extended beyond railroads. In order to promote land development, he needed to study land values and so turned to mineralogy. Here his interests were in developing Virginia's considerable deposits of coal and iron. Coal was increasingly valuable as a fuel source to replace wood in steam boilers and as an aid in the manufacture of iron. Iron was of course used in myriad products, including rails and cars for the new railroads. As early as 1866, Imboden had written to James D. Davidson of Lexington: "We are going to wake up that part of Rockbridge [County] in a short time by digging a mint of money out of its hills and mountains. I know of no such opening in

Virginia just now for big returns on a comparatively small capital. Won't some of you Lexington gentlemen want to take a little stock in the Rockbridge Mining Company and help develop your country's wealth, and pocket good dividends?"[17]

In 1872 Imboden published a twenty-eight-page pamphlet based on his findings. Entitled *The Coal and Iron Resources of Virginia*, it was for many years regarded as a primary reference source on the subject. In it Imboden stressed Virginia's abundant coal and iron, detailed production figures, and discussed railroad construction as a means of exploiting these resources. He claimed that the coal and iron interests of the state were "full of promise of a great and prosperous future for our people."[18]

Imboden now decided to open his own firm to promote the sale of land, and in the fall of 1872 he established a business known as Imboden's Office of Virginia Lands, with headquarters at 902 Main Street in Richmond. At the same time he became involved in a number of business enterprises, including the Lehigh Granite Quarry and the Goochland and Pittsylvania Asbestos Mines.

As an active businessman and promoter, Imboden sought foreign capital. In the spring of 1873 he sailed to London to solicit British investment in Virginia land. He remained in Britain seven months, his primary goal to secure financial backing for the coal mining development in southwestern Virginia. On April 21 the directors of the Foreign and Colonial Estates Exchange Agency gave a dinner in his honor at the Westminster Palace Hotel. Imboden addressed the gathering at some length, praising the relationship between Britain, his own state, and the United States. He stated the great interest of Virginia in encouraging emigration from Britain and he noted the state's extensive coal and iron resources, which he said were larger than those of Pennsylvania and had only that year been united by the Chesapeake & Ohio Railroad. Imboden must have had some success in this endeavor as two Britons, Lord Hardy and geologist David Thomas Ansted, joined several Pennsylvania investors in establishing the Gauley Coal Company, an investment group for coal mining operations.[19]

Imboden returned from England to supervise operations in the United States, both from his office in Richmond and another in New York City. By the end of 1873 the Gauley Coal Company had purchased the Hawk's Nest Coal Mines, at the time the largest along the Chesapeake & Ohio Railroad. Gauley Coal also owned the Victoria Furnace at Goshen, the important railroad town thirty-six miles southwest of Staunton.[20]

Imboden's brother Frank joined him in his business, in both Richmond and New York. During 1872–1874 Frank Imboden was the elected captain and commander of the Richmond Light Infantry Blues, a volunteer military formation formed prior to 1793. Frank continued his close association into the mid-1880s with his brother in development of land, timber, and coal in both southwest Virginia and in upper North Carolina. In October 1873 George William Imboden also joined his older brother in the Gauley Coal Company. He too had developed an interest in mineral exploration and exploitation.[21]

Imboden was now one of the premier experts on mineral exploitation in Virginia. In October 1875 Governor James L. Kemper wrote Imboden, asking that he assist the Count A. de Beausacy, a prominent foreign investor interested in purchasing iron and coal lands in Buchanan County. In making the request Kemper noted, "you are better acquainted with the mineral lands of that section than any other gentleman known to me." As testimony of Imboden's knowledge and reputation, in December 1875 the Mineralogical Society of Roanoke College at Salem unanimously elected him an honorary member and invited him to speak to the university on the anniversary of its founding on February 23.[22]

Imboden also dabbled in inventions. In October 1875 he learned that the U.S. Patent Office had approved his railway car lifter. It provided a means whereby the wheels (or trucks) on individual cars might be adjusted for tracks of differing widths (or gauges). This was important because there was then little standardization in railroads, especially in the South, which had a wide variety of short lines. The lifter operated on compressed air, which could be generated by the steam locomotive. Imboden had demonstrated his invention at the 1874 Annual Fair of the Virginia State Horticulture Society. He was also granted a patent for a device to accelerate the draft in steam boiler fires.[23]

Life was not all calm, however. On November 20, 1875, Imboden was accosted and beaten by his former comrade-in-arms Bradley T. Johnson. Imboden claimed that he had an appointment with former Governor Wise and was about to leave for his office when an old friend stopped by. Imboden believed that this delay saved his life, as it meant that he was in a more populated area when Johnson and W.L. Royall accosted him. Newspaper accounts, however, have the attack taking place at the Byrd Street Train Depot and Imboden waiting for a train for St. Louis to attend the Pacific Railroad Convention.

Johnson subsequently admitted that after locating Imboden, he had gone up to him and said, "General Imboden, I have been looking for you." Johnson then pulled a belt (identified in articles as a "cowhide") from his sleeve and struck Imboden across the face five or six times in rapid succession. Imboden then defended himself. Imboden later claimed that Johnson had planned to kill him. Royall testified that Johnson's only intent was to use the belt and that he had purchased it for Johnson for the express purpose of "cowhiding" him.

Johnson and Imboden had both fought in the First Battle of Manassas/Bull Run and then served together as brigadiers under Jubal Early. Late in the war Johnson and Brig. Gen. John McCausland had burned Chambersburg, Pennsylvania, in retaliation for Hunter's destruction in the Shenandoah Valley. Imboden found this action not in keeping with his own principles, and he and Johnson came to develop an intense dislike of one another, abetted by sharp political differences.

In any case, according to a policeman who intervened, Johnson pulled a pistol as the two men scuffled. Imboden claimed he had seized the pistol before the policeman separated the two men and arrested Johnson. Newspaper coverage universally condemned Johnson, who was duly fined twenty dollars for assault and forced to provide a bond of one thousand dollars "to keep the peace for twelve months."[24]

Imboden, who had caught his train and proceeded on to St. Louis, there spoke to nine hundred delegates to the National Railroad Convention, pointing out the close relationship between coal mining and railroads. He also used the opportunity to promote land development and his own inventions. Imboden was in the city for several weeks and apparently exhausted his financial resources. He wrote that he had been forced to borrow twenty-three dollars for fare home.[25]

During the period May 10, 1876–November 10, 1877, an important international exhibition took place in Philadelphia to celebrate the centennial of the Declaration of Independence. In August 1874 Imboden was appointed to the Centennial State Board of Virginia, with the task of insuring that Virginia products and industries were well represented at the Centennial Exhibition. Imboden was a logical choice for this position because of his wide-ranging knowledge of resources, industrial activities, and transportation facilities of his native state.[26]

In early April Imboden left for Philadelphia to establish himself there and make acquaintances that might be useful to him in land and railroad promotion. Apparently he was successful in making personal contacts, for in April 1876 the Executive Committee of the Exhibition selected him as a member of the Board of Judges for the Centennial.[27]

Imboden served in this capacity during the entire six months of the Exhibition. He did not spend all that time in Philadelphia, but commuted back to Richmond from time to time. In May 1876, in a letter from Richmond, he expressed satisfaction that his car lifter was gaining acceptance in the railroad industry. Both the Chesapeake & Ohio and Clover Hill Railroad Companies were building their cars in conformity with his model. He expected the Philadelphia & Reading Railroad to follow suit and use it on their own rolling stock.[28]

Certainly Imboden's presence in Philadelphia was useful in promoting his invention, and in July 1876 the car lifter went on display at the Exhibition. In addition to the Philadelphia and Reading, the Baltimore & Ohio and Erie Railroads also had it under consideration. Unfortunately for Imboden, the utility of the car lifter was soon obviated by the industry's realization of the necessity to standardize gauges across the country. The car lifter was no longer necessary when its patent expired in 1892.[29]

Imboden also may have designed an improved coal car, but his inventive interests were not limited to railroads. In August 1876 steam-powered cars for inner-city transportation were introduced in Philadelphia. Imboden then came up with his own design for an improved street car engine and passenger car, known by the ungainly title of "Imboden vibrating steam sub-motor." One of these steam engines was built by the Graysport Foundry and machine shops for the Oakland & East Liberty Passenger Railway in Pittsburgh. The passenger car was built by the Jackson & Sharp Company of Wilmington, Delaware. The engine and car were designed to operate on sharp curves around street corners. The whole consisted of a steam engine of twelve–fifteen horsepower, with an open cab on top of the boiler for the operator, and a "horse cart" behind. Reportedly the steam engine was designed to pull its own car as well as an extra loaded car on any "street road of not over 250 feet grade to the mile."[30]

On October 4, 1876, the Commission appointed Imboden as one of the marshals of the Centennial National Tournament, which took place at the Exhibition grounds on Maryland and Virginia Day, October 19. On the last day of the Exhibition, Imboden was presented with a special bronze medal for his services.[31]

Despite all his activities and recognition, Imboden's finances were precarious. He wrote to his friend Maj. John McCue in October 1876, "The last year has been one of the hardest I ever went through. Indeed there were times when I could not see which way to turn & live." Imboden blamed his dire financial straits in part on his brother Frank: "During my 7 months [sic] absence in Europe, when everything looked flourishing Frank rushed into two or three things that sunk several thousand dollars and swamped the big end of all I made out of the one Coal Co. I did organize in London. He went to N. York 2 years ago nearly $1500 in my debt . . . and to keep him alive there in the 2 years I paid nearly $400 more. He is now here, on his way to So West Va. with a party of rich men and I believe has arrangements concluded that will enable him to pay me off during the winter, besides realizing for me a considerable sum on that Wise County Land."[32]

Imboden remained interested in politics, and in the 1876 presidential election he supported Rutherford B. Hayes over the conservative Samuel J. Tilden. Imboden believed that "Hayes would be as generous to the South as Tilden and better able to reconcile Northerners to his policy." Imboden predicted in a letter from Philadelphia, "Hayes will sweep the country. Mark it." Tilden carried Virginia, but Imboden was correct: in the disputed election, the electoral commission elected Hayes.[33]

During his time in Pennsylvania, Imboden made a number of useful contacts. He was pleased that there were those in the state who were willing to invest in land, mining, and railroads in southwestern Virginia. In 1877 he was drawn to Pittsburgh, in large part because of its importance as a railroad center. He hoped that he might learn lessons there that could be applied to his own state. That same year Imboden's son, John Daniel Jr., died at age fourteen.

Imboden was in Pittsburgh when he received word in September 1877 that he had been elected vice president for Virginia to the permanent free exhibition in Philadelphia. Located in the National Immigration Machinery Hall at Fairmont Park, it was in effect a continuation of the Centennial Exhibition. With a representative of each state on its board, the exhibition would showcase a variety of state products in order to attract investment.[34]

Imboden continued to travel, most of the time by railroad, as he actively promoted the economic development of southwestern Virginia. He spent time in Pennsylvania, New York, North Carolina, and Tennessee. By now Imboden was embittered over his financial straits and clearly hoped he might benefit personally from development of the region. He wrote to J. Marshall McCue from Pittsburgh, "Your letters of the last 2 or 3 years have satisfied me that a man is making a d———n fool of himself who gives his time to other people's affairs. It doesn't pay in money & nothing else is worth working for. I gave some of the best years of my life to the public & you know, for you have told me so over and over again, that I have not ½ doz. friends left in all the Valley of Va. I worked so hard for. No use to ask me again to help anybody outside of the very, very few I am under direct personal obligation to."[35]

Imboden's chief interest remained his own state and the promotion of coal and iron resources of southwestern Virginia. As Richmond was far removed from that area, in 1880 Imboden moved to southwestern Virginia, to Abingdon, the country seat of rural Washington County and its largest town. With a population of only 715 people in 1870, Abingdon was in the heart of the coal and iron region and was also a major timber producer. Imboden lived in Abingdon for about five years and returned there after a short stay in Bristol. The town, which Daniel Boone had named "Wolf Hills" in 1753 and later had been known as "Black's Foot," had been incorporated as "Abingdon" in 1778. One historian referred to it as "located in the heart of the Holston Valley in a beautiful and fertile country."[36]

Imboden's continued research into the area proved valuable. He was one of the first individuals to call attention to the valuable coal and ore deposits in Dickinson, Russell, Washington, and Wise Counties and to promote their development and the building of railroads to tap these resources. He also pointed out the rich coal and iron resources in the area around White Top Mountain, also known as Iron Mountain, the tallest in Virginia.[37]

Imboden saw Big Stone Gap as an industrial center. Hidden away in the Cumberland Mountains northwest of Bristol, it lay at the Three Forks of Powell's River, near a gap between Stone and Little Stone Mountains. The presence of coal there was well known from 1749, when Dr. Thomas Walker of Albemarle County explored the western parts of the Colony of Virginia. But exploitation of these resources had to await the coming of railroads to make Wise County readily accessible.[38]

Imboden traveled by rail to Bristol, the nearest railroad point, and then by horseback across the mountains to study the coal and iron resources of the area. Impressed by what he found, he set out to try to map out a "grand design" for southwest Virginia. Imboden believed iron could be manufactured profitably where coal was available, and the area contained substantial quantities of both in close proximity to one another. The coking coal was also of a high quality. Water was abundant and the climate was excellent. The problem was Wise County's isolation. It could take ten days by wagon to travel between Big Stone Gap and Abingdon, only fifty miles away. But Imboden was certain it would become "one of the great iron producing districts of the United States," perhaps even "the greatest."

Imboden now devoted much of his energy to establishing a planned community near Abingdon in southwest Virginia. The impetus for this probably came from M.B. Wood, a leading citizen of Estillville. Wood wrote Imboden in March 1880:

> I am more and more impressed with the importance of securing those lands around Big Stone Gap. Laying aside all selfish and ulterior motives, it is important, if there is to be built a town, that the lands should be controlled by some intelligent persons so that it may be properly laid out. . . . I have no doubt that we would be able to dispose of the lots during the summer and realize hansomely [sic] on the investment, besides reserving several valuable corner lots for ourselves. . . . While your great abilities are engaged in bringing before the world the great resources of this section and making fortunes for your company, I can attend to our smaller private affairs. . . . I feel and believe this is an opportunity we cannot afford to let slip."[39]

Imboden then began making major purchases of land for "certain gentlemen of means." He bought one tract of twenty-one thousand acres for only thirty-five cents an acre and never offered more than one dollar an acre. In several weeks' time he had purchased over forty-seven thousand acres. An inventory he made of his property in May 1880 showed that John Daniel and Frank Imboden owned a one-sixth interest in a tract of over one hundred thousand acres in Wise County. Imboden was also to share in profits from the development of other land.[40]

That June Imboden arranged for a visit to the area by a government geologist, Professor Stevenson, who undertook a scientific analysis of the resources. Apparently Stevenson's report satisfied Imboden and his friends. Wood expressed himself "perfectly delighted" with it. He did all he could to encourage Imboden, playing on his vanity and urging him to approach the governor in Richmond for convict labor to work on the railroad: "Your energy, zeal, and great good sense entitle you to success. I believe you are building to yourself a name that will be cherished and revered throughout all this hill country when the names of many politicians who are striving to write their names on the pages of history are forgotten."[41]

On March 30, 1882, the Virginia Senate passed a bill incorporating the town of Imboden in Wise County. On April 4 the bill was amended in the House to change the name from "Imboden" to "Mineral City." The Senate agreed to the amendment two days later.[42]

Development rested on adequate transportation, and Imboden sought to attract entrepreneurs to the area from Kentucky, the North, and even Britain. He hoped to have railroad track from Bristol to Big Stone Gap complete by 1881, so that he could "pour down through S.W. Va. an immense supply of the finest coke made." Imboden remained in the area for a time to oversee the progress of the railroad. He loved the area and thought Wise County a "gloriously secluded region." He delighted in it "as much as a sea voyage for its solitude," while at the same time he sought to turn it into an industrial site. Others were not so certain and expressed concern over the magnitude of Imboden's plans.[43]

As he had sought to expand the Virginia Central Railroad before the Civil War, Imboden aggressively promoted expansion of the Virginia & Tennessee Railroad into the coal-producing areas of southwestern Virginia. At Bristol the Virginia & Tennessee joined the East

Tennessee & Virginia Railroad, which went through Knoxville and then on to Chattanooga.

The Virginia & Tennessee was promoted in Lynchburg in 1831 as the proposed "Lynchburg & New River Railroad." Incorporated in 1848, it was renamed the "Virginia & Tennessee Railroad" the next year when the state government also authorized a state subscription for its financing. The line was completed to Forest in March 1852 and to Big Lick (now Roanoke) by November. In 1854 it had reached Abingdon and by October 1856 the line extended to Bristol. In December 1864, Maj. Gen. George Stoneman's Union troops had burned the railroad depot at Abingdon along with much of the town.[44]

In 1868 the Virginia & Tennessee had been in receivership. Almost taken over by its competitor the Baltimore & Ohio, it had however merged in 1870 with the Southside and the Norfolk & Petersburg Railroads. The new corporation, known as the Atlantic, Mississippi, & Ohio Railroad, had 479 miles of track. The new line was sold in 1881 and reorganized as the Norfolk & Western Railway Company. Between 1881 and 1892 the Norfolk & Western built three new lines into the coalfields of Virginia and West Virginia. Unfortunately for Imboden, the expected boom did not begin to materialize until 1890, when the South Atlantic & Ohio Railroad finally arrived.[45]

When the Norfolk & Western began building its New River branch line into the coalfields, Imboden settled in Abingdon. He traveled widely to promote the products of the Connelsville Coke & Iron Company. During September and October 1881 he was general agent for the Tinsalia Coal & Iron Company and did the same for its products.

Imboden had been one of the charter partners of the Bristol Coal & Iron Narrow Gauge Railroad Company, approved in December 1879. In November 1881 he became president of the Bristol & North Carolina Narrow Gauge Railway Company, which the next year became the Tennessee & North Carolina Railroad Company. Its main office was in Elizabethton, Tennessee, and while Imboden was in that place, on July 19, 1883, he was badly injured when he was kicked by a horse. For several weeks he was incapacitated from broken bones and a crushed foot.[46]

In July 1883 Tennessee governor William B. Bate selected Imboden as his state's representative to expositions at Louisville and Boston.

Imboden's job was to promote mining and railroads in order to enhance Tennessee's industrial progress. This was precisely the activity Imboden loved, and he represented Tennessee at the September 10, 1883, opening of the Louisville Exposition and also at the subsequent Boston Exposition. Probably because of frequent travels to Bristol and Elizabethton, Imboden transferred his residence to Bristol sometime in 1885. In 1886 he traveled to New York to meet with prospective investors there and inform them that the Kentucky Railroad would cooperate with their development plans.[47]

Certainly one of Imboden's most important contributions to the mining industry of Virginia was a report that he wrote at the behest of the U.S. Bureau of Statistics. This three hundred–page effort, which brought him considerable professional recognition, was a comprehensive survey and statistical analysis of Virginia's mineral potential. It proved so popular that the U.S. Congress ordered the printing of an additional twenty-five thousand copies.[48]

Imboden also found time to write a number of articles on the Civil War. His first effort, "Reminiscences of Lee and Jackson," appeared in November 1871 in *Galaxy Magazine*. In 1876 the *Southern Historical Society Papers* published his article on Maj. Henry Wirz and the treatment of Union prisoners of war at Andersonville. Imboden wrote an article on the Battle of Piedmont and Hunter's Raid, published as "Fire, Sword, and the Halter" in the *Philadelphia Weekly Times*. Later it appeared as a chapter in the *Annals of the War* in 1879. Imboden also wrote five articles for the *Century Magazine* in "The Century War Series." This later was published as the four-volume *Battles and Leaders of the Civil War* (1887–1888). Imboden's articles were: "Jackson at Harpers Ferry," "Incidents of the First Bull Run," "Stonewall Jackson in the Shenandoah," "The Confederate Retreat from Gettysburg," and "The Battle of New Market, Va." The Staunton *Vindicator* also published his article about the Battle of Piedmont, entitled "An Augusta Battlefield," and Imboden wrote another two-part article about the same battle in the *Confederate Veteran Magazine*.

Constantly traveling, Imboden visited Richmond, Washington, Philadelphia, and New York in the spring of 1887. That summer he moved back to Abingdon and in March 1888 he became general manager of the Damascus Enterprise Company and the Mineral Bureau of

Southwest Virginia, Eastern Tennessee, and Western North Carolina. This involved promotion of the region's natural resources and creation of a planned community there.[49]

In the first part of 1888, with Imboden regularly traveling between Abingdon and Richmond, his wife developed a serious heart condition that required constant care. In mid-May Imboden wrote his friend J.H. McCue that Annie was failing rapidly and that he expected to be called home at any time. He said he wanted to be with her in Richmond, but he had to be in Abingdon earning a living for the family. Annie Imboden died in Richmond on July 5 and was buried there. Their only child now at home, Helen, was fourteen.[50]

His efforts at Big Stone Gap having failed, Imboden found a new location for his "steel city" in Washington County. Inhabited at the time of Imboden's arrival by a dozen families, the site was originally known as "Mock's Mill." Imboden changed the name to "Damascus." In 1886 Imboden, together with T.P. Trigg, G.W. Litchfield, William Aston, Walter Preston, A.J. Forbes, A.D. Reynolds, R.J. Reynolds, James M. Barker, and other associates, formed the Damascus Enterprise Company. On May 21, 1887, the Virginia Legislature passed an act incorporating the company with stock not to exceed five hundred thousand dollars and shares set at one hundred dollars each. The company then purchased the land that today forms most of the city of Damascus. By 1890 the land had been cleared of its laurel and rhododendron, surveyed, marked into lots and streets, and offered up for sale.[51]

Imboden's promotional pamphlet introduced Damascus in these words: "Fifteen miles by railway survey Southeast of Abingdon, Va. and twenty-eight miles East from Bristol, Tennessee, at the confluence of Beaverdam Creek and the Laurel fork of Holston river the site of a city, wholly in Virginia, has been purchased, paid for and laid out for business purposes on the level lands, but the adjacent uplands of the Company suitable for fine residences has not been surveyed. The proposed city will be called 'Damascus,' after the oldest continuously inhabited city in the world."[52]

Washington County, Imboden said, "has been at all times regarded as one of the finest counties in the State of Virginia, and has been especially noted for the intelligence, virtue and patriotism of its inhabitants." He touted the area as an agricultural region with streams and springs, and "surrounded by picturesque and fertile uplands and densely wooded hills. In short the country is an ideal home for the industrious farmer, and enterprising stockman." The level land above the floodplain had all been surveyed and laid out into "streets, blocks, and building lots." Imboden noted the nearby mountains had vast stores of iron ore, manganese (a much-sought-after ore used in steelmaking), and timber. The Laurel and Beaverdam provided a fine water supply, and there were "very large springs of crystal-clear, and cold free stone water."

After extolling the virtues of the site, Imboden pointed out that Damascus was close by the coking and fuel coalfields of southwestern Virginia counties, all features that led to its selection "as the very best in the United States for a *modern* 'Damascus,' destined to become as famous, we believe, as its ancient namesake in Asia, as a *steel* producing city, and also a centre of general modern manufacturing."

In his effort to tout the qualities of the area, Imboden was not above using Henry Mock, who had sold land to the company. Mock had settled there in 1841, and in 1887 he was ninety-four but still "hale and hearty." Three times married, he had fathered thirty-two children, the youngest being thirteen. Imboden, the promoter, announced that twenty-nine of the children were still alive, "all vigorous, both men and women."

At Damascus coking coal and steel-making ore were less than a hundred miles apart. Imboden pointed out the high quality of the iron in the area, which was largely free of phosphorous, and the presence of significant deposits of manganese. He also extolled the large amount of lumber available, mostly white pine of fine quality, but also white oak, poplar, and chestnut. Damascus would be an ideal location to harvest and ship this high-grade wood.

Finally, the topography was such that those wishing to exploit the resources of the region by constructing rail lines would have to come through Damascus. "Lines from the Ohio river through Buchanan and Dickinson to the great Southwestern Virginia Coalfield, aiming for the South Atlantic Coast States, will be forced by the same inexorable 'law of least resistance' to seek the 'portal' at 'Damascus.'" The Damascus Enterprise Company expected to see the first line constructed and in operation from Abingdon to Damascus in 1888. Imboden also announced that seven acres of land some twenty feet higher than the general land of the town had been set aside for a large hotel and cottages, "which we think can be made one of the most attractive summer resorts any where in these mountains always so attractive to low-landers."[53]

By mid-1888 the rail line to Damascus was nearing completion. Unfortunately for Imboden and the town, the iron deposits turned out to be on the surface only, dooming his dream of "a new steel city." However, the abundant timber resources alone did justify construction of a railroad line through the Laurel Gap and development of the town.[54]

Probably in reaction to a failure to secure adequate support for his project, Imboden wrote to J.H. McCue on February 11, 1889: "All the American people are absorbed in two things—partisan politics amongst the leaders and a *money* mania has possession of the masses."[55] Imboden wrote William S. Stuart, an old friend and owner of the Greenbriar White Sulphur Springs resort, that he intended to construct "works and mills" around Damascus, that Pennsylvania investors had bought large tracts of timberland there, and that he expected to complete the railroad line by the fall of 1889.[56]

Imboden now married for the fifth, and final, time. While in Chattanooga in the fall of 1889, he had met Florence (Johnson) Crockett (1852–1908). Possibly they had met even earlier. The daughter of Lafayette and Harriet Johnson of Lynchburg, she was a widow with two young sons. Imboden was now sixty-seven; Florence was but thirty-eight. The two were married in Chattanooga on May 22, 1890, and soon moved to Damascus.[57]

By this time, Imboden had sold his home in Richmond and decided to live permanently at Damascus. Imboden and his new wife were Episcopalians, and Florence Imboden started a Sunday school there. Largely through her efforts an Episcopal church was constructed in 1891. It soon burned but was replaced several years later.[58]

Imboden was among those active in erecting the Lee statue on Monument Boulevard in Richmond, and he was one of twenty-two Confederate generals present in a pouring rain on October 27, 1887, for a parade and cornerstone-laying ceremony. On May 29, 1890, when the statue was officially dedicated, Imboden again participated, riding in a carriage with other Confederate generals as an honored guest.[59]

In 1892, on Imboden's insistence, the name of the post office at Mock's Mill was changed to "Damascus." By that date, the streets of the town had been laid out and plans had been developed for a hotel and numerous businesses. Foundations had been laid for the hotel on a knoll near the railroad trestle and building materials had been purchased for it. The hotel was never completed; it was lost in the great national Panic of 1893.[60]

This economic depression occurred during the second Grover Cleveland administration. Overproduction and an economic downturn in Europe led to a drop in prices for agricultural products, and this in turn sharply reduced the purchasing power of the nation's farmers. New railroad construction came to an end, as within the year a reported 15,000 businesses failed, more than 150 banks closed their doors, and 4,000,000 workers were jobless. Among the railroads going under was the Abingdon Coal & Iron Railway Company. Imboden's plans for Damascus came to a halt.[61]

Imboden's attendance at the Columbian Exposition in Chicago during July–September 1892 was his last involvement with promotional traveling, and he now settled into retirement. His finances had dwindled, although he did secure a modest income from a recently established plant to bottle spring water at Damascus.

Imboden's mind remained active, and he continued to be interested in scientific research and economic development. In September 1894, he replied to a letter from his brother Frank about employing electricity to burn lime. He noted that improvement in the national economy had allowed the raising of $4 million in Boston and New York to finish the Virginia & North Carolina Railroad between Petersburg and Raleigh. He was also hopeful for the local line, writing that Colin Campbell "who has bought our little R.R." was "very sanguine that our road would be built right off. If so we will soon be OK." He also hoped that "Jim [his brother James] & I will get the tie and timber contracts, and lots will begin to sell here again." His brother George had sent him two checks for $50 each "to pay expenses," but Imboden declined to accept them as a present, choosing instead to accept them as a loan and sending him a draft on the treasury for that amount. The money had, however "eased me up immensely." He had also written two articles on the Civil War, which he believed would be accepted and would bring in a total of $150. If so, "I shall be all right for the winter." He hoped also that the bank would not sue on some claims, but if they did he had been told by the lawyers that "execution" would be delayed for a year and he could probably get by with paying $50. Indeed, Imboden believed himself secure enough in his finances that he had "ordered my first suit since 1890," for $12. Imboden reported that agricultural production in the South was booming and he expected that in another year the region would be "more prosperous than at any time since the war." Given the large number of bank failures of the previous year that would greatly assist the people and farmers.[62]

On August 13, 1895, Imboden became sick while at home in Damascus. He died two days later, on August 15, of intestinal complications. He was seventy-three. He had told his brother George, who had arrived in Damascus a few days before he became ill and who was with him when he died, that he wanted to be buried at Damascus with "a plain slab at his grave—J. D. Imboden, founder of Damascus." George Imboden noted that he was not certain how his brother left his business, "but I think it is in bad shape." Imboden's body was temporarily interred at Damascus, but in 1908 it was removed to Hollywood Cemetery in Richmond to lie with some of his children and eighteen thousand Confederate comrades-in-arms.[63]

An obituary cited Imboden's contributions during the Civil War but noted he was a man of "broad information and remarkable intellectual powers." It called him "the pioneer" in the development of the iron and coal resources of southwest Virginia, observing that he first called attention to the valuable deposits in Wise and the adjoining counties: "The importance of his influence in this direction cannot be estimated. It has simply resulted in bringing about the present state of affairs through which there comes so much hope of the future." The article went on to note that it was Imboden who secured investment in the area and caused the South Atlantic & Ohio and the Clinch Valley division of the Norfolk & Western Railroads to be built. He also caused various enterprises, "leading to a complete development of the resources of this region," to be established. Another obituary noted Imboden's role in establishing the rail line connecting Abingdon to Damascus.[64]

Four of Imboden's brothers survived him. Imboden had remained particularly close to George William, the next oldest, throughout his life. A lifelong Democrat and lawyer, George Imboden resumed the practice of law after the war. In 1866 he and his wife moved to Crittenden County, Kentucky. They lived there until 1869, when they moved to

The Imboden family in Saltville, Virginia, in the spring of 1885. Top row (left to right): Eliza Catherine "Kate" Gibson (General Imboden's sister), Isabella Wunderlich Imboden (General Imbdoen's mother), and Brig. Gen. John D. Imboden. Middle row (left to right): Capt. Francis "Frank" M. Imboden, Jacob "Jake" P. Imboden, and Col. George W. Imboden (all brothers of General Imboden). Bottom row (left to right): Frank Howard Imboden (son of General Imboden), Marie Bell Gibson Hobbs (General Imboden's niece, holding baby), and George Gibson (General Imboden's nephew). (Courtesy of Gibson T. Hobbs Jr.)

the lower James River in Virginia for a year. In 1870 they again moved, this time to Ansted in Fayette County, West Virginia. During 1873–1879 he worked for the Gauley Coal Company opening coal mines. George Imboden's first wife died in 1869, and he then married Angia Mildred Dickenson. Imboden was president of the Fayette County Court during 1881–1885 and elected the first mayor of the town of Ansted in 1891. He was successively elected recorder of the town until 1907. He continued to practice law but devoted much of his time to managing his extensive property. Imboden died at Ansted on January 8, 1922, and is buried there.[65]

Frank, John Imboden's second younger brother, was in business with John for a time in Kentucky, Louisiana, and Virginia. He then worked closely with John in promoting timber and coal development. Frank married Nantie Palmer of Saltville on October 20, 1881, in Saltville, Virginia. In 1885 Frank left the United States for Honduras. His wife and family joined him there the next year. On their return to the United States, they lived in Colorado and Arizona, where Frank continued his work in land exploration and mining. The last survivor of the Imboden brothers, Frank died on June 7, 1929. He left six children.[66]

James (Jim) Imboden, not yet eighteen when the Civil War began, rose to be a sergeant major in the 18th Virginia Cavalry. In 1870 he married Elizabeth Shepherd Smith of Albemarle County. They had nine children over the next eighteen years. In 1881 he moved his family to Glade Springs, near Saltville. He worked for his brother John Daniel at Damascus and also followed such trades as timber cutting, building railroads, and farming. He died in Clarendon (now Arlington), Virginia, on April 1, 1928, and is buried in Arlington National Cemetery.[67]

Imboden's youngest brother, Jacob Peck (Jake) Imboden, entered VMI at the end of March 1864. Six weeks later, as a member of D Company in the Corps of Cadets, he fought in the Battle of New Market and was wounded by a shell fragment. He then served until the end of the war with Col. John S. Mosby's Partisan Rangers. He graduated from VMI in 1867. He married Johnnie Meems of Kentucky, but she soon died, and he then married Anna Stuart Dickenson of West Virginia, sister of his brother Frank's second wife. They had three children. In the early 1880s Jake Imboden was also involved in mining in West Virginia and Missouri, and he advanced to become superintendent of a gold mine in north Georgia.

Jake organized the December 1885 expedition to Honduras that included his older brother Frank; John Daniel Imboden's son Frank Howard, who was struggling to find a career; and George William Gibson, his nephew. The party included a chemist, an assayer, and mining engineers. Jake represented a New York City firm that controlled several mines in the area.[68]

In Honduras Jake became U.S. consul at Yuscaran, where the mining enterprise was located. There he married for a third time, in 1890, and had four additional children. On December 3, 1893, he and his friend Dr. Gold were in a boarding house in San Pedro when Jake was shot by Honduran nationalist Joasquin Hernández, who had gotten into an argument with Gold earlier. Hernández apparently had been drinking heavily and was determined to kill "gringos." Gold had been Hernández's target, but Imboden was shot when he went to his friend's rescue. Jake's abdominal wound proved fatal. He died two days later and was buried in San Pedro Cemetery, near Puerto Cortez, Honduras.[69]

Imboden's sister Kate married John Thomas Gibson. He died in 1862 of typhoid at John D. Imboden's home in Staunton while serving in the Confederate Army. They had two children.[70]

Frank Howard Imboden, the only natural son of John Daniel Imboden to reach adulthood, studied engineering at Virginia Agricultural and Mechanics College (now VPI) in Blacksburg, Virginia. He left college without graduating and went to Honduras with his uncles, where he married a native of Honduras, Carmelata Ramdales. They had five children. Frank died in Honduras on June 15, 1915.

John Daniel Imboden's son George William died on December 12, 1862. Russie, Imboden's daughter, never married and died in Roanoke on May 15, 1930. Nanine Carrington, Imboden's first daughter by his second wife, married in 1892 and died in New Orleans in 1947. In July 1895, Imboden's last child, his daughter Helen, married John Trout of Roanoke, but he died that December.[71]

Conclusion

John Daniel Imboden was not someone who sought out a military career. Had he wanted that, he would have fought in the Mexican-American War, and possibly perished there with his brother Benjamin. He came to military service only as a consequence of the Civil War, or as he put it, "in defense of Virginia."[1]

Imboden the soldier was controversial. In his postwar writing he often exaggerated his role and stretched the truth—as in the case of reporting events or conversations, especially with Lee and Jackson, that probably did not occur. Yet Imboden was of some significance in the war. Indeed, even for that war with its generals in their twenties, he advanced rapidly, especially as he had no prewar military service and had to learn most of the military arts on the job. Imboden was ambitious, and he did not hesitate to trumpet his military accomplishments. Nor did he conceal his desire for higher command.

Imboden's rapid rise to brigadier general demonstrates his military competence. He played an important role in the First Battle of Bull Run/Manassas, and he carried out two bold raids into West Virginia in independent command. While he often lacked initiative and dash, perhaps partly attributable to his lack of military background, he was also a prudent commander who did not expend his men needlessly.

Incurring Lee's wrath early in the Gettysburg Campaign, Imboden redeemed himself in the Confederate retreat by bringing away safely the vast bulk of Lee's supply train. He fought well against General Sigel in the subsequent Shenandoah Valley Campaign, especially in events leading up to the Battle of New Market, where he secured time for General Breckinridge to mobilize his resources. That he did not do as well against Sigel's successors, Hunter and Sheridan, cannot be held against him as his command had been steadily whittled away, and his men were poorly armed and indifferently mounted. At least some of the criticism directed toward Imboden by his superiors in the Confederate Army is unwarranted.

The Battle of Piedmont was probably the least successful of Imboden's stand-up fights. Had he and General Vaughn showed greater initiative in that battle, the outcome might have been different. He did distinguish himself in the subsequent Battle of Lynchburg, however. As commander of Confederate prisons in the South late in the war, Imboden showed himself both a capable administrator and one of moral courage and humanity, concerned about the prisoners in his charge. He has not received appropriate credit for his efforts to improve their conditions.

Clearly Imboden the military leader had the support of his men. When he left the Staunton Artillery early in the war, a number of those in his battery sought to follow him in his new assignment. Part of his success with his men came from his unwillingness to impose strict discipline, a fact noted by General Early and many others. But the nature of his command in large part precluded the sort of strict discipline that was possible in the regular Confederate line units.

Following the war Imboden proved himself an able writer and publicist, regardless of his embellishments. Certainly Imboden lived long enough to be one of the chief spokesmen for the Lost Cause.

An idealist who sought the greater good for the greater number of people and who wanted to advance the general economic well-being of his native state, Imboden's greatest contribution to Virginia was in promoting its economic development. In a biographical sketch he wrote in 1894, late in his life, Imboden placed far more emphasis on his postwar role than his Civil War record. He gave the latter as follows: "Entered military service in defense of Virginia as Captain of Staunton Artillery Apr 17th 1861. Commanded Shenandoah Valley District as Brig. General of Cavalry from July 23d 1863 till Dec. 1864. On account of broken health ordered by Confederate States President Davis to light out in Georgia. Was surrendered there May 3rd 1865."[2]

There is no mention here of battles or accomplishments. In describing his postwar service, however, Imboden emphasizes at great length his civic contributions. He wrote of his activities from 1867 in "studying and explaining" the mineral resources of Virginia. He was, he asserted, "The first to discover the coking qualities of the vast deposits of the highest grade known of Bituminous Coals of S.W. Va. the principal seam of which the Bureau of the Geological Survey at Washington has renamed on the U.S. maps of the region the '*Imboden Seam,*'" (emphasis in original).[3]

Samples of this coal were exhibited at the Columbian Exposition and were there judged to be unsurpassed by any others shown. Imboden claimed, "The discovery by Genl. Imboden of the quality of S.W. Va. Coals in 1880 has led to investments of all kinds for the development of that region of more than $50,000,000." His "startling reports" of 1880 were subsequently validated by others. "Towns & large industrial plants now exist in what was then an almost impenetrable wilderness in the Great Cumberland Mountain range dividing Va and Ky." He then described his promotional efforts in Britain leading to the formation of the English company that opened the great Hawk's Nest Coal Mines and his own work in getting that started. He then described his activities with the 1876 Centennial Exhibition and the 1892 Columbian Exposition in Chicago. Imboden finished the sketch by noting his report on the coal and iron resources written in 1886 and the congressional order for the printing of twenty-five thousand additional copies. Imboden makes no mention here of any writings on the Civil War.

It is somewhat ironic that Imboden is mostly remembered, even in Virginia, as a Civil War general who later wrote of his experiences. It is not the legacy he would have sought for his amazing life.

Notes

Introduction

1. Imboden to Gen. Marcus J. Wright, 16 April 1884, T. Gibson Hobbs Jr. Collection, Lynchburg, Va.
2. West Virginia became a state on June 20, 1863. Until that date, it is correct to refer to it as a region, western Virginia.
3. William C. Davis, *The Battle of New Market* (Baton Rouge, La.: Louisiana State Univ. Press, 1975), p. 18.
4. Robert K. Krick, *Conquering the Valley: Stonewall Jackson at Port Republic* (New York: William Morrow, 1996), p. 284.
5. James I. Robertson Jr., *Stonewall Jackson: The Man, the Soldier, the Legend* (New York: Macmillan, 1997), p. 827.
6. Letter from Imboden, *Everett (Pennsylvania) Republican,* 24 December 1894.

1. Early Life to the Civil War

1. William Couper, *History of the Shenandoah Valley,* vol. 1 (New York: Lewis Historical Publishing Co., 1952), p. 139.
2. Ibid.; William Douglas Hager, "The Civilian Life and Accomplishments of John Daniel Imboden," (Master's thesis, James Madison University, 1988), pp. 5–7.
3. Helen McGuire Trout, Imboden Family Genealogy, Imboden Papers, Alderman Library, University of Virginia; Kathryn E. Pellinen, Imboden Genealogy Records, family collection; Elizabeth S. Doenges, Imboden Genealogy Records; Jean S. Mitchell, Imboden Genealogy Records; Imboden Family Records, Genealogical Department of the Church of Jesus Christ of Latter-day Saints; *Augusta County Deed Book,* vol. 29 (1796), p. 194.
4. Mitchell Genealogy; Trout Genealogy.
5. Imboden Family Bible and Imboden Family Records, T. Gibson Hobbs Jr. Collection, Lynchburg, Va.

6. Bureau of the Census, *1920 Census, Augusta County, Virginia;* Joseph A. Waddell, *Annals of Augusta County, Virginia* (Bridgewater, Va.: C.J. Carrier Co., 1958), p. 442.
7. Boutwell Dunlap to Col. Joseph R. Anderson, 1 January 1916, Imboden Papers, Virginia Military Institute, Lexington, Va..
8. Boutwell Dunlap to Col. Joseph R. Anderson, 1 June 1916, Frank Imboden Papers, Preston Library, Virginia Military Institute; Hobbs Records; Michael B. Chesson, *Richmond after the War, 1865–1890* (Richmond: Virginia State Library, 1891), p. 11.
9. *Catalogue of the Trustees, Faculty and Students of Washington College. Lexington, Va. For Session 1841–42* (Lexington, Va.: Printed at the "Gazette" Office, A. Waddill, Printer, 1842).
10. Ibid.
11. Virginia Legislature, *Journal of the House of Delegates of the Commonwealth of Virginia,* Doc. no. 1 (Richmond, 1839–1840), p. 18, in Hager, "Imboden," p. 24.
12. *Catalogue of Washington College, Session 1841–1842.*
13. *Journal of the House of Delegates,* p. 18, in Hager, "Imboden," p. 24; *Catalogue of Washington College, Session 1841–1842.*
14. Imboden to Smith, 19 November 1863, Archives, Virginia Military Institute, Lexington, Va.
15. Owen F. Norton, *A History of Rockbridge County, Virginia* (Baltimore, Md.: Regional Publishing Co., 1980), p. 261; Hager, "Imboden," pp. 25–26.
16. Hager, "Imboden," p. 27. On Crozet see Robert F. Hunter and Edwin L. Dooley, *Claudius Crozet: French Engineer in America, 1790–1864* (Charlottesville, Va.: Univ. Press of Virginia, 1989).
17. Imboden to Hon. John Boyd Thatcher, 31 July 1894, Imboden Papers, Manuscript Division, Library of Congress.
18. Hager, "Imboden," p. 32.
19. Imboden to Hon. John Boyd Thatcher, 31 July 1894, Imboden Papers, Manuscript Division, Library of Congress; Hobbs Records.
20. Letters to William Hager from the Grand Lodge of Virginia, 17 Jun, 1 August, 10 Sep 1986, Records of the Grand Lodge of Virginia, A.F. & A.M., Richmond, Va.; Hobbs Collection; Hager, "Imboden," pp. 36–38.
21. John N. McCue, comp., *The McCues of the Old Dominion* (Mexico, Mo.: Missouri Printing and Publishing, 1912), p. 44; Hobbs Records.
22. Waddell, *Annals of Augusta County, Virginia,* p. 442.
23. Robert L. Semes, "Two Hundred Years at Rockbridge Alum Springs," *Proceedings of the Rockbridge Historical Society* , vol. 7 (Verona, Va.: McClure Printing Co., Inc., 1970), pp. 46–54.
24. Mrs. William Bushman, 1973 Imboden Genealogical Report, Staunton, Va.
25. Imboden to J.M. McCue, 1 October 1854, Archives of Margaret I. King

Library, University of Kentucky, Lexington, Ky.; John H. McCue, *The McCues of Old Dominion*, p. 44; Waddell, *Augusta County*, p. 415; in Hager, "Imboden," pp. 39–42; Mrs. William Bushman, 1973 Imboden Genealogical Report, Staunton, Va.

26. Imboden to J. Marshall McCue, 11 January 1848, James Blythe Anderson Papers, Margaret I. King Library Archives, University of Kentucky, Lexington, Ky.

27. Hager, "Imboden," p. 60.

28. Hobbs Records and Hager, "Imboden," pp. 61–62.

29. Barton H. Wise, *The Life of Henry A. Wise of Virginia, 1806–1876* (New York: Macmillan, 1899), p. 137.

30. Couper, *Shenandoah Valley*, vol. 2, pp. 809–11.

31. Augusta County Will Book, 28, 148 (Public records at Staunton, Va.); Hager, "Imboden," p. 63.

32. F.N. Boney, *John Letcher of Virginia: The Story of Virginia's Civil War Governor* (University, Ala.: Univ. of Alabama Press, 1966), pp. 42–43.

33. Imboden to Eliza Imboden, 27 January 1851, Imboden Papers, Alderman Library, University of Virginia, Charlottesville, Va.

34. Imboden to Eliza Imboden, 9 March 1851, ibid.

35. Couper, *Shenandoah Valley*, vol 2, pp. 811.

36. Arthur Chester Cole, *The Whig Party in the South* (Washington, D.C.: American Historical Association, 1913), p. 316; Imboden to the *Richmond Times*, 25 August 1895.

37. Letcher to Imboden, 7 August 1852, Imboden Papers, Alderman Library, University of Virginia, Charlottesville, Va.

38. Wise, *Life of Henry A. Wise*, p. 177.

39. Hager, "Imboden," pp. 70–71.

40. Alexander Cole, *The Whig Party in the South* (Washington, D.C.: American Historical Association, 1913), p. 325.

41. Hobbs Records.

42. Staunton *Spectator*, 4 May 1857; Boney, *Letcher*, p. 70; Hager, "Imboden," pp. 73–74.

43. Augusta County Common Law Order Book, 46 (1858): 162.

44. Mary Watters, *The History of Mary Baldwin College, 1842–1942* (Staunton, Va.: Mary Baldwin College, 1942), pp. 56, 419.

45. Hobbs Records.

46. Richard Hamrick, Staunton Historical Society Records, Staunton, Va.; Hager, "Imboden," p. 142.

47. Helen Trout Genealogy.

48. The commission is in the Imboden Papers, Alderman Library, University of Virginia; William H. Baylor to Imboden, 25 August 1858, ibid.; Hager, "Imboden," p. 81.

49. McCue, *McCues of the Old Dominion*, p. 39; James Blythe Anderson Papers,

11 January 1848, Archives, Margaret I. King Library, University of Kentucky, Lexington, Ky.

50. Francis Curtis, *The Republican Party: A History of Its Fifty Years' Existence and a Record of its Measures and Leaders, 1854–1894*, vol 1 (New York: G.P. Putnam's Sons, 1904), p. 309.

51. Robert J. Driver Jr., *The Staunton Artillery and McClanahan's Battery* (Lynchburg, Va.: H.E. Howard, 1988), p. 1.

52. Imboden to Col. Francis H. Smith, 12 December 1859, Imboden Papers, Archives, Preston Library, Virginia Military Institute, Lexington, Va.

53. Driver, *Staunton Artillery*, p. 1.

54. Ibid.

55. *Staunton Spectator*, 10 January 1860.

56. Ibid.

57. *Staunton Spectator*, 28 February 1860.

58. George Ruskell to Imboden, 10 and 27 April 1860, Imboden Papers, Alderman Library, University of Virginia, Charlottesville, Va.; *Staunton Spectator*, 24 April 1860.

59. Driver, *Staunton Artillery*, p. 2.

60. Floyd to Imboden, 16 January 1860, Imboden Papers, Alderman Library, University of Virginia, Charlottesville, Va.

61. Hobbs Records and Imboden to John R. Kilby, 25 February 1861, Imboden Papers, Manuscript Division, Library of Congress.

62. *Acts of the General Assembly of the State of Virginia* (Richmond, Va.: William F. Ritchie, 1861), pp. 227–28; 273–74.

63. Couper, *Shenandoah Valley*, vol 2, p. 848; Executive Committee of the Union Club to Imboden, 9 Sep 1860, Imboden Papers, University of Virginia Library, Charlottesville, Va.

64. Gary B. Nash, et al., *The American People: Creating a Nation and a Society*, 2nd ed. (New York: Harper & Row, 1990), p. 499.

65. Imboden to Eliza Imboden, 9 March 1851, Imboden Papers, Alderman Library, University of Virginia, Charlottesville, Va.

66. Waddell, *Augusta County*, p. 455.

67. Imboden to McCue, 3 December 1860, McCue Family Papers, Special Collections, Alderman Library, University of Virginia, Charlottesville, Va.

68. John D. Imboden, "Jackson at Harpers Ferry in 1861," *Battles and Leaders of the Civil War*, vol. 1 (New York: Castle Books, 1914), p. 111.

69. Waddell, *Augusta County*, p. 456; Michael G. Mahon, *The Shenandoah Valley, 1861–1865: The Destruction of the Granary of the Confederacy* (Mechanicsburg, Pa.: Stackpole Books, 1999), pp. 14–15; Imboden to John H. McCue, 12 February 1861, McCue Family Papers, Special Collections, Alderman Library, University of Virginia, Charlottesville, Va.

70. Imboden to John H. McCue, no date, in Mahon, *The Shenandoah Valley*, p. 17.

2. Initial Military Service

1. On the plan see John D. Eisenhower, *Agent of Destiny: The Life and Times of Winfield Scott* (New York: The Free Press, 1997), pp. 385-87.
2. For more details on the family genealogy see Hager, "Imboden," pp. 5-12.
3. Undated clipping from unidentified newspaper, Imboden Collection, Alderman Library, University of Virginia, Charlottesville, Va.; Hager, "Imboden," p. 129.
4. Post-31 October 1899 Letter, ibid.; Imboden to Davis, 8 May 1862 in *War of the Rebellion: Official Records of the Union and Confederate Armies* [Hereinafter cited as *ORA*], ser. 2, vol. 3 (Washington, D.C., 1898), pp. 869-70.
5. Post-31 October 1899 Letter, Imboden Papers, Alderman Library, University of Virginia, Charlottesville, Va.
6. Family Bible, Hobbs Records.
7. Jacob Imboden to General Francis H. Smith, 19 March 1864, Imboden Papers, Preston Library, Virginia Military Institute, Lexington, Va.
8. Imboden to J.H. McCue, nd. (but postmarked 31 October 1889), Archives, Margaret I. King Library, University of Kentucky.
9. Driver says that this was the case in *Staunton Artillery*, p. 2, but in his own article on the raid Imboden says that Wise merely told him to gather the men for a meeting: Imboden, "Jackson at Harpers Ferry in 1861," *Battles and Leaders*, vol. 1, p. 111.
10. In his article on the raid, Imboden does not say who suggested utilizing the railroads: Imboden, "Jackson at Harpers Ferry in 1861," *Battles and Leaders*, vol. 1, p. 111. Another article on the raid credits Imboden, however: "The Confederacy Mounts Its Iron Horse," *Ties: The Southern Railroad System Magazine* 15 (April 1961): 16.
11. Imboden, "Jackson at Harpers Ferry in 1861," *Battles and Leaders*, vol. 1, pp. 111-12; Boney, *Letcher*, p. 112.
12. Imboden, "Jackson at Harpers Ferry in 1861," *Battles and Leaders*, vol. 1, pp. 112-13.
13. Charles C. Osborne, *Jubal: The Life and Times of General Jubal A. Early, C.S.A., Defender of the Lost Cause* (Chapel Hill, N.C.: Univ. of North Carolina Press, 1992), pp. 49-50.
14. Ibid., p. 50.
15. Imboden, "Jackson at Harpers Ferry in 1861," *Battles and Leaders*, vol. 1, pp. 113-14; Waddell, *Augusta County*, p. 457.
16. Driver, *Staunton Artillery*, pp. 3, 6, and 14.
17. Ibid., p. 3.
18. Imboden, "Jackson at Harpers Ferry in 1861," *Battles and Leaders*, vol. 1, p. 115.
19. Ibid.
20. Ibid., pp. 115-17.
21. Ibid.; Robertson, *Stonewall Jackson*, p. 228; *Richmond Enquirer*, 23 April

1861; Millard A. Bushong, *General Turner Ashby and Stonewall Jackson's Valley Campaign* (Waynesboro, Va.: Self-published, 1992), p. 33.

22. Imboden, "Jackson at Harpers Ferry in 1861," *Battles and Leaders,* vol. 1, p. 118.

23. Ibid., pp. 119–20.

24. Ibid; also Bryon Farwell, *Stonewall, A Biography of General Thomas J. Jackson* (New York: W.W. Norton, 1982), p. 156.

25. Patricia L. Faust, ed., *Historical Times Illustrated Encyclopedia of the Civil War* (New York: Harper and Row, 1986), p. 391.

26. Imboden, "Jackson at Harpers Ferry in 1861," *Battles and Leaders,* vol. 1, p. 121; Farwell, *Stonewall,* p. 160.

27. Quoted in Farwell, *Stonewall,* p. 157.

28. Imboden, "Jackson at Harpers Ferry in 1861," *Battles and Leaders,* vol. 1, pp. 120–21.

29. Ibid., p. 121.

30. Imboden, "Jackson at Harpers Ferry in 1861," *Battles and Leaders,* vol. 1., p. 122.

31. Ibid., pp. 121–22; Lt. Col. George Deas to Col. R.S. Garnett, 23 May 1861, *ORA,* ser. 1, vol. 2, p. 868.

32. Festus P. Summers, *The Baltimore and Ohio in the Civil War* (New York: G.P. Putnam's Sons, 1939), p. 65.

33. Ibid., p. 127.

34. Ibid., p. 123. The figure on the trains taken is from Driver, *Staunton Artillery,* p. 6.

35. Farwell, *Stonewall,* p. 158.

36. Robertson, *Stonewall Jackson,* p. 229; see also Farwell, *Stonewall,* p. 158.

37. Thomas, "The Military Career of John D. Imboden," (Master's thesis, University of Virginia, 1965), pp. 30–33; James Morton Callahan, *History of West Virginia, Old and New,* vol. 1 (Chicago and New York: The American Historical Society, 1923), p. 390; Harold R. Woodward, *Defender of the Valley: Brigadier General John Daniel Imboden, C.S.A.* (Berryville, Va.: Rockbridge Publishing, 1996), p. 30.

38. Robertson, *Stonewall Jackson,* pp. 827–28

39. Faust, ed., *Encyclopedia of the Civil War,* p. 728.

40. Ibid., pp. 123–24.

41. Ibid., p. 400. An excellent recent assessment of Johnston's early Civil War service is Steven H. Newton, *Joseph E. Johnston and the Defense of Richmond* (Lawrence, Kans.: Univ. Press of Kansas, 1998).

42. Ibid., pp. 124–25; John D. Imboden, "Incidents of the First Bull Run," *Battles and Leaders of the Civil War,* vol. 1, (New York: Castle Books, 1914), p. 229.; R.M. Johnston, *Bull Run: Its Strategy and Tactics* (New York: Houghton Mifflin, 1913), p. 29.

3. First Battle of Manassas

1. Johnson to S. Cooper, 18 Jun 1861, *ORA*, ser. 1, vol. 2, p. 937; Driver, *Staunton Artillery*, p. 6; Imboden, "Incidents of the First Bull Run," p. 229.
2. Driver, *Staunton Artillery*, p. 6.
3. Faust, *Historical Times Illustrated Encyclopedia of the Civil War*, p. 52. Bee was posthumously promoted to brigadier general.
4. Robertson, *Stonewall Jackson*, pp. 247–50; Patterson to Lt. Col. E. Townsend, 3 July 1861, *ORA*, ser. 1, vol. 2, p. 157.
5. Bruce Catton, *This Hallowed Ground: The Story of the Union Side of the Civil War* (Garden City, New York: Doubleday and Co., 1956), p. 46.
6. Driver, *Staunton Artillery*, p. 7; Imboden "Incidents of the First Bull Run," p. 229.
7. Driver, *Staunton Artillery*, p. 7.
8. Faust, *Historical Times Illustrated Encyclopedia of the Civil War*, p. 459.
9. S. Cooper to Johnston, 18 June 1861, *ORA*, ser. 1, vol. 2, pp. 934–35.
10. Imboden, "Incidents of the First Bull Run," p. 230.
11. Johnston, *Bull Run*, p. 111; Susan P. Lee, *Memoirs of William Nelson Pendleton, D.D.* (Philadelphia, Pa.: J.P. Lippincott Co., 1893), p. 148.
12. Driver, *Staunton Artillery*, p. 7.
13. Imboden, "Incidents of the First Bull Run," p. 230.
14. Ibid.
15. Ibid., p. 231.
16. Imboden, "Incidents of the First Bull Run," pp. 231–32.
17. Ibid., pp. 232–33.
18. Faust, *Historical Times Illustrated Encyclopedia of the Civil War*, p. 248.
19. Imboden's report of 22 July 1861 to Brig. Gen. W.H. Whiting, commanding 3d Brigade of the Army of the Shenandoah, published in the *Richmond Dispatch*, 26 July 1862; Frank Moore, ed., *The Rebellion Record: A Diary of American Events*, vol. 2 (New York: G.P. Putnam, 1862); Imboden, "Incidents of the First Bull Run," p. 233.
20. Imboden, "Incidents of the First Bull Run," p. 233.
21. Imboden's Report of 22 July 1861 in Moore, *Rebellion Record*, vol. 2, p. 44.
22. Imboden, "Incidents of the First Bull Run," p. 233; Driver, *Staunton Artillery*, p. 9.
23. Imboden, "Incidents of the First Bull Run," p. 233; Cary Crockett, "The Battery That Saved the Day," *Field Artillery Journal* (January-February, 1940): 26–33.
24. Imboden, "Incidents of the First Bull Run," pp. 233–34.
25. Imboden's Report of 22 July 1861 in Moore, *Rebellion Record*, vol. 2, p. 44.
26. Driver, *Staunton Artillery*, p. 9.
27. Johnston, *Bull Run*, pp. 197–98.
28. Imboden, "Incidents of the First Bull Run," p. 234. Later in the same ac-

count, Imboden reported the time the battery was alone as a "full three-quarters of an hour." Ibid., p. 237.

29. Wade Hampton, a wealthy South Carolina planter, had organized the unit. A mix of infantry, cavalry, and artillery, the legion lost 121 of its 600 men in the battle, and Hampton himself was wounded. Faust, *Historical Times Illustrated Encyclopedia of the Civil War,* p. 335.

30. *Charleston (S.C.) News and Courier,* 13 July 1885.

31. Driver, *Staunton Artillery,* p. 10.

32. Ibid.; Imboden, "Incidents of the First Bull Run," pp. 234, 238.

33. Imboden, "Incidents of the First Bull Run," pp. 234, 238.

34. Driver, *Staunton Artillery,* p. 10; Imboden, "Incidents of the First Bull Run," p. 234.

35. Beauregard to S. Cooper, 26 August [14 October] 1861, *ORA,* ser. 1, vol. 2, p. 491.

36. Faust, ed., *Encyclopedia of the Civil War,* p. 92.

37. Imboden, "Incidents of the First Bull Run," p. 234.

38. Imboden's Report of 22 July 1861 in Moore, *Rebellion Record,* vol. 2, p. 44; Faust, ed., *Encyclopedia of the Civil War,* p. 92.

39. Driver, *Staunton Artillery,* p. 11.

40. Imboden, "Incidents of the First Bull Run," pp. 235–36.

41. Ibid., p. 236.

42. Hampton denies this was his unit. Charleston, S.C., *News and Courier,* 13 July 1885.

43. Imboden, "Incidents of the First Bull Run," p. 236.

44. Ibid., p. 237.

45. "Report of Capt. John D. Imboden, of the Staunton Artillery," 22 July 1861, in Moore, *Rebellion Record,* vol. 2, p. 45.

46. Imboden, "Incidents of the First Bull Run," p. 237.

47. Faust, *Historical Times Illustrated Encyclopedia of the Civil War,* p. 52.

48. Faust, *Historical Times Illustrated Encyclopedia of the Civil War,* p. 92; Imboden, "Incidents of the First Bull Run," p. 238.

49. Beauregard to S. Cooper, 26 August [14 October] 1861, *ORA,* ser. 1, vol. 2, p. 491.

50. Jackson's Report, 23 July 1861, *ORA,* ser. 1, vol 2, p. 480.

51. Joseph E. Johnston, *Narrative of Military Operations During the Civil War* (New York: D. Appleton, 1874); reprint, New York: Da Capo, 1959), p. 46.

52. Imboden's Report of 22 July 1861 in Moore, *Rebellion Record,* vol. 2, p. 44.

53. Ibid.

54. Imboden, "Incidents of the First Bull Run," p. 238.

55. Driver, *Staunton Artillery,* p. 13.

56. Imboden, "Incidents of the First Bull Run," p. 239. Northrup's response is printed in *Battles and Leaders of the Civil War,* vol. 1, p. 261.

57. Driver, *Staunton Artillery,* p. 14.

58. Ibid.
59. Ibid.
60. Faust, *Encyclopedia of the Civil War*, p. 763.
61. Ibid., p. 822.
62. Ibid.; and Driver, *Staunton Artillery*, p. 24.
63. Driver, *Staunton Artillery*, p. 14.
64. Ibid., pp. 14–16.
65. Letter, 2 November 1861, ibid; also, Imboden to Billy [?] 3, 21 October 1861, Archives of Margaret I. King Library, University of Kentucky, Lexington.
66. Letter of 7 November 1861, ibid.
67. Ibid., p. 16.
68. Ibid.
69. Ibid., p. 17.
70. Paul H. Silverstone, *Warships of the Civil War Navies* (Annapolis, Md.: Naval Institute Press, 1989), p. 82; Naval History Division, Navy Department, *Civil War Naval Chronology, 1861–1865*, vol. 1 (Washington: Government Printing Office, 1971), p. 39; Driver, *Staunton Artillery*, p. 17.
71. Driver, *Staunton Artillery*, p. 17.
72. Ibid.
73. Ibid., p. 18.
74. Ibid.
75. Ibid.

4. Forming a Partisan Command

1. Driver, *Staunton Artillery*, p. 18.
2. Virgil Carrington Jones, *Gray Ghosts and Rebel Raiders* (New York: Holt, 1956), p. 385.
3. Maj. Charles Marshall to Messrs. Robbins, et al., 8 August 1862, *ORA*, ser. 2, vol. 4, p. 842. A Union circular of 20 November 1862, signed by Lt. Col. William Ludlow, agent for exchange of prisoners, said that "The body of Confederate troops known by the designation of Partisan Rangers and whose officers are commissioned by the Confederate government and who are regularly in the service of the Confederate State are to be exchanged when captured." Ibid., p. 739.
4. Chilton to Briscoe, 18 June 1861, *ORA*, ser. 4, vol. 1, p. 395.
5. Jones, *Gray Ghosts and Rebel Raiders*, p. 76.
6. Albert Castel, "The Guerrilla War," *Civil War Times Illustrated* (October 1974): 9; Jones, *Gray Ghosts and Rebel Raiders*, p. 80.
7. Francis M. Imboden Papers, Archives, Preston Library, Virginia Military Institute; Faust, *Encyclopedia of the Civil War*, pp. 838–39; J.D. Imboden to Davis, and F.M. Imboden to H.A. Wise, 8 May 1862, *ORA*, ser. 2, vol. 3, pp. 869–70; Wise to Jefferson Davis, 13 May 1862, *ORA*, ser. 2, vol. 3, pp. 869–70; U.S. Army

War Department, General Orders No. 118, 27 August 1863, *ORA,* ser. 2, vol. 4, p. 437.
   8. Imboden to Frank Imboden, 29 April 1862, Imboden Papers, Alderman Library, University of Virginia.
   9. Randolph to Imboden, 7 May 1862, Imboden Papers, Alderman Library, University of Virginia.
   10. Faust, "Loring-Jackson Controversy," *Encyclopedia of the Civil War,* pp. 447–48.
   11. Roger U. Delauter Jr., *62nd Virginia Infantry* (Lynchburg, Va.: H.E. Howard, 1988), pp. 2–3.
   12. Casteel, "The Guerilla War," p. 9.
   13. *Richmond Dispatch,* 8 May 1862.
   14. Ibid.
   15. Jones, *Gray Ghosts and Rebel Raiders,* p. 83.
   16. Delauter, *62nd Virginia Infantry,* p. 2.
   17. Hiram L. Opie Jr. to Imboden, 11 May 1862, Imboden Papers, Alderman Library, University of Virginia.
   18. Sender unknown to Imboden, postmarked 1 July 1862, Imboden Papers, Alderman Library, University of Virginia.
   19. On this battle see Lowell Reidenbaugh, *Jackson's Valley Campaign: The Battle of Kernstown* (Lynchburg, Va.: H.E. Howard, 1996).
   20. John D. Imboden, "Stonewall Jackson in the Shenandoah," in *Battles and Leaders of the Civil War,* vol. 2 (New York: Castle Books, 1956), p. 285.
   21. Faust, *Encyclopedia of the Civil War,* p. 460.
   22. Ibid., p. 249. On Ewell see Donald C. Pfanz, *Richard S. Ewell, A Soldier's Life* (Chapel Hill, N.C.: Univ. of North Carolina Press, 1998).
   23. Jackson to Chilton, 7 March 1863, *ORA,* ser. 1., vol. 12, pt. 1, pp. 470–71; Jones, *Gray Ghosts and Rebel Raiders,* p. 76; Faust, *Encyclopedia of the Civil War,* p. 460.
   24. Lee to Jackson, 8 May 1862, *ORA,* ser. 1, vol. 12, pt. 3, p. 883.
   25. Faust, *Encyclopedia of the Civil War,* p. 460.
   26. Imboden, "Stonewall Jackson in the Shenandoah," pp. 286–88.
   27. Imboden, "Stonewall Jackson in the Shenandoah," pp. 288–89; Robertson, *Stonewall Jackson,* p. 398; Faust, *Encyclopedia of the Civil War,* p. 293.
   28. Faust, *Encyclopedia of the Civil War,* p. 834; Imboden, "Stonewall Jackson in the Shenandoah," pp. 289, 291.
   29. Imboden, "Stonewall Jackson in the Shenandoah," p. 290.
   30. Ibid., pp. 290–91.
   31. Frémont's Report, 30 December 1865, *ORA,* ser. 1, vol. 12, pt. 1, p. 11.
   32. Imboden, "Stonewall Jackson in the Shenandoah," pp. 291–92.
   33. Darrell L. Collins, *The Battles of Cross Keys and Port Republic, June 8–9, 1862* (Lynchburg, Va.: H.E. Howard, 1993), pp. 49–82.
   34. Robertson, *Stonewall Jackson,* pp. 428–29.

35. Ibid., pp. 431–38.
36. Imboden, "Stonewall Jackson in the Shenandoah," 291–92.
37. Ibid., p. 293.
38. Driver, *Staunton Artillery*, p. 68; Imboden, "Stonewall Jackson in the Shenandoah," p. 293.
39. Johnson, ed., *Battles and Leaders*, vol 2., pp. 293–95.
40. Krick, *Conquering the Valley*, pp. 284–85. In quoting an unflattering review of Imboden's claim by N.B. Douglas, Krick notes that Douglas incorrectly referred to "Sandie" Pendleton as "Sandy."
41. Edward M. Alfriend, "Recollections of Stonewall Jackson," *Lippincott's Magazine*, vol. 69 (1902): 586.
42. Robertson, *Stonewall Jackson*, p. 443; Farwell, *Stonewall*, p. 327.
43. Imboden, "Stonewall Jackson in the Shenandoah," p. 295.
44. Ibid., pp. 296–97.
45. Ibid., p. 297.
46. Ibid.

5. The 1st Virginia Partisan Rangers (1862–1863)

1. Driver, *Staunton Artillery*, p. 70
2. Capt. Harding to Imboden, 7 July 1862, Imboden Papers, Alderman Library, University of Virginia.
3. Faust, *Encyclopedia of the Civil War*, p. 465; Roger U. Delauter Jr., *McNeill's Rangers* (Lynchburg, Va.: H.E. Howard, 1986), pp. 1–18.
4. Callahan, *History of West Virginia*, vol. 1, p. 374.
5. Ibid., p. 385; Faust, *Encyclopedia of the Civil War*, p. 300.
6. Imboden to Russell, 1 Sep 1862, *ORA*, ser. 1, vol. 12, pt. 3, pp. 949–50; Imboden to Brig. Gen. T.J. Jackson, 27 Sep 1862, ibid., ser. 1, vol. 19, pt. 2, p. 630.
7. Lee to Davis in Robert E. Lee, *Lee's Dispatches: Unpublished Letters of General Robert E. Lee, C.S.A. to Jefferson Davis and the War Department of the Confederate States of America, 1862–65. From the Private Collection of Wymberley Jones de Renne of Wormsloe, Georgia*, ed. with an introduction by Douglas Southall Freeman (New York: G.P. Putnam's Sons, 1915), p. 50.
8. Imboden to Russell, 1 Sep 1862, *ORA*, ser. 1, vol. 12, pt. 3, p. 950.
9. Jenkins to Lt. Col. H.H. Fitzhugh, 19 Sep 1862, *ORA*, ser. 1, vol. 12, pt. 2, pp. 757–61; Imboden to Russell, 1 Sep 1862, ibid., ser. 1, vol. 12, pt. 3, pp. 949–51; Imboden to Brig. Gen. T.J. Jackson, 27 Sep 1862, ibid., ser. 1, vol. 19, pt. 2; Genevieve Brown, "A History of the Sixth Regiment West Virginia Volunteers," *West Virginia History*, vol. 9, p. 329.
10. See Stephen W. Sears, *George B. McClellan, The Young Napoleon* (New York: Ticknor & Fields, 1988).
11. Jones, *Gray Ghosts and Rebel Raiders*, p. 117.

12. Imboden to Brig. Gen. T.J. Jackson, 27 Sep 1862, *ORA*, ser. 1, vol. 19, pt. 2, pp. 630–31.
13. A.J. Borman to Governor Pierpoint, 4 Sep 1862, *Calendar of State Papers*, vol. 11, p. 389; quoted in Thomas, "Military Career of Imboden," p. 80.
14. Driver, *Staunton Artillery*, p. 80.
15. Delauter, *McNeill's Rangers*, p. 23.
16. Delauter, *McNeill's Rangers*, p. 23; Delauter, *62nd Virginia Infantry*, pp. 3–4.
17. Lee to Imboden, 6 October 1862, Imboden Papers, Alderman Library, University of Virginia.
18. Delauter, *62nd Virginia Infantry*, p. 4.
19. Delauter, *62nd Virginia Infantry*, p. 5; Delauter, *McNeill's Rangers*, p. 25.
20. Message of the President C.S.A. in Thomas, "The Military Career of John D. Imboden," p. 87; also in Roger U. Delauter Jr., *18th Virginia Cavalry* (Lynchburg, Va.: H.E. Howard, 1985), p. 1.
21. Imboden to Sec. of War James Seddon, 13 January 1863, along with enclosures, *ORA*, ser. 2, vol. 5, pp. 808–10.
22. Delauter, *18th Virginia Cavalry*, pp. 1–3, 8.
23. Imboden to Davis, 9 December 1862, *ORA*, ser. 2, vol. 5, pp. 780–81.
24. Lee to Imboden, 20 January 1863, *ORA*, ser. 1, vol. 21, p. 1102.
25. Imboden to Lt. Gen. Thomas J. Jackson, 18 November 1862, *ORA*, ser. 1, vol. 19, pt. 2, pp. 156–59; Brig. Gen. Benjamin F. Kelley to Maj. G.M. Bascom, November 1862, ibid., pp. 159–60.
26. Ibid., p. 159.
27. Lee to Randolph, 11 November 1862, in Clifford Dowdey and Louis Manarin, eds., *The Wartime Papers of R.E. Lee* (Boston: Little, Brown, 1961), pp. 338
28. R.H. Milroy to Governor, West Virginia, *Calendar of State Papers*, vol. 11, p. 403.
29. Jones, *Grey Ghosts and Rebel Raiders*, p. 131.
30. In Woodward, *Defender of the Valley*, p. 66.
31. Circular signed by William H. Ludlow, HDQS Dept. of Virginia, Ft. Monroe, Va., 30 November 1862, *ORA*, ser. 2, vol. 4, p. 739.
32. Ron Watson Curry, "The Newspaper Press and the Civil War," *West Virginia History*, vol. 6, pp. 234–35.
33. Imboden to Milroy, *Calendar of State Papers*, vol. 11, pp. 405–6, in Thomas, "Military Career of Imboden," pp. 88–89.
34. Milroy to Imboden, ibid., vol. 11, p. 407.
35. R.E. Lee to Jefferson Davis, 26 February 1863, *ORA*, ser. 1, vol. 25, pt. 2, pp. 642–43.
36. John O. Casler, *Four Years in the Stonewall Brigade* (Dayton, Ohio: Morningside Books, 1971), pp. 126–34.
37. Cooper to Imboden, 23 December 1862, *ORA*, ser. 1, vol. 21, p. 1076.

38. Imboden's Service Record, National Archives, in Thomas, "Military Career of Imboden," p. 90.
39. Hobbs Records.

6. The Spring 1863 Jones-Imboden Raid into West Virginia

1. *Staunton Vindicator,* 20 February 1863.
2. Delauter, *62nd Virginia Infantry,* p. 7.
3. Lee to Imboden, 10 January 1863, *ORA,* ser. 1, vol. 21, p. 1086.
4. Anderson, *Genealogy,* p. 461.
5. Lee to W.E. Jones, 27 January 1863, *ORA,* ser. 1, vol. 25, pt. 2, p. 598.
6. In writing Imboden to endorse the plan, Maj. Gen. Samuel Jones credited McNeill with originating it. Jones to Imboden, 8 March 1863, *ORA,* ser. 1, vol. 25, pt. 2, p. 659.
7. Imboden to Lee, 2 March 1863, *ORA,* ser. 1, vol. 25, pt. 2, pp. 652–53.
8. Ibid., p. 653.
9. Ibid.
10. Abstract in *ORA,* ser. 1, vol. 25, pt. 2, p. 657.
11. Edward G. Longacre, *Mounted Raids of the Civil War* (New York: Bison Books, 1975), p. 123.
12. Colonel William L. Jackson gave this as the chief reason for the raid. See John A. McNeil, "The Imboden Raid and Its Effects," *Times-Dispatch,* 2 September 1906 in *Southern Historical Society Papers,* vol. 34 (1906):301–2.
13. Imboden to Lee, 2 March 1863, *ORA,* ser. 1, vol. 25, pt. 2, 652–53; Lee to Imboden, 26 March 1863, ibid., p. 685.
14. Imboden to Lee, 2 March 1863, *ORA,* ser. 1, vol. 25, pt. 2, p. 652; Lee to Jones and Imboden, 26 March 1863, ibid., pp. 684–85.
15. Lee to Imboden, 26 March and 7 April 1863, *ORA,* ser. 1, vol. 25, pt. 2, pp. 685–86, and 711–12.
16. Jones to Lee, 17 March and 13 April 1863, *ORA,* ser. 1, vol. 25, pt. 2, pp. 670, 717–18.
17. Faust, *Historical Times Illustrated Encyclopedia of the Civil War,* p. 404; Douglas Southall Freeman, *Lee's Lieutenants: A Study in Command* (New York: Charles Scribner's Sons, 1970), p. 323.
18. Freeman, *Lee's Lieutenants,* vol. 3, pp. 323–24.
19. S. Jones to W. Jones and Imboden, 19 March 1863; to Imboden, 20 March 1863, *ORA,* ser. 1, vol. 25, pt. 2, pp. 676–78.
20. Lee to Imboden, 21 and 26 March 1863, ibid., pp 679, 685.
21. S. Jones to Lee, 28 March and 2 April 1863; Ibid., pp. 689–90, 701; to Secretary of War Seddon, 4 April 1863, ibid., p. 702.
22. John A. McNeil, "The Imboden Raid and Its Effects," pp. 295, 302–3.
23. Lee to Jones, 7 April 1863, *ORA,* ser. 1, vol. 25, pt. 2, pp. 710–11.

24. Ibid.; Lee to Imboden, 7 April 1863, *ORA*, ser. 1, vol. 25, pt. 2, pp. 711–12; Jones to Lee, 26 May 1863, ibid., vol. 25, pt. 1, p. 119.

25. Halleck to Schenck, 29 April 1863, *ORA*, ser. 1, vol. 25, pt. 2, p. 295. The figure for Schenck's effective strength is from John Bigelow Jr., *The Campaign of Chancellorsville: A Strategic and Tactical Study* (New Haven, Conn.: Oxford Univ. Press, 1910), p. 467.

26. Maj. Gen. A.E. Burnside to Maj. Gen. H.W. Halleck, 29 April 1863, *ORA*, ser. 1, vol. 25, pt. 2, p. 299; Brig. Gen. William Barry to Maj. Gen. H.W. Halleck, 5 May 1863, ibid., 428–29; Maj. Gen. Robert C. Schenck to Brig. Gen. William Barry, 8 May 1863, ibid., 453; Festus P. Summers, "The Jones-Imboden Raid," *West Virginia History*, vol. 1, p. 27; Bigelow, *Campaign of Chancellorsville*, p. 467.

27. Summers, "The Jones-Imboden Raid," p. 17.

28. W. Jones to Lee, 26 May 1863, *ORA*, ser. 1, vol. 25, pt. 1, p. 16.

29. W. E. Jones to S. Jones, 14 April 1863, *ORA*, ser. 1, vol. 25, pt. 2, p. 722; S. Jones to Lee, 25 April 1863, ibid., pp. 750–51.

30. Maj. Gen. S. Jones to Imboden, 11 April 1863, *ORA*, ser. 1, vol. 25, pt. 2, p. 716; H. Childon, 1 Jun 1863, ibid., vol. 25, pt. 1, pp. 98–99; McNeil, "The Imboden Raid and Its Effects," pp. 303–5.

31. Imboden to R.H. Chilton, 1 June 1863, *ORA*, ser. 1, vol. 25, pt. 1, p. 99; McNeil, "The Imboden Raid and Its Effects," p. 306.

32. Imboden to Chilton, 1 June 1863, *ORA*, ser. 1, vol. 25, pt. 1, pp. 99–100; McNeil, "The Imboden Raid and Its Effects," p. 307; Theodore F. Lang, *Loyal West Virginia from 1861 to 1865* (Baltimore, Md.: The Deutsch Publishing Co., 1895), p. 107; Bigelow, *The Campaign of Chancellorsville*, pp. 460–61.

33. Imboden to Chilton, 1 June 1863, *ORA*, ser. 1, vol. 25, pt. 1, p. 100.

34. Imboden reported the three Confederates so badly wounded that they had to be left behind in private homes; Ibid.; McNeil says only that there were no Confederate killed or seriously wounded: McNeil, "The Imboden Raid and Its Effects," pp. 307–8.

35. Imboden to Chilton, 1 June1863, *ORA*, ser. 1, vol. 25, pt. 1, p. 100.

36. Gen. Order No. 20, 25 April 1863, in CSA Military Leaders Collection: Imboden, Eleanor S. Brockenbrough Library, The Museum of the Confederacy.

37. Imboden to Chilton, 1 June 1863, *ORA*, ser. 1, vol. 25, pt. 1, p. 100.

38. Ibid., p. 101; Edward G. Longacre, *Mounted Raids of the Civil War* (New York: Bison Books, 1975), p. 132.

39. Roberts to Col. W.H. Chesebrough, 21 May 1863, *ORA*, ser. 1, vol. 25, pt. 1, pp. 91–92; Imboden to Chilton, 1 June 1863, ibid., p. 101.

40. Imboden to Chilton, 1 June 1863, *ORA*, ser. 1, vol. 25, pt. 1, p. 100.

41. W.E. Jones to Imboden, 27 April 1863, *ORA*, ser. 1, vol. 15, pt. 1, p. 105; Jones to Lee, 26 May 1863, ibid., pp. 116–17; Brig. Gen. B.F. Kelley to Lt. Col. Cheseborough, 28 April 1863, ibid., pp. 107–8; Capt. Martin Wallace to James Cosgrove, 11 June 1863, ibid., p. 108–10; William N. McDonald, *A History of the Laurel Brigade: Originally the Ashby Cavalry of the Army of Northern Virginia and*

Chew's Battery (Baltimore, Md.: K.S. McDonald, Sun Job Print. Office, 1907), pp. 121–22; Bigelow, *The Campaign of Chancellorsville*, p. 462.

42. Jones to Lee, 26 May 1863, *ORA*, ser. 1, vol. 25, pt. 1, pp. 115–17.

43. Roberts to Halleck, 24 April 1863, *ORA*, ser. 1, vol. 25, pt. 2, p. 246; Halleck to Roberts, 24 April 1863, ibid.

44. Jones to Lee, 26 May 1863, *ORA*, ser. 1, vol. 25, pt. 1, p. 117–18; *ORA*, vol. 2, p. 239; Lee to R.S. Garnett, ibid., ser. 1, vol. 2, p. 239.

45. Green to Capt. Walter Martin, 26 May 1863, *ORA*, ser. 1, vol. 25, pt. 1, pp. 127–28; Theodore F. Lang, *Loyal West Virginia from 1861 to 1865* (Baltimore, Md.: Deutsch Publishing, 1895), p. 260.

46. Jones to Lee, 26 May, *ORA*, ser. 1, vol. 25, pt. 1, pp. 117–18.

47. Curtin to Stanton, 28 April 1863, *ORA*, ser. 1, vol. 25, pt. 2, p. 279; Lincoln to Curtin, 28 April 1863, ibid.

48. Green to Capt. Walter Martin, 26 May 1863, *ORA*, ser. 1, vol. 25, pt. 1, pp. 127–28; Jones to Lee, 26 May, ibid., p. 118; Summers, "The Jones-Imboden Raid," p. 20.

49. Harman to Brig. Gen Jones, 26 May 1863, *ORA*, ser. 1, vol. 25, pt. 1, p. 134; George Baylor, *Bull Run to Bull Run; Or, Four Years in the Army of Northern Virginia* (Richmond, Va.: B.F. Johnson Publishing Co., 1900), pp. 137ff.

50. Capt. Frank A. Bond to Capt. Walter K. Martin, 25 May 1863, *ORA*, ser. 1, vol. 25, pt. 1, p. 126; Bigelow, *The Campaign of Chancellorsville*, p. 465.

51. Jones to Lee, 26 May 1863, *ORA*, ser. 1, vol. 25, pt. 1, p. 118; Judge Advocate General J. Holt, 5 June 1863, *ORA*, ser. 2, vol. 2, pp. 611–12; *Wheeling Intelligencer*, 6 May 1863; Summers, "The Jones-Imboden Raid," p. 24.

52. Jones to Lee, 26 May 1863, *ORA*, ser. 1, vol. 25, pt. 1, p. 119; Summers, "The Jones-Imboden Raid," p. 24.

53. Dowdey and Manarin, *The Wartime Papers of R.E. Lee*, pp. 450–51.

54. Imboden to Chilton, 1 June 1863, *ORA*, ser. 1, vol. 25, pt. 1, p. 102.

55. Imboden to Brig. Gen. A.G. Jenkins, *ORA*, vol. 25, pt. 1, p. 98; Bigelow, *The Campaign of Chancellorsville*, p. 466; on the Confederate occupation of Weston, see Roy Bird Cook, *Lewis County in the Civil War, 1861–1865* (Charleston, W.Va.: Jarrett Publishing Co., 1924), pp. 62ff.

56. Imboden to Jenkins, 3 May 1863, *ORA*, ser. 1, vol. 25, pt. 1, p. 98.

57. Frank M. Imboden, War Diary, 1863, Imboden Papers, Alderman Library, University of Virginia.

58. Ibid., and Hobbs Records. A different picture is presented in Driver, *Staunton Artillery*, p. 74.

59. Imboden to Chilton, 1 June 1863, *ORA*, ser. 1, vol. 25, pt. 1, pp. 102–3.

60. Jones to Lee, 26 May 2863, *ORA*, ser. 1, vol. 25, pt. 1, pp. 119–20.

61. Ibid., pp. 119–20; McNeil, "The Imboden Raid and Its Effects," p. 309; Bernard Gainer, "Early Oil Development in West Virginia," *West Virginia History*, vol. 21, p. 85.

62. Jones to Lee, 26 May 1863, *ORA*, ser. 1, vol. 25, pt. 1, p. 120.

63. Imboden to Chilton, 1 June 1863, *ORA*, ser. 1, vol. 25, pt. 1, p. 103.
64. Ibid.
65. Ibid.
66. Ibid., p. 104.
67. Maj. Gen. Jones to Imboden, 14 May 1863, *ORA*, ser. 1, vol. 25, pt. 1, pp. 105–6; James Earl Brown, "Life of Brigadier General John McCausland," *West Virginia History*, vol. 4, pp. 256–57.
68. Jones to Lee, 26 May 1863, *ORA*, ser. 1, vol. 25, pt. 1, p. 119.
69. Ibid., p. 120.
70. Imboden to Chilton, 1 June 1863, *ORA*, ser. 1, vol. 25, pt. 1, p. 104.
71. Imboden to Chilton, 1 June 1863, *ORA*, ser. 1, vol. 25, pt. 1, pp. 102, 104; McNeil, "The Imboden Raid and Its Effects," p. 309; Lang gives the total for the raid as 3,100 head of cattle and 1,500 horses. Lang, *Loyal West Virginia*, p. 197.
72. Longacre, *Mounted Raids of the Civil War*, p. 145.
73. Lee endorsement of 15 June 1863, *ORA*, ser. 1, Vol. 25, pt. 1, p. 106.
74. Roberts to Brig. Gen. Kelley, 1 May 1863, *ORA*, ser. 1, vol. 25, pt. 2, p. 351; Roberts to Maj. Gen. Schenck, 6 May 1863, ibid., p. 436.
75. McNeil, "The Imboden Raid and Its Effects," p. 312.
76. General Orders No. 22, 17 May 1863, in CSA Military Leaders Collection: Imboden, Eleanor Brockenbrough Library, The Museum of the Confederacy.
77. William Chesebrough to Averell, 18 May 1863, *ORA*, ser. 1, vol. 25, pt. 2, p. 503.
78. Ibid., p. 502.
79. Faust, *Encyclopedia of the Civil War*, pp. 31–32.
80. Lang, *Loyal West Virginia*, p. 108.
81. Ibid., pp. 108–9.
82. Ibid., p. 109; Callahan, *History of West Virginia*, vol. 1, p. 87.

7. The Gettysburg Campaign

1. S. Jones to Imboden, 14 May, 1863, *ORA*, ser 1, vol. 25, pt. 2, pp. 799–800; Lee to Imboden, 23 May 1863; Ibid., p. 819; Driver, *Staunton Artillery*, p. 74.
2. Jones to Lee, 28 May 1863, *ORA*, ser. 1, vol. 25, pt. 2, p. 831.
3. Delauter, *62nd Virginia Infantry*, p. 16.
4. Edwin B. Coddington, *The Gettysburg Campaign: A Study in Command* (New York: Charles Scribner's Sons, 1984), pp. 15–17; Douglas Southall Freeman, *Lee's Lieutenants*, vol. 2 (New York: Charles Scribner's Sons, 1943), p. 710.
5. Lee to Imboden, 7 and 10 June 1863; to Ewell, 10 June 1863, *ORA*, ser. 1, vol. 27, pt. 3, pp. 865–66; Jack L. Dickinson, *Jenkins of Greenbottom: A Civil War Saga* (Charleston, W.Va.: Pictorial Histories Publishing Co., 1988), p. 59.
6. General Orders No. 23, 2 June 1863, CSA Military Leaders: Imboden, Eleanor S. Brockenbrough Library, The Museum of the Confederacy.
7. "Organization of the Army of Northern Virginia at the Battle of Gettysburg,"

ORA, ser. 1, vol. 27, pt. 2, p. 291; Callahan, *History of West Virginia*, vol. 1, p. 387; Walter S. Sanderlin, *The Great National Project: A History of the Chesapeake and Ohio Canal* (Baltimore: Johns Hopkins Press, 1946), pp. 321–23; Coddington, *The Gettysburg Campaign*, p. 105; Delauter, *62nd Virginia Infantry*, p. 17; Delauter, *18th Virginia Cavalry*, pp. 6–7.

8. Lee to Jefferson Davis, 20 June 1863, *ORA*, ser. 1, vol. 27, pt. 2, pp. 296–97; to Adjutant General Samuel Cooper, 31 July 1863, ibid., p. 307.

9. Lee to Imboden, 20 and 23 June 1863, *ORA*, ser. 1, vol. 27, pt. 3, pp. 905–6, 924.

10. Lee to Jones, 20 June 1863, *ORA*, ser. 1, vol. 27, pt. 3, p. 906.

11. Lee to Imboden, 20 June 1863, *ORA*, ser 1., vol. 27, pt. 3, pp. 905–6; Rual Purcell Anderson, *Genealogy Spaid, Anderson, Whitacre, and a Number of Allied Families, Also Historical Facts and Memories* (Strasburg, Va.: Shenandoah Press, 1975), p. 448.

12. Tyler to Maj. Gen. Hooker, 20 June 1863, *ORA*, ser. 1, vol. pt. 2, 27, p. 25.

13. Coddington, *Gettysburg Campaign*, p. 107; Lee to Imboden, 20 June 1862, *ORA*, ser. 1, vol. 27, pt. 3, pp. 905–6.

14. Coddington, *Gettysburg Campaign*, pp. 196–97.

15. "Civil War Diary of Francis Marion Imboden," Hobbs Collection transcription.

16. Lee to Cooper, 31 July 1863, *ORA*, ser. 1, vol. 27, pt. 2, p. 307.

17. "Civil War Diary of Francis Marion Imboden," entry of 29 June 1863; Lee to Imboden, 1 July 1863, *ORA*, ser. 1, vol. 27, pt. 3, pp. 907–8; William Hall, "The Battle of McConnellsburg," *Fulton Democrat*, 4 April 1888.

18. James Longstreet, *From Manassas to Appomattox, Memoirs of the Civil War in America* (Philadelphia: J.B. Lippincott, 1896), pp. 359, 546.

19. "Civil War Diary of Frank M. Imboden," 30 June, 1 July 1863.

20. Delauter, *18th Virginia Cavalry*, p. 7; Coddington, *Gettysburg Campaign*, pp. 197–98.

21. Coddington, *Gettysburg Campaign*, pp. 244–45.

22. "Civil War Diary of Frank M. Imboden,"3 July 1863; Anderson, *Genealogy*, p. 449.

23. Col. Watson A. Fox to Maj. Gen. Nelson Randall, 10 Sep 1863, *ORA*, ser. 1, vol. 27, pt. 2, pp. 272–73.

24. John D. Imboden, "The Confederate Retreat from Gettysburg," *Battles and Leaders of the Civil War*, vol. 3 (New York: Castle Books, 1956), p. 420.

25. Ibid., pp. 420–21.

26. Imboden, "The Confederate Retreat from Gettysburg," p. 421.

27. Lee to Cooper, 31 July 1863, *ORA*, ser. 1, vol. 27, pt. 2, p. 309; Lee to Imboden, 4 July 1863, ibid., vol. 27, pt. 3, pp. 966–67; Imboden, "The Confederate Retreat from Gettysburg," pp. 422–23.

28. J.E.B. Stuart to R.H. Chilton, 20 August 1863, *ORA*, ser. 1, vol. 27, pt. 2, p. 699.

29. Imboden, "The Confederate Retreat from Gettysburg," p. 423.
30. John W. Schildt, *Roads from Gettysburg* (Chewsville, Md.: Self-published, 1979), p. 28.
31. Imboden, "The Confederate Retreat from Gettysburg," p. 423-24; Anderson, *Genealogy,* p. 449.
32. Imboden, "The Confederate Retreat from Gettysburg," pp. 423-24; Faust, *Encyclopedia of the Civil War,* pp. 569, 660.
33. Imboden, "The Confederate Retreat from Gettysburg," p. 424.
34. Anderson, *Genealogy,* p. 449.
35. Woodward, *Defender of the Valley,* p. 81-82.
36. Anderson, *Genealogy,* p. 449; "Civil War Diary of Francis M. Imboden," 4 June 1863.
37. Imboden, "The Confederate Retreat from Gettysburg," *Battles and Leaders,* vol.3, p. 425; E.P. Alexander, *Military Memoirs of a Confederate: A Critical Narrative* (New York: Charles Scribner's Sons, 1907), p. 438.
38. Coddington, *The Gettysburg Campaign,* pp. 544-48.
39. Ibid., pp. 547-49.
40. Lee to Cooper, 31 July 1863, *ORA,* ser. 1, vol. 27, pt. 2, p. 309.
41. Coddington, *The Gettysburg Campaign,* pp. 549-52.
42. Ibid., p. 552.
43. Imboden, "The Confederate Retreat from Gettysburg," p. 425.
44. D.N. Couch to J.C. Kelton, 15 July 1863, *ORA,* ser. 1., vol. 27, pt. 2, p. 214; L.B. Pierce to D.N. Couch, 5 July 1863, ibid., p. 280; J.E.B. Stuart to R.H. Chilton, 20 August 1863, ibid., p. 703; Coddington, *The Gettysburg Campaign,* pp. 552, 814; Thomas believed more than a hundred wagons were taken: Thomas, "The Military Career of Imboden," p. 115; Coddington implies the engagement was on July 7; Private Baker and both Imbodens have it occurring on July 5; Anderson, *Genealogy,* p. 449; "Civil War Diary of Frank M. Imboden," 5 July 1863.
45. Imboden, "The Confederate Retreat from Gettysburg," p. 425; Anderson, *Genealogy,* p. 449.
46. Schildt, *Roads from Gettysburg,* p. 80.
47. Imboden, "The Retreat from Getttysburg," p. 426; Anderson, *Genealogy,* p. 450; Coddington, *The Gettysburg Campaign,* p. 566.
48. Imboden, "The Retreat from Gettysburg," pp. 426-27; Coddington has this engagement occurring on July 8: Coddington, *The Gettysburg Campaign,* p. 552; again, Baker and Imboden are in agreement that it was on July 6.
49. Anderson, *Genealogy,* p. 449.
50. Imboden, "The Confederate Retreat from Gettysburg," p. 427; Anderson, *Genealogy,* p 450.
51. Anderson, *Genealogy,* p. 450.
52. "Civil War Diary of Frank M. Imboden," 6 July 1863.
53. Lee to Cooper, 31 July 1863, *ORA,* ser. 1, vol. 27, pt. 2, p. 309.
54. Coddington, *The Gettysburg Campaign,* p. 552.

55. Coddington, *The Gettysburg Campaign*, pp. 552–53.
56. Imboden, "The Confederate Retreat from Gettysburg," p. 427; Anderson, *Genealogy*, p. 450.
57. Delauter, *62nd Virginia Infantry*, p. 19; "Civil War Diary of Frank M. Imboden," 7 July 1863.
58. Imboden, "The Confederate Retreat from Gettysburg," p. 428.
59. Coddington, *The Gettysburg Campaign*, p. 554.
60. Anderson, *Genealogy*, p. 450.
61. Ibid.
62. Ibid., p. 451.
63. Lee to Pickett and Imboden, 9 July 1863, *ORA*, ser. 1, vol. 27, pt. 3, pp. 986–87.
64. Imboden, "The Confederate Retreat from Gettysburg," pp. 428–29.
65. Lee to Imboden, 13 July 1863, Special Collections, Library, Washington and Lee University.
66. Coddington, *The Gettysburg Campaign*, pp. 566–69.
67. Ibid., pp. 571–73.
68. John L. Collins, "A Prisoner's March from Gettysburg to Staunton," *Battles and Leaders of the Civil War*, vol. 3, p. 432.
69. Ibid.
70. Ibid., pp. 432–33.
71. "Civil War Diary of Frank M. Imboden," 16, 17 July 1863.
72. Anderson, *Genealogy*, p. 451.
73. Lee to Imboden, 16 July 1863, *ORA*, ser. 1, vol. 27, pt. 3, p. 1011.
74. "Civil War Diary of Frank M. Imboden," 31 July 1863.
75. Lee to Imboden, 21 and 30 July 1863, *ORA*, ser. 1, vol. 27, pt. 3, pp. 1032 and 1051.

8. Imboden's Second West Virginia Raid

1. John D. Imboden, "The Battle of New Market," *Battles and Leaders of the Civil War*, vol. 3, p. 480.
2. R.E. Lee, *Lee's Dispatches: Unpublished Letters*, p. 123.
3. Report of Maj. Gen. Henry W. Halleck to Sec. of War E.M. Stanton, 15 November 1863, *ORA*, ser. 1, vol. 29, pp. 7–8; Averell to Brig. Gen. Kelley, 30 August 1863, ibid., p. 32; Maj. Gen. S. Jones to Gen. S. Cooper, 28 and 30 August 1863, ibid., p. 43.
4. Lee to Imboden, 10 Sep 1863, *ORA*, ser. 1, vol. 29, pt. 2, p. 709.
5. Dowdey and Manarin, *The Wartime Papers of Lee*, pp. 556–57, 587.
6. Imboden to Lee, 13 Sep 1863, *ORA*, ser. 1, vol. 29, pt. 1, p. 105.
7. Lee to Imboden, 17 August 1863, *ORA*, ser. 1, vol. 29, pt. 2, p. 650; Charles Marshall to Imboden, 21 Sep 1863, ibid., p. 739.

8. Imboden to W.S. Pilcher, 8 Sep 1863, Pilcher Papers, Eleanor S. Brockenbrough Library, Museum of the Confederacy.
9. Extract from "Record of Events," 4th Brigade, Department of West Virginia, *ORA*, ser. 1, vol. 29, pt. 1, p. 105; "Civil Ear Diary of Frank M. Imboden, 11 Sep 1863; Gen. Imboden reported 138 men captured. Imboden to Gen. Lee, 13 Sep, 1863, ibid., pp. 105–7; Anderson, *Genealogy*, p. 452.
10. Thomas, "The Military Career of Imboden," p. 93.
11. Imboden, "The Battle of New Market," p. 480.
12. Delauter, *62nd Virginia*, p. 22.
13. Imboden to Lee, 13 September, 10 October 1863, *ORA*, ser. 1, vol. 29, pt. 1, pp. 107 and 197.
14. Delauter, *62nd Virginia*, p. 21.
15. Imboden to Lee, 1 October 1863, *ORA*, ser. 1., vol. 29, pt. 1, pp. 197–98.
16. Imboden to Lee, 1 October 1863, *ORA*, ser. 1, vol. 29, pt. 1, pp. 197–98.
17. Delauter, *62nd Virginia*, pp. 21–22.
18. Captain F.B. Berkeley, "Imboden's Dash into Charlestown," *Baltimore Sunday Sun*, 30 August 1903, in *Southern Historical Papers*, vol. 31, pp. 11–12; Jefferson County Historical Society, vol. LIV (December 1988): 15–16, cited in Woodward, *Defender of the Valley*, p. 92.
19. Anderson, *Genealogy*, pp. 454–55.
20. Berkeley, "Imboden's Dash into Charlestown," p. 14; Imboden to Lee, 19 October 1863, *ORA*, ser. 1, vol. 29, pt. 1, pp. 490–91.
21. Berkeley, "Imboden's Dash into Charlestown," p. 14; Imboden to Lee, 19 October 1863, *ORA*, ser. 1, vol. 29, pt. 1, p. 91; Driver, *Staunton Artillery*, p. 81.
22. Berkeley, "Imboden's Dash into Charlestown," pp. 12–16.
23. Berkeley, "Imboden's Dash into Charlestown," pp. 14–15; Imboden to Lee, 19 October 1863, *ORA*, ser. 1, vol. 29, pt. 1, p. 491.
24. Berkeley, "Imboden's Dash into Charlestown," p. 15; Imboden to Lee, 19 October 1863, *ORA*, ser. 1, vol. 29, pt. 1, p. 491; Driver, *Staunton Artillery*, p. 82.
25. Driver, *Staunton Artillery*, pp. 81–82.
26. Berkeley, "Imboden's Dash into Charlestown," p. 16.
27. Imboden to Lee, 19 October 1863, *ORA*, ser. 1, vol. 29, pt. 1, pp. 491–92.
28. Imboden to Lee, 19 October 1863, *ORA*, ser. 1, vol. 29, pt. 1, pp. 491–92; Ibid., p. 411; Delauter, *62nd Virginia Infantry*, p. 22.
29. Dowdey and Manarin, *The Wartime Papers of Lee*, p. 614.
30. Ibid., and Lee to Imboden, 23 October 1863, *ORA*, ser. 1, vol. 29, pt. 1, p. 492.
31. Callahan, *History of West Virginia*, vol. 1, pp. 374, 385.
32. Delauter, *18th Virginia Cavalry*, p. 12.
33. Dowdey and Manarin, *The Wartime Papers of Lee*, pp. 617–18.
34. Imboden to Col. R.H. Chilton, 14 November 1863, *ORA*, ser. 1, vol. 29, pt. 1, pp. 547–48; Echols to Maj. C.S. Stringfellow, 19 November 1863, ibid., pp.

528–32; Report of Union Casualties, ibid., p. 503; Averell to Kelley, 14 November 1863, ibid., p. 504; Averell to Melvin, 17 November 1863, ibid., p. 507.

35. Maj. Gen. Samuel Jones to James A Seddon, 8, 9, and 10 November 1863, *ORA*, ser 1, vol. 29, pt. 1, p. 526; Echols to Maj. C.S. Stringfellow, 19 November 1863, ibid., 532.

36. Imboden to Maj. Gen. Francis Smith, 9 and 11 November 1863; Archives, Virginia Military Institute; Imboden to Col. R.H. Chilton, 14 November 1863, *ORA*, ser. 1, vol. 29, pt. 1, pp. 548–49; Averell to Capt. T. Melvin, 17 November 1863, ibid., pp. 505–8; Robert J. Driver Jr., *Lexington and Rockbridge County in the Civil War* (Lynchburg, Va.: H.E. Howard, 1989), pp. 50–51; *Lexington Gazette*, 18 November 1863.

37. Averell to Kelley, 14 November 1863 and to Melvin, 17 November 1863, *ORA*, ser. 1, vol. 29, pt. 1, pp. 504, 507.

38. Imboden to Col. R.H. Chilton, 19 November 1863, *ORA*, ser. 1, vol. 29, pt. 1, pp. 643–44; Delauter, *62nd Virginia Infantry*, p. 23.

39. Imboden to Messrs. Williams, Bell & Hollis, 27 November 1863, Imboden Papers, Manuscript Division, Library of Congress.

40. Delauter, *62nd Virginia Infantry*, p. 24.

41. Imboden to Massie, 13 December 1863, Archives, Virginia Military Institute.

42. Benjamin F. Kelley to G.W. Cullum, 18 February 1864, *ORA*, ser. 1, vol. 29, pt. 1, p. 921; Averell to Halleck, 21 December 1863, ibid., p. 928; Imboden, "The Battle of New Market," p. 480; Beverly Stanard, *Letters of a New Market Cadet*, edited by John G. Barrett and Robert K. Turner Jr. (Chapel Hill, N.C.: Univ. of North Carolina Press, 1961), p. 22 note.

43. Stanard, *Letters of a New Market Cadet*, pp. 21, 23 (note); Driver, *Lexington and Rockbridge County*, p. 55.

44. Driver, *Lexington and Rockbridge County*, p. 52.

45. Ibid., p. 53.

46. Early to W.H. Taylor, 24 December 1863, *ORA*, ser. 1, vol. 29, pt. 1, p. 970; Imboden to Maj. Scott Shipp, 29 December 1863, Archives, Virginia Military Institute; Freeman, *Lee's Lieutenants*, p. 326; Charles C. Osborne, *Jubal: The Life and Times of General Jubal A. Early, C.S.A., Defender of the Lost Cause* (Chapel Hill, N.C.: Univ. of North Carolina Press, 1992), p. 217; Wise, *The Military History of the Virginia Military Institute from 1861 to 1865* (Lynchburg, Va.: J.-P. Bell, 1915), pp. 264–75.

47. Lee to Early, 22 December 1863, *ORA*, ser. 1, vol. 29, pt. 2, p. 889.

48. Imboden to Jackson, 13 December 1863, *ORA*, ser. 1, vol. 29, pt. 1, p. 958.

49. Delauter, *McNeill's Rangers*, pp. 60–61.

50. Jack W. Maddex Jr. *The Virginia Conservatives, 1867–1879: A Study in Reconstruction Politics* (Chapel Hill, N.C.: Univ. of North Carolina Press, 1970), p. 25.

51. Frank Imboden, War Diary, 1863, Imboden Papers. Alderman Library, University of Virginia.

9. The 1864 Shenandoah Valley Campaign

1. Jack L. Dickinson, *Jenkins of Greenbottom: A Civil War Saga* (Charleston, W.Va.: Pictorial Histories Publishing, 1988), p. 68; Delauter, *62nd Virginia Infantry*, p. 25.
2. Osborne, *Jubal*, p. 221.
3. Freeman, *Lee's Lieutenants*, vol. 3, pp. xv, 327.
4. Ibid.
5. Freeman, *Lee's Lieutenants*, vol. 3, p. 327.
6. Lee to Imboden, 10 Sep 1863, *ORA*, ser. 1, vol. 29, pt. 2, p. 709.
7. Imboden to R.H. Chilton, 12 February 1864, *ORA*, ser. 1, vol. 33, p. 1167.
8. Ibid.
9. Comment in forwarding Imboden's letter, 12 February 1864, *ORA*, ser. 1, vol. 33, p. 1168.
10. Lee to Early, 15 February 1864, ibid.; Freeman, *Lee's Lieutenants*, vol. 3, p. 328.
11. Lee to Davis, 13 January 1864, *ORA*, ser. 1, vol. 33, p. 1086.
12. Freeman, *Lee's Lieutenants*, vol. 3, p. 328; Delauter, *62nd Virginia*, p. 25.
13. Freeman, *Lee's Lieutenants*, vol. 3, pp. 328–29; Delauter, *62nd Virginia*, pp. 25–26.
14. Delauter, *62nd Virginia*, pp. 25–26.
15. Delauter, *McNeill's Rangers*, pp. 61–63.
16. N. Harrison to J. Seddon, 26 January 1864, *ORA*, ser. 1, vol. 51, pt. 2, pp. 813–14; S. Jones to J. Seddon, 4 February 1864, ibid., p. 816; J. Seddon to S. Jones, 11 February 1864, ibid., p. 820; S. Jones to J. Seddon, 14 February 1864, ibid., ser. 1, vol. 33, p. 1172; Special Orders 78, 2 April 1864, ibid., p. 1255; Freeman, *Lee's Lieutenants*, vol. 3, p. 324.
17. R.E. Lee to President Jefferson Davis, 27 January 1864, *ORA*, vol. 33, p. 1124; Special Orders No. 46, 25 February 1864, ibid., pp. 1198; Freeman, *Lee's Lieutenants*, vol. 3, p. 325.
18. Imboden to Lee, 20 March 18643, *ORA*, ser. 1, vol. 33, pp. 1231, 1239; Delauter, *62nd Virginia Infantry*, p. 26.
19. Delauter, *McNeill's Rangers*, p. 64.
20. Robert E. Denney, *Civil War Prisons and Escapes: A Day to Day Chronicle* (New York: Sterling Publishing, 1993), pp. 144–45.
21. Delauter, *62nd Virginia Infantry*, p. 27.
22. Imboden to Lee, 10 March 1864, *ORA*, ser. 1, vol. 33, pt. 1, p. 1215.
23. Lee to Davis, 25 March 1864, *Lee's Dispatches*, p. 143.
24. Lee to Imboden, 18 April 1864, *ORA*, ser. 1, vol. 33, pp. 1287–88.
25. Franz Sigel, "Sigel in the Shenandoah Valley in 1864," *Battles and Leaders of*

the Civil War, vol. 4, p. 488; Frank J. Welcher, *The Union Army, 1861–1865: Organization and Operations*, vol. 1 of *The Eastern Theater* (Bloomington, Ind.: Indiana Univ. Press, 1989), p. 201.

26. Davis, *The Battle of New Market*, pp. 193–95.

27. Lee to Davis, 30 April 1864, *ORA*, ser. 1, vol. 33, p. 1331; Lee to Breckinridge, ibid., vol. 37, pt. 1, p. 707.

28. Lee to Breckinridge, 4 May 1864, *ORA*, ser. 1, vol. 37, pt. 1, p. 712.

29. Imboden to Lee, 2 May 1864, Charles S. Venable Papers #2213, Manuscripts Department and Southern Historical Collection, University of North Carolina at Chapel Hill; also, *ORA*, ser. 1, vol. 51, pt. 2, p. 885.

30. Imboden, "The Battle of New Market," p. 481.

31. Lee to Davis, 6 June 1864 in *Lee's Dispatches*, p. 217.

32. Imboden, "The Battle of New Market," *Battles and Leaders of the Civil War*, vol. 3, p. 480; Imboden wrote after the fact that, "as District Commander," he had called out the cadets; Imboden to Col. J. Marshall McCue, CSA Military Leaders Collection: Imboden, Eleanor S. Brockenbrough Library, The Museum of the Confederacy; Imboden to Smith, 22 April 1864, Archives, Virginia Military Institute.

33. Imboden to Breckinridge, 3, 4 and 5 May 1864; Breckinridge to Imboden, 5 May 1864, *ORA*, ser. 1, vol. 37, pt. 1, pp. 710, 715–17.

34. Lee to Breckinridge, 7 May 1864, *ORA*, ser. 1, vol. 37, pt. 1, p. 722; Davis, *The Battle of New Market*, p. 32.

35. Imboden to Breckinridge, 8 May 1864, *ORA*, ser. 1, vol. 37, pt. 1, p. 724.

36. McNeill to Sec. of War J.A. Seddon, 7 May 1864, *ORA*, ser. 1, vol. 37, pt. 1, p. 60.

37. Delauter, *McNeill's Rangers*, p. 66.

38. Imboden, "The Battle of New Market," p. 481; Imboden to Breckinridge, 8, 9 (2) May 1864, *ORA*, ser. 1, vol. 37, pt. 1, pp. 724, 726; Franz Sigel, "Sigel in the Shenandoah Valley in 1864," *Battles and Leaders of the Civil War*, vol. 3, p. 488; Welcher, *The Union Army*, p. 201.

39. Imboden to Breckinridge, 11 May 1864, *ORA*, ser. 1, vol. 37, pt. 1, p. 71; Delauter, *McNeill's Rangers*, pp. 68–69; Delauter, *18th Virginia Cavalry*, p. 17.

40. Milton W. Humphreys, *A History of the Lynchburg Campaign* (Charlottesville, Va.: Michie Co., 1924), pp. 1–29.

41. Lang, *Loyal West Virginia*, p. 112.

42. Smith to Breckinridge, 11 May 1864 (2), *ORA*, ser. 1. Vol. 37, pt. 1, p. 730.

43. Sigel to Adjutant General, U.S. Army, 12 May 1864, *ORA*, ser. 1, vol. 37, pt. 1, pp. 444–48.

44. Imboden, "Battle of New Market," p. 481.

45. Imboden to Breckinridge, 11 May 1864, *ORA*, ser. 1, vol. 37, pt. 1, p. 71; Thomas A. Lewis, *The Shenandoah in Flames* (Alexandria, Va.: Time-Life Publications, 1987), p. 28.

46. Lewis, *The Shenandoah in Flames*, p. 28.

47. Imboden, "The Battle of New Market," *Battles and Leaders,* vol. 4, p. 491.
48. Imboden, "The Battle of New Market," p. 481; Sigel, "Sigel in the Shenandoah Valley," p. 488.
49. Imboden, "The Battle of New Market," p. 481
50. Robert Grier Stephens Jr., ed., *Intrepid Warrior: Clement Anselon Evans, Confederate General from Georgia: Life, Letters, and Diaries of the War Years* (Dayton, Ohio: Morningside Books, 1992), p. 398.
51. Imboden, "The Battle of New Market," pp. 480–81; Lee to Breckinridge, 14 May 1864, *ORA,* ser. 1, vol. 37, pt. 1, p. 735.
52. Maj. Gen. Francis H. Smith to Breckinridge, *ORA,* sec. 1, vol. 37, pt. 1, p. 730.
53. Imboden to Breckinridge, 12, 13 (2), 14 May 1864, *ORA,* ser. 1, vol. 37, pt. 1, pp. 731, 733, 735.
54. William C. Davis, *The Battle of New Market* (Baton Rouge, La.: Louisiana State Univ. Press, 1975), pp. 195–97. Davis's figure of 735 cavalry in Breckinridge's command includes 20 men under Lt. Col. John S. Mosby, but Mosby operated independently against Sigel, and his Rangers were not part of Breckinridge's force. Mosby's raids in Sigel's rear did, however, contribute to Sigel's hesitation and lack of confidence.
55. Imboden, "The Battle of New Market," p. 481; Richard R. Duncan, *Lee's Endangered Left: The Civil War in Western Virginia, Spring of 1864* (Baton Rouge, La.: Louisiana State Univ. Press, 1998), pp. 110–1.
56. Henry A. Du Pont, *The Campaigns of 1864 in the Valley of Virginia and the Expedition to Lynchburg* (New York: National Americana Society, 1925), p. 9; Davis, *The Battle of New Market,* pp. 68–69.
57. Delauter, *18th Virginia Cavalry,* p. 19.
58. Imboden, "The Battle of New Market," *Battles and Leaders,* vol. 4, pp. 481–82.
59. Imboden, "The Battle of New Market," p. 482.
60. Davis, *The Battle of New Market,* p. 98.
61. Imboden, "The Battle of New Market," p. 482. Troop figures vary widely. Davis gives the 62d at 448 men: Davis, *The Battle of New Market,* p. 196.
62. Imboden, "The Battle of New Market," 483.
63. Ibid., p. 483.
64. Ibid., p. 484.
65. Delauter, *18th Virginia Cavalry,* p. 21.
66. Delauter, *62nd Virginia Infantry,* p. 30.
67. Davis, *The Battle of New Market,* pp. 200–1.
68. Sigel to Adjutant-General, 15 May 1864, *ORA,* ser. 1, vol. 37, pt. 1, p. 76.
69. Edward Raymond Turner, *The New Market Campaign* (Richmond, Va.: Whitlet & Shepperson, 1912), p. 98.
70. Turner, *The New Market Campaign,* p. 42.

71. Delauter, *18th Virginia Cavalry*, p. 21; William Couper, *History of the Shenandoah Valley*, vol. 2, p. 930.
72. Du Pont, *The Campaign of 1864*, p. 32.
73. W. Birdbeck Wood and Sir James E. Edmonds, *Military History of the Civil War* (New York: Putnam, 1960), p. 195.
74. "Report on Casualties in the Action of May 15th 1864," Cleveland, Ohio: The Western Reserve Historical Society, MSS 3123, Cont. 5, Folder 1.
75. Delauter, *18th Virginia Cavalry*, pp. 21–22; Sigel, "Sigel in the Shenandoah Valley," p. 490.
76. Sigel, "Sigel in the Shenandoah Valley," p. 489.
77. Imboden, "The Battle of New Market," p. 485.
78. Imboden to Breckinridge, 19 and 20 May 1864, *ORA*, ser. 1, vol. 37, pt. 1, p. 743; Lang, *Loyal West Virginia*, pp. 112–16; Welcher, *The Union Army*, pp. 202–3.
79. Davis, *The Battle of New Market*, Appendix B, pp. 198–201, gives ninety-two casualties for the 62d. Delauter estimated losses at 95: Delauter, *62nd Virginia Infantry*, p. 32; Imboden claimed 241 killed and wounded for the 62d and that losses in that regiment and Corps of Cadets were half the Confederate total for the battle: Imboden, "The Battle of New Market," p. 484, also Delauter, *18th Virginia Cavalry*, p. 21.
80. Freeman, *Lee's Lieutenants*, vol. 3, pp. 515–16.
81. Imboden to Col. Marshall McCue, 1 October 1883, CSA Military Leaders: Imboden, Eleanor S. Brockenbrough Library, The Museum of the Confederacy; Marshall Moore Brice, *Conquest of a Valley* (Charlottesville, Va.: Univ. of Virginia Press, 1965), p. 24; Imboden, "The Battle of New Market," p. 485; John D. Imboden, "The Battle of Piedmont," *Confederate Veteran*, vol. 31 (1923), p. 459.
82. Wise, *Military History of the Virginia Military Institute*, pp. 345, 351.

10. Destruction of the Valley

1. Faust, *Encyclopedia of the Civil War*, p. 376.
2. Welcher, *The Union Army*, p. 203; Imboden to Col. J. Marshall McCue, 1 October 1883, CSA Military Leaders Collection: Imboden, Eleanor S. Brockenbrough Library, The Museum of the Confederacy.
3. Charles M. Blackford, *Campaign and Battle of Lynchburg* (Lynchburg, Va.: J.P. Bell Co., 1901), pp. 6–7.
4. Welcher, *The Union Army*, p. 203.
5. Brice, *Conquest of a Valley*, p. 12.
6. Faust, *Encyclopedia of the Civil War*, pp. 455–56.
7. Imboden to Breckinridge, 17 May 1864, *ORA*, ser. 1, vol. 37, pt. 1, p. 739.
8. Imboden to Breckinridge,19 May 1864, *ORA*, ser. 1, vol. 37, pt. 1, p. 744.
9. Wise, *Military History of the Virginia Military Institute*, p. 351.
10. Duncan, *Lee's Endangered Left*, pp. 139–40.

11. Welcher, *The Union Army*, p. 203; Brice, *Conquest of a Valley*, pp. 15–16. Brice gives Hunter's strength at 10,000 men and 22 guns. Writing two decades after the war, Imboden listed it at 9,000 infantry, 2,500 cavalry, and 32 guns. Imboden to Col. J. Marshall McCue, 1 October 1883, CSA Military Leaders Collection: Imboden, Eleanor S. Brockenbrough Library, The Museum of the Confederacy.

12. Imboden, "The Battle of Piedmont," p. 459; Milton W. Humphreys, *History of the Lynchburg Campaign* (Charlottesville, Va.: S.N. Michie Co., 1924), p. 29.

13. Brice, *Conquest of a Valley*, p. 26.

14. Imboden to Cooper, *ORA*, ser. 1, vol. 37, pt. 1, p. 748.

15. Imboden to Lee, 2 May 1864, *ORA*, ser. 1, vol. 51, pt. 2, p. 885; Brice, *Conquest of a Valley*, pp. 24–25.

16. *Staunton Vindicator*, 27 May 1864.

17. Brice, *Conquest of a Valley*, p. 26.

18. Imboden to Lee, 25 and 27 May 1864, *ORA*, ser. 1, vol. 37, pt. 1, pp. 748–49; also Venable Papers, #2213, University of North Carolina at Chapel Hill.

19. Gary C. Walker, *Hunter's Fiery Raid through Virginia's Valley* (Roanoke: A & W Enterprises, 1992), p. 35; Richard B. Kleese, *Shenandoah County in the Civil War: The Turbulent Years* (Lynchburg, Va.: H.E. Howard, 1992), p. 68.

20. Harry Gilmore, *Four Years in the Saddle* (New York: Harper and Brothers, 1865), pp. 161–62.

21. Walker, *Hunter's Fiery Raid*, p. 35; Welcher, *The Union Army*, p. 203.

22. Kleese, *Shenandoah County*, p. 68.

23. Imboden to Col. J. Marshall McCue, 1 October 1883, CSA Military Leaders Collection: Imboden, Eleanor S. Brockenbrough Library, The Museum of the Confederacy.

24. Brice, *Conquest of a Valley*, pp. 27–29.

25. Imboden to W. E. Jones, 29 May, 186, *ORA*, ser. 1, vol. 37, pt. 1, p. 749.

26. Report of Capt. J. Jones, 30 June 1864, *ORA*, ser. 1, vol. 51, pt. 1, p. 1225; Imboden, "The Battle of New Market," p. 485; Brice, *Conquest of a Valley*, pp. 28–29.

27. Brice, *Conquest of a Valley*, pp. 29–30.

28. Brice, *Conquest of a Valley*, p. 31; Imboden to Col. J. Marshall McCue, 1 October 1883, CSA Military Leaders Collection: Imboden, Eleanor S. Brockenbrough Library, The Museum of the Confederacy.

29. Walker, *Hunter's Fiery Raid*, pp. 59, 62, 64; Brice, *Conquest of a Valley*, p. 20.

30. Imboden to Col. J. Marshall McCue, 1 October 1883, CSA Military Leaders Collection: Imboden, Eleanor S. Brockenbrough Library, The Museum of the Confederacy.

31. Imboden to Lee, 1 June 1864 and Lee's endorsement of 2 June 1864, *ORA*, ser. 1, vol. 51, pt. 2, pp. 981–82.

32. Imboden, "The Battle of Piedmont," p. 459; Imboden to Col. J. Marshall

McCue, 1 October 1883, CSA Military Leaders Collection: Imboden, Eleanor S. Brockenbrough Library, The Museum of the Confederacy; Humphreys, *Lynchburg Campaign*, p. 33. Figures given for the artillery vary, according to source.

33. Imboden, "The Battle of New Market," p. 485; Brice, *Conquest of a Valley*, pp. 33–38.

34. Imboden to Col. J. Marshall McCue, 1 October 1883, CSA Military Leaders Collection: Imboden, Eleanor S. Brockenbrough Library, The Museum of the Confederacy.

35. Imboden to Col. J. Marshall McCue, 1 October 1883, CSA Military Leaders Collection: Imboden, Eleanor S. Brockenbrough Library, The Museum of the Confederacy.

36. Ibid; and Imboden, "The Battle of New Market," p. 485.

37. Walker, *Hunter's Fiery Raid*, p. 85; Humphreys, *Lynchburg Campaign*, pp. 33–34.

38. Imboden to Col. J. Marshall McCue, 1 October 1883, CSA Military Leaders Collection: Imboden, Eleanor S. Brockenbrough Library, The Museum of the Confederacy; Brice, *Conquest of a Valley*, p. 39.

39. Brice, *Conquest of a Valley*, p. 21; Welcher, *The Union Army*, pp. 203–4.

40. Imboden to Col. J. Marshall McCue, 1 October 1883, CSA Military Leaders Collection: Imboden, Eleanor S. Brockenbrough Library, The Museum of the Confederacy.

41. Ibid.

42. Ibid.

43. Ibid. Also, Brice, *Conquest of a Valley*, pp. 42–45; Alexander K. McClure, *The Annals of the War Written by Leading Participants North and South* (Philadelphia, Pa.: Times Publishing, 1878), p. 174.

44. John N. Opie, *A Rebel Cavalrymen with Lee, Stuart and Jackson* (Chicago, Ill.: W.B. Conkey, Co., 1899), p. 219; Brice, *Conquest of a Valley*, pp. 47–48.

45. Imboden to Col. J. Marshall McCue, 1 October 1883, CSA Military Leaders Collection: Imboden, Eleanor S. Brockenbrough Library, The Museum of the Confederacy; Brice, *Conquest of a Valley*, pp. 48–49.

46. Imboden to Col. J. Marshall McCue, 1 October 1883, CSA Military Leaders Collection: Imboden, Eleanor S. Brockenbrough Library, The Museum of the Confederacy.

47. McClure, *The Annals of the War*, p. 173; Brice, *Conquest of a Valley*, pp. 40–41; Humphreys, *Lynchburg Campaign*, p. 35.

48. Brice, *Conquest of a Valley*, p. 55.

49. Imboden to Col. J. Marshall McCue, 1 October 1883, CSA Military Leaders Collection: Imboden, Eleanor S. Brockenbrough Library, The Museum of the Confederacy. Estimates of Confederate strength vary widely. Vaughn gave it at 5,600 men, including 800 for Imboden; Vaughn to B. Bragg, 6 June 1864, *ORA*, ser. 1, vol. 37, pt. 1, p. 151.

50. Imboden to Col. J. Marshall McCue, 1 October 1883, CSA Military Lead-

ers Collection: Imboden, Eleanor S. Brockenbrough Library, The Museum of the Confederacy.

51. Ibid.; Brice, *Conquest of a Valley,* pp. 48–49.

52. Humphreys, *Lynchburg Campaign,* p. 35; Imboden article in the *Staunton Vindicator,* 13 July 1894.

53. Imboden to Col. J. Marshall McCue, 1 October 1883, CSA Military Leaders Collection: Imboden, Eleanor S. Brockenbrough Library, The Museum of the Confederacy.

54. *Staunton Vindicator,* 13 July 1894.

55. Ibid.

56. Ibid.; Imboden to Col. J. Marshall McCue, 1 October 1883, CSA Military Leaders Collection: Imboden, Eleanor S. Brockenbrough Library, The Museum of the Confederacy; Brice, *Conquest of a Valley,* p. 51.

57. Ibid.

58. Brice, *Conquest of a Valley,* pp. 55–56, 61–62.

59. Ibid., pp. 52–53.

60. Humphreys, *Lynchburg Campaign,* pp. 44–45; Brice, *Conquest of a Valley,* pp. 70–74.

61. Humphreys, *Lynchburg Campaign,* p. 42.

62. Imboden to Col. J. Marshall McCue, 1 October 1883, CSA Military Leaders Collection: Imboden, Eleanor S. Brockenbrough Library, The Museum of the Confederacy.

63. Humphreys, *Lynchburg Campaign,* pp. 42–44.

64. Ibid. pp. 44–45. Emphasis in original.

65. Ibid., p. 50.

66. Ibid., pp. 51, 53.

67. Brice, *Conquest of a Valley,* p. 81; Humphreys, *Lynchburg Campaign,* p. 52.

68. Ibid.

69. Brice, *Conquest of a Valley,* pp. 74–75.

70. Ibid., p. 77.

71. Ibid., pp. 75–79.

72. Robert Leroy Hilldrup, "Romance of a Man in Gray," *West Virginia History,* vol. 22, pp. 182–83.

73. Imboden to Col. J. Marshall McCue, 1 October 1883, CSA Military Leaders Collection: Imboden, Eleanor S. Brockenbrough Library, The Museum of the Confederacy.

74. Ibid.

75. Vaughn to Lee, 5 June 1864, *ORA,* ser. 1, vol. 37, pt. 1, p. 150; Imboden to Col. J. Marshall McCue, 1 October 1883, CSA Military Leaders Collection: Imboden, Eleanor S. Brockenbrough Library, The Museum of the Confederacy.

76. Vaughn to Seddon, 5 June 1864, *ORA,* ser. 1., vol. 51, pt. 2, p. 990.

77. Seddon to Bragg, 6 June 1864, ibid.

78. Charles T. O'Ferrall, *Forty Years of Active Service* (New York: The Neale Publishing Co., 1904), pp. 101–4; Brice, *Conquest of a Valley,* 89–90.
79. Charles Culbertson, "Mary Julia and the General," *Mary Baldwin Magazine,* 5.1 (August 1991): 4–5.
80. J. Lewis Peyton, *History of Augusta County, Virginia* (Bridgewater, Va.: C.-J. Carrier, 1953), p. 237; Culbertson, "Mary Julia and the General," pp. 5–6.
81. Welcher, *Union Army, 1861–1865,* p. 205.
82. Ibid., pp. 204–5.
83. Humphreys, *Lynchburg Campaign,* p. 53.
84. Welcher, *Union Army,* 204; Imboden, "Battle of New Market," p. 486.
85. Lee to Davis, 6 June 1864, *Lee's Dispatches,* pp. 217–18.
86. Duffié's report, 9 July 1864, *ORA,* ser. 1, vol. 37, pt. 1, pp. 139–140.
87. Ibid., p. 140.
88. Blackford, *The Campaign and Battle of Lynchburg, Va.,* p. 14.
89. Imboden to Smith, 15 June 1864, Archives, Virginia Military Institute; Thomas, "The Military Career of Imboden," p. 142; George Morris and Susan Foutz, *Lynchburg in the Civil War: The City—The People—The Battle* (Lynchburg, Va.: H.-E. Howard, 1984), p. 39; Humphreys, *Lynchburg Campaign,* pp. 54–55.
90. McClure, *The Annals of the War Written by Leading Participants North and South,* p. 175; Blackford, *Campaign and Battle of Lynchburg,* pp. 36–37,
91. Humphries, *History of the Lynchburg Campaign,* p. 54.
92. Letcher to Imboden, 20 April 1877, Imboden Papers, Alderman Library, University of Virginia; *Lexington Gazette,* 15 July 1864; Duncan, *Lee's Endangered Left,* pp. 214–29.
93. Duffié's Report, 9 July 1864, *ORA,* ser. 1, vol. 37, pt. 1, pp. 140–45; Hunter to Duffié, 11 June 1864, ibid., p. 625.
94. Duffié's Report, 9 July 1864, *ORA,* ser. 1, vol. 37, pt. 1, pp. 140–41; Imboden's Reports, 11, 12 June 1864, ibid., pp. 151–52.
95. Imboden's Report, 13 June 1864, in F. Nicholls to B. Bragg, 13 June 1864, *ORA,* ser. 1, vol. 37, pt. 1, p. 760.
96. Duncan, *Lee's Endangered Left,* pp. 238, 252; Cooper, *One Hundred Years at VMI,* vol. 3, pp. 45–46; Humphreys, *Lynchburg Campaign,* pp. 59–60; Morris and Foutz, *Lynchburg in the Civil War,* p. 136.
97. Freeman, *Lee's Lieutenants,* vol. 3, pp. 510, 523–24.
98. Blackford, *Campaign and Battle of Lynchburg, Va.,* pp. 17–18.
99. Early to Breckinridge, 16 June 1864, *ORA,* ser. 1, vol. 37, pt. 1, pp. 762–63.
100. Imboden's Reports 14 (4), 16 (4), 17 June 1864, *ORA,* ser. 1, vol. 37, pt. 1, pp. 155–60; Blackford, *Campaign and Battle of Lynchburg, Va.,* pp. 17–19; Freeman, *Lee's Lieutenants,* vol. 3, pp. 524–25; J.C. Wise, *History of VMI,* pp. 358–59.
101. Breckinridge to Bragg, 15 June 1864, *ORA,* ser. 1, vol. 40, pt. 2, p. 658.
102. Special Orders No. 137, 13 June 1864, *ORA,* ser. 1, vol. 37, pt. 1, p. 760.
103. Early to Bragg, 17 June 1864, *ORA,* ser. 1., vol. 51, pt. 2, p. 1020.

104. Humphreys, *Lynchburg Campaign*, p. 61; Blackford, *The Campaign and Battle of Lynchburg, Va.*, p. 20.
105. Jubal A. Early, *Autobiographical Sketch and Narrative of the War Between the States* (Philadelphia, Pa.: J.B. Lippincott, 1912), p. 374.
106. Humphreys, *Lynchburg Campaign*, p. 63; Duncan, *Lee's Endangered Left*, pp. 271–72.
107. Imboden to Breckinridge, 17 June 1864, *ORA*, ser. 1, vol. 37, pt. 1, pp. 159–160; report of Duffié, 9 July 1864, ibid., p. 141.
108. Blackford, *The Campaign and Battle of Lynchburg*, pp. 22–23, 30–31.
109. Report of Gen. Hunter, 8 August 1864, *ORA*, ser. 1, vol. 37, pt. 1, p. 99.
110. Hunter's report of 8 August 1864, *ORA*, ser 1, vol. 37, pt. 1, pp. 99–100.
111. Duffié report, 18 June 1864, *ORA*, ser. 1, vol. 37, pt. 1, p. 650; Humphreys, *Lynchburg Campaign*, pp. 67–68; Blackford, *The Campaign and Battle of Lynchburg, Va.*, p. 25; Imboden, "The Battle of New Market," p. 486.
112. *ORA*, ser. 1, vol. 37, pt. 1, p. 766; Humphreys, *Lynchburg Campaign*, p. 63; Osborne, *Jubal*, p. 265.
113. Humphreys, *Lynchburg Campaign*, pp. 69–70.
114. Ibid., pp. 70–72.
115. Delauter, *18th Virginia Cavalry*, p. 27.
116. Freeman, *Lee's Lieutenants*, vol. 3., pp. 526–27; Welcher, *The Union Army*, pp. 206–7.

11. Final Confederate Service

1. Freeman, *Lee's Lieutenants*, vol. 3, pp. 557–58.
2. Delauter, *62nd Virginia Infantry*, p. 37.
3. Freeman, *Lee's Lieutenants*, vol. 3, pp. 557–58.
4. Ibid., vol. 3, p. 559.
5. Sigel to Adjutant General, U.S. Army, 5 July 1864, *ORA*, ser. 1, vol. 37, pt. 1, p. 176; Delauter, *62nd Virginia Infantry*, p. 37.
6. Ibid.; Bell I. Wiley, *The Life of Johnny Reb: The Common Soldier of the Confederacy* (Baton Rouge, La.: Louisiana State Univ. Press, 1943), p. 25; John D. Imboden, "Statement of General John D. Imboden to General D. H. Murray on January 12, 1876, Regarding the Treatment of Prisoners at Andersonville," *Southern Historical Society Papers*, vol. 1, p. 187.
7. Freeman, *Lee's Lieutenants*, vol. 4, p. 559.
8. Freeman, *Lee's Lieutenants*, vol. 3, pp. 560–64.
9. Osborne, *Jubal*, p. 270; Freeman, *Lee's Lieutenants*, vol. 3, pp. 562–64.
10. Freeman, *Lee's Lieutenants*, vol. 3, p. 565.
11. Ibid., pp. 566–68.
12. Delauter, *18th Virginia Cavalry*, p. 28.
13. Ibid., p. 29.
14. Ibid.

15. Early, *Autobiographical Sketch,* p. 400.
16. Grant to Sherdian, 7 August 1864, *ORA,* ser. 1, vol. 43, pt. 1, p. 719; Return of Casualties, ibid., vol. 37, pt. 1, pp. 288–290.
17. Early, *Autobiographical Sketch,* p. 401.
18. Ibid.
19. Ibid., p. 404.
20. Report of Brig. Gen. Bradley Johnson, 10 August 1864, *ORA,* ser. 1, vol. 43, pt. 1, p. 7.
21. Anderson, *Genealogy,* p. 461.
22. Freeman, *Lee's Lieutenants,* vol. 3, p. 573.
23. Delauter, *18th Virginia Cavalry,* p. 43.
24. Ransom to S. Cooper, 22 August 1864, *ORA,* ser. 1, vol. 43, pt. 1, pp. 1003–4.
25. Bragg to Early, 29 August 1864, *ORA,* ser. 1, vol. 43, pt. 1, p. 1008.
26. Freeman, *Lee's Lieutenants,* vol. 3, pp. 575–76.
27. Early, *Autobiographical Sketch,* pp. 419–20.
28. *Proceedings of the Clarke County Historical Association,* vol. 15: 13; Early, *Autobiographical Sketch,* p. 406; Anderson, *Genealogy,* p. 459.
29. Early, *Autobiographical Sketch,* pp. 415–16; Sheridan to L. Thomas, 13 Sep 1864, *ORA,* ser. 1., vol. 43, pt. 1, pp. 60–61 and note.
30. John Imboden to Frank Imboden, 22 Sep 1864, Imboden Papers, Alderman Library, University of Virginia.
31. Freeman, *Lee's Lieutenants,* vol. 3, p. 568.
32. Grant to Sheridan, 27 August 1864, *ORA,* ser. 1, vol. 43, pt. 1, p. 917.
33. Delauter, *18th Virginia Cavalry,* pp. 33–34.
34. Delauter, *62nd Virginia Infantry,* p. 42.
35. Ibid., p. 42.
36. Sheridan to H. Halleck, 24 November 1864, *ORA,* ser. 1, vol. 43, pt. 1, p. 37.
37. Kean, Robert G. *Inside the Confederate Government: The Diary of Robert Garlick Hill Kean, Head of the Bureau of War,* Edward Younger, ed., (New York: Oxford Univ. Press, 1975); Entry for 20 August 1864, p. 204.
38. Delauter, *62nd Virginia Infantry,* p. 43.
39. Ibid.; Thomas A. Lewis, *The Guns of Cedar Creek* (New York: Harper & Row, 1988), p. 288.
40. Delauter, *18th Virginia Cavalry,* p. 36; Delauter, *62nd Virginia Infantry,* p. 44.
41. Delauter, *62nd Virginia Infantry,* p. 44.
42. Ibid., pp. 44–45.
43. Osborne, *Jubal,* p. 384; Mildred K. Bushong, *Old Jube: A Biography of General Jubal A. Early* (Boyce, Va.: Carr Publishing, 1955), pp. 267–72; Delauter, *18th Virginia Cavalry,* p. 36.
44. Delauter, *18th Virginia Cavalry,* p. 37.

45. Imboden to Maury, 12 January 1876, in *Southern Historical Society Papers*, I: 187–88.
46. Records of the War Department, Collection of Confederate War Records, National Archives, Washington, D.C., in Thomas, "Military Career," p. 146.
47. J. Withers to Imboden, 6 December 1864, *ORA*, ser. 1, vol. 43, pt. 2, p. 937; Delauter, *18th Virginia Cavalry*, p. 37
48. Delauter, *18th Virginia Infantry*, pp. 37–38; Delauter, *62nd Virginia Infantry*, p. 45.
49. Delauter, *18th Virginia Cavalry*, p. 38.
50. Imboden to R.E. Lee, 4 January 1865, Records of the War Dept, Collection of Confederate War Records, National Archives, Washington, D.C.
51. Winder, Special Orders No. 1 & 2, January 1865, *ORA*, ser. 2, vol. 8, p. 12; Imboden, "Statement . . . Regarding the Treatment of Prisoners at Andersonville," *Southern Historical Society Papers*, vol. 1, p. 187; Arch Frederic Blakey, *General John H. Winder, C.S.A.* (Gainesville, Fla.: Univ. of Florida Press, 1991), p. 2; Faust, *Historical Times Illustrated Encyclopedia of the Civil War*, p. 836.
52. James M. McPherson, *Battle Cry of Freedom: The Civil War Era* (New York: Oxford Univ. Press, 1988), pp. 792–93.
53. Blakey, *General John H. Winder*, p. 182.
54. Ibid., p. 197.
55. Faust, *Historical Times Illustrated Encyclopedia of the Civil War*, p. 837; Imboden to Maury, 12 January 1876, *Southern Historical Society Papers*, vol. 1, pp. 192–93.
56. Imboden, "Statement . . . Regarding the Treatment of Prisoners at Andersonville," p. 188.
57. Ibid., pp. 188–89.
58. Ibid., p. 189.
59. Henderson to Imboden, 23 January 1865, *ORA*, ser. 2, vol. 8, pp. 117–18; Imboden to Henderson and General Order No. 2, 15 February 1865, ibid., pp. 121–22.
60. Imboden to Maury, 12 January 1876, *Southern Historical Society Papers*, vol. 1, p. 189.
61. Ibid., p. 190.
62. Ibid., pp. 190–91.
63. Ibid., p. 191.
64. Ibid., pp. 191–92.
65. Ibid., p. 192.
66. Ibid., pp. 192–94.
67. Ibid., pp. 194–96.
68. Ibid., p. 195.
69. Ibid.; Imboden to Hon. John Boyd Thatcher, 31 July 1894; Parole Pass in Imboden Papers, Alderman Library, University of Virginia; G.W. Imboden to Trout, 25 Sep 1900; unsigned order of 5 May 1865, *ORA*, ser. 2, vol. 8, p. 535.

70. Ibid., p. 195.
71. George W. Imboden to Helen Imboden Trout, 25 Sep 1900, Imboden Papers, Alderman Library, University of Virginia.

12. Post–Civil War Career

1. Waddell, *Augusta County*, p. 507.
2. Imboden "Treatment of Prisoners," p. 192.
3. *Lynchburg Virginian*, 30 September 1865.
4. Ibid., 14 November 1865.
5. Woodward, *Defender of the Valley*, p. 156.
6. Company Charter, Virginia State Library and Archives, Richmond, Va., in Woodward, *Defender of the Valley*, p. 156.
7. Imboden to R.E. Lee, 20 November 1865, Archives, Washington & Lee University Library.
8. Imboden to E.M. L'Engle, 13 April 1866, L'Engle Papers, #425, Manuscripts Department and Southern Historical Collection, the University of North Carolina at Chapel Hill.
9. *Lynchburg Virginian*, 2 October 1866.
10. *Lexington Gazette and Banner*, 18 December 1867.
11. Imboden to J.M. Leech, Esqr., 16 August 1869, Archives, Library, Washington & Lee University.
12. Imboden to J.M. Letcher, 16 August 1869, Archives Library, Washington & Lee University, Lexington.
13. Imboden to E.W. Hubbard, 31 July 1867, and 13 Sep 1869. Hubbard Papers, #360, Manuscripts Department and Southern Historical Collection, University of North Carolina at Chapel Hill.
14. Imboden to Col. E.W. Hubbard, 13 September 1869, Hubbard Papers No. 360, Archives, University of North Carolina Library, Chapel Hill.
15. Imboden to Annie Lockett, 8 December 1870, Imboden Papers, Alderman Library, University of Virginia.
16. John F. Stover, *The Railroads of the South, 1865–1900: A Study in Finance and Control* (Chapel Hill, N.C.: Univ. of North Carolina Press, 1955), p. 68.
17. Bruce S. Greenwalt, ed., "Virginians Face Reconstruction: Correspondence from the James Dorman Davidson Papers 1865–1880," *Virginia Magazine of History and Biography*, 78.4 (October 1979): 458.
18. John D. Imboden, *The Coal and Iron Resources of Virginia: Their Extent, Commercial Value, and Early Development Considered* (Richmond, Va.: Clemmitt & Jones, 1872), p. 3.
19. Flyer from "Foreign and Colonial Estates Exchange Agency Limited," undated document in Imboden Papers, Alderman Library, University of Virginia; Imboden to the Hon. John Boyd Thacher, 31 July 1894, Imboden Collection,

Manuscript Division, Library of Congress; *Roanoke Times,* 2 June 1935; Hager, "Imboden," p. 104.

20. Hobbs Records.

21. John A. Cutchins, *A Famous Command: The Richmond Light Infantry Blues* (Richmond: Garrett & Massie, 1934), p. 175; Hobbs Records.

22. Kemper to Imboden, 19 October 1875; Mineralogical Society to Imboden, 13 December 1875. Both in Imboden Papers, Alderman Library, University of Virginia.

23. Scientific American to Imboden, and Patent Office Department to Imboden, both 23 October 1875, Imboden Papers, Alderman Library, University of Virginia.

24. *Richmond Daily Dispatch,* 22, 23, 24 November and 3, 5 December 1875; *Lynchburg Virginian,* 24 November 1875.

25. Imboden to Annie Imboden, 24, 26 and 27 November and 1 December 1875, Imboden Papers, Alderman Library, University of Virginia.

26. A.D. Goshorn to Imboden, 27 August 1874, Imboden Papers, Manuscript Room, University of Virginia Library.

27. Executive Committee of Centennial Exhibition to Imboden, 22 April 1876; Exhibition pass, both in Imboden Papers, Alderman Library, University of Virginia.

28. Imboden to Col. E.W. Hubbard, 22 May 1876, Hubbard Papers No. 360, Manuscripts Department and Southern Historical Collection, University of North Carolina at Chapel Hill.

29. Hager, "Imboden," pp. 108–10.

30. Imboden to J.H. McCue, 6 August 1876, Special Collections 47M63, Archives, Margaret I. King Library, University of Kentucky. Hager, "Imboden," p. 109; There is a detailed description of the invention in an undated article, probably from an Altoona, Pennsylvania newspaper, which was pasted into the Imboden Family Bible in the T. Gibson Hobbs Collection. The article was reprinted in the *Staunton Spectator,* 24 September 1878.

31. Centennial Commission to Imboden, 4 October and 10 November 1876, Imboden Papers, Alderman Library, University of Virginia.

32. Imboden to McCue, 3 October 1876, ibid.

33. Maddex, *Virginia Conservatives,* p. 138; Imboden to J.H. McCue, 18 June 1876, Special Collections 47M63, Archives of Margaret I. King Library, University of Kentucky, Lexington, Ky.

34. Lee Crandall to Imboden, 10 September 1877, Imboden Papers, Alderman Library, University of Virginia; Hager, "Imboden," p. 147.

35. Imboden to McCue, 17 July 1879, ibid.

36. Hager, "Imboden," pp. 112, 117; Lewis Preston Summers, *History of Southwest Virginia, 1746–1786: Washington County, 1777–1870* (Richmond, Va.: J.L. Hill Printing Co., 1903), p. 136.

37. Hager, "Imboden," p. 113.

38. Patricia Hickin, "Seat of Empire! Such Big Stone Gap Will Unquestionably Be Unless an Earthquake Swallows It," *Virginia Cavalcade*, 21.1 (Summer 1971): 23.
39. Wood to Imboden, 1 March 1880, Imboden Papers, Alderman Library, University of Virginia.
40. Imboden to Messrs. Vance and Wood, 16 March, 1880, ibid; List of property owned, 12 May 1880, ibid.
41. Wood to Imboden, no date, ibid.
42. *Journal of the House of Delegates of the State of Virginia, For the Extra Session of 1882* (Richmond, Va.: R.F. Walker, Superintendent Public Printing, 1882), pp. 125, 145, 151, 173.
43. Hickin, "Seat of Empire!", pp. 26–27.
44. Railroad File, Miscellaneous Papers, Rockbridge County Historical Society, Archives, Washington & Lee University.
45. Hickin, "Seat of Empire," pp. 26–27; Railroad File, Rockbridge Historical Society, Archives, Washington & Lee University.
46. Imboden to J.H. McCue, 18 November 1881, Imboden Papers, Alderman Library, University of Virginia; 19 July 1883, Special Collection 47M63, Archives, Margaret I. King Library, University of Kentucky; Edward Henson, *General Imboden and the Economic Development of Wise County, 1880–81* (NP: The Historical Society of Southwest Virginia, 1965), p. 8.
47. Bates to Imboden, 30 July 1883, Imboden Papers, Alderman Library, University of Virginia; Hager, "Imboden," p. 119.
48. Imboden to Thatcher, 31 July 1894, Imboden Papers, Alderman Library, University of Virginia.
49. Imboden to J.H. McCue, 26 December 1887, Special Collection 47M63, Archives, Margaret I. King Library, University of Kentucky; "Damascus and the Damascus Enterprise Company, in Washington Co., Va." 1887 pamphlet; *Journal of the House of Delegates of the State of Virginia, For the Extra Session of 1882* (Richmond, Va.: R.F. Walker, Superintendent Public Printing, 1882), pp. 125, 145, 151, 173.
50. Imboden to J.H. McCue, 14 May 1888, Special Collection 47M63, Margaret I. King Library Archives, University of Kentucky.
51. Louis Fortune Hall, *A History of Damascus, Virginia, 1793–1950*, (NP), pp. 11–12.
52. "Damascus and The Damascus Enterprise Company, in Washington Co., Va." (pamphlet, dated 1887).
53. Ibid.
54. Hager, "Imboden," p. 121; Summers, *Washington County*, p. 692; Hall, *A History of Damascus, Virginia, 1793–1950*, p. 11.
55. Imboden to McCue, 11 February 1889, Special Collection 47M63, Archives, Margaret I. King Library, University of Kentucky.
56. Imboden to McCue, 23 August 1889, ibid.

57. Family Bible.
58. Hall, *A History of Damascus, Virginia,* p. 12.
59. *Southern Historical Society Papers,* vol. 17, pp. 190–266.
60. Summers, *Washington County,* p. 692; Hager, "Imboden," p. 122.
61. Hall, *A History of Damascus, Virginia,* p. 15.
62. Imboden to the Hon. John Boyd Thacher, 31 July 1894, Imboden Collection, Manuscript Division, Library of Congress; J.D. Imboden to F.M. Imboden, 17 September 1894, Hobbs Records.
63. George Imboden to John W. Carroll, 23 September 1895, copied by Gibson Hobbs from the original, Hobbs Collection, Lynchburg, Virginia.
64. Undated article in unidentified paper, Imboden Collection, Alderman Library, University of Virginia
65. Undated clipping from unidentified newspaper, ibid.
66. Frank Imboden to Joseph R. Anderson, 18 January 1904; Frank Imboden to VMI Superintendent W.H. Cocke, 11 December 1926, Archives, Virginia Military Institute; Imboden Family Bible.
67. Helen Trout Genealogy.
68. Jacob Imboden to VMI superintendent Smith, 19 March 1864; John Imboden to Smith, 27 January 1864; John Imboden to Joseph R. Anderson, 18 January 1904, Archives, Virginia Military Institute; Family Bible; Hobbs Records; *New Orleans Daily Picayune,* 16 July 1885.
69. Ibid.; Frank Bliss Imboden to VMI superintendent, 20 March 1939, Imboden Papers, Preston Library, VMI; Frank Howard Imboden to Imboden, 16 September 1875 and 29 July 1878, Imboden Papers, Alderman Library, University of Virginia; Consular Agent J.M. Mitchell Jr. to U.S. Minister to Guatemala W. Godfrey Hunter, 16 December 1899, U.S. Department of State, Record Group 59: Diplomatic Dispatches, Central America, vol. 43; *New Orleans Times Democrat,* 14 December 1899.
70. Imboden Family Papers, T. Gibson Hobbs, Lynchburg, Va..
71. Hobbs Records.

Conclusion

1. Imboden to the Hon. John Boyd Thacher, 31 July 1894, Imboden Collection, Manuscript Division, Library of Congress.
2. Ibid.
3. Ibid.

Bibliography

Manuscript Collections

Anderson, James Blythe. Papers. Archives of Margaret I. King Library, University of Kentucky, Lexington, Ky.
Augusta County Historical Society, Stanton, Va.
CSA Military Leaders Collection. Eleanor S. Brockenbough Library, The Museum of the Confederacy, Richmond, Va.
Hubbard, E.W. Papers. Manuscripts Department and Southern Historical Collection. University of North Carolina at Chapel Hill.
Imboden, John Daniel. Papers. Archives of Preston Library, Virginia Military Institute, Lexington, Va.
Imboden, John Daniel. Papers. Archives of Washington & Lee University Library, Lexington, Va.
Imboden, Francis Marion. Civil War Diary. Transcription. T. Gibson Hobbs Jr. Collection, Lynchburg, Va.
Imboden, John Daniel. Papers. Manuscript Room of Alderman Library, University of Virginia, Charlottesville, Va.
Imboden, John Daniel. Papers. National Archives of Library of Congress, Washington, D.C.
Imboden, John Daniel. Papers. Special Collections, Margaret I. King Library, University of Kentucky, Lexington, Ky.
Imboden Family Records. Genealogical Department, The Church of Jesus Christ of Latter-day Saints.
L'Engle, E.M. Papers. Manuscripts Department and Southern Historical Collection, University of North Carolina at Chapel Hill.
McCue, J. Marshall. Papers. Virginia Historical Society, Richmond, Va.
McCue Family Papers. Special Collections, Alderman Library, University of Virginia, Charlottesville, Va.
Mss #3123. The Western Reserve Historical Society, Cleveland, Ohio.

Pilcher, Eleanor S. Papers. Brockenbrough Library, Museum of the Confederacy, Richmond, Va.
Venable, Charles S. Papers. Manuscripts Department and Southern Historical Collection, University of North Carolina at Chapel Hill.
VMI Archives. Virginia Military Institute, Lexington, Va.
U.S. National Archives. *War Department Records.* Washington, D.C.: U.S. Government Printing Office.

Private Collections

Bushman, Mrs. William. Imboden Genealogy, Staunton, Va.
Doenges, Elizabeth S. Imboden Genealogy, Bartlesville, Okla.
Grand Lodge of Virginia, A.F. & A.M. Richmond, Va.
Hamrick, Richard. Imboden Materials and Photographs, Staunton, Va.
Hobbs, T. Gibson, Jr. Imboden Family Collection, Lynchburg, Va.
———. Imboden Family Bible (handwritten entries beginning with George and Isabella Imboden), Lynchburg, Va.
Mitchell, Jean S. Imobden Genealogy, La Feria, Tex.
Pellinen, Kathryn E. Imboden Genealogy, Anoka, Minn.
Trout, Helen McGuire. 1733 Genealogy and Notes, Imboden Family in U.S.A. 1948. Collection of T. Gibson Hobbs Jr. Lynchburg, Va.

Unpublished Government Documents

U.S. Department of State. Record Group 59. Diplomatic Dispatches, Central America. Vol. 43.

Published Government Materials

State of Virginia. *Acts of the General Assembly of the State of Virginia.* Richmond,1861.
State of Virginia. *Journal of the House of Delegates of the Commonwealth of Virginia.* Richmond, 1839–1840, 1882 (Extra Session).
U.S. Government Printing Office. *Statistical Abstract of the United States: 1885.* Washington, D.C.: U.S. Government Printing Office, 1986.
U.S. Government Printing Office. *The War of the Rebellion: A Compilation of the Official Records of the Union and Confederate Armies.* 128 vols. Washington, D.C.: U.S. Government Printing Office, 1880–1902.

Public Records

Augusta County Common Law Order Book. Staunton, Va, 1858.
Augusta County Deed Book. Staunton, Va., 1796.
Augusta County Will Book. Staunton, Va., 1847.

Bibliography 353

Newspapers

Charleston, S.C. *The News and Courier* (13 July 1885).
Charlottesville, Va. *Advocate* (2 April 1836).
Everett, Pa. *The Everett Republican* (14 December 1894).
Lexington, Va. *Gazette and Banner* (18 December 1867).
Lexington, Va. *Lexington Gazette* (18 November 1863; 15 July 15).
Lexington, Va. *Union* (22 September 1832).
Lynchburg, Va. *Lynchburg Virginian* (29 May 1830; 22 September 1831; 30 September 1865; 14 November 1865; 29 January 1866; 24 November 1875).
New Orleans, La. *Daily Picayune* (16 July 1885).
New Orleans, La. *The Times Democrat* (14 December 1899).
Richmond, Va. *The Dispatch* (1862).
Richmond, Va. *The Enquirer* (1861).
Richmond, Va. *Richmond Daily Dispatch* (22, 23, 24 November, and 3, 5, December 1875).
Richmond, Va. *Times* (25 August 1895).
Richmond, Va. *Whig* (2 October 1832).
Roanoke, Va. *Whig* (2 October 1832).
Staunton, Va. *Staunton Spectator* (4 May 1857; 10 January 1860; 28 February 1860; 24 April 1860; 24 September 1878).
Staunton, Va, *Staunton Vindicator* (13 July 1894).
Wheeling, W.Va., *Wheeling Intelligencer* (29 April, 6 May 6 1863).

Books, Articles, and Theses

Abbott, Haviland. "General John D. Imboden." *West Virginia History* 21, no. 2 (January 1960): 88–122.
Alexander, E.P. *Military Memoirs of a Confederate: A Critical Narrative.* New York: Charles Scribner's Sons, 1907.
Alfriend, Edward M. "Recollections of Stonewall Jackson." *Lippincott's Magazine* 69 (1902): 586.
Anderson, Rual Purcell. *Genealogy Spaid, Anderson, Whitacre, and a Number of Allied Families, also Historical Facts And Memories.* Strasburg, Va.: Shenandoah Press, 1975.
Andrews, Matthew Page. *Virginia: The Old Dominion.* Garden City, N.Y.: Doubleday, Doran & Co., 1937.
Barnard, John Gross. *The Confederate States of America and the Battle of Bull Run.* New York: D. Van Nostrand, 1900.
Baylor, George. *Bull Run to Bull Run; Or, Four Years in the Army of Northern Virginia.* Richmond, Va.: B.F. Johnson, 1900.
Beckelheimer, Christine. "Fayette County, West Virginia, and the War Between the States." *United Daughters of the Confederacy Magazine* (April 1986): 39–41.
Berkeley, Captain Francis B. "Imboden's Dash into Charlestown." *Baltimore Sun-*

day Sun (August 30, 1903). *Southern Historical Society Papers* 31 (1903): 11–18.

Bigelow, John, Jr. *The Campaign of Chancellorsville: A Strategic and Tactical Study.* New Haven, Conn.: Oxford Univ. Press, 1910.

Black, Robert C. *The Railroads of the Confederacy.* Chapel Hill, N.C.: Univ. of North Carolina Press, 1952.

Blackford, Charles M. *The Campaign and Battle of Lynchburg.* Lynchburg, Va.: J.P. Bell Co., 1901. Also published as "The Campaign and Battle of Lynchburg." *Southern Historical Society Papers* 30 (1902): 279–314.

Blakey, Arch Frederic. *General John H. Winder, C.S.A.* Gainesville, Fla.: Univ. of Florida Press, 1991.

Boney, F. N. *John Letcher of Virginia: The Story of Virginia's Civil War Governor.* University, Ala.: Univ. of Alabama Press, 1996.

Boykin, Edward. *Beefsteak Raid.* New York: Funk & Wagnalls, 1960.

Brice, Marshall Moore. *Conquest of a Valley.* Chrlottesville, Va.: Univ. of Virginia Press, 1965.

Bright, Simeon Miller. "A Study in Confederate Guerilla Warfare." *West Virginia History* 12 (1950): 338–94.

Brown, Genevieve. "A History of the Sixth Regiment, West Virginia Infantry Volunteers." Master's thesis, West Virginia University, 1936.

———. "A History of the Sixth Regiment West Virginia Volunteers." *West Virginia History* 9 (1948): 315–68.

Brown, James Earl. "Life of Brigadier General John McCausland." *West Virginia History* 4 (1943): 239–93.

Bushong, Millard A. *General Turner Ashby and Stonewall Jackson's Valley Campaign.* Waynesboro, Va.: Self-published, 1992.

———. *Old Jube: A Biography of General Jubal A. Early.* Boyce, Va.: Carr Publishing, 1955.

Callahan, James Morton. *History of West Virginia, Old and New.* 3 vols. Chicago and New York: The American Historical Society, 1923.

Catalogue of the Trustees, Faculty and Students of Washington

Catlett, James M. and T.B. Warder. *Battle of Young's Branch, or Manassas Plain, Fought July 21, 1861.* Richmond, Va.: Enquirer Book and Job Press, 1862.

Catton, Bruce. *This Hallowed Ground: The Story of the Union Side of the Civil War.* Garden City, New York: Doubleday and Co., 1956.

Chambers, Lenior. *Stonewall Jackson.* New York: W. Morrow, 1956.

Chesson, Michael B. *Richmond after the War, 1865–1890.* Richmond: Virginia State Library, 1891.

Coddington, Edwin B. *The Gettysburg Campaign. A Study in Command.* New York: Charles Scribner's Sons, 1984.

Cole, Arthur Charles. *The Whig Party in the South.* Washington, D.C.: American Historical Association, 1913.

College. Lexington, Va. For Session 1841–42. Lexington, Va.: Printed at the "Gazette" Office, A. Waddill, Printer, 1842.

Collins, Darrell L. *The Battles of Cross Keys and Port Republic, June 8–9, 1862.* Lynchburg, Va.: H.E. Howard, 1993.
Collins, John L. "A Prisoner's March from Gettysburg to Staunton." In *Battles and Leaders of the Civil War.* Vol. 3. New York: Castle Books, 1956, p. 429–33.
Commager, Henry Steele. *The Blue and the Gray.* Vols. 1 and 2. Indianapolis, Ind.: Bobbs-Merrill, 1950.
"The Confederacy Mounts its Iron Horse." *Ties: The Southern Railway System Magazine* 15, no. 5 (April 1961): 16–17.
Cook, Roy Bird. *Lewis County in the Civil War, 1861–1865.* Charleston, W.Va.: Jarrett Publishing Co., 1924.
Couper, William. *History of the Shenandoah Valley.* 3 vols. New York: Lewis Historical Publishing Co., 1952.
Crockett, Gary I. "The Battery That Saved the Day." *Field Artillery Journal* 30 (January-February 1940): 26–33.
Crute, Joseph H., Jr. *Confederate Staff Officers.* Powhatan, Va.: Derwent Books, 1982.
Culbertson, Charles. "Mary Julia and the General." *Mary Baldwin Magazine* 5, no. 1 (August 1991): 4–6.
Cunnigham, Frank. *Knight of the Confederacy: General Turner Ashby.* San Antonio, Tex.: Naylor, 1960.
Curry, Ron Watson. "The Newspaper Press and the Civil War." *West Virginia History* 6 (1945): 225–64.
Curtis, Francis. *The Republican Party: A History of Its Fifty Years' Existence and a Record of its Measures and Leaders, 1854–1894.* 2 Vols. New York: G.P. Putnam's Sons, 1904.
Cutchins, John A. *A Famous Command: The Richmond Light Infantry Blues.* Richmond, Va.: Garrett and Massie, 1934.
Davis, Burke. *Jeb Stuart, The Last Cavalier.* New York: Holt, Rinehart & Winston, 1963.
Davis, William C. *Battle at Bull Run: A History of the First Major Campaign of the Civil War.* Garden City, N.Y.: Doubleday, 1977.
———. *The Battle of New Market.* Baton Rouge, La.: Louisiana State Univ. Press, 1975.
Delauter, Roger U., Jr. *18th Virginia Cavalry.* Lynchburg, Va.: H.E. Howard, 1985.
———. *62nd Virginia Infantry.* Lynchburg, Va.: H.E. Howard, 1988.
———. *McNeill's Rangers.* Lynchburg, Va.: H.E. Howard, 1986.
Denney, Robert E. *Civil War Prisons and Escapes: A Day to Day Chronicle.* New York: Sterling Publishing, 1993.
Dickinson, Jack L. *Jenkins of Greenbottom: A Civil War Saga.* Charleston, W.Va.: Pictorial Histories Publishing Co., 1988.
Dowdey, Clifford and Louis Manarin, editors. *The Wartime Papers of R.E. Lee.* Boston: Little, Brown, 1961.
Driver, Robert J., Jr. *Lexington and Rockbridge County in the Civil War.* Lynchburg, Va.: H.E. Howard, 1989.

———. *The Staunton Artillery and McClanahan's Battery.* Lynchburg, Va.: H.E. Howard, 1988.
Duncan, Richard R. *Lee's Endangered Left: The Civil War in Western Virginia, Spring of 1864.* Baton Rouge, La.: Louisiana State Univ. Press, 1998.
Du Pont, Henry A. *The Campaign of 1864 in the Valley of Virginia and the Expedition to Lynchburg.* New York: National Americana Society, 1925.
Early, Jubal A. *Autobiographical Sketch and Narrative of the War Between the States.* Philadelphia, Pa.: J.B. Lippincott, 1912.
Evans, Clemont A. *Confederate Military History.* 12 Vols. Atlanta: Confederate Publishing Co., 1899.
Farwell, Bryon. *Stonewall: A Biography of General Thomas J. Jackson.* New York: W.W. Norton, 1982.
Faust, Patricia L., editor. *Historical Times Illustrated Encyclopedia of the Civil War.* New York: Harper and Row, 1986.
Fish, Carl Russell. *The Restoration of the Southern Railroads.* Madison, Wis.: Univ. of Wisconsin Press, 1919.
Freeman, Douglas Southall. *Lee's Lieutenant's: A Study in Command.* 3 Vols. New York: Charles Scribner's Sons, 1970.
French, Steve. "'Hurry was the Order of the Day': Imboden and the Wagon Train of the Wunded." *North & South* 2, no. 6 (June 1999): 35–42.
Gainer, Bernard. "Early Oil Development in West Virginia." *West Virginia History* 21 (January 1960): 84–87.
Gilmore, Harry. *Four Years in the Saddle.* New York: Harper and Brothers, 1865.
Govan, Gilbert E. and James W. Livingood. *A Different Valor: General Joseph E. Johnston, C.S.A.* Indianapolis, Ind.: Bobbs-Merrill, 1956.
Greenwalt, Bruce S., ed. "Virginians Face Reconstruction: Correspondence from the James Dorman Davidson Papers 1865–1880." *Virginia Magazine of History and Biography* 78, no. 4 (October 1979): 447–63.
Hager, William D. "The Civilian Life and Accomplishments of John Daniel Imboden." Master's thesis, James Madison University, 1988.
Hall, Louise Fortune. *A History of Damascus, Virginia, 1793–1950.* Abingdon, Va.: John Anderson Press, 1950.
Hall, William Hall. "The Battle of McConnellsburg." *Fulton Democrat* (4 April 1888).
Hanson, Joseph Mills. *Bull Run Remembers.* Manassas, Va.: National Capital Publishers, 1953.
Henderson, G.F.R. *Stonewall Jackson and the American Civil War.* New York: Grosset & Dunlap, 1943.
Henry, Robert Selph. *The Story of the Confederacy.* New York: New Home Library, 1936.
Henson, Edward L. "General Imboden and the Economic Development of Wise County, 1880–81." Historical Society of Southwest Virginia, 1965. Pamphlet.
Hess, James W. *Guide to Manuscripts and Archives in the West Virginia Collection.* Morgantown, W.Va.: West Virginia University Library, 1974.

Hickin, Patricia. "Seat of Empire! Such Big Stone Gap Will Unquestionably Be Unless an Earthquake Swallows It." *Virginia Cavalcade* 21, no. 1 (Summer 1971): 22–33.
Hilldrup, Robert Leroy. "Romance of a man in Gray." *West Virginia History* 22 (1961): 166–83.
Humphreys, Milton W. *A History of the Lynchburg Campaign*. Charlottesville, Va.: Michie Co., 1924.
Imboden, John D. "The Battle of New Market." *Battles and Leaders of the Civil War*. Vol. 4. New York: Castle Books, 1956, pp. 480–86.
———. "The Battle of Piedmont." *Confederate Veteran* 31 (1923): 459–61; 32(1924): 18–20.
———. *The Coal and Iron Resources of Virginia: Their Extent, Commercial Value, and Early Development Considered*. Richmond, Va.: Clemmitt & Jones, 1872.
———. "The Confederate Retreat from Gettysburg." *Battles and Leaders of the Civil War*. Vol. 3. New York: Castle Books, 1956, pp. 420–29.
———. "Damascus and the Damascus Enterprise Company in Washington Co., Va." N.p., 1887.
———. "Fire, Sword, and the Halter." In *The Annals of the War Written by Leading Participants North and South*. Edited by Alexander K. McClure. Philadelphia, Pa.: Times Publishing, 1878, pp. 169–83.
———. "Incidents of the the First Bull Run." *Battles and Leaders of the Civil War*. Vol. 1. New York: Castle Books, 1956, pp. 229–39.
———. "Jackson at Harpers Ferry in 1861." *Battles and Leaders of the Civil War*. Vol. 1. New York: Castle Books, 1956, pp. 111–25.
———. "Reminiscences of Lee and Jackson." *Galaxy Magazine* 12, no. 5 (November 1871):41, 627–34.
———. "Report." *The Rebellion Record*. Vol. 2. New York: B.B. Russell, 1862, pp. 43–45.
———. "Statement of General John D. Imboden to General D.H. Murray on January 12, 1876, Regarding the Treatment of Prisoners at Andersonville." *Southern Historical Society Papers*, 1, no. 3 (March 1876): 187–201.
———. "Statement of General J.D. Imboden." *Southern Historical Society Papers* 1 (January–June 1876): 187–96.
———. "Stonewall Jackson in the Shenandoah." *Battles and Leaders of the Civil War*. Vol. 2. New York: Castle Books, 1956, pp. 282–98.
Johnston, Angus J. II. "Disloyalty on Confederate Railroads in Virginia." *Virginia Magazine of History and Biography* 63 (1955): 410–26.
———. *Virginia Railroads in the Civil War*. Chapel Hill, N.C.: Univ. of North Carolina Press for the Virginia Historical Society, 1961.
Johnston, Joseph E. *Narrative of Military Operations During the Civil War*. New York: Da Capo, 1959. Reprint.
Johnston, R.M. *Bull Run: Its Strategies and Tactics*. New York: Houghton Mifflin, 1913.
Jones, Virgil Carrington. *Gray Ghosts and Rebel Raiders*. New York: Holt, 1956.

Kean, Robert G. *Inside the Confederate Government: The Diary of Robert Garlick Hill Kean, Head of the Bureau of War.* Edited by Edward Younger. New York: Oxford Univ. Press, 1975.
Kelley, Robert. *The Shaping of the American Past.* Englewood Cliffs, N.J.: Prentice Hall, 1975.
Kellogg, Sanford C. *The Shenandoah Valley and Virginia, 1861 to 1865.* New York: Neale Publishing Co., 1903.
Kleese, Richard B. *Shenandoah County in the Civil War: The Turbulent Years.* Lynchburg, Va.: H.E. Howard, 1992.
Krick, Robert K. *Conquering the Valley. Stonewall Jackson at Port Republic.* New York: William Morrow, 1996.
———. *Lee's Colonels.* Dayton, Ohio: Morningside Bookshop, 1979.
Lang, Theodore F. *Loyal West Virginia from 1861 to 1865.* Baltimore, Md.: The Deutsch Publishing Co., 1895.
Lee, Robert E. *Lee's Dispatches. Unpublished Letters of General Robert E. Lee, C.S.A. to Jefferson Davis and the War Department of the Confederate States of America, 1862–65. From the Private Collection of Wymberley Jones de Renne of Wormsloe, Georgia.* Edited with an introduction by Douglas Southall Freeman. New York: G.P. Putnam's Sons, 1915.
Lee, Susan P. *Memoirs of William Nelson Pendleton, D.D.* Philadelphia, Pa.: J.P. Lippincott Co., 1893.
Leonard, Cynthia Miller, compiler. *The General Assembly of Virginia: July 30, 1819–January 11, 1978: A Bicentennial Register of Members.* Richmond, Va.: Published for the General Assembly of Virginia by the Virginia State Library, 1978.
Lewis, Thomas A. *The Shenandoah in Flames.* Alexandria, Va.: Time-Life Publications, 1987.
Longacre, Edward G. *Mounted Raids of the Civil War.* New York: Bison Books, 1975.
Longstreet, James. *From Manassas to Appomattox, Memoirs of the Civil War in America.* Philadelphia: J.B. Lippincott, 1896.
Lorant, Stefan. *The Glorious Burden.* Lenox, Mass.: Authors Edition, Inc., 1976.
Loth, Calder, ed. *The Virginia Landmarks Registrar.* 3d ed. Charlottesville, Va.: Univ. Press of Virginia, 1986.
Maddex, Jack P., Jr. *The Virginia Conservatives, 1867–1879: A Study of Reconstruction Politics.* Chapel Hill, N.C.: The Univ. of North Carolina Press, 1970.
Mahon, Michael G. *The Shenandoah Valley, 1861–1865: The Destruction of the Granary of the Confederacy.* Mechanicsburg, Pa.: Stackpole Books, 1999.
May, C. E. *Life Under Four Flags in the North River Basin of Virginia.* Verona, Va.: McClure Printing Co., 1976.
McClure, Alexander K., ed. *The Annals of the War Written by Leading Participants North and South.* Philadelphia, Pa.: Times Publishing, 1878.
McCue, John N., compiler. *The McCues of the Old Dominion.* Mexico, Mo.: Missouri Printing and Publishing, 1912.
McDonald, Archie P. *Make Me a Map of the Valley: The Civil War Journals of Stonewall Jackson's Topographer.* Dallas, Tex.: Southern Methodist Univ. Press, 1973.

Bibliography 359

McDonald, William N. *A History of the Laurel Brigade: Originally the Ashby Cavalry of the Army of Northern Virginia and Chew's Battery.* Baltimore, Md.: Sun Job Printing Office, 1907.
McNeil, John A. "The Imboden Raid and Its Effects." *Times-Dispatch* (September 1, 1906), reprinted in the *Southern Historical Society Papers* 34 (1906): 294-312.
McPherson, James M. *Battle Cry of Freedom: The Civil War Era.* New York: Oxford Univ. Press, 1988.
Mitchell, Joseph B. *Decisive Battles of the Civil War.* New York: Putnam, 1955.
Morris, George and Susan Foutz. *Lynchburg in the Civil War: The City—the People—the Battle.* Lynchburg, Va.: H.E. Howard, 1984.
Morton, Owen F. *A History of Rockbridge County, Virginia.* Baltimore, Md.: Regional Publishing Company, 1980.
Naisawald, L. Van Loan. *Grape and Canister.* New York: Oxford Univ. Press, 1960.
Newton, Steven H. *Joseph E. Johnston and the Defense of Richmond.* Lawrence, Kans.: Univ. Press of Kansas, 1998.
Nicolay, John G. *The Outbreak of the Rebellion.* New York: Charles Scribner's Sons, 1881.
O'Ferrall, Charles T. *Forty Years of Active Service.* New York: The Neale Publishing Co., 1904.
Opie, John N. *A Rebel Cavalrymen with Lee, Stuart and Jackson.* Chicago, Ill.: W.B. Conkey, Co., 1899.
Ormsby, R. McKinley. *A History of the Whig Party.* 2nd ed. Boston: Crosby, Nichols & Company, 1860.
Osborne, Charles C. *Jubal: The Life and Times of General Jubal A. Early, C.S.A., Defender of the Lost Cause.* Chapel Hill, N.C.: Univ. of North Carolina Press, 1992.
Page, Thomas Nelson. *Robert E. Lee, Man and Soldier.* New York: Scribners, 1923.
Peyton, J. Lewis. *History of Augusta County, Virginia.* Bridgewater, Va.: C.J. Carrier, 1953.
Pfanz, Donald C. *Richard S. Ewell, A Soldier's Life.* Chapel Hill, N.C.: Univ. of North Carolina Press, 1998.
Pond, George E. *The Shenandoah Valley in 1864.* New York: Charles Scribner's Sons, 1883.
The Rebellion Record: A Diary of American Events. Vol. 2. Edited by Frank Moore. New York:. G.P. Putnam, 1862.
Register of Former Cadets. Lexington, Va.: Virginia Military Institute, 1927, 1957.
Rhodes, Charles Dudley. "John Daniel Imboden." *Dictionary of American Biography.* Vol. 9. Edited by Dumas Malone. New York: 1932, pp. 460-61.
Roberts, Joseph K. *Annotated Geological Bibliography of Virginia.* Richmond, Va.: The Dietz Press for The Alderman Library, University of Virginia, 1942.
Robertson, James I., Jr. *Stonewall Jackson: The Man, the Soldier, the Legend.* New York: Macmillan, 1997.
Rockbridge Retired Teachers Association, eds. *A Brief History of Education in Rockbridge County-Lexington-Buena Vista: 1748-1980.* Lexington and Buena Vista, Va.: Rockbridge Retired Teachers Association, 1980.

Sanderlin, Walter S. *The Great National Project: A History of the Chesapeake and the Ohio Canal.* Baltimore, Md.: Johns Hopkins Press, 1946.
Schildt, John W. *Roads from Gettysburg.* Chewsville, Md.: Self published, 1979.
Sigel, Franz. "Sigel in the Shenandoah Valley in 1864." In *Battles and Leaders of the Civil War.* Vol. 4. New York: Castle Books, 1956, pp. 487–91.
Silverstone, Paul H. *Warships of the Civil War Navies.* Annapolis, Md.: Naval Institute Press, 1989.
Simms, Henry H. *The Rise of the Whigs of Virginia: 1824–1840.* Richmond: The William Byrd Press, 1929.
Simpson, Craig M. *A Good Southerner: The Life of Henry A. Wise of Virginia.* Chapel Hill, N.C.: Univ. of North Carolina Press, 1985.
Stackpole, Edward J. "The Day 18,000 Rebels marched on Washington." *Civil War Times* 2 (February, 1961): 5–6, 19.
Stanard, Beverly. *Letters of a New Market Cadet.* Edited by John G. Barrett and Robert K. Turner Jr. Chapel Hill, N.C.: Univ. of North Carolina Press, 1961.
Steele, Matthew Forney. *American Campaigns.* 2 Vols. Washington, D.C.: United States Infantry Association, 1909.
Stephens, Robert Grier, Jr., ed. *Intrepid Warrior: Clement Anselon Evans, Confederate General from Georgia: Life, Letters, and Diaries of the War Years.* Dayton, Ohio: Morningside Books, 1992.
Stevenson, James Hunter. *Boots and Sattles.* Harrisburg, Pa.: Patriot Publishing Co., 1879.
Stover, John F. *The Railraods of the South, 1865–1900: A Study in Finance and Control.* Chapel Hill, N.C.: Univ. of North Carolina Press, 1955.
Summers, Festus P. *The Baltimore and Ohio in the Civil War.* New York: G.P. Putnam's Sons, 1939.
———. "The Jones-Imboden Raid." *West Virginia History* 1, pp. 15–29.
Summers, Lewis Preston. *History of Southwest Virginia, 1746–1786: Washington County, 1777–1870.* Richmond, Va.: J.L. Hill Printing Company, 1903.
Swift, General Eben. "The Military Education of Robert E. Lee." *Virginia Magazine of History and Biography* 35, pp. 97–160.
Thomas, Clayton Malcolm, III. "The Military Career of John D. Imboden." Master's thesis, University of Virginia, 1965.
Tucker, Glenn. *High Tide at Gettysburg.* New York: Konecky & Konecky, 1958.
Turner, Edward Raymond. *The New Market Campaign.* Richmond, Va.: Whitlet & Shepperson, 1912.
Turner, George Edgar. *Victory Rode the Rails: The Strategic Place of the Railroads in the Civil War.* Indianapolis: Bobbs-Merrill, 1953.
U.S. Navy, Naval History Division. *Civil War Naval Chronology, 1861–1865.* Washington, D.C.: Government Printing Office, 1971.
Vandiver, Frank. *Jubal's Raid: General Early's Famous Attack on Washington in 1864.* Westport, Conn.: Greenwood Press, 1960.
———. *Mighty Stonewall.* New York: McGraw-Hill, 1957.

———. *Rebel Brass: The Confederate Command System*. Baton Rouge, La.: Louisiana State Univ. Press, 1956.
Waddell, Joseph A. *Annals of Augusta County Virginia: From 1726 to 1871*. Staunton, Va.: C. Russell Caldwell, 1902.
Walker, Gary. *Hunter's Fiery Raid Through Virginia's Valley*. Roanoke: A&W Enterprise, 1989.
Watters, Mary. *The History of Mary Baldwin College, 1842–1942*. Staunton, Va.: Mary Baldwin College, 1942.
Wayland, John Walter. *The German Element of the Shenandoah Valley of Virginia*. Harrisonburg, Va.: C.J. Carrier, 1978.
Weems, John Edward. *To Conquer a Peace: The War Between the United States and Mexico*. Garden City, N.Y.: Doubleday, 1974.
Welcher, Frank J. *The Union Army, 1861–1865. Organization and Operations*. Vol. 1. *The Eastern Theater*. Bloominmgton, Ind.: Indiana Univ. Press, 1989.
Wiley, Bell I. *The Life of Johnny Reb: The Common Soldier of the Confederacy*. Baton Rouge, La.: Louisiana State Univ. Press, 1943.
Wilson, Howard McKnight. *The Tinkling Spring, Headwater of Freedom: A Study of the Church and Her People, 1732–1952*. Fishersville, Va.: The Tinkling Spring and Hermitage Presbyterian Churches, 1954.
Wilshin, Francis F. *Manassas: National Battlefield Park, Virginia* (National Park Service Historical Handbook Series No. 15). Washington, D.C.: National Park Service, 1953.
Wise, Barton H. *The Life of Henry A. Wise of Virginia, 1806–1876*. New York: The MacMillan Co., 1899.
Wise, Jennings C. *The Military History of the Virginia Military Institute from 1861 to 1865*. Lynchburg, Va.: J.P. Bell, 1915.
Wood, W. Birdbeck, and Sir James E. Edmonds. *Military History of the Civil War*. New York: Putnam, 1960.
Woodward, Harold R., Jr. *Defender of the Valley: Brigadier General John Daniel Imboden, C.S.A.* Berryville, Va.: Rockbridge Publishing, 1996.

Index

Abercrombie, John J., 45
Abingdon Coal & Iron Railway Company, 307
Alfriend, Edward M., 89
Anaconda Plan, 24
Anderson, John L., 252
Anderson, Joseph R., 18, 252
Anderson, Richard, 271
Anderson, S.R., 72
Anderson, William D., 16
Andersonville Prison, 280–87, 290, 303
Antietam, Battle of, 98
Armentrout, George, 65
Armistead, David T., 294
Armistead, Lewis, 151
Ashby, Richard, 28–29, 31,
Ashby, Turner, 28–29, 31, 41–42, 48, 71–72, 77, 79–83, 86–88, 92
Aston, William, 304
Atlantic, Mississippi, & Ohio Railroad, 302
Augusta Female Seminary, 12
Averell, William W., 137–38, 174, 177, 183–88, 190–91, 199–200, 202, 225, 235, 242, 244, 247–48, 253, 255, 259, 269–70, 273
Aylett, William R., 161

Baker, L.S., 153

Baker, Narval, 144, 155–56, 161–62, 164–66, 171, 180, 271–72, 279
Baldwin, James, 30
Balthis, William L., 31, 68
Baltimore & Ohio Railroad, 34–35, 39, 41, 70, 72, 92, 96–100, 103, 108, 112–15, 118–19, 123, 126, 129, 131, 137–38, 143–44, 172–73, 176–78, 184, 199, 202, 223, 263–64, 270, 297, 302
Banks, Nathaniel P., 76, 78–83, 200
Barbour, Alfred M., 28–29, 34
Barker, James M., 304
Bartlett, J.H., 201
Bartow, Francis S., 52, 54, 56–57, 61
Bate, William B., 302
Baylor, William S.H., 16, 31, 35, 38, 40
Beall, D.E., 177
Beauregard, Pierre G.T., 21, 46–48, 50, 57–58, 62, 64, 72, 75
Beausacy, Count A., de, 295
Bee, Barnard E., 45, 48–57, 61–62
Bell, John, 18
Benjamin, Judah P., 64, 73, 81
Berkeley, Carter, 182, 237, 239, 260
Berkeley, Frank B., 180, 229
Berkley, H.M., 230, 237,
Beverly (West Virginia), skirmish at, 121–23

Birney, James C., 8
Black, J.L., 161–62
Blackford, Charles, 250
Blenker, Louis, 85
Blue, Monroe, 108, 228
Blue Ridge Railroad Company, 10
Bonaparte, Napoléon, 70
Boone, Daniel, 299
Boyd, William H., 187, 202, 207–8
Bradford, Hill C., 65
Bragg, Braxton, 115, 178, 245, 254, 271–72,
Brandt, Logan, 65
Breckinridge, John C., 18, 197, 201–2, 204–6, 208–10, 212–22, 224, 248, 250, 254–56, 259, 262–63, 269, 313
Bristoe Station Campaign, 178–79
Bristol & North Carolina Narrow Gauge Railway Company, 302
Brown, John, 14–15, 36, 41
Browne, W.H., 230, 237
Bryan, Thomas A., 228, 230, 235, 239, 240
Buchanan, James, 11, 13–14, 20–21
Buford, John, 147–48, 151, 163–65
Bull Run (Manassas), First Battle of, 46–62
Burke, Jesse S., 77
Burnside, Ambrose E., 71, 101, 119
Butler, Benjamin F., 39, 200
Byrd, John T., 184

Cabell, W.L., 64
Callahan, James, 41, 96, 183
Campbell, Colin, 307
Carrington, Nanine, 311
Carter, Welby, 31
Casler, John D., 108
Caton, Bruce, 45
Cedar Creek, Battle of, 275–76
Centennial Exhibition, 296–98, 314
Chamberlain, Joshua, 148
Chambliss, John R., 163

Charles Town (West Virginia), skirmish at, 180–81
Chesapeake & Ohio Canal, 72, 144
Chesapeake & Ohio Railroad, 294–95, 297
Chew, Robert L., 21
Chilton, R.H., 70
Chrisman, George, 227, 234
Christian, Gilbert, 2
Christian, Lucy, 2
Clay, Henry, 8
Cloyd's Mountain, Battle of, 205, 224
Cobb, Howell, 285, 287
Coddington, Edwin, 165
Collins, John L., 170–71
Columbian Exposition, 307, 314
Connelsville Coke & Iron Company, 302
Cooper, Samuel, 48, 108, 163, 225, 278
Corley, James L., 166
Couch, Darius, 159
Couper, William, 218
Cox, Jacob D., 71
Cranford, Samuel, 233–34
Crook, George, 200, 205–6, 223, 225, 235, 242, 244–45, 247–48, 253, 255, 257–59, 268–69, 273
Cross Keys, Battle of, 85–86, 88
Crozet, Claudius, 5, 10
Curtin, Andrew G., 127
Custer, George A., 149, 157, 278

Dabney, Robert, 87
Damascus Enteprise Company, 303–4
Davidson, James D., 190, 293
Davis, Jefferson, 20–21, 24–25, 61–62, 75, 81, 97, 102–3, 108, 129, 152, 174, 195–97, 216, 247
Davis, T. Sturgis, 173, 179–80, 188, 201, 206, 220, 227, 234
Delauter, Roger, 218
Diller, Eleanor, 1
Dimmock, Charles, 29

Douglas, Stephen A., 14, 18
Douthat, Henry C., 249–50
Doyle, Robert, 228
Drake, R.T.W., 31
Dred Scott, 14
Dred Scott v. Sanford, 13–14
Driver, Robert J., Jr., xii, 40
Droop Mountain, Battle of, 184–85, 197
Duffié, Alfred N., 248–52, 257–59
Dunn, A.C., 117, 120–21, 133–34
Du Pont, Henry A., 217–18, 225, 233, 235, 240–42, 258

Early, Jubal, 115, 149, 165, 190–92, 193–97, 250, 253–54, 256–69, 270–75, 277–78
East Tennesse & Virginia Railroad, 302
Echols, John, 184–85, 191, 209, 213, 217, 220, 248, 254, 262, 269, 291
Elzey, Arnold, 85, 259, 262
Erie Railroad, 297
Erwin, William D., 146
Evans, Nathan G., 52, 54
Ewell, Richard, 65, 79, 81–82, 85–87, 89–90, 140, 143, 145, 148–49, 157–58, 162–63, 168–69, 178, 197, 253

Falling Waters, skirmish at, 45
Farragut, David G., 75
Farwell, Bryon, 40
Fernsler, Catherine W., 2
Fillmore, Millard, 11
Finley, Samuel B., 237
Fisher's Hill, Battle of, 274
Flournoy, Thomas S., 82, 192
Floyd, John B., 17
Fontaine, Edmund, 28
Foote, Andrew H., 75
Forbes, A.J., 304
Fort Pickens, 21
Fort Sumter, 21–22
Frazier, William, 6–7

Freeman, Douglas Southall, 194, 253, 266, 271
Frémont, John C., 11, 76, 78–81, 83–87, 89–91, 222
French, William H., 161, 163
Fulkerson, Samuel V., 77
Funsten, Oliver R., 28–29, 31

Garber, Asher W., 31, 54
Garner, R.R., 72
Garnett, Richard B., 77–78, 151
Garnett, Robert S., 96
Gartell, Lucius J., 282
Gauley Coal Company, 294–95
Gettysburg, Battle of, 147–50
Gibson, George William, 310
Gibson, John Thomas, 25–26, 311
Giddings, John C., 37
Gilham, William, 72
Gilmor, Harry, 112, 173, 175, 178–82, 192, 194, 196, 201, 207, 209–10, 220, 223, 226, 268
Given, Alexander, 233
Glazebrook, L.W., 292
Goochland and Pittsylvania Asbestos Mines, 294
Gordon, John B., 254, 257, 262–63, 265, 269, 275, 277
Gosport (Norfolk) Navy Yard, 29–30
Grant, Ulysses S., 75, 170, 200, 202, 223–25, 227, 247–48, 253, 262, 267, 272–74, 286–87
Gratton, Mrs. Robert, 229
Green, John S., 126
Greenland Gap (West Virginia), fighting at, 125–26
Gregg, David M., 149, 271

Hager, William D., xii
Hall, William, 104
Halleck, Henry W., 103, 118, 126, 156–57, 168, 227, 275
Hampton, Wade, 55–56, 60, 153, 247, 271

Hancock, Winfield Scott, 149
Harding, John F., 94
Hardy, Lord, 294
Harman, Asher W., 126–31
Harman, Nathan G., 67
Harman, John A., 28, 38–39, 71, 166
Harman, Michael, 291
Harman, Thomas L., 16, 30–31, 59, 65
Harman, William H., 16, 30–31, 35, 38, 201–2
Harney, William S., 35, 39
Harnsberger, Henry, 227, 234
Harper, Kenton, 30–31, 33, 35–39
Harpers Ferry Federal Arsenal, 14–15, 26–35
Harriet Lane, 67
Hart, Benjamin, 291
Hart, James F., 153–54, 159, 161–62
Hawk's Nest Coal Mines, 195, 314
Hayes, Rutherford B., 205, 298
Heintzelman, Samuel, 55
Henderson, G.F.R., 40
Henderson, H.A.M., 282
Henkel, Elon, 208
Henry, Judith, 57
Hernández, Joasquin, 311
Heth, Henry, 169
Higginbotham, John, 120
Higgins, Jacob, 203
Hill, Ambrose P., 145–47, 150, 168–69, 178–79
Hill, Daniel H., 256
Hill, Hannibal, 276
Hobbs, T. Gibson, Jr., xii
Hobson, McNary, 175–76
Hoke, Robert F., 160
Holmes, Theophilus Hunter, 72
Hood, John B., 163
Hooker, Joseph, 115, 140–41, 143, 145
Hopkins, Luther, 153
Hotchkiss, Jedediah, xi, 167, 275
Huffman, John S., 120

Hull, George W., 81
Humphreys, Milton, 242
Hunter, David, 55, 222–29, 232–33, 235–36, 239–53, 255–60, 262, 269, 296, 313
Hunter, George, 257

Imboden, Angia Mildred Dickinson, 309
Imboden, Anna Stuart Dickinson, 310
Imboden, Annie Harper Lockett, 292–93, 304
Imboden, Benjamin, 2, 7
Imboden, Carmelata Ramdales, 311
Imboden, David, 2
Imboden, Edna Paulding Porter, 291–92
Imboden, Elizabeth Shepherd Smith, 310
Imboden, Eliza Catherine ("Kate"), 2–3, 311
Imboden, Eliza McCue ("Dice"), 6–7, 9, 11, 110
Imboden, Florence Crockett, 306
Imboden, Francis Marion ("Frank"), 2–3, 25–26, 71, 130, 146, 156, 158, 163–64, 171–72, 175–76, 182, 234, 284, 288, 295, 298, 301, 30, 310
Imboden, Frank Howard, 6, 11, 310, 311
Imboden, George William (1793–1875), 2, 130–31
Imboden, George William (1836–1922), 2–3, 16, 25–26, 30, 65, 68, 88, 97, 112, 121, 124, 132, 143, 154, 159, 167, 172, 179, 181, 186, 201, 209–10, 220, 231–33, 268, 278–79, 287, 295, 307–10
Imboden, George William (1857–1862), 11, 110, 311
Imboden, Helen Maguire, 293, 311
Imboden, Henry, 2
Imboden, Isabella ("Bel"), 6

Index 367

Imboden, Isabella Wunderlich, 2, 130–31
Imboden, Jacob Peck ("Jake"), 2–3, 25–26, 209, 310–11
Imboden, James Adam ("Jim"), 2, 25–26, 307, 310
Imboden, Janie ("Jennie") Crawford, 6, 11
Imboden, Johannes, 1
Imboden, John D.: recollections of events called into question, xi-xii; birth and childhood, 1–3; student at Washington College, 4–5; fondness for VMI, 5; and the practice of law, 5–7, 17; marries Eliza McCue, 6; and militia service, 7, 13, 15–16; and politics, 7–9; and railroad promotion, 8; service in the Virginia House of Delegates, 9–11; fails to win election to Congress, 12; marries Mary McPhail, 12; interested in investing in land in Florida, 17; director of Virginia Arms Manufacturing Co., 18; and slavery, 19; and secession, 20–21, 25; helps arrange prisoner exchange of his brother Frank, 26, 71; and effort to seize Harpers Ferry, 26, 28–34; at Harpers Ferry, 34–43; describes Thomas J. Jackson, 38; describes "capture" of B&O trains, 39–41; activities prior to First Battle of Bull Run, 44–46; role in First Battle of Bull Run, 48–62; injured, 59; at Manassas, 61–65; in eastern Virginia, 65–68; leaves the Staunton Artillery, 68; forms Partisan Rangers, 69–74; during Jackson's Valley Campaign, 78–81, 83–85, 91–93; in Battle of Port Republic, 87–90; 93–95; raids into West Virginia (1862), 95–101, 103–6; 102–3, 107–10; promoted to brigadier general, 110; in Jones-

Imboden Raid (1863), 111–25, 127, 129–37; 139–40; in Gettysburg Campaign, 140–56; 158–67, 170, 172; in Battle of Williamsport, 160–65; receives command of the Valley District, 172; 173–79; raid into West Virginia (October 1863) 180–84; 184–92, 193–99; in 1864 Shenandoah Valley Campaign, 199–210; in Battle of New Market, 210–20; faces offensive by General Hunter, 221–33; and Battle of Piedmont, 233–38; 241–43; in subsequent fighting, 244–47; in Lynchburg Campaign, 247, 249–50, 252, 254, 256–57, 259–62; in Early's descent on Washington, 262–64; ill from typhoid, 264; resumes command of Northwestern Brigade, 268–69; 270–72; on medical leave, 272; 273–76; relinquishes command of the Northwestern Brigade, 278; on prisoner-of-war duty, 279–87; paroled, 287; regains health, 288; subpoenaed for Wirz trial, 290; wife Mary dies, 290; works for National Express Transportation Company, 291; marries Edna Porter, 291; works in Virginia land promotion, 292; wife Edna dies, 292; marries Annie Lockett, 293; active in promotion of Virginia natural resources, 293–95; publishes *The Coal and Iron Resources of Virginia*, 294; travels to London, 294; invents railroad car lifter, 295; incident involving Bradley T. Johnson, 295–96; involvement with Philadelphia Centennial Exhibition, 296–98; inventions, 297–98; interest in politics, 298; promotes economic

development of southwestern Virginia, 299–303; writes articles on Civil War; wife Annie dies; general manager of Damascus Enterprise Company, 304–5; marries Florence Crockett, 306; attends Columbian Exposition, 307; death, 308, 310; assessment of, 311–14
Imboden, John Daniel, Jr., 13, 298
Imboden, John H., 2
Imboden, Johnnie Meems, 310
Imboden, Martha Russel ("Russie"), 6, 11, 311
Imboden, Mary Wilson McPhail, 12, 290
Imboden, Nanine Carrington ("Nannie"), 13
Imboden, Nanine Palmer, 310
Imboden, Mary Francis Tyree, 25
Imboden, Mary Wilson, 13
Imboden, Polly Jane, 2
Imboden, Susan B., 2
Imboden's Office of Virginia Lands, 294
Iverson, Alfred, 163, 165

Jackson, Thomas J., 36–45, 49, 52, 56–59, 62–63, 66, 71–73, 76; Valley Campaign, 76–91; 92–93, 98, 105, 115, 117, 140, 148, 217, 253, 261
Jackson, William L., 117, 120–21, 130, 185–86, 190–92, 223, 226, 259, 272, 279
James River & Kanawha Canal, 227, 251
Jenkins, Albert G., 97, 130, 140, 205–6, 224, 247
Johnson, Andrew, 289
Johnson, Bradley T., 259, 262, 265, 267–68, 270, 272, 295–96
Johnson, Edward, 79–80
Johnson, Harriet, 306

Johnson, Lafayette, 306
Johnston, Joseph E., 42–45, 48–49, 60, 62, 64–65, 73, 81, 95, 199–200, 286–87, 291
Jones, Abram, 146
Jones, Beuhring H., 230, 237
Jones, James F., 228, 230
Jones, John Marshall, 161–62
Jones, Roger, 34
Jones, Samuel, 115–17, 120, 133, 139, 144, 174, 185, 191, 195–97
Jones, William E., 111–20, 125–36, 140, 227–33, 235–43, 245–47, 262

Kansas-Nebraska Act, 10
Kelley, Benjamin F., 98–99, 106, 131
Kemper, James L., 151, 291, 293, 295
Kenly, John R., 82, 130
Kernstown: First Battle of, 77–78; Second Battle of, 269
Kershaw, Joseph B., 271–72, 277
Keyes, Erasmus, 55
Kilpatrick, Judson, 157–58, 161, 163–65, 281
Kimball, Nathan, 77
Krick, Robert K., xi, 89

Lang, D.B., 123, 177
Lang, Theodore F., 138
Lang, Theodore S., 212–14
Latham, George, 121
Lee, Edwin G., 225–26, 245–46
Lee, Fitzhugh, 163–65, 191–92, 194, 271
Lee, Robert B., 64
Lee, Robert E., 36–37, 41, 76, 80, 91, 95, 97–101, 103, 105–6, 108, 111, 114–17, 119, 129, 132–33, 135, 139–41, 143–53, 156–58, 163, 165–69, 172–75, 176, 178–79, 183–84, 190–91, 194–202, 207–8, 220, 222–23, 225–26, 229, 236, 242–45, 247–48, 253, 260, 265,

267, 271–72, 277, 279, 283, 286–87, 291, 306, 313
Lehigh Granite Quarry, 294
Letcher, John, Jr., 5, 9–10, 12, 28, 30, 36, 38, 73, 114, 251
Lexington, destruction of, 251
Lincoln, Abraham, 14, 18–21, 22, 31, 39, 46, 74–75, 127, 156–67, 169, 197, 266, 289
Litchfield, G.W., 304
Lockett, Augusta, 292
Lockett, Howard, 292
Lomax, Lunsford, 271–73
Longstreet, James, 145–49, 167–69, 178, 199, 253
Loring, William W., 72–73, 96
Lough, Jacob H., 74
Louisa Railroad Company, 8–10
Lynchburg, Battle of, 254–60

MacDonald, Angus, 42
Magruder, John, 75
Mallory, W.B., 31
Manassas Gap Railroad, 10, 28, 31, 46, 48–49, 82, 210
Marr, John Quincy, 36
Mary Baldwin College, 13
Massie, James W., 36–37, 189
McCausland, John, 133, 205–6, 223–25, 247, 250–51, 254, 256–60, 265, 267–68, 270–72, 296
McClanahan, John H., 112, 120, 136, 143, 151, 153–54, 159, 173, 179–80, 196, 201, 207, 209, 212, 215, 217–19, 221, 230, 235, 237, 240, 244, 260
McClellan, George B., 62, 75–76, 78, 83, 92, 96–101, 123
McCue, Franklin, 6
McCue, John Howard, 5, 7, 9, 19, 306
McCue, John Marshall, 7, 13, 18, 176, 292, 298, 299
McCulloch, Ben, 71

McDonald, Angus, 96
McDowell, Battle of, 80–81
McDowell, Irwin, 46–48, 50, 52, 57–58, 60, 62, 75–78, 83–84, 222
McDowell, James, 8
McLaughlin, William, 213, 216–17
McNeill, John H., 94–95, 99, 108, 112, 116, 126, 143, 162, 173, 176, 179–80, 188–89, 192, 196, 198, 201–4, 209, 220, 223, 228
McPhail, C.C., 65
McPhail, George W., 150, 281
Meade, George G., 145–49, 157–58, 168–69, 173, 178–79, 200, 225
Mexican-American War, 6–7
Mick, John, 198
militia, origins and characteristics of, 13
Milroy, Robert, 78, 80, 102–7, 119, 143
Mineralogical Society of Roanoke College, 295
Monocacy, Battle of, 264–65
Moor, Augustus, 210, 212–13, 235, 240–41, 247
Moorman, M.N., 188
Mosby, John Singleton, 26, 223, 243, 310
Mowry, George W., 232
Mulligan, James A., 124, 176, 186–87, 191

National Express Transportation Company, 291
New Market, Battle of, 210–20
Nicholls, Francis T., 251–52
Norfolk & Petersburg Railroad, 302
Norfolk & Western Railroad, 302, 308
Northrup, L.B., 64
Northwestern Railroad, 113, 131

O'Ferrall, Charles, 245–46
Office of Virginia Lands, 191

Opie, Hiram, 74
Opie, John N., 228, 234
Orange & Alexandria Railroad, 10, 28, 31, 46, 178, 223, 248–49, 254
Otis, Charles, 245–46

Parsons, Job, 102
Partisan Ranger Act, 70–71, 196
Partisan Rangers (described), 69–70, 107
Patterson, Robert, 36, 43–45, 48
Patton, George S., 117, 120–21, 123, 174
Patton, John M., 86
Pearce, John T., 203
Pegram, John, 277
Pemberton, John C., 170
Pender, William, 154
Pendleton, Alexander, 88–89
Pendleton, William N., 49
Peters, William E., 250, 270
Phares, J.F., 122
Philadelphia & Reading Railroad, 297
Pickett, George E., 146–49, 166
Piedmont, Battle of, 236–43
Piedmont Railroad, 279
Pierce, Franklin, 10
Pierce, Lewis B., 158–59
Pierpont, Francis H, 96, 99, 129
Pillow, Gideon, 282, 285
Poague, William T., 88
Points, J.J., 53
Polk, James K., 6, 8
Porter, David C., 292
Porter, Elizabeth Beale, 292
Porter, N.D., 291
Port Republic, Battle of, 86–91
Potts, James M., 208
Powell, William H., 276
Preston, Margaret, 190
Preston, Walter, 304
Price, Samuel, 192
Purcell, Charles W., 291

Quinn, Timothy, 210, 213, 226

Ramseur, Stephen D., 254, 257–58, 260, 262–63, 269
Randolph, Beverly, 228
Randolph, George W., 71, 106
Ransom, Robert, 255, 259–60, 262, 268, 271–72
Reynolds, A.D., 304
Reynolds, R.J., 304
Richardson, William H., 15
Richmond, Nathaniel P., 163
Richmond & Danville Railroad, 279
Richmond Dispatch, 73
Richmond Enquirer, 34
Rickett, James, 265
Roberts, Benjamin S., 119, 123, 125–26, 130–31, 135, 137
Robertson, Beverly H., 92, 140, 146, 157, 163
Robertson, Charles, 230
Robertson, James I., xi, 40–41, 89
Rockbridge Mining Company, 294
Rodes, Robert E., 262–63, 266, 273
Rosecrans, Williams S., 96
Rosser, Thomas, 196
Royall, W.L., 296
Russell, C.W., 97

Scales, Alfred, 154
Schenck, Robert, 78, 80, 118
Scott, John, 31
Scott, W.C., 90
Scott, Winfield, 10, 24, 43, 46
Seddon, James A., 108, 110, 117, 245
Sedgwick, John, 157–58
Seward, William, 21
Sexton, Rufus, 83
Shellar, George, 282
Sheridan, Philip H., 223, 247, 268–69, 271–78, 286, 313
Sherman, William T., 55, 200, 281, 285
Shields, James, 77–78, 81, 83–91

Shipp, Scott, 213, 216
Shotwell, Randolph, 155–56
Shumate, Joseph, 60–61
Siders, W.A., 54
Sigel, Franz, 199–210, 212–20, 222–24, 263, 269, 313
Simpson, Benjamin L., 179–81
Smith, Francis H., 5, 15, 190, 202, 250
Smith, George H., 112, 143, 179, 182, 193–94, 201, 204, 206–7, 209–12, 216, 220
Smith, Gustavus W., 68
Smith, W.P., 41
Smith, William, 192
Snyder, Mary Jane, 97
South Atlantic & Ohio Railroad, 302, 308
Southside Railroad, 302
Spectator (Staunton newspaper), 12, 17, 31, 111, 246
Stahel, Julius, 200, 218, 225, 227, 233, 240, 243–44
Stanton, Edwin, 275
Staunton, Hunter's destruction of, 246
Staunton Academy, 3, 25
Staunton Artillery, 15–16, 25, 28–31, 33, 35, 43–45, 49–59, 63–69, 71, 74, 93, 313
Steuart, George, 85, 90
Stevens, Thaddeus, 289
Stevenson, James H., 208
Stone, Henderson, 101
Stoneman, George, 119, 302
Stringfellow, W.W., 244
Stuart, Alexander H., 20
Stuart, James E.B., 41–42, 48, 61, 99–101, 145, 147–49, 153, 158–59, 163–65, 167–68, 178, 180, 196
Stuart, William S., 306
Sullivan, Jeremiah C., 200, 225, 240, 248, 259
Swamp Dragoons, 198–99, 201
Taliafero, William B., 72

Tanner, Robert, 242
Taylor, Richard, 86, 88, 90
Taylor, Zachary, 8
Tazewell, Littleton W., 8
Tennessee & North Carolina Railroad Company, 302
Thoburn, Joseph, 240–41
Thomas, Clayton M., III, xii, 40
Tilden, Samuel J., 298
Tinsalia Coal & Iron Company, 302
Toombs, Robert, 19
Torbert, Alfred T.A., 157, 279
Tredegar Iron Works, 18
Trigg, T.P., 304
Trimble, Isaac R., 65, 85–86, 90
Trout, John, 311
Turk, Randolph, 225
Turner, Edward R., 217
Tyler, Daniel, 48
Tyler, Erastrus B., 77, 89
Tyler, Nat, 26
Tylor, Daniel, 144
Tyree, William, 25

U.S. Military Academy, West Point, 36, 41, 42, 45–46, 52, 65, 69, 79, 138, 222, 262

Vaughn, John C., 230–33, 239, 241–42, 244–45, 247, 249–50, 252, 254, 259, 262, 272, 313
Victoria Furnace, 295
Vindicator (Staunton newspaper), 225
Virginia & Tennessee Railroad, 10, 189–90, 199–201, 205, 223, 251, 253, 255, 301
Virginia Arms Manufacturing Co., 17–18
Virginia Central Railroad, 9–11, 28–31, 79, 191, 220, 222, 246–47, 273, 278, 301
Virginia Institute for Education of the Deaf and the Dumb and of the Blind, 5, 9

Virginia Land and Aid Immigration Company, 292
Virginia Lands and Southern Real Estate Generally, 292
Virginia Military Institute, 3–5, 15, 25–26, 31, 36–37, 69, 73, 78, 81, 179, 185–86, 189–91, 202, 208–9, 213–14, 216–17, 220–21, 224, 251, 253–54, 256, 262, 310

Waddell, Joseph, 289
Walker, Gilbert C., 293
Walker, Lindsay, 61
Walker, Thomas, 300
Wallace, Lew, 264–65
Warren, Gouverneur K., 157–58, 179
Washington, John, 49
Washington College (Washington and Lee University), 4, 7, 251, 291
Wells, George D., 247
Wharton, Gabriel C., 173, 201, 209, 213, 217, 220, 248, 250, 254, 259
White, Elijah, 112
White, Robert, 179, 187–88, 201, 220, 234

Whiting, William H.C., 65, 67–68, 91–92
Williamsport, Battle of, 159–65
Wilson, James H., 287
Winchester: First Battle of (May 25, 1862), 83; Third Battle of (September 19, 1864), 273
Winchester & Potomac Railroad, 33
Winder, Charles, 88–89, 91
Winder, John H., 278–83
Wirz, Heinrich, 281–84, 290, 303
Wise, Henry, 13, 26, 28–30, 71
Wolfe, John P., 216
Wood, M.B., 300
Woodson, Charles H., 216
Woodward, Harold K., Jr., xi, 41, 89
Woolson, Constance, 106
Wright, Horatio G., 275
Wynkoop, John E., 175, 210, 241, 252

Yoakum, Michael, 198
Yorktown, Siege of, 76
Young, P.M.B., 153–54, 159